cut here

Internet Resources

Web Browsers

Internet Explorer:

http://www.microsoft.com/ie/download

Netscape Navigator:

http://www.netscap

Int

Outlook Express:

http://www.microsoft.com/ie/download

Netscape Messenger:

http://www.netscape.com/computing/download

Web-Based Mail Services

http://www.hotmail.com

http://www.iquest.net

http://www.netaddress.com

http://altavista.iname.com

http://www.rocketmail.com

http://mail.yahoo.com

http://www.iname.com

Search Engines

http://www.lycos.com

http://www.infoseek.com

http://www.altavista.com

http://www.snap.com

http://www.deja.com

http://www.dogpile.com

News Sites

http://www.abcnews.com
http://www.nbcnews.com
http://www.cbsnews.com
http://www.cnn.com
http://www.foxnews.com
http://www.newsweek.com
http://www.washingtonpost.com
http://www.nytimes.com
http://www.chicagotribune.com
http://www.usatoday.com

Online Auction Sites

http://www.ebay.com
http://www.onsale.com
http://www.auctionuniverse.com
http://www.bid.com
http://www.firstauction.com
http://www.webauction.com
http://www.zauction.com

Web Chat Rooms

http://www.talkcity.com
http://www.chatting.com
http://chat.yahoo.com
http://chat.earthweb.com
http://www.wbs.net

The Complete Idiot's Guide to the Internet, Sixth Edition

QUE®

201 W. 103rd Street, Indianapolis, IN 46290

THE COMPLETE IDIOT'S GUIDE® TO

The Internet,

Sixth Edition

Peter Kent

Que®

201 W. 103rd Street, Indianapolis, IN 46290

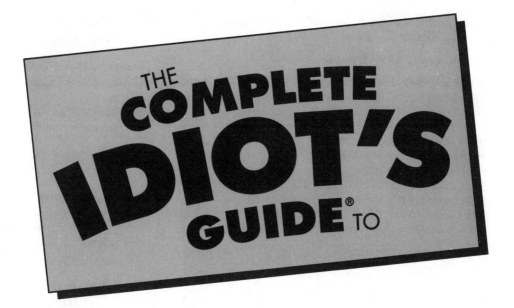

The Complete Idiot's Guide to the Internet, Sixth Edition

International Standard Book Number: 0-7897-2120-1

Library of Congress Catalog Card Number: 99-63002

Printed in the United States of America

First Printing: *August 1999*

01 00 99 4 3 2 1

Trademarks

All terms mentioned in this book that are known to be trademarks or service marks have been appropriately capitalized. Que cannot attest to the accuracy of this information. Use of a term in this book should not be regarded as affecting the validity of any trademark or service mark.

Warning and Disclaimer

Every effort has been made to make this book as complete and as accurate as possible, but no warranty or fitness is implied. The information provided is on an "as is" basis. The authors and the publisher shall have neither liability nor responsibility to any person or entity with respect to any loss or damages arising from the information contained in this book.

Executive Editor
Greg Wiegand

Acquisitions Editor
Stephanie McComb

Development Editor
Sarah Robbins

Managing Editor
Thomas F. Hayes

Project Editor
Lori A. Lyons

Technical Editor
Bill Bruns

Illustrator
Judd Winick

Indexer
Christine Nelsen

Proofreader
Maribeth Echard

Layout Technician
Brad Lenser

Interior Design
Nathan Clement

Cover Design
Michael Freeland

Copy Writer
Eric Borgert

Contents at a Glance

Table of Contents

About the Author

Peter Kent is the author of around 40 computer and business books, including *Poor Richard's Web Site: Geek-Free, Commonsense Advice on Building a Low-Cost Web Site* (Top Floor Publishing). His work has appeared in numerous publications, from the *Manchester Guardian* to *Internet World*, the *Dallas Times Herald* to *Computerworld*, and has won him two Excellence in Journalism Awards from the Society of Professional Journalists.

Dedication

To Nick & Chris, partners in crime.

Acknowledgments

Thanks to the huge team at Que (see the list of people on the Credits Page) who helped me put this book together. There's a lot more to writing a book than just, well, writing. I'm very grateful to have people willing and able to do all the stuff that comes after the words are on the computer screen. Thanks also to Connie Brenden for her assistance.

Tell Us What You Think!

As the reader of this book, *you* are our most important critic and commentator. We value your opinion and want to know what we're doing right, what we could do better, what areas you'd like to see us publish in, and any other words of wisdom you're willing to pass our way.

As an Associate Publisher for Que, I welcome your comments. You can fax, email, or write me directly to let me know what you did or didn't like about this book—as well as what we can do to make our books stronger.

Please note that I cannot help you with technical problems related to the topic of this book, and that due to the high volume of mail I receive, I might not be able to reply to every message.

When you write, please be sure to include this book's title and author as well as your name and phone or fax number. I will carefully review your comments and share them with the author and editors who worked on the book.

Fax: 317-581-4666

Email: `office_que@mcp.com`

Mail: Greg Wiegand
Que
201 West 103rd Street
Indianapolis, IN 46290 USA

Introduction

Welcome to *The Complete Idiot's Guide to the Internet, Sixth Edition*. That's six editions in just five and a half years. Sometimes it's hard to imagine that, to most people just five years ago, the Internet was little more than some weird computer thing they'd heard about on television. Now it's become a necessity for many of us—it's hard to imagine life without it. Not for you, though. If you're reading this book, chances are you're what's known in Internetspeak as a *newbie*—a newcomer. Well, I've got good news for you.

If you're just now learning about the Internet, in one way you're lucky. In 1993, most Internet users were computer geeks, and that was okay because you needed a high degree of geekhood to get anything done on the Internet. For the average business or home computer user, getting an Internet account was like stepping into a time warp. One moment you were in your whiz-bang, multimedia, mouse-clicking, graphical user interface—Windows, OS/2, or the Macintosh—and the next minute you were back in the 1970s, working on a dumb UNIX terminal (dumb being the operative word), typing obscure and arcane—not to mention funky and strange—UNIX commands. You probably found yourself wondering, "What's this `ftp ftp.microsoft.com` thing I have to type?" or "What's *grep* all about and why do I care?" or "Why can't UNIX programmers actually *name* their programs instead of giving them two- or three-letter acronyms?" (Acronyms are so important in the UNIX world that there's even an acronym to describe acronyms: TLA, Three Letter Acronym.)

Most Internet users today don't need to know the answers to these ancient questions. These days the majority of new users are firmly in the 1990s—if not quite the 21st Century—working in the graphical user interfaces they love (or love to hate, but that's another issue). Since 1993, thousands of fancy new Internet access programs have been written. Today, it's easier to get on the Internet, and it's easier to get around after you are there.

So, Why Do You Need This Book?

Even if you've never stumbled along the information superhighway (or "infotainment superhighway," as satirist Al Franken calls it), you've almost certainly heard of it. A recent survey found that although only 2.3 percent of American high school students could tell you the name of the countries bordering the United States, 93.7 percent knew how to get to the Penthouse Online Web site—and more know how to download bootleg MP3 copies of just about any band's new releases ("MP3?," you're thinking—don't worry, we'll cover that in Chapter 7).

Chances are, though, that if you've picked up this book, you are not an experienced international traveler along the highways and byways of this amazing system called the Internet. You probably need a little help. Well, you've come to the right place.

Yes, the Internet is far easier to get around now than it was in 1993, but there's still a lot to learn. The journey will be more comfortable than it was then, and you can travel much farther.

Now, I know you're not an idiot. What you do, you do well. But right now, you don't do the Internet, and you need a quick way to get up and running. You want to know what the fuss is about, or maybe you already know what the fuss is about and you want to find out how to get in on it. Well, I'm not going to teach you how to become an Internet guru, but I will tell you the things you really *need* to know, such as

- How to get up and running on the Internet
- How to send and receive email messages
- How to move around on the World Wide Web (and what is the Web, anyway?)
- How to find what you are looking for on the Internet
- Why the Recording Industry of America is terrified of MP3
- What "push" is all about, how to push what you want pushed, and where to push it
- Protecting life and limb on the information superhighway fast lane
- How to participate in Internet discussion groups (this could take over your life and threaten your relationships if you're not careful)
- How to make your fortune in cyberspace

I am, however, making a few assumptions. I'm assuming that you know how to use your computer, so don't expect me to give basic lessons on using your mouse, switching between windows, working with directories and files, and all that stuff. There's enough to cover in this book without all that. If you want really basic beginner's information, check out *The Complete Idiot's Guide to PCs* (also from Que), a great book by Joe Kraynak.

How Do You Use This Book?

I've used a few conventions in this book to make it easier for you to follow. For example, things you type, press, click, and select appear in bold like this:

type **this**

If I don't know exactly what you'll have to type (because you have to supply some of the information), I'll put the unknown information in italic. For example, you might see the following instructions. In this case, I don't know the filename, so I made it italic to indicate that you have to supply it.

type **this *filename***

Also, I've used the term "Enter" throughout the book, even though your keyboard might have a "Return" key instead.

Finally, Internet addresses are in a monospace type font. They'll look something like this:

```
http://www.microsoft.com/
```

In case you want a greater understanding of the subject you are learning, you'll find some background information in boxes. You can quickly skip over this information if you want to avoid all the gory details. On the other hand, you might find something that will keep you from getting into trouble. Here are the special icons and boxes used in this book.

Check This Out

These boxes contain notes, tips, warnings, and asides that provide you with interesting and useful (at least theoretically) tidbits of Internet information.

Techno Talk

The Techno Talk icon calls your attention to technical information you might spout off to impress your friends, but that you'll likely never need to know to save your life.

Part 1

Start at the Beginning

You want to start, and you want to start quickly. No problem. In Part 1, you're going to do just that. First, I'll give you a quick overview of the Internet, and then I'll have you jump right in and use the two most important Internet services: email and the World Wide Web. (The Web is so important these days that many people think the Internet is the Web. I'll explain the difference in Chapter 1, "The Internet: What's It All About?") By the time you finish this part of the book, you'll be surfing around the Web like a true cybergeek—and you'll be ready to move on and learn the other Internet services.

The Internet: What's It All About?

In This Chapter

- The obligatory "What is the Internet?" question answered
- A quick history of the Internet
- What sort of information flies across the Internet
- Internet services, from Archie to the World Wide Web
- Getting a connection to the Internet
- Four types of Internet connections
- The difference between the Internet and the online services

Yes, this is the obligatory "What is the Internet?" chapter. But before you skip ahead, let me tell you that I'll be covering some other subjects, too, and that I promise not to go into too much detail about Internet history. Quite frankly, most people are tired of hearing about the history of the Internet; they just want to get on the Net and get something done. However, for those of you who might have been too busy preparing for the end of civilization on 01/01/00 to pay attention to anything else, here's my abbreviated history of the Internet:

1. The Internet was created by the U.S. military-industrial complex in the late 1960s as a way of enabling government researchers who were working on military projects to share computer files.

2. The Internet *wasn't* set up to figure out how computer networks could be made to survive nuclear war. Or maybe it *was*. I still haven't figured out this one. Although the nuclear war story is common knowledge, some people involved in the early days of the Internet say it's untrue. I'll admit that I've repeated the nuclear war story in earlier books, as have a gazillion other Internet authors, but then I read an article by one of the founders of the Internet claiming that nuclear survivability wasn't the initial purpose of the Internet. Since then I've seen it said, by authoritative sources, that it was. Either way, at some stage in the Internet's early life, testing survivability became an important purpose.
3. Everyone and his dog in academia jumped on the bandwagon. The Internet became a sort of secret academic communication link, connecting hundreds of academic institutions, while America went on watching *Starsky and Hutch* and *The Dukes of Hazzard*, not realizing what was going on.
4. Eventually, the people in the press figured out what was happening. Granted, it took them almost a quarter of a century, but during that time they were busy being spoon-fed by our political institutions, and the Internet didn't have a public relations company.
5. In 1993, the press started talking about the Internet. In 1994 and 1995, it was about all they could talk about.
6. Ordinary Americans—and then ordinary Brits, Aussies, Frenchies, and others all around the world—began to wake up and realize that the Internet might be worth looking into. And look into it they did—by the millions.
7. The World Wide Web appeared on the scene at the same time that thousands of software companies started producing Internet programs that could be used by people who don't regard Jolt Cola as the equivalent of a fine wine—in other words, by the average nongeek. The Internet was transformed, if not exactly overnight, certainly within a year.
8. The Internet today has become a haven for all the people the U.S. military-industrial complex loathes: pinkos, body piercers, eco-anarchists, people who wear clothing more suited to the opposite sex, and Democrats. Along with, of course, all sorts of ordinary people, businesses, schools, churches, and the like.
9. The Internet now serves as the world's largest chain letter and get-rich-quick-scheme forum, a true testament to the human spirit.

That's my quick history of the Internet. If you want more, you'll have to look elsewhere. I want to move on to what *today's* Internet is.

Okay, Then, What Is the Internet?

Let's start with the basics. What's a computer network? A computer network is a system in which computers are connected so they can share "information." (I'll explain what I mean by that word in a moment.) There's nothing particularly unusual about this in today's world. Millions of networks exist around the world. True, they are mostly in the industrialized world, but you won't find a nation in the world that doesn't have at least a few. (I don't know that for sure, but I can't think of one.)

The Internet is something special, though, for two reasons. First, it's the world's largest computer network. Second, it's pretty much open to anyone with the entrance fee—and the entrance fee is constantly dropping. Many users have free accounts and many more are paying as little as $10 to $20 a month, sometimes for "unlimited" usage. (Unlimited, in Internetspeak, is a euphemism meaning "if your computer can manage to connect to the service, and if the service's computers let you stay connected, you can use it as much as you want.") Consequently, millions of people all over the world are getting online.

Just how big is the Internet? Many of the numbers thrown about in the past few years are complete nonsense. In 1993, people were saying 25 million. Considering that the majority of Internet users at the time were in the United States, and that 25 million is 10% of the U.S. population, and that most people in this great nation thought that the Internet was some kind of hairpiece sold through late-night infomercials, it's highly unlikely that anywhere near 25 million people were on the Internet. In fact, they weren't.

These days, estimates vary all over the place, ranging from the high tens of millions to the low hundreds of millions. Late in 1997 I saw advertisements claiming 80 million, probably based on the reasoning that it was 40 million a few months ago, so it must be more than 80 million by now. In January of 1998, Nua Internet Surveys estimated more than 100 million; and today they're claiming 159 million. The truth is that nobody knows how many people are using the Internet. I believe, however, that many of the claims are gross exaggerations. Also, remember that many users are only infrequent visitors to cyberspace, visiting just now and again, maybe once a week or so. That little bit of information might not be important to the average user, but it *is* worth bearing in mind if you plan to set up shop on the Internet, as I'll discuss in Chapter 21, "Making Money on the Internet."

Cyberspace

The term *cyberspace* means the area in which you can move around online. When you are on the Internet, on an online service, or even connected to a computer BBS (bulletin board system), you are in cyberspace.

One way or another, though, a whole lot of people are out there; the numbers are definitely in the tens of millions.

What Exactly Is Information?

What, then, do I mean by information? I mean anything you can send over lines of electronic communication, and that includes quite a lot these days (and seems to include more every day). I mean letters, which are called *email* on the Internet. I mean reports, magazine articles, and books, which are called *document files* on the Internet. I mean music, which is called *music* (or MP3 files) on the Internet.

You can send your voice across the Internet; you'll learn how to do that in Chapter 14, "Internet Conferences: Voice on the Net, Whiteboards, and More." For now let me just say that you'll find it much cheaper than talking long-distance on the phone (although most certainly not as easy), as long as you can find someone to talk to. You can also grab computer files of many kinds (programs, word-processing files, clip art, sounds, and anything else that can be electronically encoded) from huge libraries that collectively contain literally millions of files.

A Word About Numbers

When I first started writing about the Internet, I tried to be specific; I might have said "2.5 million files." However, I've given up that practice for two reasons. First, many of the numbers were made up, not by me, but by Internet gurus who were trying to be specific and made educated guesses. Second, even if the numbers were correct when I wrote them, they were too low by the time the book got to the editor, much too low by the time the book got to the printer, and ridiculously low by the time the book got to the readers. But you can be pretty sure that at least 2,536,321 files are available for you to copy—give or take a million.

Information could also be a type of conversation. You want to talk about the tragedy in Kosovo? There's a discussion group waiting for you (whatever side you might take!). Do you want to meet like-minded souls with a passion for daytime soap operas? They're talking right now. Feel the need to hear what Monica's got to say, but don't want to pay for the book? Plenty of people are willing to fill you in with the details.

Anything that can be sent electronically is carried on the Internet, and much that can't be sent now probably will be sent in a few months. "Such as?" you ask. How about a three-dimensional image of your face? In the next year or so, special face scanners will appear on the scene. You'll be able to scan your face, and then send a three-dimensional image of your face to someone, or use the image for your chat *avatar*. You'll learn about avatars in Chapter 13, "Yak, Yak, Yak: Chatting in Cyberspace."

The Internet Services

The following list provides a quick look at the Internet services available to you. This list is not exhaustive. Other services are available, but these are the most important ones:

- **Email** This is the most used Internet service. Hundreds of millions of messages—some estimates say more than a billion (another of those completely unconfirmable figures)—wing their way around the world each day, among families, friends, and businesses. The electronic world's postal system is very much like the real world's postal system, except that you can't send fruit, bombs, or this month's selection from the Cheese of the Month club. (You can, however, send letters, spreadsheets, pictures, sounds, programs, and more.) This method is much quicker and cheaper, too. And the mailman isn't armed. Come to think of it, it's not much like the real world's postal system, but in principle it's very similar: helping people communicate with others all over the world. See Chapter 2, "The Premier Internet Tool: Email," and Chapter 3, "Advanced Email: HTML and Encryption," for more information about this essential service.
- **Chat** Chat's a bit of a misnomer. Not much chatting goes on, but you'll see an awful lot of typing. You type a message, and it's instantly transmitted to another person, or to many other people, who can type their responses right away. If you enjoy slow and confusing conversations in which it's tough to tell who's talking to whom, in which the level of literacy and humor is somewhere around fourth grade, and in which many of the chat-room members claiming to be handsome and successful businessmen are actually spotty teenage boys...you'll love chat! (Okay, maybe I'm being a little harsh; some people enjoy chat. On the other hand, some people enjoy eating monkey brains and going bungee-jumping, too.) You'll learn more about chatting in Chapter 13.
- **Internet Phones** Install a sound card and microphone, get the Internet phone software, and then talk to people across the Internet. This service is not very popular today, and to be quite honest, despite all the hype, it probably won't be popular anytime soon, either. But just think: You can, in some cases, make international phone calls for nothing. (I've given up predicting imminent success for this service. I'll discuss some of the reasons why in Chapter 14.)
- **FTP** The whole purpose of the Internet was to transfer files from one place to another, and for years, FTP was how it was done. FTP provides a giant electronic library of computer files; you'll learn how to use it in Chapter 12, "The Giant Software Store: FTP."

- **Gopher** Poor old Gopher. If not crippled, he's at least been hobbled. Just a couple of years ago this service (which you'll learn about in Chapter 16, "Gopher and Telnet: Still Alive, but Barely") was supposed to revolutionize the Internet by converting a command-line computer system to a menu system. You wouldn't have to remember and use arcane commands anymore; you could just use the arrow keys or type a number corresponding to a menu option. Then along came the World Wide Web.
- **World Wide Web** The Web is driving the growth of the Internet because it's cool! (Are you sick of that word yet?) Containing pictures, sounds, and animation, the Web is a giant *hypertext* system in which documents around the world are linked to one another. Click a word in a document in, say, Sydney, Australia, and another document (which might be from Salzburg, Austria) appears. You'll begin learning about this amazing system in Chapter 4, "The World of the World Wide Web."
- **Telnet** Very few people use Telnet, but it can be quite useful. Telnet provides a way for you to log on to a computer that's connected somewhere out there on the Internet—across the city or across the world. When logged on, you'll probably be using arcane commands or a text-based menu system. You might be playing one of the many role-playing *MUD* games (that stands for Multiple User Dungeons or Multiple User Dimensions) or even perusing a library catalog. Most people are too busy using the Web, but you can read about Telnet in Chapter 16.
- **Newsgroups** Newsgroups are discussion groups. Want to hear the latest theory about why American teenagers are arming themselves to the teeth? Want to learn an unusual kite-flying technique? Want to learn about...well, anything really? You'll find probably more than 40,000 internationally distributed newsgroups, and you'll find out how to work with them in Chapter 9, "Newsgroups: the Source of All Wisdom," and Chapter 10, "Your Daily News Delivery." (I broke my "no specific numbers rule" there, but 40,000 is fairly close, at least for the moment; the number grows by thousands every year.)
- **Mailing lists** If 40,000 discussion groups are not enough for you, here are 150,000 more. (This number is more of a guess. One large directory lists 90,000 mailing lists. Certainly many, many more mailing lists exist, along with thousands of Web forums.) As you'll learn in Chapter 11, "Yet More Discussion Groups: Mailing Lists and Web Forums," mailing lists are another form of discussion group that works in a slightly different manner—you send and receive messages using your email program. Web forums are discussion groups located at Web sites. In these forums, you read and submit messages using your Web browser.
- **Push programs** These systems are so named because information from the Internet is "pushed" to your computer. Rather than your going out onto the Internet to find information, information is periodically sent to your computer without your direct intervention (all you need to do is state what information

you want to retrieve and how often). *Push* is another Internet misnomer (I don't get to pick these names!); this system is really a scheduled-pull system, as I'll explain in Chapter 8, "Push Information to Your Desktop." I'll also explain why *Scientific American* is wrong when it says Push is an "innovation that might improve work. "These services are all tools, not reasons to be on the Internet. As a wise man once said, "Nobody wants a 1/4-inch drill bit; they want a 1/4-inch hole." Nobody wants a car, either; they want comfortable, affordable transportation. Nobody wants the Web, FTP, or Telnet; they want...well, what do they want? As you read this book, you'll get ideas for how you can use the Internet tools for profit and pleasure (along with a good measure of incidental frustration, unfortunately). Chapter 22, "Ideas," gives loads of examples of how real people use the Internet.

Getting on the Net

So, you think the Net sounds great. How do you get to it, though? You might get Internet access in a number of ways:

- Your college provides you with an Internet account.
- Your company has an Internet connection from its internal network.
- You've signed up with an online service such as America Online (AOL), CompuServe, The Microsoft Network (MSN), or Prodigy.
- You've signed up with a small, local Internet service provider.
- You've signed up with a large, national Internet service provider such as PSINet, Earthlink, or SpryNet.
- You've signed up with one of the phone companies, such as AT&T, Sprint, or MCI WorldCom.
- You've signed up with a Free-Net or other form of free community computer network.

The Internet is not owned by any one company. It resembles the world's telephone system: Each portion is owned by someone, and the overall system hangs together because of a variety of agreements among those organizations. So, you'll find no single *Internet, Inc.* where you can go to get access to the Internet. No, you have to go to one of the tens of thousands of organizations that already have access to the Internet and get a connection through it.

At this stage, I'm going to assume that you already have some kind of Internet connection. But if you don't, or if you're considering finding another Internet account or a replacement, you can learn more about finding a connection (and about those Free-Nets) in Appendix D, "Finding Internet Access and the Right Equipment."

The Difference Between the Internet and Online Services

I often hear the questions, "What's the difference between the Internet and AOL, or CompuServe, or whatever?" and "If I have an AOL account, do I have an Internet account?" Services such as AOL (America Online), CompuServe, Prodigy, GEnie, MSN (The Microsoft Network), and so on, are not the same as the Internet. They are known as *online services*. Although they are similar to the Internet in some ways (yes, they are large computer networks), they are different in the sense that they are private clubs.

For instance, what happens when you dial into, say, CompuServe? Your computer connects across the phone lines with CompuServe's computers, which are all sitting in a big room somewhere. All those computers belong to CompuServe (well, now they belong to America Online, which recently bought CompuServe). Contrast this with the Internet. When you connect to the Internet, you connect to a communications system that's linked to millions of computers, which are owned by tens of thousands of companies, schools, government departments, and individuals. If the Internet is like a giant public highway system, the online services are like small private railroads.

However, at the risk of stretching an analogy too far (I'm already mixing metaphors, so why not?), I should mention that these private railroads let you get off the tracks and onto the public highway. In other words, although AOL, CompuServe, and the others are private clubs, they do provide a way for you to connect to the Internet. So, although the barbarians on the Internet are held at the gates to the private club, the private club members can get onto the Internet.

The online services view themselves as both private clubs and gateways to the Internet. As Russ Siegelman of The Microsoft Network stated, Microsoft wants MSN to be "the biggest and best content club and community on the Internet." So, it's intended to be part of the Internet—but a private part. In fact, although I (and many others) call these services "online services," Microsoft now refers to MSN as an "Internet Online Service."

To summarize:

- The Internet is a public highway system overrun with barbarians.
- Online services are private railroads or exclusive clubs...or something like that.
- Even if you use the Internet, you can't get into the online services unless you're a member.
- If you are a member of the online services, you can get onto the Internet.

The answer to the second question I posed earlier, then, is "yes." If you have an online-service account (at least with the services mentioned here), you also have an Internet account. Interestingly, these services are now being merged into the Internet.

In particular, MSN is making great efforts to appear as an integral part of the Internet. Parts of MSN are already open to the public. People on the Internet can now access the private areas in MSN if they sign up for the service. They don't have to dial into a phone number provided by Microsoft; they can get onto the Internet any way they like and then use their World Wide Web browser to get into MSN.

What Do You Need?

What does it take to get onto the infotainment superhypeway? Many of you already have Internet accounts; our high-priced research shows that most readers buy this book after they have access to the Internet (presumably because they got access and then got lost). However, I want to talk about the types of accounts (or connections) that are available because they all work in slightly different ways. This discussion will help ensure that we are all on the same wavelength before we get going.

Several types of Internet connections include

- Permanent connections
- Cable connections
- Dial-in direct connections (PPP, SLIP, and CSLIP)
- Dial-in terminal connections (shell accounts)
- Mail connections

Generally, if you ask an online service or service provider for an account these days, you're given a dial-in direct connection, even though it isn't called that. Different service providers use slightly different terms, and the terminology can become blurred. The following sections define each one, which should clarify things a little.

Service Provider

A service provider is a company that sells access to the Internet. You dial into its computer, which connects you to the Internet. The online services are an anomaly. Strictly speaking, they are Internet service providers because they provide Internet access. However, they aren't normally called service providers; they're simply known as online services. The companies known as service providers generally provide access to the Internet and little, if anything, more. The online services, on the other hand, have all sorts of file libraries, chat services, news services, and so on within the private areas of the services themselves.

Permanent Connections

If you have a permanent connection, your computer connects directly to a TCP/IP (Transmission Control Protocol/Internet Protocol) network that is part of the Internet. To be a little more specific, what is most likely is that your organization has a large computer connected to the network, and you have a terminal or computer connected to that computer. This sort of connection is often known as a *dedicated connection* or sometimes as a *permanent direct connection.*

You might have a special form of permanent connection from your phone company, an ISDN or DSL connection. ISDN is an Albanian term that means "Yesterday's Technology Tomorrow." I'd stay clear of ISDN if I were you, for a couple of reasons. Although it's very old technology, the U.S. phone companies never quite figured out how to use it, so if you ask them to install one it might take a long time to get it, be very expensive, you might lose a bush or two while the phone company digs up your yard (I was lucky—my neighbor lost his bush instead), and then there's a good chance it might not work anyway. As for DSL, it's faster than ISDN, and a more recent technology, but it can be very expensive (ranging from $40 a month to $130 a month, with setup fees going as high as $520). And, well, I just don't trust the phone companies on this one. Anyway, if you're lucky, there's a better option—cable.

Cable Connections

There's a new form of permanent connection. Until recently, permanent connections were used only within companies and educational institutions—you wouldn't have one at home. But if you sign up for Internet access through your cable company, you might have a permanent connection. (A few cable companies sell Internet connections that are not permanent connections, connections that are unidirectional; you need a phone line for outgoing data, and use the cable for incoming data.) For the last six months, I've been lucky enough to have cable-modem access. The modem is connected to a network node of 240 other homes in my area; it's like a company network in many ways. I don't have to dial in to the Internet; as soon as I start my computer, I'm automatically connected to the Internet.

Cable connections are fantastic; they're very fast, and although they're more expensive than dial-in connections (I pay $40 a month), the increased speed more than makes up for the cost. In fact *Wired* magazine recently rated cable systems at the very top of their comparison table, with an index value of more than 3,400, compared with a value of 100 for a fast dial-up connection.

I've also found my cable connection to be the most reliable Internet service I've ever had (and I've had a lot) (except, that is, for the nine-day period that it died completely). There were around 200,000 Americans with cable connections by the end of 1998. The cable companies claim there'll be two to three million by the end of 1999. If you can get a cable connection, go for it; you'll be glad you did.

What's a Protocol?

A protocol defines how computers should talk to one another. A protocol is like a language: If a group of people agree to speak French (or English or Spanish), they can all understand one another. Communication protocols provide a similar set of rules that define how modems, computers, and programs can communicate.

Permanent connections are often used by large organizations, such as universities and corporations. The organization has to set up special equipment to connect its network to the Internet, and it has to lease a special telephone line that can transfer data very quickly. Because that organization has a leased line, it is always connected to the Internet, which means there's no need to make a telephone call and use a modem to reach the service provider's computer. Instead, the user simply logs on to the Internet from his terminal.

Dial-In Direct Connections (PPP, SLP, and CSLIP)

Dial-in direct connections are often referred to as PPP (Point-to-Point Protocol), SLIP (Serial Line Internet Protocol), or CSLIP (Compressed SLIP) connections (PPP is the most common form these days). Like the permanent connection, this is also a TCP/IP connection, but it's designed for use over telephone lines instead of a dedicated network. This type of service is the next best thing to the permanent connection. Although a permanent connection is out of the price range of most individuals and small companies, a dial-in direct connection is quite cheap, often available for $20–$25 a month for unlimited use. (I've seen them as low as $12 a month.) After you've connected across your dial-in direct connection, though, you'll use it in the same way you would use a permanent connection. (You might have a permanent connection at work, and a dial-in direct connection at home, but you use the same skills and techniques in both places.)

A dial-in direct connection is a *dial-in* service. That is, you must have a modem, and you have to dial a telephone number given to you by the service provider or online service. The following figure shows an example of one type of software you can run while working with a dial-in direct or permanent connection. The figure shows Microsoft's FTP site, a large file library that's open to the public, displayed within Netscape Navigator 4.5 (you learn about using FTP through a browser in Chapter 12). The main reason I'm showing you this right now is so that you can compare it to the horrible-looking dial-in terminal connection I'll talk about next. With a dial-in direct connection, you can use all the nice GUI (Graphical User Interface) software that the computer industry has spent billions of dollars on over the last few years. With a dial-in terminal account, you're back in the 1970s.

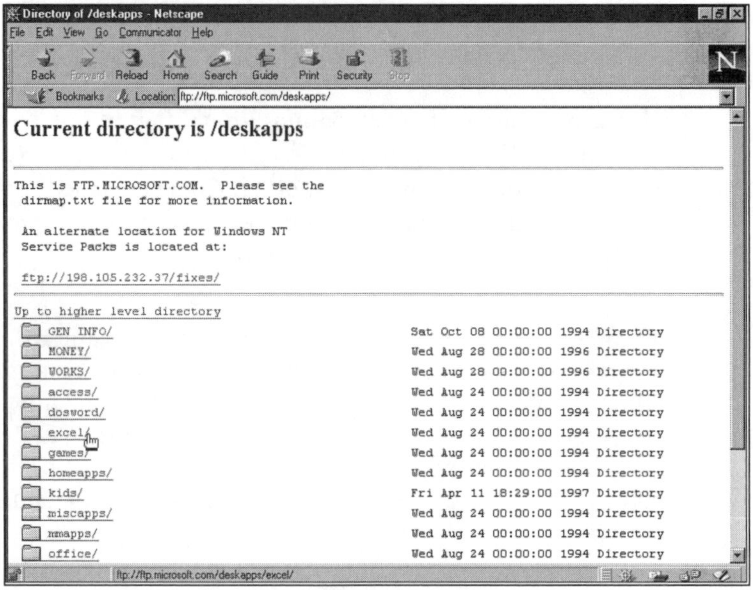

Microsoft's FTP site as viewed from a program running in a dial-in direct connection (SLIP, CSLIP, or PPP) or a permanent connection. To change directories or transfer a file, just click with the mouse.

Dial-In Terminal Connections (Shell Accounts)

With a dial-in terminal connection, you also have to dial into the service provider's computer. When the connection is made, your computer becomes a terminal of the service provider's computer. All the programs you use are running on the service provider's computer. That means that you can transfer files across the Internet to and from your service provider's computer, but not to and from yours. You have to use a separate procedure to move files between your computer and the service provider's.

If you want to see just how ugly this sort of connection is, take a look at the next figure. This figure shows Microsoft's FTP site, the same service you saw in the first figure, in a simple serial communications program (specifically Windows's Hyperterminal). If you're working with a dial-in terminal connection, you have to remember all the commands you need to use to get around, or you'll soon be lost. There's no pointing and clicking here; you'll have to type arcane commands such as `ls -l ""|more"`.

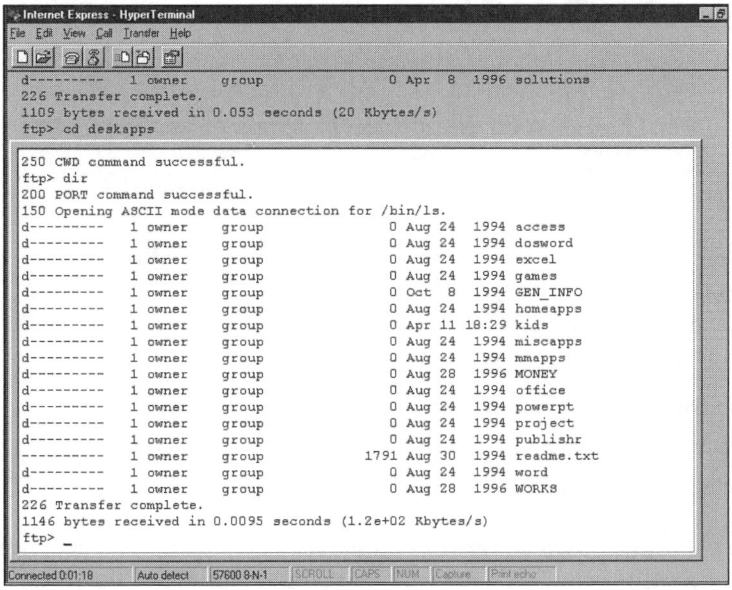
Internet Express - HyperTerminal
File Edit View Call Transfer Help
d--------- 1 owner group 0 Apr 8 1996 solutions
226 Transfer complete.
1109 bytes received in 0.053 seconds (20 Kbytes/s)
ftp> cd deskapps
250 CWD command successful.
ftp> dir
200 PORT command successful.
150 Opening ASCII mode data connection for /bin/ls.
d--------- 1 owner group 0 Aug 24 1994 access
d--------- 1 owner group 0 Aug 24 1994 dosword
d--------- 1 owner group 0 Aug 24 1994 excel
d--------- 1 owner group 0 Aug 24 1994 games
d--------- 1 owner group 0 Oct 8 1994 GEN_INFO
d--------- 1 owner group 0 Aug 24 1994 homeapps
d--------- 1 owner group 0 Apr 11 18:29 kids
d--------- 1 owner group 0 Aug 24 1994 miscapps
d--------- 1 owner group 0 Aug 24 1994 mmapps
d--------- 1 owner group 0 Aug 28 1996 MONEY
d--------- 1 owner group 0 Aug 24 1994 office
d--------- 1 owner group 0 Aug 24 1994 powerpt
d--------- 1 owner group 0 Aug 24 1994 project
d--------- 1 owner group 0 Aug 24 1994 publishr
---------- 1 owner group 1791 Aug 30 1994 readme.txt
d--------- 1 owner group 0 Aug 24 1994 word
d--------- 1 owner group 0 Aug 28 1996 WORKS
226 Transfer complete.
1146 bytes received in 0.0095 seconds (1.2e+02 Kbytes/s)
ftp> _
Connected 0:01:18
Auto detect
57600 8-N-1
SCROLL
CAPS
NUM
Capture
Print echo

Back at Microsoft's FTP site, this time with a dial-in terminal account. Now, what was the command to change the directory?

Who uses this sort of connection? Up until 1993, and well into 1994, most Internet users did. It wasn't until the middle of 1994 that people began using dial-in direct accounts and the more convenient GUI software. Today, few users in the industrialized world use dial-in terminal connections, unless perhaps they're using a free Internet account or studying at Podunk University. In the third world, this type of account might be more common, so many users in poorer countries are still using dial-in terminal connections.

Techno Talk

Clearing Up the Confusion

A dial-in terminal connection is often called a *dial-up connection*. That term can be confusing because you have to dial a call before connecting to a PPP or SLIP account as well. To differentiate between the two, some service providers call a dial-in terminal connection an interactive service, which seems only slightly less ambiguous, or a shell account. Wherever I mention this sort of account (which isn't often), I call it a dial-in terminal connection because you dial the call to your service provider, and after it's connected, your computer acts as a terminal of the other computer.

Mail Connections

A mail connection enables you to send and receive Internet email and, perhaps, read the Internet newsgroups. But you can do nothing more. This is hardly a real Internet account, so I've ignored it in this book. I'll assume you have one of the first three types of accounts.

What Do You Have?

So, what kind of connection do you have, and why do you care? We're interested only in the permanent, dial-in direct, and dial-in terminal connections. The first two connections are the most important for the following reasons:

- They are easier to use.
- You use both in pretty much the same way.
- You probably have one of these connections.

If you have an Internet account provided by your employer at work and you access it across your network connection, you have a permanent connection. How do you connect? Ask your system administrator. You might have to log on in some way, or you might find that you are permanently logged on. If your company has set up the network so that you can connect using your graphical user interface—Windows, the Macintosh, a UNIX graphical user interface, or OS/2—you can use all the fancy Internet software that's available for your particular operating system.

If you have an account through one of the major online service providers, you have a dial-in direct account: PPP, SLIP, or CSLIP (almost certainly PPP, but it makes little difference). You must use the software the online service provider gives you to dial in and connect, but after you're connected properly, you can use whatever Internet software you want. (You'll learn about various programs as you go through the book.) With any of these accounts, you'll be using GUI software with windows, dialog boxes, and so on. In fact, you can use the same sort of software as the permanent connection users.

The dial-in terminal connection is the nasty "I'll use it if I absolutely have to" connection. If you are completely broke and have to use the very cheapest service you can find (perhaps a free service, one of the Free-Nets I talk about in Appendix D) or if, perhaps, you are at a college that hasn't yet upgraded its Internet access, you might have to work with a dial-in terminal (shell) account. If so, you'll find yourself working at the command line, where you have to know a bunch of geeky little UNIX commands to get around.

When I wrote the first edition of this book in 1993, it was based on this sort of account, because it was pretty much the only type of account available. These days, most users are working with a graphical user interface instead of the command line, so this book is based on the newest software. However, if you are still working with a command-line account (if you have a dial-in terminal account, or if your company or college has given you a dumb terminal connected to a UNIX computer connected to the Internet), you can still get help.

Almost the entire first edition of *The Complete Idiot's Guide to the Internet* is available to you using an email responder, a special program that automatically sends you information when you send it an email message. The first edition has all the old command-line information that's required if you're using a dial-in terminal connection. When you get to a subject in which you need more information about the UNIX command line, I'll tell you where to send an email message and what to put in the body of that message. You automatically receive a response that includes the relevant chapter from the book. See Appendix E, "The Email Responder," for more information about using the autoresponder.

I Have AOL (CompuServe, MSN, or Such), but Where's the Internet?

I've told you that the online services provide access to the Internet, but when you first install their software and connect to the service, the Internet connection might not be enabled. You might see a message telling you that if you want to connect to the Internet, you'll have to download some more software. Follow the instructions to do so. Just in case, though, here's how to find out more about setting up an Internet connection on the three most popular online services:

- **America Online** Log on, and then click the **Internet** bar in the Welcome window, or click the **Internet Connection** bar in the Channels window, or use the keyword **INTERNET**.
- **CompuServe** Log on, and then click the **Internet** button in the main menu, or use the GO word **INTERNET**.
- **CompuServe 2000** The new CompuServe 2000 integrates the Internet more fully with the online service, so in effect as soon as you connect, you're on. But you can find more information about their Internet services by clicking the big **Internet** button on the toolbar.
- **The Microsoft Network** Log on, then select **Communicate**, **Internet Center**.

You Want Help Setting Up?

Unfortunately, I can't help you with the initial setup of your software. There are too many systems to cover. So here's my (very general) advice: If your service provider or online service can't help you set up, find another one!

Don't let me frighten you. In many cases, the initial software installation is quite easy. You simply run some kind of setup program and follow any instructions, and in a few minutes, you'll be up and running. (If you're just now learning about the

Internet, you're lucky. Installing this fancy GUI Internet software back in the early days was a real nightmare.)

Some providers—in particular, many of the small service providers—are not terribly helpful. However, things are certainly better than they were a few years ago, when many service providers had the attitude "we give you the account to connect to; it's up to you to figure out how to do it!" These days, most providers are making more of an effort. But if you run into a service provider that isn't willing to explain, absolutely clearly, what you need to do to connect, you should move on. This is a very competitive business, and you can find many good companies that are willing to help you.

The Promise of the Internet

For several years, a variety of companies and organizations have been promising that soon we would all be using very fast connections to the Internet. And for several years I've been saying, "not this century." I'd like to crow "told you so," but the pleasure is lessened somewhat by the fact that my prediction was so easy to make. I still don't understand how anyone could have predicted fast connections would become widespread in such a short time.

Still, that time is nearing. No, not next year, and probably not even in 2001, the first year of the twenty-first century. But by then the move will be in full swing, and it won't be too long after then that really fast connections will become commonplace.

Many of us are already using fast connections. If you're lucky enough to have a cable connection, or lucky enough to have an ISDN connection that actually works, or perhaps a DSL connection, you're one of the privileged few. And you can more easily see the promise of the Internet. You see, the Internet is not really a multimedia system, not for most people at least. If you're using a modem connection, you're not going to spend too much time viewing news videos online. But if you're using a high-speed connection, viewing videos is no longer a drag.

For many of us, the Internet has become completely integrated into our daily lives. We get our news online, we research just about any subject you can imagine online (when you know what you're doing, it's surprising just how quickly you can find information, from maps and driving locations to product information and answers to trivia questions). We communicate with family and colleagues online, we buy online, we sell online, we check our email 20 or 30 times a day…if you're reading this book you probably don't understand just how important the Internet has become to many of us. But spend a little time online, learn what you can do with this fantastic new media, and you'll soon see. Then imagine that it all works tens or hundreds of times faster…that's the promise of the Internet.

That's All, Folks!

I don't need to talk any more about getting an Internet account. Most of you already have an account, so it's time to move on and get down to the meat of the subject: how to work with the account you have. If, on the other hand, you don't have an account yet, flip to Appendix D, in which I explain how to find Internet access and tell you what computer equipment you need. Even if you do have an account, you might want to look at this appendix because you might eventually want to swap to a cheaper or more reliable service. Moving along, I'll assume that you have an Internet account that you are completely happy with and that you know how to log on to that account. (Check with your system administrator or look in your service documentation if you need information about logging on to the Internet.)

The Least You Need to Know

- The Internet is the world's largest computer network, a huge public information highway.
- The Internet's motto might be "Designed by the military-industrial complex, used by the people they hate!"
- You can do many things on the Internet: send email, join discussion groups, grab files from electronic libraries, cruise the World Wide Web, and much more.
- Four types of Internet connections are available: mail connections, which aren't much good; dial-in terminal connections, which are better, but you're working with the command line or text menus; and permanent connections and dial-in direct (SLIP and PPP) connections, both of which are much better.
- The Internet is a public system. The online services, such as America Online, CompuServe, and The Microsoft Network, are private services with gateways to the Internet.
- A member of an online service can use the Internet, but an Internet user cannot use an online service unless he joins that service.
- You can get Internet access through your company or school, a small local Internet service provider, a giant Internet service provider (such as AT&T or PSINet), or an online service.

Chapter 2

The Premier Internet Tool: Email

In This Chapter

- Which email program are you using?
- All about email addresses
- Setting up your email program
- Sending a message
- Retrieving your messages—then what
- Sending files across the Internet
- Avoiding fights

Some of you might think the title of this chapter is a joke. It's not. Although email might not be exciting, cool, or compelling, it is the most popular and, in many ways, the most useful Internet service. More people use email on any given day than use any other Internet service. Tens of millions of messages fly across the wires each day. According to *Wired* magazine, publishing via email—newsletters, bulletins, even small books—is growing very quickly, perhaps more quickly than publishing on the World Wide Web.

Despite all the glitz of the Web (you'll learn about that glitz in Chapter 4, "The World of the World Wide Web," Chapter 5, "More About the Web," Chapter 6, "Forms, Applets, and Other Web Weirdness," and Chapter 7, "Web Multimedia"), the potential of Internet Phone systems (Chapter 14, "Internet Conferences: Voice on the Net,

Whiteboards, and More"), and the excitement—for some—of the many chat systems (Chapter 13, "Yak, Yak, Yak: Chatting in Cyberspace"), email is probably the most productive tool there is. Email is a sort of Internet workhorse, getting the work done without any great fanfare.

After spending huge sums of money polling Internet users, we've come to the conclusion that the very first thing Internet users want to do is send email messages. Sending email messages is not too threatening, and it's an understandable concept: You're sending a letter. The only differences are that you don't take it to the post office and that it's much faster. So that's what I'm going to start with: how to send an email message.

Dial-In Terminal (Shell) Accounts

If you are working with a dial-in terminal account (also known as a shell account), this information on email—beyond the basic principles—won't help you much. To learn more about working with email with your type of account, you can use the autoresponder to get the mail chapters from *The Complete Idiot's Guide to the Internet*. Of course, to use the autoresponder, you need to be able to send an email message! So, if necessary, ask your service provider how to send the first message. When you've got that figured out, send email to `CIGInternet@mcp.com` with **allmail** in the Subject line to receive the email chapters.

What Email System?

Which email system do you use? If you are a member of an online service, you have a built-in mail system. But if you are not a member of one of the major online services, who the heck knows what you are using for email! I don't. For that matter, even with an online service, there are different options; CompuServe, for instance, offers a number of different programs you can use.

Basically, it all depends on what your service provider set you up with. You might be using Netscape, a World Wide Web browser (discussed in Chapter 4) that has a built-in email program. Or perhaps you're using Microsoft Exchange, which comes with Windows 95 and NT4, or if you are working with a very recent version of Windows

95 (yes, there are different versions of Windows 95, but we won't get into that) or Windows 98, you might be using Outlook Express. You could be using Eudora, which is one of the most popular email programs on the Internet, or perhaps Pegasus. Or you might be using something else entirely. Luckily, the email concepts are all the same, regardless of the type of program you are using—even if the buttons you click are different.

Start with What You Were Given

I suggest you start off using the email program that you were given when you set up your account. You might be able to use something else later. If you'd like to try Eudora later, go to `http://www.qualcomm.com/`. (You'll see how to use a URL, one of these Web addresses, in Chapter 4.) A free version called Eudora Light is available for the Macintosh and Windows. My current favorite is AK-Mail, a shareware email program (`http://akmail.com/`). You can find Pegasus at `http://www.pegasus.usa.com/`.

To POP or Not to POP

POP (Post Office Protocol) is a very common system used for handling Internet email. A POP server receives email that's been sent to you and holds it until you use your mail program to retrieve it. However, POP's not ubiquitous; some online services and many companies do not use POP.

Why do you care what system is used to hold your mail? After all, all you really care about is the program you use to collect and read the mail, not what arcane system your company or service provider uses. However, the POP issue becomes important if you want to change mail programs. In general, the best and most advanced email programs are designed to be used with POP servers. So, if you need some specific email features and have decided you want to switch to another mail program, you might find you can't do so.

Suppose that you have an America Online or CompuServe account. The mail programs provided by these systems are quite basic. They lack many features that programs such as AK-Mail and Eudora have, such as advanced filtering. (Filtering allows you to automatically carry out actions on incoming email depending on the characteristics of that mail. For instance, you could set up the program to automatically delete all the email messages received from your boss. That way you won't be lying when you tell him you didn't receive his message.) But you might be stuck with what you've got. At the time of this writing, you could not use a POP program with an America Online account, so you couldn't install Eudora or AK-Mail or any other POP program. On the other hand, CompuServe now does provide POP mail, but you have to sign up for this optional service (it's free; use **GO POPMAIL** to find more information). On the other hand, CompuServe 2000, the brand-new CompuServe software release, *does* not have a POP system, for some bizarre reason. This is a classic case of a software upgrade introducing new bugs. (This sort of design screwup is sometimes called a "buglike feature.")

Another common mail system, IMAP (Internet Message Access Protocol), is generally used by corporate networks, not Internet service providers. If you're using a corporate network, you probably won't have much choice about which mail program you can use.

You Have a New Address!

I recently discovered how to spot an absolute beginner on the Internet: He often talks about his email number, equating email with telephones. They are both electronic, after all. However, you have an *email address*. That address has three parts:

- Your account name
- The "at" sign (@)
- Your domain name

What's your account name? Usually, it is the name you use to log on to your Internet account. For instance, when I log on to my CompuServe account, I have to type `71601,1266`. That's my account name. When I log on to MSN, I use `CIGInternet`, and on AOL, I use `PeKent`. (Note that the CompuServe account name is a special case; when using this account in an email address, I have to replace the comma with a period, such as this: `71601.1266@compuserve.com`.)

After your account name, you use the @ sign. Why? How else would the Internet mail system know where the account name ends and the domain name starts?

Finally, you use the domain name, which is the address of your company, your service provider, or your online service. Think of it as the street part of an address: one street (the domain name) can be used for thousands of account names.

Where do you get the domain name? If you haven't been told already, ask the system administrator or tech-support people. (Later in this chapter, you learn the domain names of the larger online services.)

Techno Talk

Account Names: They're All the Same

CompuServe calls the account name a *User ID*, MSN calls it a *Member Name*, and AOL calls it a *Screen Name*. In addition, you might hear the account name called a *username* or *logon ID*. All these names mean the same thing: the name by which you are identified when you log on to your account. However, I discovered that some large service providers (mainly the phone companies, for some reason, who "don't quite get it") do something a little odd. You get some strange number as the account name, and you get another name to use when accessing your email. Someone at AT&T's WorldNet gave me a flip answer as to why they do this, using a sort of "well, of course, we *have* to do this, but you probably wouldn't understand" tone of voice; I wasn't convinced.

A Word About Setup

You might need to set up your email system before it will work. In many cases, this setup has already been done for you. If you are with one of the online services, you don't need to worry—it's done for you. Some of the Internet service providers also do all this configuring stuff for you. Others, however, expect you to get into your program and enter some information. It doesn't have to be difficult. The following figure shows some of the options you can configure in Netscape Messenger, the new email program that comes—along with Navigator—as part of the Netscape Communicator package, but the options will be similar in other programs.

Check This Out

Pronouncing Your Email Address

Here's the correct way to say an email address out loud. You say "dot" for the periods and "at" for the @ sign. Therefore, `pkent@topfloor.com` is "p kent at topfloor dot com."

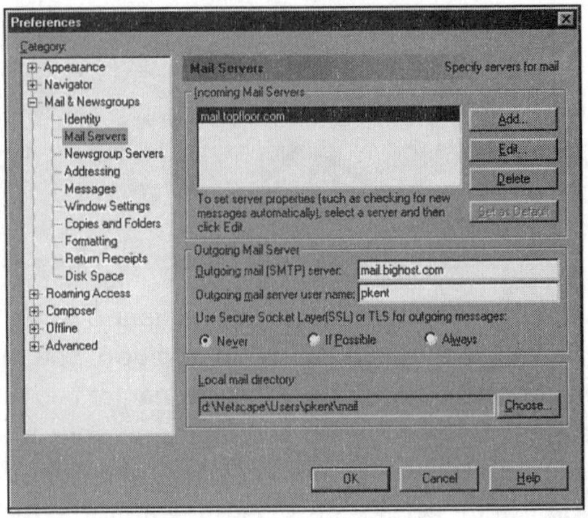

One of several mail-related panels in Netscape Messenger's Preferences dialog box, in which you can configure the mail program before you use it.

Whatever program you have, you might have to enter the following information:

- **Incoming Mail Server** This is usually a POP account, although if you're on a corporate network it might be an IMAP (Internet Message Access Protocol) account. When you connect to your service provider, your email program needs to check with the mail server (a program running on your service provider's system) to see whether any mail has arrived. This mail server holds the messages that arrive for you until your mail program asks for them. Your account name is usually the same as the account name that you use to log on to your service. You might need to enter the full account name and the server hostname (for instance, in Netscape Messenger, I enter `pkent`, my account name, in the Mail Server User Name box, and then enter the server name—`topfloor.com`—in the Incoming Mail Server text box, and click the **POP** option button). On some systems, such as Eudora, you might have to enter the account name and server name all together in one box.
- **SMTP (Simple Mail Transfer Protocol) Server** This mail program is used to send mail. While the POP account holds your incoming mail, the SMTP server transmits your messages onto the Internet. This time you'll enter a hostname (`mail.usa.net`, for instance) or maybe a number (something such as `192.156.196.1`) that your service provider has given to you.
- **Password** You'll need to enter your password so the email program can check the POP for mail. This password is generally the same one you use to log onto the system. Some programs, however, don't request your password until the first time you log on to retrieve your mail.
- **Real Name** This is, yes, your actual name. Most mail programs will send your name along with the email address when you send email in the From line of the message.

- **Return or Reply To Address** You can make the email program place a different Reply To address on your messages. For instance, if you send mail from work but want to receive responses to those messages at home, you'd use a different Reply To address. If you do this, be sure you enter the full address (such as `pkent@topfloor.com`).
- **All Sorts of Other Stuff** You can get a good mail program to do all sorts of things. You can tell it how often to check the POP to see whether new mail has arrived, choose the font you want the message displayed in, and get the program to automatically include the original message when you reply to a message. You can even tell it to leave messages at the POP server after you retrieve them. This might be handy if you like to check your mail from work; if you configure the program to leave the messages at the POP, you can retrieve them again when you get home, using the program on your home machine. You can also define how the program will handle attachments, but that is a complicated subject that I'll get to in the later section "Sending Files Is Getting Easier."

What Else Can I Do with My Mail Program?

You might be able to do lots of things. Check your documentation or Help files, or browse through the configuration dialog boxes to see what you can do. Note, however, that the online services' email programs generally have a limited number of choices. Email programs such as Eudora, Pegasus, AK-Mail, and those included with Netscape Communicator and Internet Explorer have many more choices.

There are so many email programs around; I can't help you configure them all. If you have trouble configuring your program, check the documentation or call the service's technical support. As I've said before, if your service doesn't want to help, find another service!

Sending a Message

Now that you understand addresses and have configured the mail program, you can send a message. So to whom can you mail a message? You might already have friends and colleagues whom you can bother with your flippant "Hey, I've finally made it onto the Internet" message. Or mail me at `testmail@topfloor.com`, and I'll send a response back to you. (To do that, I'll use something called an *autoresponder*, a program that automatically replies to messages that it receives.)

So start your email program, and then open the window in which you are going to write the message. You might have to double-click an icon or choose a menu option that opens the mail's Compose window. For instance, in Eudora, once the program is open, you click the **New Message** button on the toolbar or choose **Message**, **New Message**.

Online Services

If you are working in one of the old CompuServe programs, choose **Mail**, **Create New Mail**. With CompuServe 2000, click the big **Create Mail** button in the toolbar. In AOL, choose **Mail**, **Compose Mail**. In MSN, you open the **Communicate** menu and select **Send or Read Email**. (If you're still working with the old version of the MSN software, click the big **Email** bar in MSN Central.) If you are using Netscape's email program, there are all sorts of ways to begin: select **File**, **New**, **Message**, for instance.

In all the email programs, the Compose window has certain common elements. Some programs have a few extras. Here's what you might find:

- **To** This line is for the address of the person you are mailing to. If you are using an online service and you are sending a message to another member of that service, all you need to use is the person's account name. For instance, if you are an AOL member and you're mailing to another AOL member with the screen name of PeKent, that's all you need to enter. To mail to that member from a service other than AOL, however, you enter the full address: `pekent@aol.com`. (I'll explain more about mailing to online services in the section "We Are All One: Sending Email to Online Services.")
- **From** Not all mail programs show this line, but it shows your email address, which is included in the message header (the clutter at the top of an Internet message). It lets the recipient know whom to reply to.

- **Reply To** You might have both a From address (to show which account the message came from) and a Reply To address (to get the recipient to reply to a different address).

Don't Cc to a List!

If you want to mail a message to a large list of people, don't put all the addresses into the Cc line. Addresses in the Cc line will be visible to all recipients, and most people don't like the idea of their email address being given away to strangers. Instead, put the list into the Bcc line. Addresses in the Bcc line will not be displayed anywhere in the email message.

- **Subject** This line is a sort of message title—a few words summarizing the contents. The recipient can scan through a list of subjects to see what each message is about. (Some mail programs won't let you send a message unless you fill in the Subject line; others, perhaps most, don't mind if you leave it blank.)
- **Cc** You can enter an address here to send a copy to someone other than the person whose address you placed in the To line.
- **Bc** This means "blind copy." As with the Cc line, a copy of the message will be sent to the address (or addresses) you place in the Bc (or Bcc) line; however, the recipient of the original message won't be able to tell that the Bcc address received a copy. (If you use Cc, the recipient of the original message sees a Cc line in the header.)
- **Attachments** This option is for sending computer files along with the message. (Again, I'll get to that later in this chapter, in the section "Sending Files Is Getting Easier.")
- **A big blank area** This area is where you type your message.

Email programs vary greatly, and not all programs have all these features. Again, the online service mail programs tend to be a bit limited. The following figures show the Compose window in two very different mail programs.

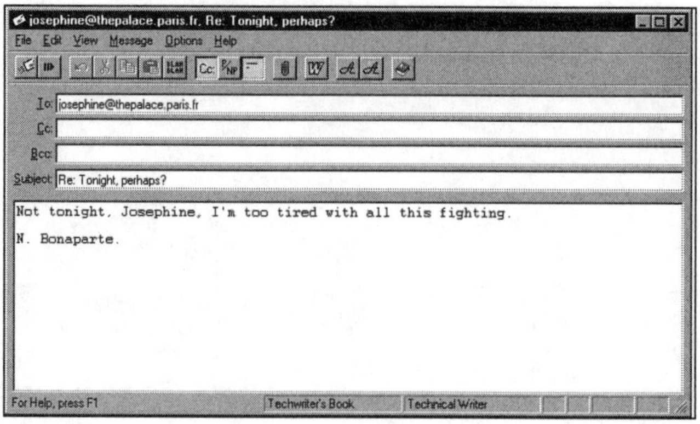

This is AK-Mail, my current favorite.

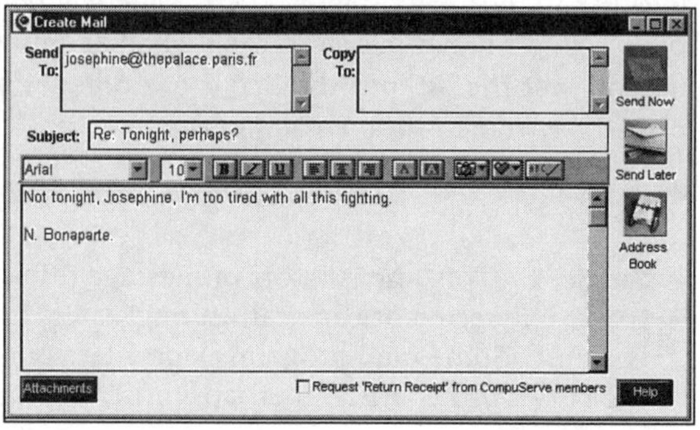

This is CompuServe 2000's mail composition window.

Go ahead and type a To address; Email `testmail@topfloor.com`, and you'll get a response. Or email to your own address. If you use an online service, you might as well use the entire Internet address (for instance, on AOL type `name@aol.com`). The message will probably go out onto the Internet and then turn around and come back to you. I'll explain those online service addresses in the next section.

We Are All One: Sending Email to Online Services

One of the especially nice things about the Internet, from an email point of view, is that because all the online services are now connected to the Internet, you can send email between online services. (Not so long ago the online services were completely separate; you could email someone on a service only if you had an account with that service.) Perhaps you have an America Online account because AOL sent you a disk in the mail. Perhaps your brother has a CompuServe account because he's a geek, and that's where the geeks have been hanging out for years. (Before you email me to complain, I've had a CompuServe account for almost 15 years.) You can send email to one another, using the Internet as a sort of bridge. How? You just have to know the other person's account name on that service and that service's domain name.

For instance, CompuServe has this Internet domain name: `compuserve.com`. Say you want to send an email message to someone at CompuServe who has the account name (or User ID as it's called on CompuServe) of `71601,1266`. You add the two together with the @ in the middle. Then you have `71601,1266@compuserve.com`. However, you can't have a comma in an Internet address. So you replace it with a period, and you end up with `71601.1266@compuserve.com`. (Some CompuServe users have "proper" email addresses, names instead of numbers. If you use CompuServe and want one of these real addresses, use **GO REGISTER**.) The following table lists a few services and tells you how to send email to them.

Table 2.1 Sending Email to Other Services

Service	Method of Addressing
America Online	Add `@aol.com` to the end of an America Online address.
CompuServe	In the User ID, replace the comma (,) with a period (.), and then add `@compuserve.com` to the end (these days many CompuServe members have Internet-style addresses, although probably most still have the old style, such as: `71601,1266`, which would be written as `71601.1266@compuserve.com`).
GEnie	Add `@genie.geis.com` to the end of a GEnie address.
MCImail	Add `@mcimail.com` to the end of a MCImail address.
Microsoft Network	Add `@msn.com` to the end of the MSN Member name.
Prodigy	Add `@prodigy.com` to the end of the user's Prodigy address.

These addresses are quite easy. Of course, there are more complicated Internet addresses, but you'll rarely run into them. However, if you have trouble emailing someone, call and ask exactly what you must type as his email address. (There's no rule that says you can't use the telephone anymore.)

Write the Message

Now that you have the address onscreen, write your message—whatever you want to say. Then send the message. How's that done? There's usually a big **Send** button, or maybe a menu option that says **Send** or **Mail**. What happens when you click the button? That depends on the program and whether you are logged on at the moment. Generally, if you are logged on, the mail is sent immediately. Not always, though. Some programs will put the message in a queue and won't send the message until told to do so. Others will send the message immediately, and if you are not logged on, they will try to log on first. Watch closely and you'll usually see what's happening. A message will let you know whether the message is being sent. If it hasn't been sent, look for some kind of **Send Immediately** menu option or perhaps

Send Queued Messages. Whether the message should be sent immediately or put in a queue is often one of the configuration options available to you.

Where'd It Go? Incoming Email

You've sent yourself an email message, but where did it go? It went out into the electronic wilderness to wander around for a few seconds or maybe a few minutes. Sometimes email messages can take a few hours to reach their destinations. Very occasionally, it even takes a few days. (Generally, the message comes back in a few minutes, especially if you're sending yourself a message, unless you mistyped the address, in which case you'll get a special message telling you that it's a bad address.)

Now it's time to check for incoming email. If you are using an online service, as soon as you log on you'll see a message saying that email has arrived. If you are already online, you might see a message telling you that mail has arrived, or you might need to check periodically; you might find a Get New Mail menu option. If you are working with an Internet service provider, you generally won't be informed of incoming mail; rather your email program has to go and check. Either you can do that manually (for instance, in Eudora, there's a **File**, **Check Mail** command), or you can configure the program to check automatically every so often.

Fancy Fonts

Some of the online services allow you to use fancy text formatting features. For example, MSN and AOL let you use colors, indents, different fonts, bold, italic, and so on. But in general these features work only in messages sent *within* the online services. Internet email is plain text—nothing fancy. Don't bother getting fancy in your Internet email because the online service's email system will strip out all that attractive stuff when the message is sent out onto the Internet. However, there is a system you can use to send formatted email, if both you and the recipient have the right type of mail program—HTML Mail. We'll take a quick look at HTML Mail in Chapter 3, "Advanced Email: HTML and Encryption."

What Now?

What can you do with your incoming email? All sorts of things. I think I'm pretty safe in saying that every email program allows you to read incoming messages. Most programs also let you print and save messages (if your program doesn't, you need another). You can also delete them, forward them to someone else, or reply directly to the sender. These commands should be easy to find. Generally you'll have toolbar buttons for the most important commands, and more options will be available if you dig around a little in the menus, too.

A Word About Quoting

It's a good idea to quote when you respond to a message. This means that you include part or all the original message. Some programs automatically quote the original message. Different programs mark quoted messages in different ways; usually, you'll see a greater than symbol (>) at the beginning of each line. The following figure shows a reply message that contains a quote from the original message.

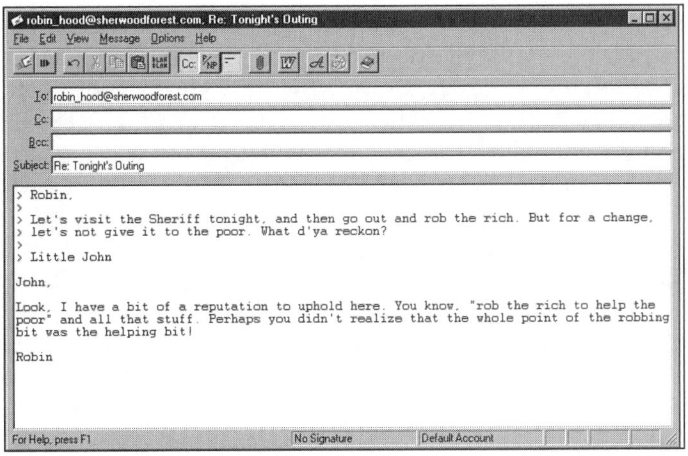

Quote the original message when responding to remind the sender what he said.

You aren't required to quote. But if you don't, the recipient might not know what you are talking about. I receive scores of messages a day and I know people who get hundreds. (Of course, the radiation emitted from their computer screens is probably frying their brains.) If you respond to a message without reminding the recipient exactly which of the 200 messages he sent out last week (or which of the five he sent to you) you are responding to, he might be slightly confused. Quoting is especially important when sending messages to mailing lists and newsgroups (discussed in Chapter 9, "Newsgroups: The Source of All Wisdom"), where your message might be read by people who didn't read the message to which you are responding.

Sending Files Is Getting Easier

I used to hate sending files. Not because it's so difficult to send files across the Internet (although it is—or at least used to be until very recently), but because it was sort of embarrassing to admit how difficult it was. Now before you misunderstand, let me say that I did know how to send files across the Internet. However, very few other people seemed to understand, and even when they did understand, they didn't seem to have software that worked properly. Unless both parties involved (the sender and the recipient) understood the process and had the correct software, things sometimes didn't work.

I recall, for instance, the incredible problems I had transferring computer files to a magazine early in 1995. It didn't matter what transmission format I used (I'll discuss that in a moment), or what program I was working with; the staff at the magazine couldn't seem to open those files—never mind that this magazine just happened to be a major Internet magazine. Today the situation is much improved, and the problems inherent in file transfers are, for many users, a thing of the past. Still, the situation isn't perfect, and problems can still occur.

Files are commonly sent across cyberspace in one of four ways:

- **MIME** Multimedia Internet Mail Extensions is a system designed to make sending files across the Internet easier. It converts the file to text, sends it with the message, and converts it back at the other end. (You can send only text files in the Internet's email system, hence the need to convert files to text.) What's the difference between uuencode and MIME? Whereas uuencode, the following method, is a sort of quick fix, MIME was intended to be a nicely integrated system that works transparently so that all you have to do is select the file you want to send, and MIME does the rest. MIME also has a method for identifying the type of file that is being transferred. (MIME is now used on the World Wide Web to identify multimedia files linked to Web pages.) MIME is the most common method used for sending files across the Internet these days. Most users now have email programs that handle the file transfer, but a few have to use utilities to convert a MIMEd file back to its original format.
- **uuencode** In this system, a computer file is converted to plain ASCII text. It might start out as a sound file or a word processing file, but when it's converted it looks like gibberish text. This process is called *uuencoding*. An encoded file can be placed into an email message and sent. The person at the other end must then either receive the message with a mail program that can convert uuencoded files back to their original format or save the message as a text file and *uudecode* it—convert it back to its original format—using a special utility. This system is falling out of favor because most email programs now handle MIME.
- **BinHex** This system is used on the Macintosh and it's very similar to uuencode. Files are converted into text and then converted back at the other end. However, it seems to be dying out (relatively speaking; please don't email me to tell me it's alive and well, and how the Macintosh is a better machine, and how

Bill Gates should be crucified for stealing Macintosh design features...). Even many Macintosh mail programs use MIME and uuencode.

- **Online Service Systems** Each of the online services has a file-transfer system. In AOL and CompuServe, you can attach a file to a message and then send that message to another member of the same online service. In MSN, you can insert all sorts of things directly into messages—pictures, formatted text, or computer files—and then send them to other MSN members.

Now, here's the problem. If you want to send a message to another person on the Internet, you might have to know which system to use. The following guidelines can help you make a good decision:

1. The first time you have to send a file to someone, just go ahead and use whatever system your mail program works with. A couple of years ago you'd have a 50-50 chance of the file getting through, but these days it will probably work. If it doesn't, though, move on to the next step.
2. Check to see whether the other person has an account on the same online service that you do. Even if you've been given an Internet email address that is obviously not an online service, ask just in case. It's more reliable to send a file between CompuServe accounts, between AOL accounts, or between MSN accounts, for instance, than to use MIME, BinHex, or uuencode. (You'll find that many people—especially geeks—have accounts on two or more services.) I used to tell people that it's far more reliable to use the online service rather than the other systems, but the gap is closing.
3. If you have to use the Internet email system, check to see which system the recipient can work with (MIME, uuencode, or BinHex). In the past I've advised that you shouldn't simply pick one and send the file because if the recipient didn't have the right software, he wouldn't be able to use the file. However, these days MIME is in fairly wide use, so if you're not able to check with the recipient first, you could try MIME, and it will probably work. (However, see the following discussion of the online services.) The most popular POP mail programs all work with MIME: Eudora, Netscape Communicator's mail program (Messenger), Pegasus, Microsoft Internet Mail, Outlook Express, and so on.
4. Consider which file-transfer systems are built into your email program. If you are lucky, the system that's built into your email program is the same system the recipient uses—however, if that were the case, you wouldn't have had a problem in the first place. However, the program might have two or more systems built in so that you can choose one or the other. For example, Eudora Light can send files using MIME or BinHex—but it can't send files using uuencode. (At least, Eudora can't do so directly. However, you'll see in a moment how to send uuencoded messages even if it's not built into your email program.) Netscape Navigator has both MIME and uuencode, so you can use either. Many mail programs work only with MIME, though.

What if you don't have a match? Or what if the recipient has an online service account? Or if you have an online service account? Some of the online services might not work with either MIME or uuencode. The major online services have recently been upgrading their mail services so you can use MIME—perhaps. You can send files to and from CompuServe using MIME, although to receive them you might have to upgrade your mail system (use the **GO NEWMAIL** command). AOL also allows file transfers to and from the Internet. Surprisingly, MSN didn't allow incoming and outgoing file attachments until recently; version 2.5 of the MSN software, which uses Outlook Express as the mail program, does work with attachments, so if you have an earlier version, you might want to upgrade.

Note, however, that even if an online service's mail system uses MIME, it might not do so properly. For instance, I found that when I sent a file from CompuServe to an Internet account the file was transferred correctly, but without a filename. CompuServe had trouble accepting incoming files that had MIME attachments, too. AOL, on the other hand, might strip out the file extension on *incoming* files, yet transfer outgoing files correctly, although the new version 4.0 seems to work well. (By the way, the online services' mail systems are very slow; I think they employ people to retype all the incoming messages. I'm not sure what they do with attachments, but attachments slow down incoming mail even further.) If you are working with a service that won't work with MIME or uuencode, you'll have to use a utility to convert the incoming file for you, which I'll discuss next.

Conversion Utilities

There are things you can do to get around incompatibilities between your mail system and the recipient's, but they might be a hassle. Say you want to send someone a file using uuencode because that's the only thing he can work with. But you have a CompuServe account, which means your email program won't automatically uudecode files. You can go to one of the software archives mentioned in Appendix C, "All the Software You'll Ever Need," and download a uuencode program. (For instance, if you use Windows, you can use a program called Wincode.) Then you use that program to convert the file to a text file, you copy the text from the file and paste it into the message, and you send the message. (And then you cross your fingers.)

How about MIME? Say someone just sent you a MIME-encoded file, but you have a mail program that won't decode MIME attachments. What can you do? Go to the software libraries and search for MIME. For instance, I use little DOS programs called Mpack and Munpack. You can save the message you received as a text file (virtually all email programs let you do this, generally with the **File**, **Save As** command), and then use Munpack to convert that text file to the original file format. (Mpack and Munpack are also available for the Macintosh and for UNIX systems.)

How about BinHex? I sometimes receive files from Macintosh users; I use a Windows program called StuffIt Expander to extract the file from BinHex. (StuffIt Expander was originally a Macintosh program, so Mac versions are available, too, of course; it also works with uuencoded files and archive files such as .sit and .zip files—see Chapter 15, "What on Earth Are All Those File Types?" for more information. You can find these programs at `http://www.aladdinsys.com/`.)

If you are lucky, though, your email program has MIME and uuencode built in, as well as some kind of command that lets you insert or attach a file. For instance, in Eudora Light, choose **Message**, **Attach File** and use the small drop-down list at the top of the Compose window to choose between **BinHex** and **MIME**. In AOL, click the **Attach** button; in CompuServe (see the next figure), use the **Mail**, **Send File** command in the main window, or click the **Attach File** button in the Create Mail window.

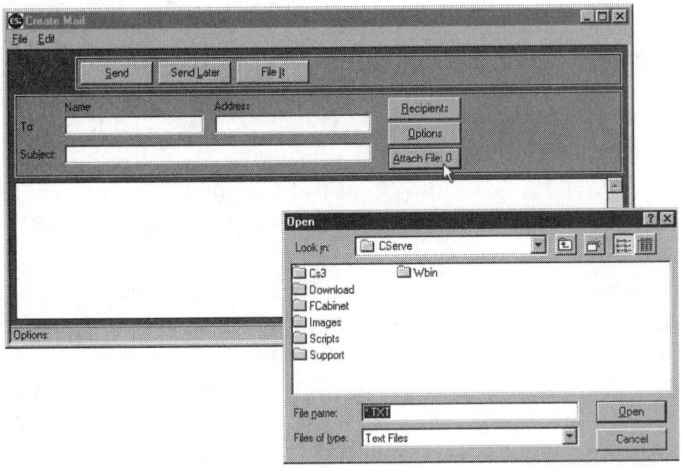

Sending a file with your email is usually as simple as clicking a button and selecting the file.

Cool Things You Can Do with Email

After you understand your email system and realize that it won't bite, you might begin to enjoy using it. The following list contains suggestions of some things you might want to do with your email program:

- **Create a mailing list** You can create a special mailing list that contains the email addresses of many people. For instance, if you want to send a message to everyone in your department (or family, or club) at the same time, you can create a mailing list. Put all the addresses in the list, and then send the message to the list. Everyone on the list receives the message, and you save time and hassle. Some programs will have a mailing list dialog box of some sort; others let you create a nickname or alias for the mailing list and then associate the addresses with it.
- **Create an address book** Virtually all email systems have address books, and they're usually quite easy to use. You can store a person's complicated email address and then retrieve it quickly using the person's real name.

- **Use aliases** An alias, sometimes known as a *nickname*, is a simple identifier you give to someone in your address book. Instead of typing `peter kent` or `pkent@topfloor.com`, for instance, you could just type a simple alias such as `pk` to address a message to that person.
- **Work with mail while you're offline** Most programs these days let you read and write email offline. The program quickly logs on to send and retrieve messages, and then logs off again automatically. This feature is of particular importance with services that charge you for the amount of time you are online.
- **Forward your mail** After being on the Internet for a while, there's a risk of attaining real geekhood by getting multiple Internet accounts, such as one with your favorite online service, one at work, one with a cheap service provider, and so on. (Right now, I have about eight, I think.) That's a lot of trouble logging on to check for email. However, some services let you forward your email to another account so that if a message arrives at, say, the account you use at home, you can have it automatically sent on to you at work. Ask your service provider how to do this; you might need to log on to your shell account to set this up (discussed in Chapter 19, "21 Questions: The Complete Internet FAQ"). Although most Internet service providers let you do this, the online services generally don't.
- **Create a vacation message** When you go on vacation, your email doesn't stop. That's why so many cybergeeks never go on vacation, or take a laptop if they do: They can't bear the thought of missing all those messages. Still, if you manage to break away, you might be able to set a special vacation message, an automatic response to any incoming mail that says basically, "I'm away, be back soon." (You get to write the response message.) Again, ask your service provider. The online services generally don't have this service.
- **Filter your files** Sophisticated email programs have file-filtering capabilities. You can tell the program to look at incoming mail and carry out certain actions according to what it finds. You can place email from your newsgroups into special inboxes, grab only the message subject if the message is very long, delete mail from certain people or organizations, and so on.

Caution: Email Can Be Dangerous!

The more I use email, the more I believe that it can be a dangerous tool. There are three main problems: 1) People often don't realize the implications of what they are saying, 2) people often misinterpret what others are saying, and 3) people are comfortable typing things into a computer that they would never say to a person face-to-face. Consequently, online fights are common both in private (between email correspondents) and in public (in the newsgroups and mailing lists).

The real problem is that when you send an email message, the recipient can't see your face or hear your tone of voice. Of course, when you write a letter, you have the same problem, but email is replacing conversations as well as letters. The U.S. Post Office is as busy as ever, so I figure email is mainly replacing conversations. That contributes to the problem because people are writing messages in a chatty conversational style, forgetting that email lacks all the visual and auditory "cues" that go along with a conversation.

In the interests of world peace, I give you these email guidelines to follow:

- **Don't write something you will regret later** Lawsuits have been based on the contents of electronic messages, so consider what you are writing and whether you would want it to be read by someone other than the recipient. A message can always be forwarded, read over the recipient's shoulder, printed out and passed around, backed up onto the company's archives, and so on. You don't have to use email—there's always the telephone. (Oliver North has already learned his lesson!)
- **Consider the tone of your message** It's easy to try to be flippant and come out as arrogant or to try to be funny and come out as sarcastic. When you write, think about how your words will appear to the recipient.
- **Give the sender the benefit of the doubt** If a person's message sounds arrogant or sarcastic, consider that he might be trying to be flippant or funny! If you are not sure what the person is saying, ask him to explain.
- **Read before you send** It will give you a chance to fix embarrassing spelling and grammatical errors and to reconsider what you've just said. (Some mail programs have spell checkers.)
- **Wait a day...or three** If you typed something in anger, wait a few days before sending it and read the message again. Give yourself a chance to reconsider.
- **Be nice** There's no need for vulgarity or rudeness (except in certain newsgroups, where it seems to be a requirement for entrance).
- **Attack the argument, not the person** I've seen fights start when someone disagrees with another person's views and sends a message making a personal attack upon that person. (This point is more related to mailing lists and newsgroups than email proper, but we are on the subject of avoiding fights.) Instead of saying, "Anyone who thinks *Days of Our Lives* is not worth the electrons it's transmitted on must be a half-witted moron with all the common sense of the average pineapple," consider saying, "You might think it's not very good, but clearly many other people find great enjoyment in this show."

You're Being Baited

Some people send rude or vicious messages because they *enjoy* getting into a fight like this where they can fight from the safety of their computer terminals. Avoid conversations with people who are obviously baiting you.

- **Use smileys** One way to add some of those missing visual and auditory cues is to add smileys—keep reading.

Smile and Be Understood!

Over the past few years, email users have developed a number of ways to clarify the meaning of messages. You might see <g> at the end of the line, for example. This means grin and is shorthand for saying, "You know, of course, that what I just said was a joke, right?" You might also see :-) in the message. Turn this book sideways, so that the left column of this page is up and the right column is down, and you'll see that this symbol is a small smiley face. It means the same as <g>, "Of course, that was a joke, okay?"

Emoticons Galore

Little pictures are commonly known as *smileys*. But the smiley face, although by far the most common, is just one of many available symbols. You might see some of the emoticons in the following table, and you might want to use them. Perhaps you can create a few of your own.

Share the Smiles

Many people call these character faces "smiley faces." But if you'd like to impress your friends with a bit of technobabble, you can call them *emoticons*. If you really want to impress your colleagues, get hold of *The Smiley Dictionary* by Seth Godin. It contains hundreds of these things.

Table 2.2 Commonly Used Emoticons

Emoticon	Meaning
:-(	Sadness, disappointment
8-)	Kinda goofy-looking smile, or wearing glasses
:->	A big smile
;-)	A wink

Emoticon	Meaning
*<|:-)	Santa Claus
:-&	Tongue-tied
:-o	A look of shock
:-p	Tongue stuck out
=:o]	Bill Clinton
,:-) or 7:^]	Ronald Reagan

(For a handy reference to smileys, see `http://www.czweb.com/smilies.htm`.) Personally, I don't like smileys much. They strike me as being just a *tiiny* bit too cutesy. However, I do use them now and again to make absolutely sure that I'm not misunderstood!

Message Shorthand

There are a couple of other ways people try to liven up their messages. One is to use obscure acronyms such as the ones in this table.

Table 2.3 Online Shorthand

Acronym	Meaning
BTW	By the way
FWIW	For what it's worth
FYI	For your information
IMO	In my opinion
IMHO	In my humble opinion
LOL	Laughing out loud (used as an aside to show your disbelief)
OTFL	On the floor, laughing (used as an aside)
PMFBI	Pardon me for butting in
PMFJI	Pardon me for jumping in
RTFM	Read the &*^%# manual
ROTFL or ROFL	Rolling on the floor laughing (used as an aside)
ROTFLMAO	Same as above, except with "laughing my a** off" added on the end. (You didn't expect me to say it, did you? This is a family book, and anyway, the editors won't let me.)
TIA	Thanks in advance
YMMV	Your mileage might vary

The real benefit of using these is that they confuse the average neophyte. I suggest that you learn them quickly, so you can pass for a long-term cybergeek.

You'll also see different ways of stressing particular words. (You can't use bold and italic in most Internet email, remember?) You might see words marked with an underscore on each side (_now!_) or, perhaps frequently, with an asterisk (*now!*).

The Least You Need to Know

- There are many different email systems, but the basic procedures all work similarly.
- Even if your online service lets you use fancy text (colors, different fonts, different styles) within the service, that text won't work in Internet messages (see Chapter 3 for information on HTML Mail, though).
- Sending files across the Internet is much easier now than it was just a year or so ago, but problems still arise; sending files within the online services is always easy.
- On the Internet, the most common file-transfer method is MIME; uuencode is also used now and then. These often are built into mail programs, or you can use external utilities to convert the files.
- In most cases these days you can just attach a file and send it—it'll probably get through okay. But things can go wrong now and then, especially if the sender or recipient is using an old program.
- Get to know all the neat little things your email program can do for you, such as create mailing lists and filter files.
- Be careful with email; misunderstandings (and fights) are common.

Chapter 3

Advanced Email: HTML and Encryption

In This Chapter

- HTML Mail: an end to plain old text messages?
- How Inbox Direct floods your inbox with HTML Mail
- Email encryption
- Public-key encryption and how it works
- Digitally signing your messages
- Why key length makes a difference

Email has changed quite a bit over the past year or so and will continue to change dramatically over the next year or so, thanks to two important systems: HTML Mail and encryption.

The first of these, HTML Mail, livens up email a little—in some cases, quite a lot. HTML Mail enables you to use different colors for the text in your messages, to work with different font sizes and styles, to create bulleted lists and centered text, and even to insert pictures and sounds.

Although encryption has been available for a few years, it was too complicated to catch on. Now email encryption—the ability to encrypt, or scramble, email messages to make them unreadable to all but the recipient—is being built into email programs, which makes it easier to use. I used to predict that everyone would be using encryption pretty soon, but I've given up on that prediction. Most people just don't seem to care. Still, the systems are available if you need them, so I'll explain what encryption can do for you and how to use it.

Banish Dull Email with HTML Mail

HTML Mail is a system in which HTML tags can be used within email messages. *HTML* means Hypertext Markup Language, and as you'll learn in the World Wide Web chapters of this book (Chapter 4, "The World of the World Wide Web;" Chapter 5, "More About the Web;" Chapter 6, "Forms, Applets, and Other Web Weirdness;" Chapter 7, "Web Multimedia;" and Chapter 20, "Setting Up Your Own Web Site"), HTML is used to create World Wide Web pages. HTML tags are the codes inserted into a Web page that tell a Web browser how to display the page. These tags can be used to modify the manner in which text appears on the page—its color, size, style, and so on—and where the text appears on the page. They can be used to create tables, insert pictures and Java applications, and plenty more. Now that HTML is coming to email, email messages can be far more than just plain text.

To use HTML Mail, you need two things. First, you need an HTML Mail program. Second (but just as important), you need to ensure that the recipient has an HTML Mail program. If you send an HTML Mail message to someone who doesn't have an HTML Mail program, that person won't see all the formatting you've added to the message. Worse, depending on the program you've used, the message the person receives might be very difficult to read because it will be full of HTML tags. (Some HTML Mail programs insert a plain-text version of the message at the beginning of the message, so a recipient who isn't using an HTML Mail program can still read the message.)

Finding an HTML Mail Program

Most recent mail programs can work with HTML Mail in some form or other. If you're working with Netscape Messenger or Microsoft Outlook, the two most commonly used programs on the Internet, you have an HTML Mail-capable program. Most other major programs also work with HTML Mail, too—Eudora and Pegasus, for instance. You can see a couple of these HTML programs at work in the following figures. Unfortunately, some of the online services' email systems use a different method. CompuServe 2000, for instance, allows you to format your messages with colors, bolding, and so on, and even to insert images. But they're not using HTML Mail, so people receiving the messages in an HTML Mail program won't be able to view them properly. If people with HTML Mail programs send formatted mail to CompuServe 2000, it won't be received in the correct format.

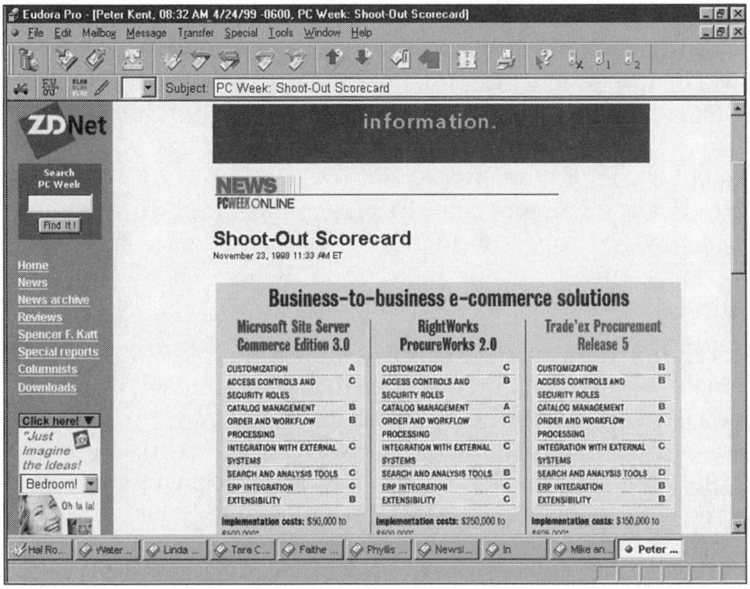

This is a Web page transmitted to a Eudora email program. Because Eudora works well with HTML Mail, it can display the page inside the message.

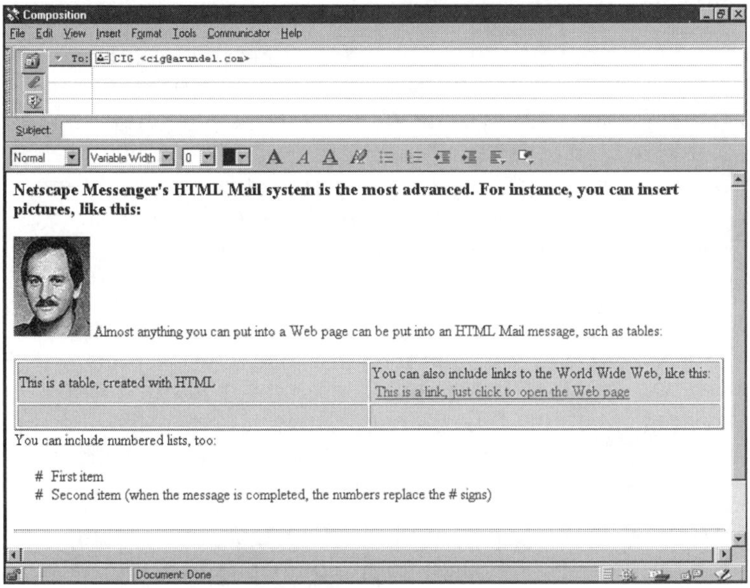

Netscape Messenger, the program that introduced HTML Mail to the world.

Different Programs, Different Abilities

Just because an email program supports HTML Mail doesn't mean that it supports it well or in the best way. Some programs can handle a few simple things, but not the more complicated processes involved with HTML Mail.

Suppose you insert an image into a message using Netscape Messenger. That image will be transferred along with the email message. If the recipient has Netscape Messenger, the image will be displayed within the message exactly where it should be. If the user has another HTML Mail program, though, the image might not be displayed in the message; it might be saved on the recipient's hard disk instead. Some HTML Mail programs won't even send the inserted image with the message. The early HTML Mail versions of Netscape's mail program (the program included with Netscape Navigator 3) inserted a link to the image instead of transferring the image itself. That caused problems, of course, because the image might be on the user's hard disk and unavailable to the recipient.

Some HTML Mail programs might be unable to display some forms of HTML Mail messages, too. For instance, the program might be able to display simple HTML Mail messages from Netscape Messenger, but not the more complicated messages used by companies delivering Inbox Direct publications (which we'll look at next). You might be able to send HTML Mail messages, but that doesn't mean the recipients can view the message properly, even if they do have an HTML Mail program.

Inbox Direct: Web Pages Delivered Directly to You

To promote its new HTML Mail standard, Netscape set up a system called Inbox Direct. Scores of companies have signed up with Netscape to provide HTML-formatted email messages to anyone who signs up at the Netscape site. These messages are in effect newsletters, and they're all free for at least an introductory period (many are free for as long as you want them). You can get information from *The New York Times, USA Today, The Melbourne Age, Rheinische Post, Correo Expansión Directo, The Financial Times, PlanetOut, ParentsPlace.com Gazette, National Geographic Online, PBS Previews*, and many more.

To sign up for one of these publications, go to `http://home.netscape.com/` and find the **In-Box Direct Free E-Magazines** link, and then just follow instructions (Chapter 4 explains how to use the Web). The publications have all been created using HTML Mail, so they'll be brightly illustrated publications, as you can see in the following figure. They will contain links to Web pages, pictures, tables, perhaps even JavaScript and Java applets (which you'll learn about in Chapter 6).

Is anyone really using HTML Mail? Yes, but I don't think HTML Mail turned into one of those "gotta have" technologies that various software companies swore it would. For instance, I recently investigated advertising on a joke email list (at least 300,000 people have subscribed to various joke mailings—after all, isn't that what the Internet is for?). Only about 8% of the subscribers to the list were receiving their daily joke in HTML Mail format. HTML Mail can be a real nuisance sometimes; many people use HTML Mail all the time, not realizing that many recipients can't see the formatting.

Many long-term Internet users do not use HTML Mail at all. I'm a newsletter publisher myself, with over 30,000 subscribers (visit `http://PoorRichard.com/newsltr/`), and I certainly don't use HTML mail, nor have I felt much pressure from my subscribers to do so. However, advertisers like HTML mail, because it allows them to insert banners and other graphical ads into the mail, so many newsletters have gone to HTML mail to please the advertisers.

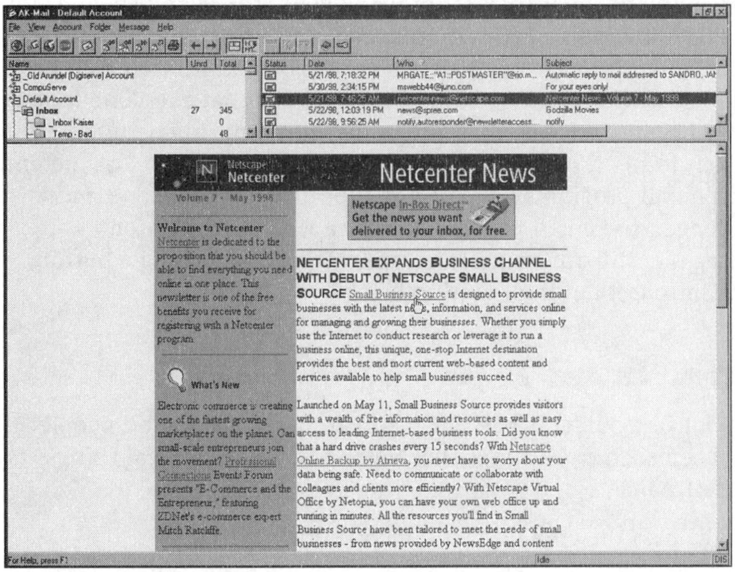

An Inbox Direct email message is formatted with HTML Mail and displayed in Netscape Messenger.

Keep Away Prying Eyes with Encryption

The other major change coming to email is the capability to encrypt messages. In other words, messages can be scrambled so that they can't be read if intercepted. Before a scrambled message can be read, it must be decrypted—that is, converted back to its original form. Then it will be legible. If all goes well, the only person who can decrypt the message is the intended recipient.

There was a great deal of interest in data encryption late in 1994 and early in 1995. Most of this interest centered around a program called *PGP* (Pretty Good Privacy). This program is able to encrypt a message so solidly that it's essentially unbreakable. It's almost certainly impossible to break a PGP-encrypted message using current computer technology, and even when technology improves a little, breaking such a message might remain prohibitively expensive. (As I'll explain, there are different levels of encryption; although it's possible to break messages encrypted using the low levels, the most secure messages cannot be broken.) For instance, breaking into a message to your Aunt Edna explaining when you're going to arrive for Christmas dinner would probably cost the CIA more than engineering a coup in a midsize Central American republic. Therefore, your mail will likely remain completely safe. (This, of course, upsets the U.S. government, along with many other governments around the world.)

I know exactly when this intense interest in PGP occurred because I made a shameless attempt to cash in on the interest by writing a book about PGP. I also know exactly when this interest subsided—about three days before my book was published. Why the sudden decline in interest in a technology that could be so useful? Because it's so hard to use.

I wrote my book based on an application called WinPGP, a Windows program that insulates the user from many of the intricacies of using PGP. Still, even using a front end such as WinPGP, PGP remained a little complicated, and I told anyone who would listen to me that "encryption won't be popular until it's built into email programs and is as easy to use as clicking a button." I'd like to say that everyone took my advice and immediately began work on email programs with built-in encryption, but actually few people listen to me (except my family, and I suspect they're just pretending). Nonetheless, such email programs have begun appearing on the scene, most notably Netscape Messenger, the email portion of Netscape Communicator. Encrypting email messages is still a little more complicated than clicking a button, but it's certainly much simpler than it all used to be.

Why Encrypt Your Email?

Email can get you in a lot of trouble. It got Oliver North in hot water, and people have lost their jobs or been sued over things they've said in email. Several things can go wrong when you use email:

- The recipient might pass the email on to someone else.
- The message can be backed up to a backup system and later read by someone other than the recipient.
- Someone could spy on you and read your email looking for incriminating comments.
- Your boss might decide to read your email, based on the idea that if it's written on company time and company equipment, it's company property (and the courts will almost certainly back him up).

The most likely scenario is that the recipient intentionally or thoughtlessly passes your message to someone who you didn't count on seeing it. Unfortunately, encryption can't help you with that problem. The second problem—that the message could be copied to a backup system— has gotten many, many people into trouble. Even if you delete a message and the recipient deletes the message, it might still exist somewhere on the network if the system administrator happened to do a backup before it was deleted. So if you are ever the subject of some kind of investigation, that message could be revived. This is more of a problem on the Internet because a message goes from your computer, to your service provider's computer, to the recipient's service provider's computer, to the recipient's computer—at least four places from which it could be copied. Finally, someone might be out to get you. Internet Email is basic text, and a knowledgeable hacker with access to your service provider's system (or the recipient's service provider's system) can grab your messages and read them.

What do you do, then? The simplest solution is to avoid putting things in email that you would be embarrassed to have others read. The more complicated solution is to encrypt your email.

Public-Key Encryption: It's Magic

Email encryption systems depend on something known as *public-key encryption*. I'd like to give you a full and detailed description of exactly how it works, but I don't know exactly how it works (I'm no mathematician, and encryption is done using the sort of math that only a geek could love), so I'll give you the simple answer: It's magic. Perhaps that's insufficient; I'll endeavor to explain a little more without getting more complicated than necessary.

First, let me describe *private-key encryption*, which you might have already used. A computer file can be encrypted—turned into a jumble of garbage characters that makes it useless—using a program that works with a *private key* (also known as a *secret key* or even simply called a *password*). The private key is a sort of code word. Tell the program the name of the file you want to encrypt and the private key, and the program uses a mathematical algorithm to encrypt the file. How can you decrypt the file? You do the same thing: Give the program the name of the encrypted file and the private key, and it uses the algorithm to reverse the process and decrypt the file. You might have used private-key encryption already, because many computer programs use it. For instance, if you use the Protect Document command in Word for Windows, you are using private-key encryption. The password that the program asks you for is, in effect, the private key.

Public-key encryption is where the process starts to get a little weird. Public-key encryption uses two keys: a private key and a public key. Through the wonders of mathematics, these keys work together. When you encrypt a file with one key (the public key, for example), the file can be decrypted only with the other key! You can't decrypt the file with the key you used to encrypt it; you must use the other key. Sounds a little odd, but that's how it works. (Okay, this is where my knowledge breaks down. Don't ask me how the mathematics work; as far as I'm concerned, it's magic!)

Public-Key Encryption and Your Email

How, then, does public-key encryption apply to email encryption? An email program with built-in encryption uses public-key encryption to encrypt your email message before it sends it. When you want to send an encrypted message to someone, you have to get that person's public key. These keys are often posted—yes, publicly—on the Internet. There's no need to worry about who has the public key because it can't be used to decrypt an encrypted message. Using the recipient's public key, you encrypt a message and send it off. The recipient then uses his private key to decode the message.

Where do you find someone's public key? It used to be complicated; you might have to go to a *key server*, a Web or FTP site that stored thousands of public keys. Or you could ask the person to send you the key. A new system is greatly simplifying the task, though. Some new email programs, such as Netscape Messenger, enable a user to include a digital "certificate," containing his public key, in what's known as a *Vcard*, a special block of information that can be tacked onto the end of an email message. The user can set up Messenger so that every time it sends a message it includes the Vcard, which includes the public key. The email program receiving the message can then extract the public key and place it into a directory of public keys (assuming, of course, that the email program can work with Vcards, and currently most can't). Netscape Communicator's Messenger email program will automatically extract certificates from incoming email. With another program, you might have to choose to save the certificate.

Outlook Express, the new program in Windows 98 and some versions of Windows 95 and NT, handles certificates a little differently. It doesn't use a Vcard, but it does attach the certificate containing the public key to a message. If you receive an email message containing a digital certificate, you can add the certificate to your address book by selecting **File**, **Properties**, clicking the **Security** tab, and clicking the **Add Digital ID to Address Book** button.

So, here's how it works:

1. Linda Tripp sends you an email message. She's using a Vcard-enabled program and has a public key in the Vcard.
2. When your email program receives the message from Linda, it extracts Linda's public key and saves it.
3. Later, you decide that you want to send a private message to Linda, one that's so sensitive it must be encrypted. So you write the message to Linda, and then click the **Encrypted** check box. (Netscape Messenger has an Encrypted check box; other programs might have a button or menu command.)
4. You click the **Send** button, and the mail program sees that you want to encrypt the file. The program looks through its list of public keys, searching for one that is related to Linda's email address. When it finds the public key, it uses the key to scramble the message, and then it sends the message across the Internet.
5. Linda's email program receives the message and sees that it has been encrypted. It takes a closer look and sees that it has been encrypted with Linda's own public key, so it uses Linda's private key to decrypt the message. Linda can now read the message.

What happens if someone other than Linda receives the message? The recipient won't be able to decrypt the message because the recipient won't have Linda's private key. Well, you assume he won't, but that's a weakness of the system. If the private key is stolen, the security is compromised. Where the system breaks down completely is that just because the message is encrypted doesn't mean Linda won't decrypt it and then share it with someone else.

Digital Signatures

You can encrypt messages with either the public or private key. Encrypt with one key, and only the matching key can decrypt it. Of course, it wouldn't be a good idea to secure a message by encrypting it with your private key. Remember, a message encrypted with your private key can be decrypted with your public key, and the public key is, well, public. However, if the message can be decrypted with your public key, it means that it must have been encrypted with the corresponding private key, your private key. If you assume that only you have access to the private key, you've just signed the message. In other words, you can sign messages by encrypting them with your private key. As long as your private key remains secure, then the recipient can be sure that the message came from you.

Just to clarify all this, remember these key points:

- To send an encrypted message to someone, use that person's public key.
- To send a signed message to someone, use your private key.
- To send an encrypted message to someone and sign it, use your private key and the recipient's public key.

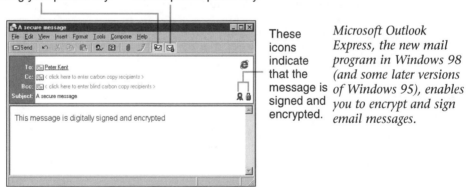

You don't have to remember all this—an email program will handle it for you. In Netscape Messenger, for instance, if you want to sign a message, click the **Signed** check box. The program will automatically encrypt your message using your private key.

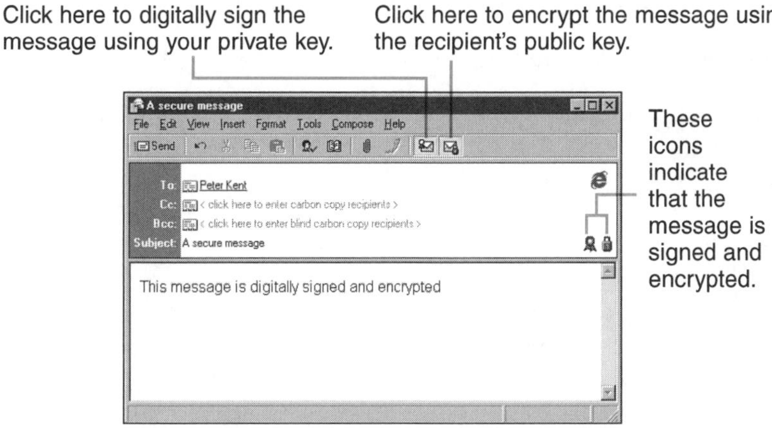

Microsoft Outlook Express, the new mail program in Windows 98 (and some later versions of Windows 95), enables you to encrypt and sign email messages.

I'm Sold; Where Do I Get My Keys?

Keep in mind that there are two types of email encryption in use. Some email programs use PGP encryption. To work with this type of encryption, you have to download PGP and create your public and private key pairs. Working with PGP can be complicated, though; if you want more information, search for PGP at one of the Web search sites (see Chapter 17, "Finding Stuff"), or go to `http://www.nai.com/`.

Probably the most common system—the system that will win the encryption war—is the one being used by Netscape Communicator in the Netscape Navigator and Netscape Messenger programs and, recently, by Microsoft in Outlook Express. This system doesn't use PGP. Rather, you must get a *personal certificate*, a special digital certificate that contains your private and public keys.

Where do you get your certificate? From a *key server*, a site with the necessary software to issue certificates. There are both public- and private-key servers. You can get a certificate from a variety of places, the two most commonly used being VeriSign (`http://www.verisign.com/`) and `Thawte` (`http://www.thawte.com/`). Install the email program you've chosen, and then go to one of these sites and follow the instructions for creating and installing the personal certificate (called a Digital ID by VeriSign) in the program. (I'd recommend Thawte; they give certificates away, whereas VeriSign charges $9.95 a year.)

Of course, to use this system, you'll need a mail program that supports it. Here are a few:

Netscape Messenger (`http://www.netscape.com/`)

Microsoft Outlook and Outlook Express (`http://www.microsoft.com/`)

Email Connection (`http://email-connection.com/`)

Frontier Technologies Email (`http://www.frontiertech.com/`)

Opensoft ExpressMail (`http://www.opensoft.com/`)

WorldSecure Client (`http://www.worldtalk.com/`)

TrustedMIME: (`http://www.sse.ie/`)

I thought that many more would soon join the fray, but this list has remained the same size for more than a year.

Different Size Keys

The size of the keys determines the security of the encryption system. For instance, the Netscape Messenger security software comes in two versions: a 40-bit version and a 128-bit version. These numbers refer to the length of the key (the code) that is used to encrypt data. The longer the key, the more secure the transmission. The 128-bit software is built into the Netscape programs sold to customers within the United States. The 40-bit software is built into Netscape programs that are sold to customers outside the United States; it's also built into most of the systems that can be downloaded from the Netscape Web site and FTP sites and the various mirror sites.

128-Bit Netscape Communicator Versions

You can download the 128-bit software from Netscape's site (previously you could get it only by buying it at a store or having it shipped to you), but you'll have to fill out a form and provide information that Netscape can check (by using the services of a couple of address-verification companies) to show that you are a resident of the United States or Canada. (Only citizens and resident aliens—green-card holders—who are living in the United States are allowed to download the software.)

Or rather, maybe you can do that. In the best tradition of the World Wide Web, Netscape keeps moving this stuff around and making it hard to find. You might be able to find information about downloading the 128-bit software; but there again, you might not. Go to `http://www.netscape.com/` and see. You can check which version you are currently using by opening Navigator or Messenger, and selecting **Help**, **About Communicator**. Then look for the RSA logo, and nearby you'll find a statement such as "This version supports International security with RSA Public Key Cryptography, MD2, MD5, RC2-CBC, RC4." The term "International" means 40-bit.

Does it matter which version you use? In most cases, no. The 40-bit software is strong enough for all but the most critical of applications. A government department using the Web to transfer information throughout the world would probably want to use 128-bit encryption, ensuring that the message is unbreakable. But for most uses, 40-bit keys are fine. Still, 40-bit keys are much weaker and could be broken by someone with the available computing resources. (The cost might be in the tens of thousands of dollars to break a message; if you think someone's willing to spend that to see what you're saying, then you need stronger encryption!)

Why, then, are there two versions of Netscape's software? The reason is ITAR, the U.S. government's International Traffic in Arms Regulations. Encryption software using keys more than 40 bits long is, as far as ITAR is concerned, on a par with armaments (SAM missiles and the like) and cannot be exported. Ridiculous, but true. (How can you stop the export of software, something that can be exported without physically moving anything?) This situation might change soon, as a federal judge recently ruled this regulation unconstitutional, so the issue is now in the hands of the courts.

How Much Stronger Is 128-Bit Encryption?

Much, much stronger. For instance, Pretty Good Privacy, Inc. says that the 128-bit PGP software creates messages that are 309,485,009,821,341,068,724,781,056 times more difficult to break than 40-bit messages. They also quote a U.S. government study that found it would take "12 million times the age of the universe, on average, to break a single 128-bit message encrypted with PGP." (That's just an average, so your mileage might vary.)

Other countries have laws that are as bad or worse. France, for instance, has banned the use of even the 40-bit version of Communicator's encryption, so Netscape Communications now produces a special "security-free" Communicator for that country.

The Law Seems to Be Slowly Crumbling

The U.S. Department of Commerce has begun allowing some companies, including Pretty Good Privacy, Inc., Netscape, and Microsoft, to export 128-bit software in some circumstances. Phil Zimmermann, the designer of PGP, recently demonstrated how ridiculous the law is by exporting the program in a legal manner; the program was exported in the form of printed text, and then scanned in another country and converted back to computer code. ITAR is gradually crumbling, so the 40-bit system might disappear eventually. And fairly recently companies such as VeriSign (and probably sometime soon Thawte) have been able to export special 128-bit certificates for Web servers. The law's changing, as the absurdity of the law becomes apparent.

Really Fancy Mail

Email is becoming, well, more than just email. There are now fancy programs that play all sorts of neat tricks, such as faxing you your email messages. Or emailing you your fax messages. One of the more popular of these systems is JFAX (`http://www.jfax.com/`). With a JFAX account, you can receive faxes and voice messages by email. The faxes are converted to image files, and the voice messages are saved as sound files. So when you receive them, you can view or listen to them. You can then forward them, save them, mark up and print the faxes, and so on.

You can send faxes, too. You simply send an email to `@jfaxsend.com`, preceding the @ with the phone number to which you want to send the fax. JFAX will then fax it out for you (they charge 5 cents per page, and a monthly fee of $12.50). This sounds pretty neat, but the main problem I can see is if you receive a lot of faxes and voice mail messages, and you access the Internet via a phone line. (For business users, with fast connections to the Internet, though, this isn't a problem.)

There's more. How about listening to your email? JFAX have a service that allows you to call in and have a computer read the message to you. You can then forward the messages to a fax machine...(just don't get your fax numbers mixed up and fax it to your email account). Of course, you might waste a lot of time listening to messages such as "$$$ One Year Guarantee!! $$$ L@@K NOW $$$ Easy Home Business. All you do is send out this exact email!" (I wonder how you pronounce L@@K...)

Some of these JFAX services are free, by the way; you can receive faxes in your email for free, for instance (you'll need to pay if you want to send them, though, and for various other features).

There are paging systems integrated with email, too. You can email messages to alphanumeric pagers, by mailing them to a particular address and providing the pager number you want to reach. There are services that send weather information, reminders, and sports scores to your email. There are programs that make it easy to send voice messages in email, too, so you can give up typing and just speak your messages. Imagine any kind of mix of email and just about anything else, and somebody has probably already created it. (If not, start looking for venture capital and you, too, can be part of the Internet startup craze.)

To find these sorts of email integration services, visit a search engine (which we discuss in Chapter 17), and search for *email fax*, *email pager*, and so on. As email takes over our lives (I've reached the point at which I simply don't have time to respond to all the mail I receive), we'll see more neat tricks being played with email, and more ways for email to extend its stranglehold.

The Least You Need to Know

- HTML Mail enables you to create email messages with colors, special fonts, pictures, tables, and more.
- Both the sender and recipient must have HTML Mail-compatible programs, or the system won't work. For the moment at least, the online services don't work with HTML Mail.
- Email encryption uses a system called public-key encryption; you'll need to get a personal certificate and install it in a compatible email program.
- Email programs that allow encryption also allow you to digitally sign messages, proving that they've come from you.
- Encryption is not legal everywhere. Some versions of the email software can be sold only in the United States.
- The longer the key, the safer the encryption, but even 40-bit keys are safe enough for most everyday use.

Chapter 4

The World of the World Wide Web

In This Chapter

- What is the Web?
- Which browser should you use?
- The home page
- Moving around the Web
- The history list and bookmarks
- Using URLs

The World Wide Web is also known as *The Web*, *WWW*, and sometimes (among really geeky company) *W3*. In really confused company, it's called *the Internet*. The World Wide Web is *not* the Internet. It's simply one software system running on the Internet. Still, it's one of the most interesting and exciting systems, so it has received a lot of press, to the extent that many people believe that the terms Web and Internet are synonymous. However, the Web seems to be taking over roles previously carried out by other Internet services; at the same time, Web programs, called *browsers*, are including utilities to help people work with non-Web services. For instance, you can send and receive email with some Web browsers and you also can read Internet newsgroups with some browsers.

What's the Web?

Imagine that you are reading this page in electronic form, on your computer screen. Then imagine that some of the words are underlined and colored. Use your mouse to point at one of these underlined words on your screen and press the mouse button. What happens? Another document opens, a document that's related in some way to the word you clicked.

That's a simple explanation of *hypertext*. If you've ever used Apple's Hypercard or a Windows Help file, you've used hypertext. Documents are linked to one another in some way, generally by clickable words and pictures. Hypertext has been around for years, but until recently most hypertext systems were limited in both size and geographic space. Click a link, and you might see another document held by the same electronic file. Or maybe you'll see a document in another file, but one that's on the same computer's hard disk, probably the same directory.

The World Wide Web is a hypertext system without boundaries. Click a link, and you might be shown a document in the next city, on the other side of the country, or even on another continent. Links from one document to another can be created without the permission of the owner of that second document, and nobody has complete control over those links. When you put a link in your document connecting to someone else's, you are sending your readers on a journey that you can't predict. They will land at that other document, from which they can take another link somewhere else—to another country, another subject, or another culture from which they can follow yet another link, and on and on.

The Web has no capacity limit, either. Web pages are being added every minute of the day, all over the world; the Web is pushing the growth of the Internet. Creating and posting a Web page is so easy that thousands of people are doing it, and more are joining them each day.

If you haven't seen the Web, this description might sound a little mundane. Okay, so one document leads to another that leads to another; what's the big deal? I try to avoid the Internet hype we've been inundated with over the past couple of years, but the Web really is a publishing revolution. Publishing to an international audience is now quick and simple. I don't mean to imply (as some Internet proponents seem to) that every Web page is a jewel that is widely read and appreciated (much of it is closer to a sow's ear than to silk), but it's a medium with which people can make their words available so that they can be widely read if they have some value.

Dial-In Terminal (Shell) Accounts

Using the Web with a dial-in direct account is very different from using it with a dial-in terminal (shell) account. If you are working with a dial-in terminal account, much of the information in this chapter won't help at all. To learn more about working with the Web with your type of account, you can use the autoresponder to get the Web chapters from the first edition of *The Complete Idiot's Guide to the Internet*. Send email to `ciginternet@mcp.com`, with `web` in the Subject line to receive the email chapters.

Let's Start

If you want to listen to a CD, you need a CD player. If you want to watch a video, you need a video player. If you want to view a Web page, you need a Web player: a *Web browser*.

The Web equation has two parts. First, a *Web server* is a special program running on a host computer (that is, a computer connected directly to the Internet). This server administers a Web site, which is a collection of World Wide Web documents. The second part is the *browser*, which is a program on your PC that asks the server for the documents and then displays the documents so that you can read them.

Servers and Clients

If you hang around on the Internet long enough, you'll hear the terms server and client used over and over. A *server* is a program that provides information that a *client* program can use in some way.

There are two big contenders in the Web browser war (yes, there's a war going on). One is Netscape Navigator. Right now, somewhere around 40% of all Web users are working with Netscape, although in the past Netscape owned 80% of the market or higher. Netscape is available in versions for Windows 3.1, Windows 95 and Windows NT, the Macintosh, and various flavors of UNIX. Netscape Navigator is now part of the Netscape Communicator suite of programs. The following figure shows the Netscape Navigator Web browser.

Netscape Navigator 4.5, part of the Netscape Communicator suite of programs.

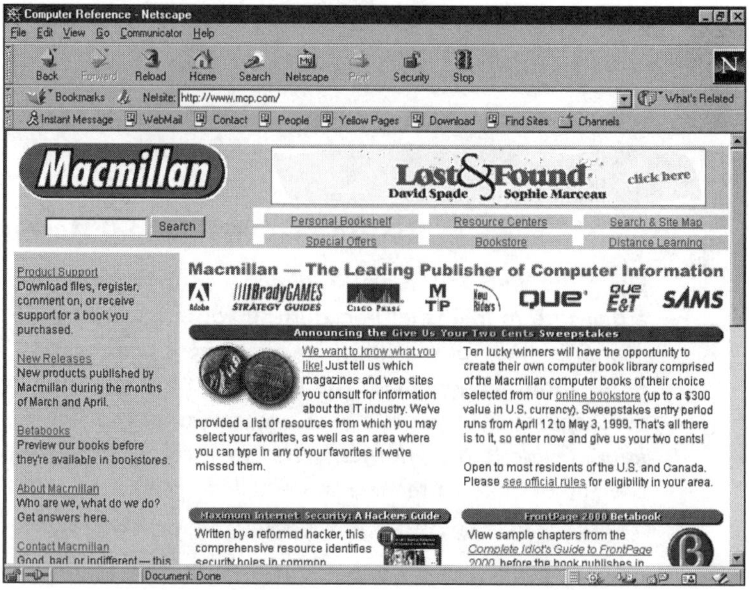

Netscape Navigator

Netscape Communications manufactures Netscape Navigator. You might think that it would be known as Navigator for short, but it's not. It's known as Netscape, mainly for historical reasons. The Netscape programmers came from NCSA (National Center for Supercomputing Applications). They originally created the first graphical Web browser, called Mosaic. Netscape was originally known as Netscape Mosaic, and the company was Mosaic Communications. Therefore, the browser was known as Netscape to differentiate it from Mosaic.

The most popular browser is Internet Explorer from Microsoft (shown in the following figure); around 60% of all Web users are working with this program. This browser is available for all flavors of Windows, and even for the Macintosh. Chances are you are using either Netscape Navigator or Internet Explorer—only a few percent of all users work with another type of browser.

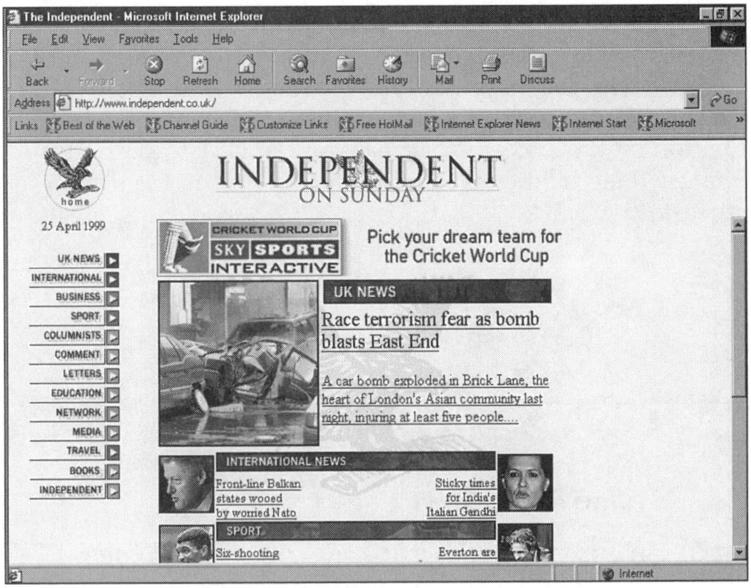

Microsoft Internet Explorer 5, Microsoft's latest weapon in the Web war with Netscape (a war that it's won).

Getting a Browser

Which browser should you use? If your service provider has given you one, I suggest you start with that. You'll probably be given either Netscape or Explorer—most likely Internet Explorer these days because CompuServe, AOL, and (of course!) Microsoft Network provide that browser to their members.

Which is the better browser? Depends what sort of bugs you prefer. Each has a different set. The actual features aren't so different, although there are a few differences. I prefer Navigator's bookmarks and history list, but I don't much like the way it keeps crashing. I like the fact that you can copy images from a Web page directly into the Clipboard with Internet Explorer, but I don't much like the way it keeps crashing. In fact, I use both browsers, and switch them around depending on what I'm doing at the time.

For now, I'm going to assume that you have a Web browser installed, and that you have opened it and are ready to start. One nice thing about Web browsers is that they all work similarly, and they look very similar, too. So whatever browser you use, you should be able to follow along with this chapter.

Browsing Begins at Home

When you open your browser, whatever page you see is, by definition, your *home page*. (I like that kind of definition; it's easy to understand.) Ideally, the home page is a page that has lots of useful links, which take you to places on the Web that you will want to go to frequently. You can create your own home page by using something called HTML, the Web document language (see Chapter 20, "Setting Up Your Own Web Site") or even using one of the fancy new customizing systems you'll find on the

Web. (Both Netscape and Microsoft have systems that automatically create customized pages for you, if you have their browsers. Go to `http://www.netscape.com/custom/index.html` for the Netscape system or `http://home.microsoft.com/` for the Microsoft system (Internet Explorer 4.5 and 5 have an Internet Start button on the Links toolbar that you can click to get to this page). I'll explain how to use these "addresses" later in this chapter, in the section "A Direct Link: Using the URLs."

Home Page, Start Page

Microsoft's programmers can't seem to decide whether to use the term *home page* or *start page*. The term home page originally meant the page that appeared when you opened your browser or when you used the Home button. Then all of a sudden, everybody was using the term to mean a person or company's main Web page (the page you see when you go to that Web site) such as NEC's home page, Netscape's home page, and so on. So Microsoft's programmers evidently thought it made more sense to rename the home page to "start page." Unfortunately, they're using *both* terms, so Internet Explorer 3, 4, and 5 have a Home button on the toolbar; Explorer 3 has a Go, Start Page menu option; some versions of Explorer 4 have a Go, Home Page menu option and a Home button, but mention start page in the options dialog box. Explorer 5, and the later versions of Explorer 4, seem to have completely replaced the term start page with home page.

Moving Around on the Web

Whatever browser you are using, you'll almost certainly find links on the home page. Links are the colored and underlined words. You might also find pictures that contain links, perhaps several different links on a picture (a different link on each part of the picture). Use your mouse to point at a piece of text or a picture; if the mouse pointer changes shape—probably into a pointing hand—you are pointing at a link. (Just to confuse the issue, some pictures contain links even though the pointer doesn't change shape.)

Click whichever link looks interesting. If you are online (I'm assuming you are), your browser sends a message to a Web server somewhere, asking for a page. If the Web server is running (it might not be) and if it's not too busy (it might be), it transmits the document back to your browser, and your browser displays it on your screen.

You've just learned the primary form of Web "navigation." When you see a link you want to follow, you click it. Simple, eh? But what about going somewhere useful, somewhere interesting? Most browsers these days either have toolbar buttons that take you to a useful Web page or come with a default home page with useful links. For example, in Netscape Navigator 4, you can click the **Guide** button to open the Guide page, or click the **Guide** button and hold it down to display a number of options that lead you to pages that help you find your way around the Internet. In Navigator 4.5, though, they removed the **Guide** button. Instead, at the Netcenter page (the page that appears each time you open your browser, unless you change your home page—which we discuss in Chapter 20), they provide a number of options:

- **Classifieds** This option takes you to the classifieds and auctions page.
- **Net Search** This option takes you to a search page.
- **Find Web Sites** This option takes you to a directory of Web pages.
- **What's Cool?** This option provides links to Web sites chosen for their usefulness or CQ—coolness quotient. (Personally, I'm getting tired of the word cool. But hey, that's my job: Internet Curmudgeon.)
- **What's New?** This option provides links to a selection of new and interesting Web sites from the people at Netscape.
- **People Finder** This option provides links to sites that can help you track down other Internet users.
- **Yellow Pages** This option displays a page from which you can select a regional Yellow Pages system and search for a business.

How Does the Browser Know Where to Go?

How does your browser know which server to request the document from? What you see on your computer screen is not quite the same document that your browser sees. Open the source document (which you can probably do using the **View, Page Source** menu option), and you'll see what the Web document really looks like. (You'll learn more about these source documents in Chapter 20.) The source document is just basic ASCII text that contains all sorts of instructions. One of the instructions says, in effect, "if this guy clicks this link, here's which document I want you to get." You don't normally see all these funky commands because the browser *renders* the page, removing the instructions and displaying only the relevant text.

Internet Explorer 3 has a special QuickLinks toolbar (click **QuickLinks** in the Address toolbar to open the QuickLinks toolbar). In Explorer 4 and 5, this toolbar is simply named the Links bar and can be opened or closed by selecting **View**, **Toolbars**, **Links**. On this toolbar, you'll find a variety of buttons designed to take you to useful starting points. (The button names vary among versions.)

Whatever browser you are using, take a little time to explore. Go as far as you want. Then come back here, and I'll explain how to find your way back to where you came from.

Link Colors

Some links change color after you click them. You won't see it right away, but if you return to the same page later, you'll find that the link is a different color. The color change indicates that the particular link points to a document that you've already seen. The "used-link" color does expire after a while, and the link changes back to its original color. How long it takes for this to happen is something that you can generally control with an option in your browser's Preferences or Options area.

The Hansel and Gretel Dilemma: Where Are You?

Hypertext is a fantastic tool, but it has one huge drawback: It's easy to get lost. If you are reading a book and you flip forward a few pages, you know how to get back. You flip back, right? But with hypertext, after a few moves through the electronic library, you can become horribly lost. How do you get back to where you came from? And where did you come from, anyway?

Over the years, a number of systems have been developed to help people find their way around this rather strange freeform medium. This table explains some tools you can use in most Web browsers to move through the pages and sites you've seen.

Table 4.1 Web Page Navigation Tools

Button	Description
Back	Click the **Back** button or choose **Back** from a menu (probably the **Go** menu) to return to the previous Web page.
Forward	Click the **Forward** button or choose the **Forward** menu option to return to a page you've just come back from.
Home	Click the **Home** button (or the **Start** button on some versions of Internet Explorer) to go all the way back to your home page or start page.
Bookmarks or Favorites	You can set bookmarks on pages you think you'll want to come back to (they're known as Favorites in Internet Explorer); bookmarks can be very helpful because you don't have to struggle to find your way back to the page the next time.
History	This is a list of pages you've seen previously. The **Back** and **Forward** commands take you back and forward through this list. You can also go directly to a page in the history list by selecting it from the **Go** menu. (In Explorer 2, you select from the **File** menu. In Explorer 4 and 5, click the small triangle on the **Back** button.)

Bookmarks

The bookmark system (known as Favorites in Internet Explorer) is an essential tool for finding your way around. Get to know it right away.

In most browsers, you can just click a button or select a menu option to place a bookmark. Each system works a little differently, of course. In Netscape Navigator, choose **Bookmarks**, **Add Bookmark** (Navigator 3), or click the **Bookmarks** button and choose **Add Bookmark** (Navigator 4), or click the Communicator menu, choose Bookmarks from the drop-down menu, and then choose Add Bookmark. The bookmark is added to the bottom of the Bookmark menu (you can move it to a folder or submenu later). In Navigator 4 and 4.5, you can even select which folder you want to put the bookmark in by clicking the **Bookmarks** button and then choosing **File Bookmark**.

In Internet Explorer, choose **Favorites**, **Add to Favorites**, and then click the **Create In** button and select the folder into which you want to place the bookmark.

Both systems have Bookmarks windows and an associated Bookmarks menu. (In Explorer, they're called the Favorites window and menu.) Creating a folder in the window automatically creates a submenu in the menu.

To open Netscape's Bookmarks window choose **Bookmarks**, **Go to Bookmarks** (Navigator 3) or **Bookmarks**, **Edit Bookmarks** (Navigator 4 and 4.5). In the latest version of Explorer, you can click the **Favorites** button in the toolbar to open a Favorites panel that appears on the left side of the browser window itself.

You can even search Bookmarks or Favorites. For instance, you can search Internet Explorer's Favorites using the Windows 95 or 98 **Find** tool on the **Start** menu. In Internet Explorer 4 or 5, open the Favorites panel, and then right-click a folder in the Favorites list and choose **Find** to search the folder.

Internet Explorer's "in-browser" Favorites panel.

Click here to open the Favorites panel.

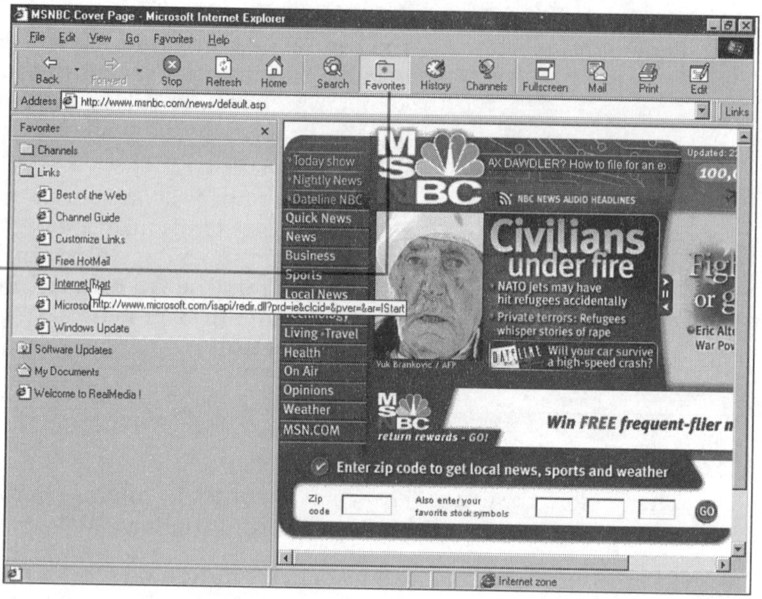

A Little History

The history list varies tremendously. Netscape 3's history list is not very helpful. It lists some, but not all, of the pages you've visited in the current session. Other browsers, including Netscape Navigator 4, show much more, often listing pages from previous sessions. Explorer, for instance, keeps a record of up to 3,000 pages (including all the pages from the current session and earlier sessions). You can view the list in a window (see the following figure) sorted by date or by name. Double-click an entry in the history list to open that Web page.

Whatever system you have, though, using the history list is simple. In Netscape Navigator, you can select an entry from the **Go** menu. To keep us on our toes, Microsoft's programmers keep moving the history list. In Internet Explorer 2, you'll find the history entries on the **File** menu; in Explorer 3 and some versions of 4, the history list is on the **Go** menu. Some later versions, and Version 5, don't have a **Go** menu; instead, click the little black triangle on the right side of the Back button, and a menu drops down showing the most recent pages you've seen.

In or Out?

In Internet Explorer 2, the History window is separate from the browser window; in Version 3 and later the history list is shown within the browser window. Click on Internet Explorer 4's **Favorites** button, and a panel opens on the left side of the browser window to display the Favorites list. But select **Favorites, Organize Favorites** to open a separate Favorites window.

You can also open the history window to see more history entries, perhaps thousands. In versions 4 and 5 of Internet Explorer, click the **History** button in the toolbar; in version 3, choose **Go**, **Open History Folder**, and in version 2, choose **File**, **More History** (sometimes I wonder what drugs these Microsoft programmers are on). In Netscape, choose **Window**, **History**; or use **Communicator**, **History** in some later versions, depending on the operating system—and in later versions still, choose **Communicator**, **Tools**, **History**.

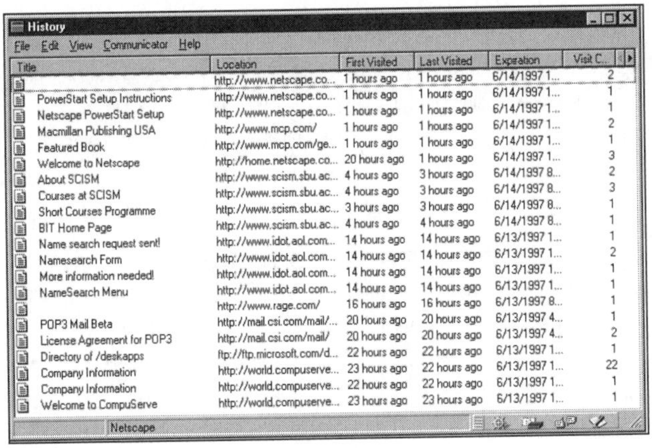

With Netscape Navigator 4's history list, you can go back days or even weeks in your Web travels. The list even indicates how long it's been since you visited the page and how often you've been there.

A Direct Link: Using the URLs

Earlier in this chapter, I mentioned a couple of URLs. *URLs* are Web addresses, such as `http://www.msn.com/` or `http://www.netscape.com/`. These addresses provide a direct link to a particular Web page. Instead of clicking links to try to find your way to a page, you can tell your browser the URL and say "go get this page."

New History List Trick

Starting with version 4, the Internet Explorer and Netscape Navigator browsers have a handy new feature that enables you to see the history list from the **Back** and **Forward** buttons. In Navigator, click the button and hold down the mouse button; in Explorer, right-click the button, or click the little downward-pointing arrow on the button. In both cases, you'll see a list of pages that you've visited.

URL

This acronym stands for Uniform Resource Locator, which is a fancy name for Web address.

Most browsers have a bar near the top in which you can type the URL of the page you want to go to. The bar's almost certainly already displayed; it's a long text box. If it's not there, someone must have removed it; in Netscape, use the **Options**, **Show Location** or **View**, **Show Location Toolbar** menu command to display the bar (depending on the version you're working with); in Internet Explorer, choose **View**, **Toolbar**, or **View**, **Toolbars**, **Address Bar**.

If you don't want the bar there all the time (after all, it takes up room that is sometimes better given to the Web pages), you can leave it turned off. If you keep it turned off, you can generally use a shortcut key to display a dialog box in which you can type a URL. In Netscape, press **Ctrl+O** to open the box (or try **Ctrl+L** if that doesn't work—earlier versions of Navigator used that shortcut; the shortcut key varies among versions); in Internet Explorer, choose **File**, **Open** or press **Ctrl+O**. In either case, you type the URL in the box that appears. If you prefer to use the Address or Location box at the top of the browser window, click in the box, type the address, and press **Enter**.

Maximizing the Web Page

Browsers have so many controls and tools that sometimes there's not enough room for the Web page. Internet Explorer 4 has a new feature. Click the **Fullscreen** button to remove almost all the controls (except a small toolbar at the top of the window), giving the Web page the maximum room. (If you're using Explorer 5, press **F11** to activate this feature—the Fullscreen button seems to have gone.) You can even remove the small toolbar using an Autohide feature similar to that used by the Windows 98 toolbar (right-click the toolbar and select **Autohide**). Actually, this feature isn't new; it's from the ancient history of the graphical Web browser (way back in 1994). It used to be called a Kiosk feature, but it disappeared for a while.

The URL Explained

A URL consists of certain distinct parts. For example, here's a long URL:

```
http://www.poorrichard.com/newsltr/instruct/subsplain.htm
```

Each part of this URL has a specific meaning:

`http://`	This part tells the browser that the address is for a Web page. The `http://` stands for *Hypertext Transfer Protocol*, the system used on the Internet to transfer Web pages. In addition to `http://`, you might see similar prefixes for an FTP site or a Gopher menu (see the following table).
`www.poorrichard.com`	This part is the hostname, the name of the computer holding the Web server that is administering the Web site you want to visit.
`/newsltr/instruct/`	This part is the directory in which the Web server has to look to find the file you want. In many cases, multiple directories will be listed, so the Web server looks down the directory tree in subdirectories. In this example, the Web server has to look in the instruct directory, which is a subdirectory of the newsltr directory.

`subsplain.htm`	This part is the name of the file you want, the Web page. These files are generally HTM or HTML files (that extension stands for Hypertext Markup Language, the coding used to create Web pages). Sometimes the URL has no filename at the end; in that case, the Web server generally sends a default document for the specified directory.

The URL is not complicated; it's just an address so your browser knows where to look for a file. The different types of URLs are identified by a different *protocol* portion of the address. The Web page URLs all begin with `http://`. This table lists some other protocols you'll see on the Internet.

Table 4.2 Other Internet Protocols

Protocol Prefix	Description
`ftp://`	The address of an FTP file library; you'll learn more about FTP in Chapter 12, "The Giant Software Store: FTP."
`gopher://`	The address of a Gopher site (see Chapter 16, "Gopher and Telnet—Still Alive, but Barely").
`news:`	The address of a newsgroup, discussed in Chapter 9, "Newsgroups: The Source of All Wisdom." Note that this pre fix doesn't have the // after the name; neither does `mailto:` (see the following entry).
`mailto:`	When you use this prefix, the browser's email program opens so you can send mail. Web authors often create links using the `mailto:` URL so that when someone clicks the link, he can quickly send a message to the author.
`telnet://`	The address of a Telnet site (see Chapter 16).
`tn3270://`	The address of a tn3270 site. This protocol is similar to Telnet and is also covered in Chapter 16.
`wais://`	The address of a WAIS site; WAIS is a little-used database-search tool, and you probably won't run into many WAIS links. In any case, most browsers don't recognize the `wais://` protocol.

Forget http://

In most browsers these days (including Netscape and Internet Explorer), you don't need to type the full URL. You can omit the `http://` piece, and the browser will assume that the `http://` piece should be added. If you type something beginning with `gopher` (as in `gopher.usa.net`, for instance) or `ftp` (as in `ftp.microsoft.com`), you can omit the `gopher://` or `ftp://` part, too. Also, in some browsers, you can even drop the `www.` and `.com` bits. For instance, in Netscape Navigator and Internet Explorer, you can type **mcp** and press **Enter** to get to the `http://www.mcp.com/` Web site (this works only if the domain ends with `.com`). The newest browsers have an auto-fill-in feature, something you might have seen in personal-finance programs. Start typing a URL, and if the browser recognizes that you've entered it before, it will fill in the rest for you.

What Will You Find on Your Web Journey?

When you travel around the Web, you'll find a lot of text documents and much, much more. As a system administrator at a Free-Net once said to me, "The Web is for people who can't read!" It was a slight exaggeration, perhaps, but his point was that, on the Web, the nontext stuff is often more important than the words.

While traveling around the Web, you'll find these sorts of things:

- **Pictures** You'll find pictures both inside the text documents and on their own. Sometimes when you click a link (at a museum site, for example), a picture—not a document—is transferred to your browser.
- **Forms** These days, most browsers are forms-compatible (Navigator and Explorer have always been forms-compatible). In other words, you can use forms to interact with the Web site to send information about yourself (to subscribe to a service, for instance), to search for information, to buy products, or to play a game, for example.
- **Sounds** Most browsers can play sounds, such as voices and music. Many Web sites contain sounds. For instance, IUMA (the Internet Underground Music Archive at `http://www.iuma.com/`) has song clips from many new bands.

Where Do I Find What I Want on the Web?

You can follow any interesting links you find, as discussed earlier in this chapter. You can also search for particular subjects and Web pages by using a Web search site, as discussed in Chapter 17, "Finding Stuff."

- **Files** Many Web sites have files you can download, such as shareware, demos of new programs, and documents of many kinds. When you click a link, your browser begins the file transfer (see Chapter 5, "More About the Web").
- **Multimedia of other kinds** All sorts of strange things are on the Web: 3D images, animations, Adobe Acrobat PDF hypertext files, videos, slideshows, 2D and 3D chemical images, and plenty more. Click a link, and the file starts transferring. If you have the right software installed, it automatically displays or plays the file. For instance, in the following figure, you can see a BubbleViewer image. (See `http://www.omniview.com/` for information about the BubbleViewer, and Chapter 6, "Forms, Applets, and Other Web Weirdness," and Chapter 7, "Web Multimedia," to learn more about multimedia.)

A BubbleViewer image in Netscape. You can move around inside the car, viewing up, down, and all around.

Speeding Up Your Journey by Limiting Graphics

The Web used to be a very fast place to move around. The first Web browsers could display nothing but text, and text transfers across the Internet very quickly. These days, though, thanks to something commonly known as "progress," things move more slowly. The things I just mentioned—pictures, video, sounds, and so on—slow down the process. Although video is the slowest thing on the Web (moving at an almost glacial pace in most cases), pictures are more of a nuisance; very few sites use video, but most use static pictures.

Most browsers provide a way for you to turn off the display of pictures. In Netscape Navigator, for instance, choose **Options**, **Auto Load Images**, and remove the check mark from the menu option to turn off images. In Netscape Navigator 4, choose **Edit**, **Preferences**, and then click the **Advanced** category and clear **Automatically Load Images**. In Internet Explorer, you can turn off images in the Options dialog box, and you can turn off sounds and video, too. Choose **Tools**, **Internet Options** and click the **Advanced** tab, and then clear the **Show Pictures** check box in the list box below **Multimedia**. (In early versions of Explorer, you have to select **View**, **Options**, and might find the Show Pictures option under the **General**. Because the images are no longer transmitted to your browser, you see the pages much more quickly.)

Of course, you often need or want to see those images. Many images have links built into them, and although some Web pages have both graphic links and corresponding text links (for people using a browser that can't display pictures), other Web pages are unusable unless you can see the pictures. However, you can usually grab the picture you need quickly. Where there should be a picture, you'll see a little icon that functions as a sort of placeholder.

In Netscape, you can right-click the placeholder and choose **Load Image** (**Show Image** in some versions) from the shortcut menu that appears. Or you can click the **Images** button in the toolbar to see all of them. To view an image when you have images turned off in Internet Explorer, right-click the placeholder and choose **Show Picture** from the shortcut menu.

There's Plenty More!

There's a lot more to say about the Web than I've said in this chapter. In fact, one could write a book about it (I already have: *Using Netscape Communicator 4*). In the next few chapters, you'll learn a few advanced Web travel tips and all about Web multimedia.

The Least You Need to Know

- The World Wide Web is a giant hypertext system running on the Internet.
- The two best browsers available are Netscape Navigator and Microsoft Internet Explorer.
- The home page (sometimes called the start page in Internet Explorer) is the page that appears when you open your browser.
- Click a link in a document to see another document. To find your way back, use the **Back** or **Home** button.
- The history list shows where you've been. In Netscape Navigator 3, it includes just some of the pages you've seen in the current session; in some other browsers, including Netscape Navigator 4 and Internet Explorer, the history list includes all the pages from the current session and many pages from previous sessions.
- A URL is a Web address. You can use the URL to go directly to a particular Web page.

Chapter 5

More About the Web

In This Chapter

- Running multiple Web sessions
- Opening files from your hard disk
- All about the cache and reloading
- Searching documents and using the pop-up menu
- Copying things you find to the Clipboard
- Saving images, documents, and files

You've seen the basic moves; now you are ready to learn more techniques to help you find your way around the Web. In the last chapter, you learned how to move around on the Web using a Web browser such as Netscape Navigator or Internet Explorer. In this chapter, you'll find out how to run multiple Web sessions at the same time, how to deal with the cache, how to save what you find, and so on. You need to know these advanced moves to work efficiently on the Web.

Multiple Windows: Ambidextrous Browsing

These days, most browsers enable you to run more than one Web session at the same time. Why would you want to do that? There could be many reasons. While you wait for an image to load in one window, you can read something in another window. Or maybe you need to find information at another Web site but don't want to "lose your place" at the current one. (Yes, you have bookmarks and the history list, but sometimes it's just easier to open another window.) You can open one or more new browser windows, as shown in the following figure, so that you can run multiple Web sessions. In this example, you can see two Internet Explorer windows. To make the one at the back take up the entire screen, I pressed F11 to use the **Fullscreen** feature (earlier versions had a **Fullscreen** button), and then right-clicked the bar and selected the **Autohide** feature (see Chapter 4, "The World of the World Wide Web").

Opening multiple windows is a good way to keep from getting lost or to do more than one thing at a time. In this illustration, one Internet Explorer sits over another that has been maximized using the Fullscreen command (press F11).

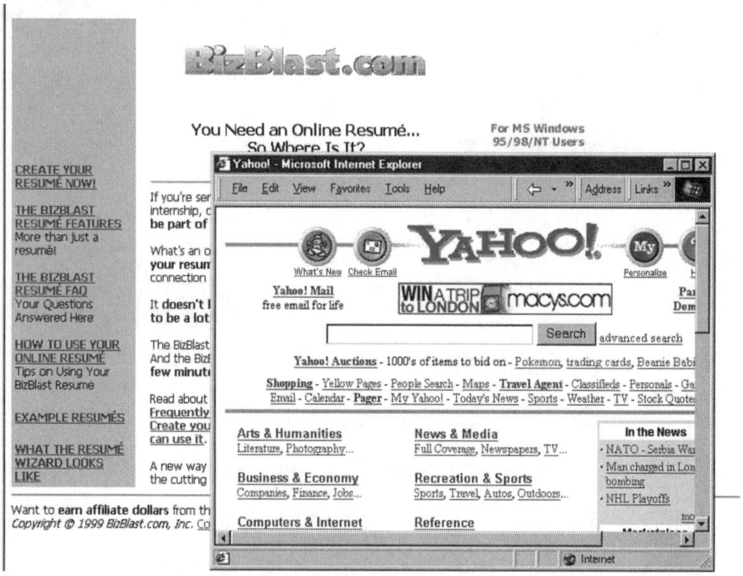

Exactly how you open a new window varies among browsers; however, most are similar. In Netscape Navigator, try these procedures:

- Right-click the link that you want to follow in a new window, and then choose **Open in New Window**. A new Netscape window opens, and the referenced document opens in that window.
- Choose **File**, **New Web Browser**, or **File**, **New**, **Navigator Window**, or press **Ctrl+N** to open a new window displaying the home page.

Internet Explorer gives you several options:

- Right-click the link you want to follow, and then choose **Open in New Window**. A new window opens, displaying the referenced document.
- Press **Tab** until the link becomes highlighted, and then press **Shift+Enter**.

- Choose **File**, **New Window** (or, in some versions, **File**, **New**, **Window**) or press **Ctrl+N** to open a new window that displays the same document as the one you've just viewed.
- Type a URL into the **Address** text box, and then press **Shift+Enter** to display that document in a new window.

You might encounter some problems when running multiple Web sessions. Web browsers are turning into real memory hogs, so you might find that you don't have enough memory to run multiple sessions or to run more than one additional session. In addition, your modem can do only so much work. If you have several Web windows open and each is transferring things at the same time, every transfer will be slower than if it were the only thing the modem had to do.

Automatic Multiple Sessions

Now and then, windows will open automatically. If you suddenly notice that the browser's Back button is disabled, it might be that when you clicked a link, a secondary window opened and you didn't notice. Web authors can create codes in their Web pages that force browsers to open secondary or targeted windows.

Your Hard Disk As Web Server?

If you enjoy working on the Web and spend most of your waking hours there, eventually, you'll end up with HTM or HTML files on your hard disk. You'll have them in your cache (discussed next), or you may save documents using the **File**, **Save As** command. Your browser provides a way to open these HTML files—generally a **File, Open** command or something similar. You'll see a typical Open box from which you can select the file you want to open.

Here's a geek trick for you. If you know the exact path to the file you want to open, and if you can type quickly, click in the **Address** or **Location** text box. Then type the entire path and filename, such as `C:/Program Files/Netscape/Navigator/ownweb.htm`. This trick should work in both Netscape and Internet Explorer. In some browsers, however, you might need to use the more formal (and older) method by entering the file path in this format:

`file:///C|/Program Files/Netscape/Navigator/ownweb.htm`. Notice that in the second format, you precede the path with `file:///` and replace the colon after the disk letter (in this case, **C**) with a pipe symbol (|).

Forward Slash or Backslash

UNIX computers use a forward slash (/) between directory names. DOS computers use a backslash(\). Because the Web was developed on UNIX computers, URLs use forward slashes. Therefore `C:/Program Files/Netscape/Navigator/ownweb.htm` is correct, even though in normal DOS notation this would appear as `C:\Program Files\Netscape\Navigator\ownweb.htm`. However, you can type it whichever way you please when you're opening a file on your hard disk or a page on the Web; both Internet Explorer and Netscape will figure it out.

HTM or HTML?

Depending to some degree on the operating system you use, the file extension of the HTML Web files might be .htm or .html. Originally, the Web was developed using UNIX computers, and Web files had the extension .html. Later, when Windows 3.1 machines started appearing on the Web, the .htm extension came into use because Windows 3.1 could work only with three-character file extensions, and many people were creating Web pages in Windows. Today, you'll see both extensions. Even though Windows 95 and 98 can accept four-letter extensions, not all Windows HTML-editing programs can, so people are still creating files with three-letter extensions. Also, many people still use Windows 3.1 machines to create Web pages.

Turbocharging with the Cache

Have you noticed that when you return to a Web document that you've previously viewed, it appears much more quickly than when you first accessed it? That's because your browser isn't taking it from the Internet; instead, the browser is getting it from the *cache*, an area on your hard disk or in your computer's RAM (memory) in which it saves pages. The cache is handy because it greatly speeds up the process of working on the Web. After all, why bother to reload a file from the Internet when it's already sitting on your hard drive? (Okay, you may think of some reasons to do so, but I'll come back to those when I talk about the Reload command.)

When the browser loads a Web page, it places it in the cache. You can generally control the size of the cache. Not all browsers let you do so, but Netscape, Internet Explorer, and many others do. When the cache fills up, the oldest files are removed to make room for newer ones. Each time the browser tries to load a page, it might look in the cache first to see whether it has the page stored. (Whether it does depends on how you set up the cache.) If it finds that the page is available, it can retrieve the page from the cache very quickly.

Putting the Cache to Work

To take full advantage of the cache's benefits, you need to do some configuring. To configure the cache in Netscape Navigator 2 or 3, choose **Options**, **Network Preferences**, and then click the **Cache** tab. In Navigator 4 and 4.5, select **Edit**, **Preferences**, and then open the **Advanced** category and click the **Cache** subcategory. The following figure shows Netscape's cache information.

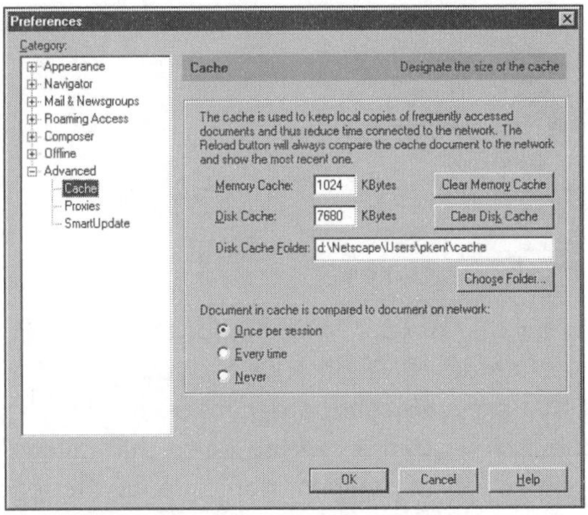

You have several options when setting up Netscape's cache.

Configure any of the available settings to meet your needs:

- **Memory Cache** You can tell Netscape how much of your computer's memory you want to assign to the cache. Netscape stores a few documents in the memory so that it can retrieve them extremely quickly. The button to the right of this option enables you to remove all the pages from the memory cache.

- **Disk Cache** You can also tell Netscape how large the disk cache should be—that is, how much of your disk space you want to give to Netscape. How much should you give? That all depends on how much disk space you have free. (I always say that you can never have too much hard disk space, money, or beer; I've been proven wrong once or twice, though.) The button to the right of this option enables you to clear out the disk cache, which is handy when you finally run out of disk space.
- **Disk Cache Folder** You can tell Netscape where to place the disk cache. If you have several hard disks, put the cache on the fastest disk or the one with the most room.
- **Document in cache is compared to document on network** Now for the complicated one. This setting tells Netscape when to verify documents. When you request a document (by clicking a link or entering a URL), Netscape can send a message to the Web server asking (basically), "Has this document changed since the last time I grabbed it?" If it has changed, Netscape downloads a new copy. If it hasn't changed, Netscape grabs the page from the cache. You can configure Netscape to ask the Web server to verify documents Once per Session (in which case, Netscape checks the first time you try to retrieve a document, but it doesn't bother after that); Every Time (so that Netscape checks every time you try to get a document, regardless of how many times you view that document in a session); or Never (in which case, Netscape doesn't even bother to check to see whether the document has been updated, unless you use the Reload command).

Techno Talk

The Hard Disk Cache

Note that you are not reserving an area of your hard disk for the cache. For instance, if you have a 30,000KB (almost 30MB) disk cache, your browser doesn't create a 30,000KB file that prevents other programs from using that disk space. You're just telling the browser that it can use up to that much disk space for the cache if it's available—if other programs don't use up the space first. When you fill up the available cache space, the browser starts clearing out older files to make way for newer ones.

- **Allow Persistent Caching of Pages Retrieved Through SSL** This feature is in earlier versions of Netscape (it's not in the latest version), and it's related to Internet security. SSL stands for secure sockets layer (which probably means no more to you than SSL, so I'm not sure why I told you that). An SSL Web browser can use secure transmission of information; the information is encrypted before being transmitted. (See Chapter 18, "Staying Safe on the Internet," for a discussion of encryption.) This feature tells the browser to cache pages that were sent in a secure manner.

Internet Explorer 5 uses a similar system. Choose **Tools**, **Internet Options**, and click the **General** tab. (As you may have noticed by now, Microsoft has to keep moving things around; in some versions of Explorer you'll need to select **View**, **Options**—or perhaps **Internet Options**—then click the General Tab, or maybe the Advanced tab.) Then click the **Settings** button under the **Temporary Internet files** area. Although Explorer's programmers (ever the innovators) have taken to referring to the cache as Temporary Internet files, it's the same thing. The following figure shows Explorer 5's settings.

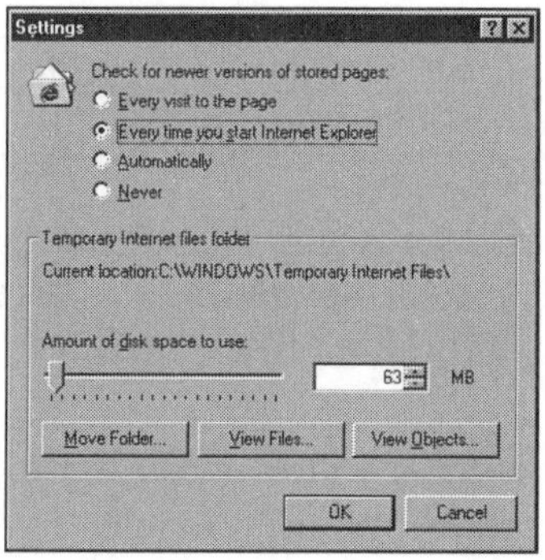

Internet Explorer enables you to modify the cache and view its contents directly.

Near the top of the box, you can tell the browser when to check to see whether there's a newer version of the file. You can tell it to check Once per Session in Explorer 3; this option is ambiguously labeled Every Time You Start Internet Explorer in Explorer 4 and 5, but it's the same thing. Or you can turn it off altogether (select Never). In Explorer 4 and 5, you also have the option to check Every Visit to the Page. And Explorer 5 has yet another option, Automatically. This starts off working the same as Every Time You Start Internet Explorer, but, in theory, the browser learns how often a particular page changes, and if it doesn't change often, eventually the browser stops checking quite so frequently.

You also can modify the size of the cache by dragging a slider to set the percentage of the drive you want to use (instead of by entering an MB value). You can select the cache directory using the **Move Folder** button, but notice that Explorer offers something extra: a **View Files** button. Click the **View Files** button to display a list of the files stored in the cache; you can double-click a file to open it in the browser. Explorer 5, and some versions of Explorer 4, also has a **View Objects** button, which opens a window containing ActiveX controls downloaded to your computer (see Chapter 6, "Forms, Applets, and Other Web Weirdness"). You can also empty the cache; in more recent versions, there's a **Delete Files** button back in the Internet Options dialog box, whereas earlier versions had an **Empty Folder** button in the cache Settings dialog box).

Decisions, Decisions

Which of the cache options should you use? I prefer Never because it makes my Web sessions *much* quicker. Whenever I tell a browser to go to a Web page that's already in the cache, it loads the page from the hard disk right away, without sending a verification message to the server first. Even if the browser doesn't have to retrieve the page again because the page hasn't changed, checking with the Web server can slow you down noticeably.

On the other hand, I have to remember to keep using the Reload command to be sure I'm viewing the latest version of the Web page. Some people might prefer to use the Once Per Session option to ensure that they are looking at a recent page.

What Is Reload?

Sometimes you want to get a file from the Web again. Reload is a "cure" for the cache. If you get a page from the cache, you are not getting the latest document. Sometimes getting the most recent document doesn't matter, but in a few cases, it does.

For instance, say you want to return to a site you visited several weeks ago. If you have a very large cache, that document might still be available. If you have the Never option button selected in the Preferences dialog box, your browser displays the old document, without checking to see whether the corresponding document stored on the Web has changed. Or perhaps you are viewing a Web document that changes rapidly, such as a stock quote page. Even if you viewed the page only a few minutes ago, it could already be out of date.

The cure for replacing those old, stale Web pages is to reload them. Click the **Reload** button or choose **View**, **Reload**. Internet Explorer's programmers, in their attempt to rename everything they can, use the term **Refresh** instead of Reload. (The fact that Reload is a term the Web's been using for several years and that Refresh has a different meaning—Netscape has a Refresh command that simply "repaints" the display using the contents of the memory cache—doesn't seem to matter to Microsoft's programmers.) Anyway, the Reload command (Refresh in Explorer) tells the browser, "Throw away the copy held in the cache and get the latest version."

You sometimes see a Reload Frame command, which reloads just one frame in a framed document. (Chapter 6 covers frames.) Netscape Navigator has a "super reload" command that few people know about. Holding down the Shift key and then selecting the Reload command says to Netscape Navigator "be absolutely sure you really do reload the page!" Navigator's Reload command has had a bug living in it for several years and in some cases doesn't reload the page. (This problem seems to be related to forms and scripts not being reloaded correctly.) Holding down the Shift key ensures that the page really is reloaded.

Long Documents: Finding What You Need

Some Web pages are large. Some are positively huge—thousands of lines long with links at the top of the document that take the user to sections lower on the same page. Many Web authors prefer to create one large page than to create lots of small linked ones, the advantage being that once the page has been transferred to your browser you can use links to move to different parts of the page very quickly.

Virtually all browsers have some kind of Find command; it's generally **Edit**, **Find**, or a Find button on the toolbar. Internet Explorer's programmers (as you might guess) have a command called **Edit**, **Find (on this page)**, which I must admit is a good idea. This command tells the browser to search the current page instead of the Web; I'm sure some new users get confused about that issue. (On the other hand, Explorer's Search toolbar button is not the same as the Find command; it's for searching the Web. You'll learn how to search the Web in Chapter 17, "Finding Stuff.")

Don't Forget Find

The Find command can come in very handy for searching long Gopher menus (see Chapter 16, "Gopher and Telnet—Still Alive, but Barely") and FTP file listings (see Chapter 12, "The Giant Software Store: FTP"), as well as large Web documents.

The Find command works in a way that's very similar to what you've probably used in other programs (in particular, in word processors). Click the **Find** button, or choose **Edit**, **Find**, and the Find dialog box opens. Type the word or words you are looking for, choose **Match Case** (if necessary), and then click **Find Next**. The browser moves the document so that the first line containing the word or words you are searching for is at the top of the window.

Remember to Right-Click

Remember to use the shortcut menus that appear when you right-click on items. Both Netscape and Internet Explorer use them, as do other browsers. The shortcut menu is a new toy in the programmer's toy box—and a very nice one at that. (The Macintosh mouse has only one button; on Macintosh browsers, you might be able to access a pop-up menu by pressing the button and holding it down.) Experiment by right-clicking links, pictures, and the background, and you'll find all sorts of useful commands, such as those listed here:

- **Copy Shortcut or Copy Link Location** This command copies the URL from the link to the Clipboard.
- **Open** This command opens the related document, just as if you clicked the link.
- **Open in New Window** This command opens a new window and loads the document referenced by the link you clicked.
- **Save Target As or Save Link As** This command transfers the referenced document and saves it on your hard disk without bothering to display it in the browser first.
- **Add Bookmark or Add to Favorites** This command places an entry for the document referenced by the link in the Bookmark or Favorites system.

Look to see what other commands are available. You'll find commands for moving back through framed documents, saving image files, saving background images as your desktop wallpaper, adding wallpaper, sending the Web page in an email message, and so on. (Which reminds me, maybe you should learn how to save such things from the Web, eh?)

Is It Worth Saving?

A lot of it is. Yes, I know that multimedia consultant and author William Horton has called the Web a GITSO (Garbage In, Toxic Sludge Out) system. Although there *is* a lot of sludge out there, it's not *all* sludge. Much of it is worth saving. And now and then that's just what you'll want to do: Save some of it to your hard disk. Let's look at two aspects of saving in particular: how to save and what you can save.

You can save many things from the Web. Most browsers work in much the same way, although one or two have a few nice little extra "save" features. Here's what you can save:

- **Save the document text** You can copy text from a browser to the Clipboard and then paste the text into another application. Or you can use the **File**, **Save As** command, which enables you to choose to save the document as plain text (that is, without all the little codes used to create a Web document; you'll look at those in Chapter 20, "Setting Up Your Own Web Site").

- **Save the HTML source document** The source document is the HTML (Hypertext Markup Language) document used to create the document that you see in your browser. The source document has lots of funky little codes, which you'll understand completely after you read Chapter 20 (perhaps not completely, but at least you'll understand the basics). After you begin creating your own Web pages (you are planning to do that, aren't you? Everyone else and his dog is), you might want to save source documents so you can "borrow" bits of them. Use **File, Save As** and choose to save as HTML.

It's Not Yours

Remember that much of what you come across on the Web is copyrighted material. Unless you are sure that what you are viewing is not copyrighted, you should assume that it is.

- **Save the text or HTML source for documents you haven't even viewed** You don't have to view a page before you save it (although to be honest, I haven't yet figured out why you would want to save it if you haven't seen it). Right-click the link and choose **Save Target As** or **Save Link As** from the shortcut menu.
- **Save inline images in graphics files** You can copy images you see in Web pages directly to your hard drive. Right-click an image and choose **Save Image As** or **Save Picture As**.
- **Save the document background** Internet Explorer even lets you save the small image that is used to put the background color or pattern in many documents. Right-click the background and choose **Save Background As**.
- **Create Windows wallpaper** Internet Explorer also lets you quickly take an image or background from a document and use it as your Windows wallpaper image. Right-click the picture or the background and choose **Set As Wallpaper**.
- **Copy images to the Clipboard** With this neat Explorer feature, you can copy images and background images directly to the Clipboard. Right-click the image, and then choose **Copy** or **Copy Background** from the shortcut menu.
- **Print the document** Most browsers have a File, Print command and maybe even a Print button. Likewise, you'll often find a Page Setup command that lets you set margins and create headers and footers.
- **Save URLs to the Clipboard** You can save URLs to the Clipboard so that you can copy them into another program. Copy the URL directly from the Address or Location text box, or right-click a link and choose **Copy Shortcut** or **Copy Link Location**. Some versions of Netscape also allow you to drag a link onto a document in another program; the link's URL will then appear in the document.

- **Grab files directly from the cache** Remember that the cache is dynamic; the browser is constantly adding files to and removing files from it. If you have something you want to save, you can copy it directly from the cache. Internet Explorer makes this process easy; simply click the **View Files** button in the Options dialog box. With Netscape, you can view the directory holding the files. However, Netscape renames files, making them hard to identify. (Explorer names each file with its URL.) You can also find special programs that will help you view and manage files in your cache; see Appendix C, "All the Software You'll Ever Need," for information about tracking down software.
- **Save computer files referenced by links** Many links do not point to other Web documents; they point to files of other formats, which opens a whole new can of worms that we'll explore right now.

Grabbing Files from the Web

I like to group nondocument files into the following two types:

- **Files that you want to transfer to your hard disk** A link might point to an EXE or ZIP file (a program file or a ZIP archive file) that contains a program you want to install on your computer. Chapter 15, "What on Earth Are All Those File Types?," deals with file formats. (See Appendix C for a list of sources of shareware programs, which would fall into this category.)
- **Files that you want to play or view** Other files are not things you want to keep; instead, they are files containing items such as sounds (music and speech), video, graphics, or word processing documents that are part of the Web site you are viewing.

Both types of files are the same in one way: Whatever you want to do with them—whether you want to save them or play them—you *must* transfer them to your computer. However, the purpose of the transfer is different, and the way it's carried out is different. When you want to play or display a file, you might have to configure a special viewer, helper application, or plug-in so that when the browser transfers the file it knows how to play or display it. Chapter 7, "Web Multimedia," covers such things in detail. For now, we're interested only in the first type of file—a file that you want to transfer and save on your hard disk.

Web authors can distribute computer files directly from their Web documents. Several years ago, pretty much the only file libraries were FTP sites (covered in Chapter 12). Now many Web sites have links to files. Companies that want to distribute their programs (shareware, freeware, or demo programs) and authors who want to distribute non-Web documents (PostScript, Word for Windows, Adobe Acrobat, and Windows Help documents, for example) can use Web sites to provide a convenient way to transfer files.

Files Can Be in Both Categories

Files can be in both the first and second categories. What counts is not so much the type of file, but what you want to do with the file and how your browser is configured. If you want to save the file on your hard disk, perhaps for later use, it would fall into the first category: save on your hard disk. If you want to view the file right now, it would fall into the second category: view in a viewer or plug-in.

Which category a file fits into also depends on the manner in which the file was saved. In its normal format, for instance, an Adobe Acrobat file (a PDF file) could fall into either category. In some compressed formats, it would fall into the first category only because you'd have to save it to your hard disk and decompress it before you could view it. (Compressed formats are explained in Chapter 15.)

Winsock?

What's this Winsock thing? Winsock is a contraction of *Windows Sockets*, the name of the TCP/IP driver used to connect Windows programs to the Internet's TCP/IP system. Just as you need a print driver to connect a Windows program to a printer, you also need a special driver to connect a program to the Internet. The term Winsock refers to programs that can connect to a TCP/IP network.

Save It

To see how you can save a file, go to TUCOWS (The Ultimate Collection of Winsock Software) at `http://www. tucows.com/`. (Its logo is two cows.) This site contains a fantastic library of Internet software for Windows and Macintosh computers.

Suppose you find a link to a program that you want to transfer. You click it as usual, and what happens? If you're using Netscape, and if the file is an EXE or COM file, you'll probably see a File Save box. If so, choose the directory into which you want to save the file (download directories are discussed in Chapter 15). Or you might see the Unknown File Type dialog box (shown in the next figure). This box appears whenever Netscape tries to transfer a file that it doesn't recognize; Netscape wants you to tell it what to do. You can click the **Save File** button to get to the Save As dialog box, and then you can proceed to tell your computer where you want to save the file.

Explorer uses a slightly different method. First, it displays a dialog box showing that a file is being transferred. After a moment or two, you'll see another dialog box (similar to the one in the following figure).

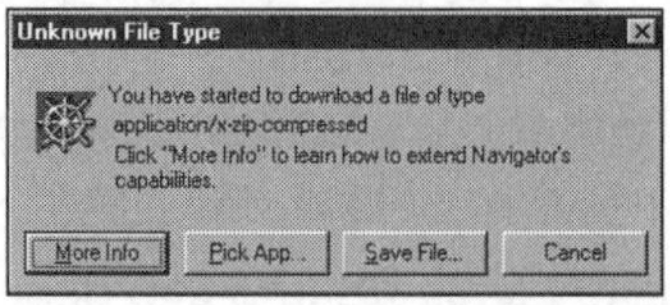

Netscape doesn't know what to do with this file type, so you have to tell it.

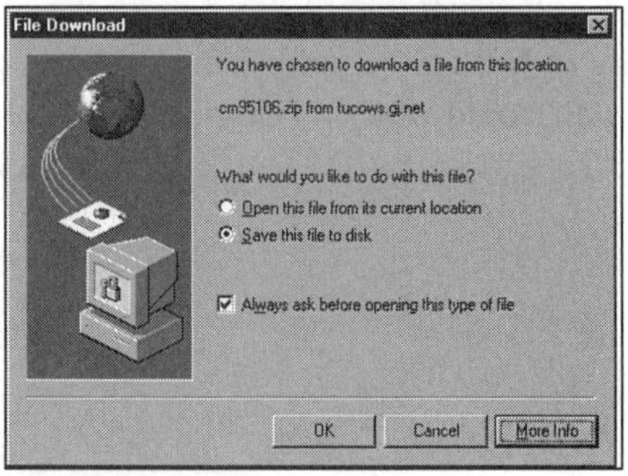

Internet Explorer uses a slightly different method for managing file transfers.

You now have two choices:

- You can tell Explorer to open it, in which case Explorer transfers the file to your desktop and runs the file. This is a pretty lousy idea, for a couple of reasons. First, if the file is a compressed archive file, you'll be expanding all files held by the archive onto the desktop, making a huge mess and mixing them in with all the other files already there. Second, the file may be a program file that will run automatically. If it contains a virus, you could be in trouble. You should check program files with virus-check software before running them. (You'll learn more about that subject in Chapter 15.)
- You can save it to disk. This is the preferable option. Choose this option and click **OK**, and the transfer will continue. After the file has been transferred to your hard disk, you'll see a Save As dialog box in which you can choose where to place the file.

Notice the check box titled Always Ask Before Opening This Type of File. If you clear the check box, the next time you download a file, Explorer will automatically transfer it and open it, even if you chose the **Save It to Disk** option button the first time. (To recheck this check box, go to Windows Explorer, and then choose **View**, **Options**—or **View**, **Folder Options**—and click the **File Types** tab. Then click the file type in the list box, click **Edit**, click **Confirm Open After Download**, and click **OK**.)

The Least You Need to Know

- If your computer has enough memory, you can open a second Web document in a new window and keep the current window open.
- You'll probably end up saving Web documents on your hard disk; you can reopen them using the **File**, **Open** command.
- The cache stores documents you've seen on your hard disk. The browser can get those documents from the cache the next time you want to see them, which speeds up work tremendously.
- The Reload command (or Refresh in Internet Explorer) throws away the version of the page held in the cache and grabs a new one from the Web site. You can configure the cache to do this automatically once every session.
- You can copy, print, and save all sorts of things from the Web: document text, the document source file, images, background images, and more.
- If you click a link to a nondocument file, your browser might ask you what to do with it. You can save it to your hard drive if you want.

Chapter 6

Forms, Applets, and Other Web Weirdness

In This Chapter

- Unexpected things you'll run into on the Web
- Using tables and forms
- Getting into password-protected sites
- Using frames and secondary windows
- Web programming: Java, JavaScript, and ActiveX
- Pushing, pulling, and multimedia

Not so long ago, the Web was filled with static documents that contained pictures and text—originally Web documents didn't even have pictures. But the Web has changed and is still changing; no longer is it just a static medium that you read. In this chapter, you're going to take a quick look at some weird and wonderful things you might find on the Web, such as tables, forms, password-protected sites, secondary or targeted windows, and frames. You'll also learn about Java, JavaScript, and ActiveX applets, as well as push and pull commands and multimedia.

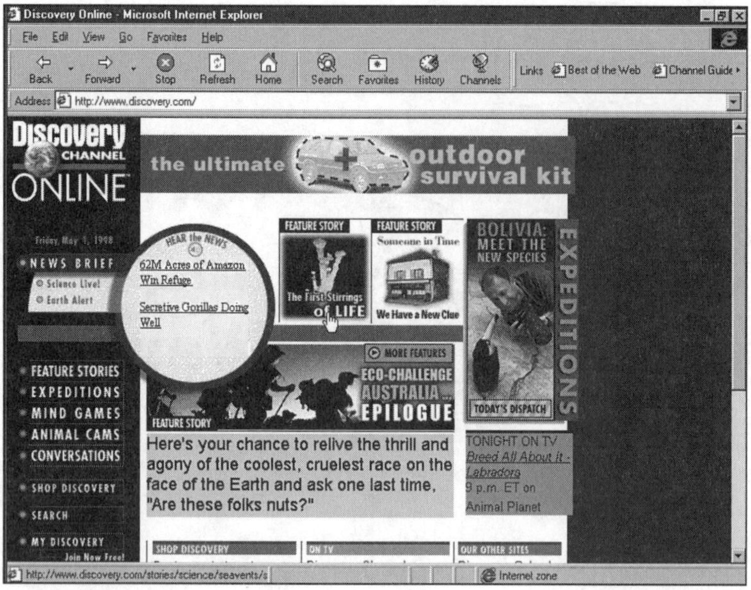

The Discovery Channel (`http://www.discovery.com/`) *page formatted using the table feature.*

Working with Tables

A *table* is...well, you know, a table. It's a set of columns and rows in which you organize text and (sometimes) pictures. Most browsers these days can display tables. So if you are using a recent one (such as Netscape or Internet Explorer), you'll have no problems. Tables are often used to display tabular data (go figure), but they can also be used as a simple page layout tool to get pictures and text to sit in the correct places. (The following figure shows a table being used in this way.) Recent improvements to the way that browsers handle tables enable Web page authors to use different background colors and different border colors in each cell.

Interactive Web Pages: Using Forms

A *form* is a special *interactive* Web document. It contains the sorts of components that you've become familiar with while working in today's graphical user interfaces: text boxes, option buttons (also known as radio buttons), command buttons, check boxes, list boxes, drop-down list boxes, and so on. You'll find forms at the search sites (see Chapter 17, "Finding Stuff"). You use them just as you would a Windows or Macintosh dialog box: You type a search word into a text box, select any necessary options by clicking option buttons and check boxes, and then click a command button.

Forms are also used to collect information (you might have to enter your name and address when downloading demo software, for instance) and make sales. You can choose the products you want to buy and enter your credit card information into a form. The next figure shows an order form at one of my Web sites.

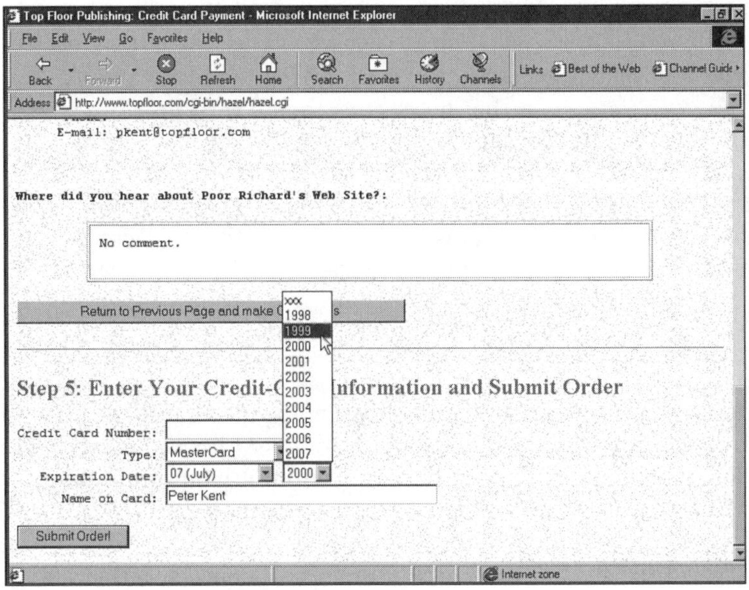

Enter all the required information, select options from the drop-down list boxes, and then click the Submit Order button.

Playing It Safe: Secure Sites

When you enter information into a form and send that information back to the Web server, there is a slight chance that it could be intercepted by someone and read. (It's not very *likely* that your information will be intercepted, but that's another story—which I'll get to in Chapter 18, "Staying Safe on the Internet".) Netscape, Internet Explorer, and some other browsers provide a way to send information *securely*. If the form you are viewing comes from a special `https://` server (a secure server), the information is *encrypted* before it's sent back from the form to the server. When the server receives the information, it decrypts the information. While the encrypted data is between your computer and the server, the information is useless; anyone who intercepted the information would end up with a load of garbled rubbish.

Just a Little Different

Forms in Web pages do function just a little differently from forms in other programs. For a start, you must click directly on an option button or check box to select it, not just on the label; in some operating systems—Windows, for instance—clicking the label will select the option or box. Although you can press **Tab** to move to the next field in a form in most browsers (or **Shift+Tab** to move to the last), this keystroke doesn't work in all browsers.

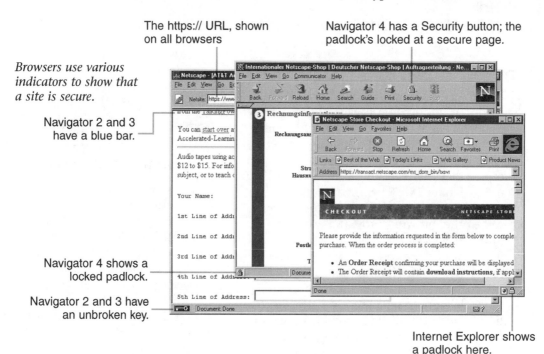

In most browsers, you know when you are at a secure site. In Internet Explorer, the little padlock icon in the lower-right corner is locked (in some versions of Explorer, no lock appears until you're displaying a secure page; in others, the lock's always there, but it's open when you're at a page that not secure). Some versions of Netscape Navigator have a key in the lower-left corner of the window; the key is whole at a secure page (it's broken on pages that are not secure). These versions of Navigator also display a blue bar just below the toolbars when the site is secure. More recent versions of Navigator (Versions 4, 4.5, and 4.6) don't have the blue bar or the key. Instead, they use a padlock icon, which is closed. You'll see the padlock icon in the lower-left corner of the browser and in the toolbar; the Security button is a padlock that changes according to the type of document displayed. Other browsers use similar but slightly different methods to indicate that you are at a secure page.

One indicator of a secure site is visible in any Web browser. As you can see in the following figure, the URL of a secure Web page begins with `https://` instead of `http://`. If you send information to this site or receive information from it, you can be sure that the information will be transmitted in a secure, encrypted manner.

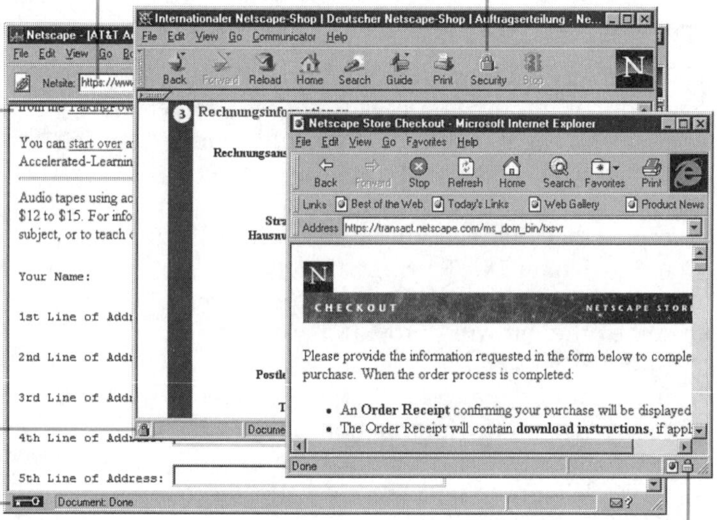
The https:// URL, shown on all browsers
Navigator 4 has a Security button; the padlock's locked at a secure page.
Navigator 2 and 3 have a blue bar.
Navigator 4 shows a locked padlock.
Navigator 2 and 3 have an unbroken key.
Internet Explorer shows a padlock here.

Browsers use various indicators to show that a site is secure.

For Your Eyes Only: Password-Protected Sites

Many Web sites are password-protected or have an area that is password-protected. You can't enter a password-protected Web site or area unless you enter a password, which is given to you when you go through a registration process (which often, although not always, includes payment of some kind).

Why do sites use passwords? They may be selling information or some other kind of data (the single most common form of sold data, and in general the most profitable, is pornography). They may have private areas for employees of a particular company or members of a club or association. But sometimes free sites that are open to the public require that you log in. This requirement is often because these sites create an account for you and save information about you. To access that account, you have to log in (see the following figure). For instance, Expedia (`http://expedia.com/`), Microsoft's travel Web site, creates accounts for people that save information about them: their email address, zip code, the airport they generally fly from, and a subscription to an email notification of travel promotions.

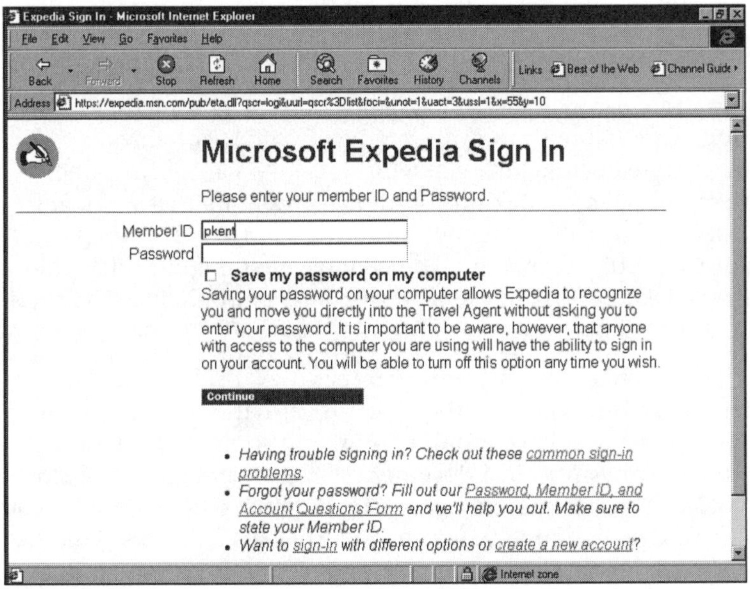

Microsoft Expedia is free, but you have to set up an account—with an account name and password—if you want to use it.

Dealing with Secondary Windows

I should know better, but once or twice I've been confused when I've suddenly discovered that Netscape Navigator's history list has disappeared. What happened? I clicked a link and then looked away for a moment. While my eyes were averted, another browser window opened automatically. I continued, unaware of what had happened.

Web authors can set up a link so that when you click it, a new window opens, and the referenced document appears in that window. It's a very handy feature when used properly. These windows are called *targeted* windows. (I prefer to use an older hypertext term: *secondary* windows.)

When a targeted window opens in Netscape Navigator, the history list disappears from the previous window because the history list is linked to a particular window. In newer versions of Navigator, you *can* still use the history list from the Go menu, although the Back button won't work. That's how it works in all versions of Internet Explorer—although the Back and Forward commands stop working in that browser, you can still access the full history list and get back to a previous page.

Public Letter to Web Authors

Dear Web authors: It's bad interface design to open a secondary window full-screen. Please open your windows slightly less than full screen, so it's obvious to your users what's going on! Signed, Confused in Denver. (Unfortunately, browsers aren't very helpful. In many cases, the Web author can't determine the screen size.)

Panes or Frames

Another new feature you might find while browsing on the Web is *frames*. (In other earlier hypertext systems, these were sometimes known as *panes*.) The following figure shows an example of frames. A framed document displays two or more documents, each within its own pane. The frames around each document might be movable (if the author set them up that way), and you might have scrollbars in each pane. Why put documents in frames? Frames can be a good way to organize a lot of information. For example, you might find a table of contents in one frame; clicking a link in the table of contents would load the specified document into the other frame.

Some browsers have a special reload command for frames: Click inside a frame and then choose **View**, **Reload Frame** to reload the contents of that one frame. Some versions of the Netscape browser also have a **Back in Frame** command with which you can move back to the previously viewed document within the frame. Navigator Version 2 had a real problem with frames, though; using the Back command took you all the way out of the frames, perhaps many steps back, rather than showing you the previous document you viewed within the frames. Internet Explorer and the more recent versions of Navigator (Navigator Version 4) have no Back in Frame command; instead, they assume that if you're using the Back command, you want to go back step by step, not all the way out of the frames.

Frames are one of the most hated features on the Web. Although they can be very useful when designed properly, too many Web authors misuse them; they put too many frames into a window or lock frame contents so you can't scroll down the page within the frame. Such authors are often working with very high-resolution monitors on which everything works fine, but things get totally messed up on lower-resolution monitors.

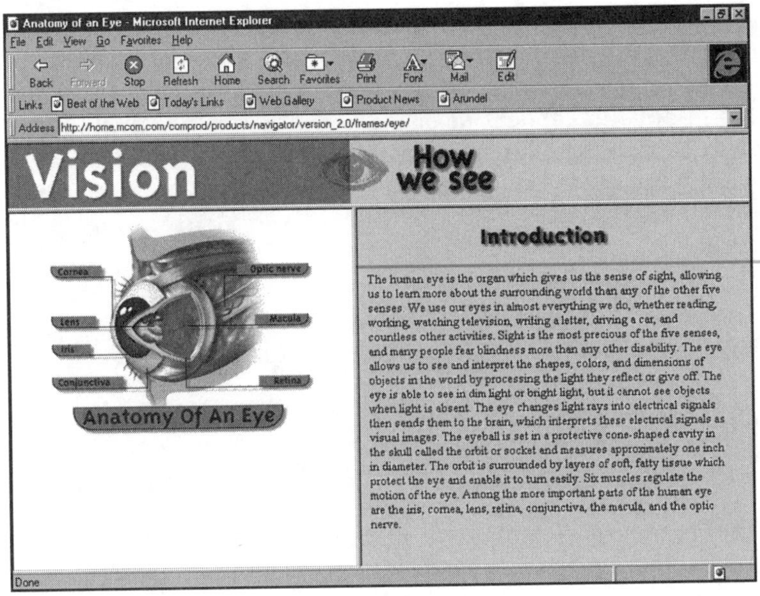

The How We See demo shows a good use of framed documents. Click parts of the eye in the left frame to see information in the right frame.

This bar divides the frames.

Animated Icons

Animated icons are becoming popular these days. These little pictures embedded into Web documents appear to be in motion. They are relatively easy for Web authors to create, so you can expect to see many more of them appearing on the Web. They add a little motion to a page (this is known in Web jargon as "making a page more compelling") without causing a lot of extra stuff to be transmitted to your computer. Unfortunately, such animations can be extremely irritating, as user research has shown. Many authors throw in animations because they're cool, without realizing that they sometimes make the page harder to read.

If you find large and complicated things in motion, you've stumbled across some kind of video or animation file format (see Chapter 7, "Web Multimedia") or perhaps a Web program created in Java or ActiveX, which we'll look at next.

Web Programs: Java, JavaScript, and ActiveX

You might have heard of Java by now. I'm not talking about a chain of coffee bars; I'm talking about a new programming language that will (if you believe the hype) make the Web more exciting, make every appliance from toasters to dishwashers talk to you in Swahili, bring about world peace, and lead to a complete and total eradication of body odor.

Java has been hyped for a couple of years, but I think it's finally becoming useful. A number of sites now have Java applets that do something useful (in the early days

Java was a toy, and the average Java applet was nothing more useful than a picture of bouncing heads). The Expedia site mentioned earlier, for instance, has Java-based maps. You can select an area to see a map showing a few hotels, and then zoom in on a particular area, or find information about one of the hotels. Java is also used to create moving banners, automatically scrolling text boxes, chat programs (see Chapter 13, "Yak, Yak, Yak: Chatting in Cyberspace"), and many other useful and not-so-useful things.

Java Interpreters

Java-compatible browsers are Java "interpreters." In effect, an interpreter is a program that can run another program, coordinating between the computer's operating system and the program. So a Java applet can run on any operating system (Windows 3.1, Windows 95, Macintosh System 7, and UNIX of various flavors) as long as there is an interpreter created for that operating system. Both Netscape Navigator and Internet Explorer are Java interpreters.

For these programs to work, you must be using a Java-compatible Web browser—and even then they might not work. Netscape 2.0 and later versions, and Internet Explorer 3.0 and later versions, are Java-compatible. The later the version, the more likely that the Java applet will function (Netscape Navigator 2, for instance, doesn't handle Java applets very well). But even if you have the very latest browser, you might still run into problems.

When you reach a Web page that has an embedded Java applet, the Java program is transmitted to your computer, and the browser then runs the program. The program might be a game of some sort, a multimedia display, a financial calculator of some kind, or just about anything else. The following figure shows one of the Java maps at Expedia.

For all the overblown projections, many Java applets remain rarely used, unreliable, and slow (and all too often pointless). Searching for interesting or useful Java applets has been an experience in frustration and disappointment for some time. The situation is improving, though, with truly useful Java applets becoming more common and more reliable.

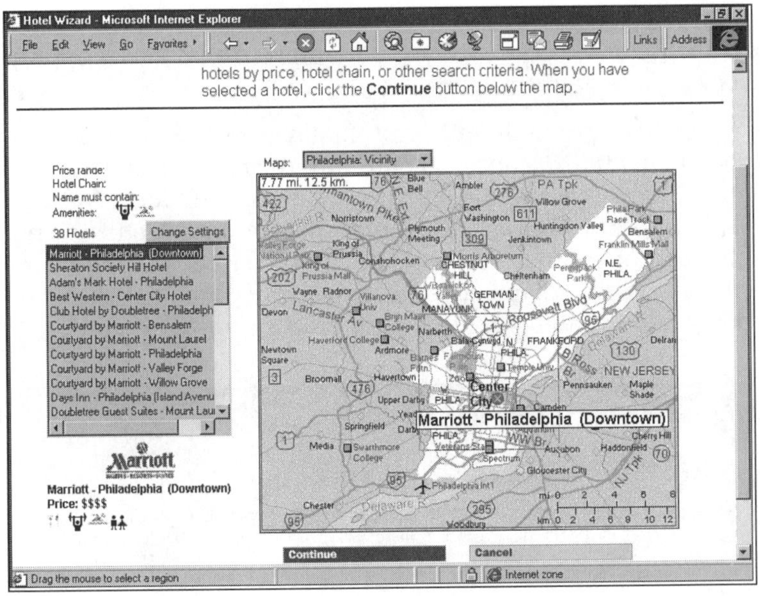

Expedia's Java maps help you find a hotel.

Applications Across the Net

You might have heard the theory that pretty soon, instead of buying software and installing it on your hard drive, you'll "rent" programs across the Internet, paying for the time you use. If this *ever* happens (and there are good reasons to suspect it won't), it will be a very long time from now. Internet connections are currently about as reliable and efficient as a drunk at a beer tasting, and until they are as reliable as the electricity supply, this system won't work. I've added this projection to my "yeah, right, don't hold your breath" list.

What About JavaScript and ActiveX?

JavaScript is Java's baby brother. It's a scripting language in which programs are written within the Web page. In other words, a JavaScript-compatible browser reads the Web page, extracts the JavaScript commands, and runs them. JavaScript is not as powerful a programming language as Java, but it's easier to create programs using JavaScript, so it's more common. You can find loads of JavaScript programs at

Developer.com (`http://www.developer.com/directories/pages/dir.javascript.html`). The following figure shows an example of a JavaScript application, taken from a book I wrote on the subject.

A competitor to Java, ActiveX is a system from Microsoft, designed to allow Web authors to easily incorporate multimedia and programs into their Web pages. Currently, the only ActiveX browser is Internet Explorer, and you can probably expect it to stay that way for a while. With Netscape as the most popular browser, there's not much incentive for Netscape Communications to add ActiveX to Netscape and help their major competitor! (On the other hand, as Internet Explorer gains Web share—which it seems to be doing fairly steadily—that situation might change.)

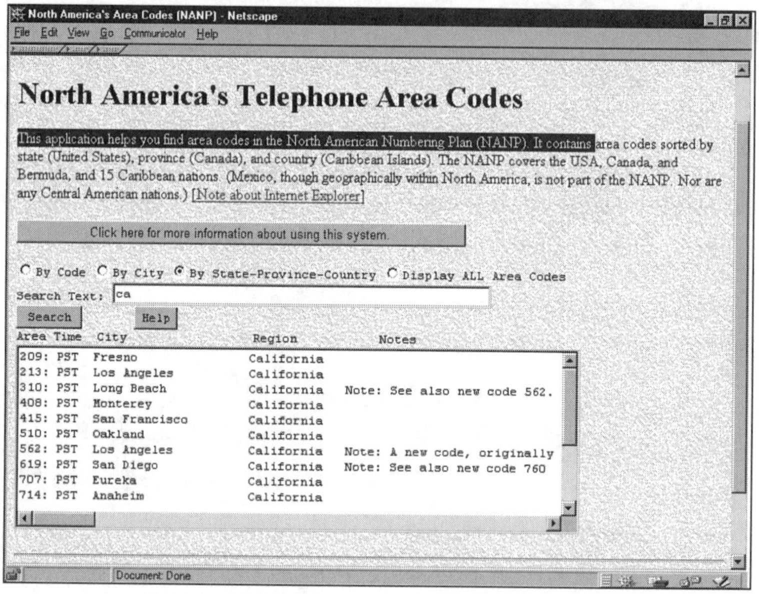

My Area Code program, written in JavaScript (`http://www.topfloor.com/javascript/areacode.htm`).

The Latest Programmer's Toy, Dynamic HTML

There's another way to make Web pages move, and that's with a new toy called Dynamic HTML (also called DHTML) and layers. A Web designer can now create different layers of information—pictures and text—and then shuffle these layers around on the page, making them visible and then invisible, to create an animation effect and even let people move things around on the page (see the alien head in the following illustration). People define Dynamic HTML differently; layering is a feature that's often used in conjunction with Dynamic HTML, although the purists may say it's a different thing. Microsoft and Netscape regard Dynamic HTML and layers as different things, too.

Dynamic HTML means Dynamic Hypertext Markup Language. You might remember from Chapter 4, "The World of the World Wide Web," that HTML is Hypertext Markup Language and is the coding used to create Web pages—you'll see it in action in Chapter 20, "Setting Up Your Own Web Site." So DHTML is sort of like HTML in motion. That's the theory, but advanced DHTML also requires programming skills, not just Web-authoring skills.

For the moment, DHTML is a programmer's toy used on few sites, although that's rapidly changing. DHTML works in both Internet Explorer 4 and 5 and Netscape Navigator 4, which means that many users don't have DHTML browsers. In any case, DHTML that works in Explorer probably won't work in Navigator and vice versa.

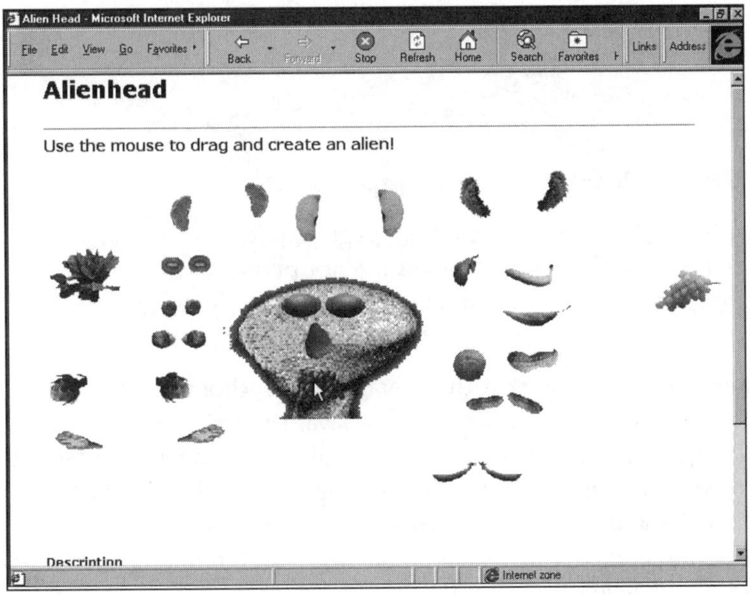

Create your own alien head through the wonders of DHTML. (You'll have to use Internet Explorer, though.)

Just a Little Shove: Pushing and Pulling

Information generally arrives at your screen because you've directly requested it by clicking a link or entering a URL. However, Web authors can set up their Web pages to use server push and client pull so you can get information without doing a thing.

The first of these, *server push*, occurs when the Web server continues sending information even though you haven't requested it. Suppose you click a link to display a Web page, and just a few minutes later, the Web page changes. Even if you don't request more information, the server sends updated information and continues to send periodic updates until you close the page.

Client pull is similar, except that the request for updates comes from the browser. For instance, you open a page. At the same time the server sends the page, it sends a special program (you don't see this; it all happens in the background). This program tells the browser when to request updates. After the defined interval, the browser sends a request to the server asking for the information. Again, these updates will continue until you leave the page.

These systems work so similarly that you usually won't know which method is being used. They are very useful when you're viewing information that changes rapidly, such as stock quotes, weather reports, news headlines, or auctions.

The Web Gets More Complicated

As you'll see in Chapter 20, creating a simple Web page is quite easy; even many of the more advanced Web-authoring techniques are not particularly complicated. Sure, there are special codes to learn, but it's all reasonably straightforward.

But the latest technologies are things that the average Web author will find much more complicated to use. Technologies such as Java, JavaScript, ActiveX, and Dynamic HTML require programming skills. As a result, it's becoming harder for Web authors to keep up with the Joneses (technologically speaking), which might be a good thing. Now they can concentrate on function instead of form, forget about the glitz, and compete by making their Web sites interesting and content-rich instead of just trying to be cool.

The Multimedia Experience

You'll find all sorts of file formats on the World Wide Web, including still pictures, video and animations, sounds, electronic documents, and 3D images. Any file format that you can play or display on your computer can be linked to a Web page.

When you click a link that takes you to one of these file formats, your browser handles the file, if it can. It displays the document or picture in the window in the normal way. If the file is a format that your browser can't handle, it has two options. Your browser might send the file directly to a program that *can* handle it (known as a *plug-in, viewer,* or *helper*), or it might ask you what to do. Chapter 7 deals with this topic.

Before I move on, though, here's a quick thought related to this issue:

The Internet is not a multimedia system!

Remember that, and you'll be saved from a lot of frustration. This statement might seem a little strange after you've been bombarded by several years of advertising and media hype about the Internet. We've all seen the TV ads in which video rolls across a computer screen within a Web browser, as quickly as if it were being displayed on a TV screen. But the Internet does *not* work that quickly, and many of its problems seem to arise from people trying to treat it as if it does.

As a multimedia system, the Internet is primitive, mainly because it's so slow. If it's "lights, cameras, action" that you're after, use the TV or go see a movie; the Internet can't compete. The Internet, despite what you might have heard, is primarily a text-based system. (What's the fastest growing area on the Internet? Email publishing!) Even the Web is primarily text. All the hype in the world won't change that. What will change that is much faster connections from people's homes to the Internet, faster Web servers, and faster and more reliable backbone connections across the Internet. But don't hold your breath, because you'll turn blue before these things appear on the scene (see Chapter 24, "The Future of the Internet," for a discussion of that issue).

The Least You Need to Know

- The Web is far more diverse than it was a year or two ago; it's much more than just text with pictures.
- You'll find lots of tables and forms.
- Framed documents allow an author to split a document into multiple pieces, each of which is displayed in its own frame.
- Java, JavaScript, and ActiveX are Web programming languages that enable authors to bring their pages to life. The new programmer's toy is Dynamic HTML.
- Client pull is a system by which a browser automatically requests updates to a page. Server push is a system by which a server automatically sends updates.
- A wide range of multimedia formats must be displayed in viewers or plug-ins; you'll learn about those in Chapter 7.

Chapter 7

Web Multimedia

In This Chapter

- How does a browser handle different file formats?
- Finding plug-ins and viewers
- Types of plug-ins and viewers you might want
- Installing plug-ins
- Installing viewers in Netscape
- Installing viewers in Internet Explorer

As the Web gets older, and as people start using it more, it's storing more and more types of computer files. You'll find animations, videos, pictures of various formats, sounds that play after they've transferred to your computer, sounds that play *as* they transfer to your computer, "slide" presentations, and all sorts of other weird and wonderful things. Think of these formats as the *multimedia* content of the Web—literally "multiple media." But as I explained in the previous chapter, the Internet is not a true multimedia system. Yes, it has many types of media, but they tend to move rather slowly!

Today's Web browsers are designed to handle any computer file format. When you click a link to a file, that file is transferred to your computer, and your browser can then use it in one of three ways:

- **On its own** The file format might be one that the browser can handle directly. Web browsers can play or display Web pages (HTM or HTML), text documents (TXT), some graphics formats (GIF, XBM, JPG, and JPEG), and some sound formats.

- **With a plug-in** The browser might open a *plug-in*, a special add-on program that plays or displays the file within the browser window.
- **With a viewer (or helper)** The browser might send the file to a *viewer* or *helper*, which is a separate program that recognizes the file format. That program then opens a window in which the file is played or displayed.

When you first get your browser, it probably won't recognize all the file formats you'll encounter. When the browser comes across a file format that it doesn't recognize, it will ask you what to do; you can then install a new plug-in or viewer to handle that file type, or simply save the file on your hard disk.

Check This Out

Two Types of Multimedia Inclusions

There are basically two ways to include a multimedia file in a Web page. The author might include the file as a *live, embedded,* or *inline object* (a file that is automatically transferred to your computer along with the Web page). For instance, an embedded file might play a background sound or display a video within the Web page. On the other hand, the author can include the file as an *external file;* you click a link, and that file alone (without a Web page) is transferred to your computer.

Check This Out

Which Plug-Ins Are Installed?

In Netscape Navigator, you can quickly find out which plug-ins are installed by choosing **Help, About Plug-Ins**. You'll see a page showing you each plug-in and its filename. You'll also find a link to the Inline Plug-Ins page, where you can download more. In some versions of Internet Explorer, you can select **Help, Product Updates**, and you'll see a Web page that lists a number of recommended plug-ins and shows you whether those plug-ins are already installed. This feature is not in Internet Explorer 5, though. Instead, select **Tools, Windows Update**, to go to the Microsoft site and find out what piece of bloated software they want you to download today.

What's Available?

Scores of plug-ins and viewers are available; you just have to know where to find them. A good starting point for Netscape Navigator plug-ins is the Netscape Navigator Components page; select **Help**, **About Plug-Ins**, and then click the **For More Information on Netscape Plug-Ins, Click Here** link near the top of the page, or go to `http://home.netscape.com/plugins/`. For Internet Explorer, use the **Help**, **Product Updates** command I just mentioned, or visit the Windows Updates site. You can also find many viewers at the sites discussed in Appendix C, "All the Software You'll Ever Need."

About now you're probably wondering whether you should use a plug-in or a viewer. In general, you'll probably prefer working with plug-ins because they allow the browser to display or play the file. In effect, a plug-in extends the capabilities of the browser, allowing it to work with a file type that it couldn't use before. A viewer, on the other hand, is a completely separate program; the Web browser remains at the previous Web page while the multimedia file is sent to the viewer. Of course, there might be cases in which a viewer is a better program and has more features than the equivalent plug-in. You might want to experiment and find out which is the more capable of the two.

Which Do You Need? Which Do You Want?

You don't need all the available viewers and plug-ins. There are hundreds already—last time I looked Netscape claimed there were almost 180 plug-ins for Netscape Navigator—and more are being added all the time. So unless you are independently wealthy and don't need to waste time working, you probably won't have time to install them all (and you probably don't have the disk space you'd need). To help you determine which plug-ins and viewers you should get, I've broken them down into a few categories and the most common file formats. You might not want to get them until you need them, though.

Music and Voice (Very Useful)

Some of the most useful plug-ins and viewers are those for music and voice. In particular, you might want RealAudio, TrueSpeech, and StreamWorks. (RealAudio is the most popular, and therefore the most useful, of these sound formats.)

Most sound formats can't play until they have been completely transferred to your disk drive (you twiddle your thumbs for 10 minutes, and then listen). The RealAudio, TrueSpeech, and StreamWorks formats play sounds as they are being transferred, though. They're used by radio stations and music libraries, for example, so you can listen to the news from National Public Radio (`http://www.npr.org`) or music from the Internet Underground Music Archives (`http://www.iuma.com`). The following illustration shows Netscape Navigator using RealAudio to play a file from the NPR site.

You Already Have Viewers

In many cases, you might already have viewers for certain file formats. For instance, if you use Windows, you can use the Windows Media Player as a viewer for MIDI files. If you use the Macintosh and have Microsoft Word, you can use Word as the viewer for Word .DOC files.

During your Internet travels, you are likely to come across these other sound formats:

- **.AU**, **.AIF**, **.AIFF**, **.AIFC**, and **.SND** These common sound formats are used on UNIX and on the Macintosh. Your browser can probably play these formats without an additional plug-in or viewer.
- **.WAV** This is the Windows sound format. Your browser can probably play files in this format without an additional plug-in or viewer.
- **.MID** and **.RMI** These are MIDI (Musical Instrument Digital Interface) formats. You might need to add a plug-in or viewer for these. (Netscape Navigator, since version 3, comes with a preinstalled plug-in that will work with MIDI files.)

The MIDI formats are not common, but they are of interest to people who, well, are interested in MIDI. Many MIDI sites on the Web have sound clips. (MIDI is a system used to create music using computers and other electronic toys.)

The RealAudio viewer playing the newscast from NPR.

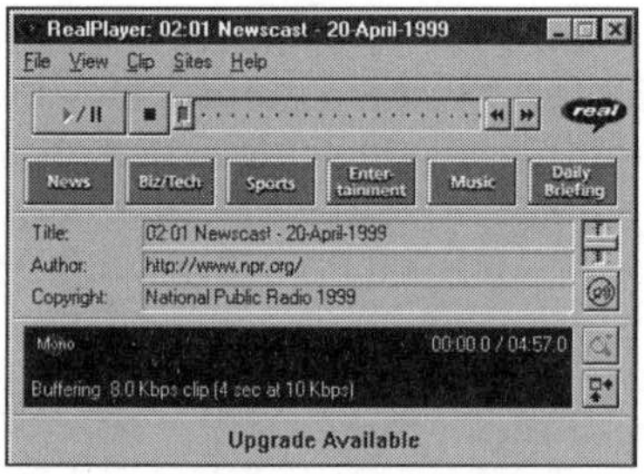

MP3

MP3 is another important sound format you should know about. While it's rare to find MP3 files set up to play across the Internet—people generally download the files and play them "offline"—it can be done. There's a service called SHOUTCAST (`http://www.shoutcast.com/`) that has hundreds of channels of "streamed" MP3 music.

What's so special about MP3? Well, MP3 files are CD-quality, and take up relatively little room. One minute of music takes up just 1MB, more or less, of disk space (the format used on audio CDs uses requires almost 10MB for each minute). MP3 is very popular, and it has the music business terrified; in fact, the Recording Industry Association of America has even tried to have an MP3 player banned.

MP3 can be used in many different ways. You can store all your music on your computer, and then create playlists. Having a weekend party? Set up a playlist to run all weekend, click the start button, and forget about the music for the next 72 hours.

You can also create custom CDs. Pick the tracks you want, convert them to audio CD, and cut your own CD. Or play the music through an MP3 player, such as Rio from Diamond Multimedia—plug the player into your computer, load the music, and away you go. Create custom cassette tapes and DAT tapes. Send your friends tracks across the Internet, and so on. The music business is terrified.

The two most popular MP3 players are WinAmp (`http://www.winamp.com/`) and MusicMatch (`http://www.musicmatch.com`). MusicMatch has the advantage of including a "ripper," software that can take tracks off your audio CDs and save them in MP3 format (WinAmp may include a ripper soon, too).

To find music, and learn about all the neat MP3 tools, visit MP3.com (`http://www.mp3.com`, of course) or one of these sites:

> Songs.com
> `http://www.songs.com`
>
> MP3 2000
> `http://www.mp3-2000.com`
>
> MP3 Now
> `http://www.mp3now.com`
>
> MPEG.ORG
> `http://www.mpeg.org`
>
> Dimension Music
> `http://www.dmusic.com`

Oh, and don't forget to check out a book I've just published, *MP3 and the Digital Music Revolution: Turn Your PC into a CD-Quality Digital Jukebox* (`http://topfloor.com/`). It comes with the MusicMatch software and hours of music.

What's the music business doing about all this? They're trying to come up with their own sound formats, such as Liquid Audio and A2B (which comes from AT&T, of all places). Of course, the problem is that most people won't want to use these sound formats, because the entire purpose of these formats is to make moving your music around *inconvenient*, to discourage piracy. But if it's inconvenient for software pirates (the music business has finally come to the realization that music is a form of software), then it's inconvenient for the rest of us, so the music business will find it hard to get people to switch. (Try this test; visit AltaVista, a search site we discuss in Chapter 7, and search for the word MP3. Then search for "Liquid Audio"; you'll quickly see which is the more popular!)

Other Document Formats (Also Very Useful)

Viewers and plug-ins are also available for a number of document formats that you'll find on the Web. In particular, the Adobe Acrobat Reader is useful. You'll also find viewers and plug-ins that display Microsoft Word, Envoy, and PostScript documents.

Adobe Acrobat is a hypertext format that predates the Web. It enables an author to create a multipage hypertext document that is contained in a single PDF file and that can be read by any Acrobat Reader, regardless of the operating system it is running on. Many authors like to use Acrobat because it gives them more control over the layout than they get when creating Web pages. It's also often used by companies that want to allow people to download forms from their Web sites; you can open the form in Adobe Acrobat Reader and then print it, and it will look exactly as the company intended (it's difficult to create high-quality forms using Web pages). For instance, most Internal Revenue Service forms are available in PDF format. You can see an example of an Acrobat file in the following figure.

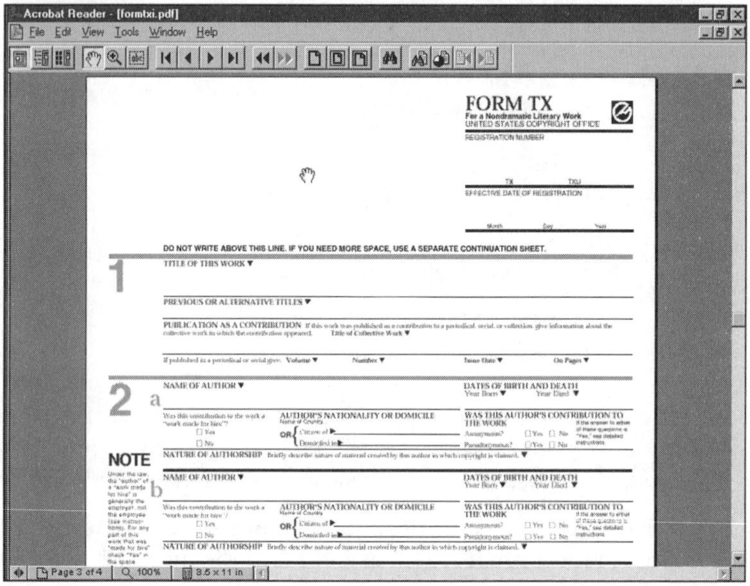

A form from the United States Copyright Office saved in an Adobe Acrobat file and displayed in the Adobe Acrobat viewer.

3D Worlds (Greatly Overrated!)

There are a number of viewers and browsers that display 3D (three-dimensional) images. Netscape Navigator has a plug-in called Live3D or Cosmo Player (depending on the version of Navigator that you are using), which might have been installed when you installed the browser. Internet Explorer has a plug-in called Microsoft VRML Viewer, which probably won't be installed with the browser—you'll have to add it later. You can download other 3D plug-ins or viewers, too.

Do you need a 3D plug-in or viewer? Probably not. After you've seen a couple of 3D sites, the novelty will quickly wear off. This is another of those much-touted technologies that hasn't yet lived up to the hype. Four years ago, it was supposed to be "the next big thing." We're still waiting. Three-dimensional images load slowly and move slowly. They are, in my opinion, unnecessary gimmicks. Perhaps one day they'll be an integral part of the Web, but for now they're little more than toys.

VRML

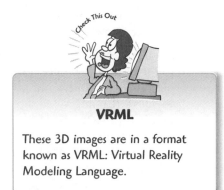

These 3D images are in a format known as VRML: Virtual Reality Modeling Language.

You can walk around these buildings and maybe even into them. This technology is cute, but slow (and not terribly exciting after you've done it once or twice).

Video (If You Can Wait)

Video is fairly popular on the Web, but it has serious drawbacks. The main problem is speed. It can take hours for anything big to transfer, and if it's small, what's the point? After waiting an eternity to watch a five-second cut from a movie, I was left with the question "Was that really worth it?" ringing in my head. However, now that I have fast access, I really do watch videos more often—news videos at the CNN site, for instance (`http://www.cnn.com/`).

Video is another of those things that requires a fast connection. If you are on a corporate network or a cable modem you are probably okay—assuming the video clip is stored on a fast server and the Internet is not as sluggish as molasses on a cold day—but if you are using a modem to connect to a service provider, you'll find video to be very slow.

Still, if you want to try video you can find many viewers and plug-ins. The most common formats are the Windows AVI and QuickTime formats (which may be built into your browser already) and MPEG. A new format, VIV, is a compressed AVI file that provides streaming video. Recently, a video format from RealNetworks has become popular (RealNetworks is the RealAudio company), too, with some news sites using it. Netscape 3.0 comes with a built-in AVI plug-in, but other AVI plug-ins and viewers have more features. Another popular player is the VivoActive player (`http://www.vivo.com/`).

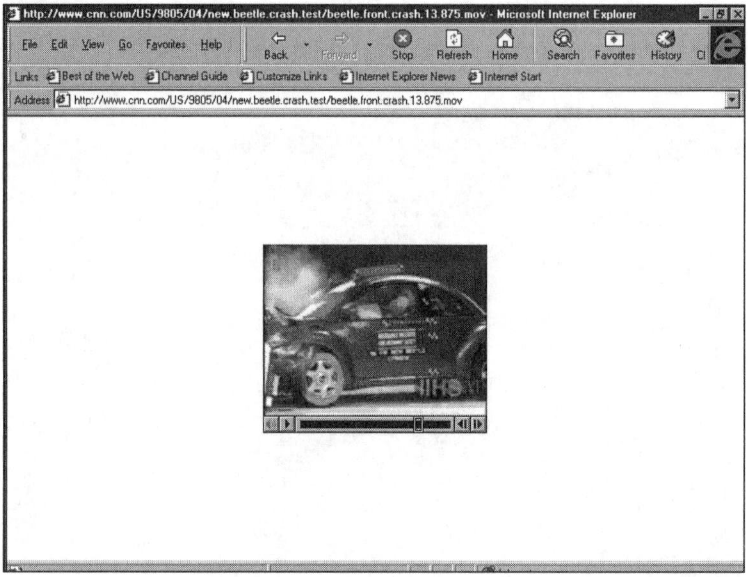

A VW Beetle crash test video from the CNN news site, displayed in the QuickTime viewer inside Internet Explorer.

Streaming Video

I mentioned RealAudio earlier; RealAudio is a streaming audio format, which means it plays as it transmits. That's the new thing in video, too. Not too long ago, you'd have to wait for a video file to transfer completely before you could play it. Now streaming video viewers and plug-ins are turning up; these viewers and plug-ins play the video as it transmits.

Animations (Here and There)

You'll find many animation plug-ins and viewers, but only a few formats are commonly used on the Web. Although it's popular these days for any software company with a proprietary file format to create a plug-in for it, very few Web authors are using animation, and only a few of the available formats are commonly used. Probably the most common animation formats are Macromedia's Authorware and Director animations, which can be viewed using the Shockwave plug-in. (How does animation differ from video? Think of video as a film; think of animation as a cartoon.)

Another very common form of animation is GIF animation. The GIF format is one of the basic image formats used on the Web, and GIF animations are created by layering several images. These animations require no plug-in or viewer, though; if a browser can display images, it can probably display GIF animations.

Other Weird File Formats

You'll find plug-ins and viewers available for all sorts of unusual file formats. Some plug-ins are not programs designed for handling particular file formats that you might come across while cruising the Web—they are more like special utilities designed to extend the features of the Web browser. For instance, there are Netscape plug-ins available for these tasks:

- **Carbon Copy** This Netscape plug-in lets you control a PC across the Internet.
- **Chemscape Chime** This is a plug-in for 2D and 3D chemical models.
- **EarthTime** This plug-in displays eight different times from cities around the world.
- **ISYS Hindsight** This plug-in keeps a record of every Web page you've seen and even allows you to search the text in those pages.
- **Look@Me** This plug-in allows you to view another user's computer screen across the Web and see what's going on (assuming that person *wants* you to see what's going on, of course).
- **Net-Install** This plug-in is designed to automate the transfer and installation of software across the Internet.

Looking for Samples?

A good place to find samples of these various multimedia formats is the Netscape plug-ins page that I mentioned earlier. For each plug-in or viewer, you'll find links to Web sites using the file format handled by that program.

As I mentioned earlier, any file type can be sent to a viewer of some kind. However, only a handful of file types are commonly used (the ones I mentioned earlier as the common formats). You'll want to install other plug-ins and viewers only if the particular file type happens to be used at the Web sites that you frequent.

You don't necessarily need to install these plug-ins or viewers right away. You can wait until you stumble across a link to one of the file formats. If your browser doesn't recognize the format, it will ask you what to do with the file. If you want to access the file, you will need to install the appropriate viewer or plug-in at that time.

Installing a Plug-In

Installing a plug-in is easy. Simply transfer the installation file from the Web and place it in a download directory (see Chapter 17, "Finding Stuff"). Then run the file (double-click it, for instance) to run the installation program. The installation program may run immediately, or you might find that a series of files are extracted from the one you downloaded, in which case you have to run a SETUP.EXE file to start the installation program. Follow the instructions to install the file. After you have installed the plug-in, your browser will be able to automatically call the plug-in anytime it needs it.

By the way, your browser might sometimes tell you when you need a plug-in. For instance, if you see the dialog box shown in the following figure (or something similar), you have displayed a Web page with an embedded file format that requires a plug-in. You can click the **Get the Plugin** button, and the browser will open another window and take you to a page with information about plug-ins.

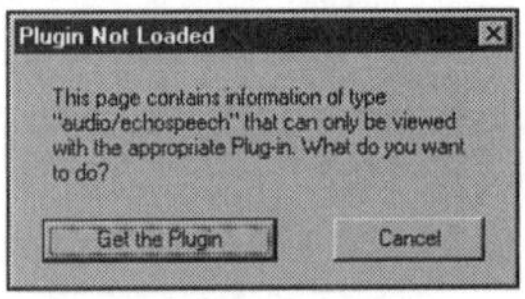

This Netscape dialog box opens when you click a link that loads a file requiring a plug-in you don't have.

Installing a Viewer

Installing a viewer is a little more complicated than installing a plug-in, but it's still not rocket science. There are generally two different types of viewer installations. One is the type used by the early versions of Netscape and by the Macintosh and UNIX versions of Netscape. In this type of installation, you tell the browser which viewer to work with for each file type. You also add information about a particular viewer to a list of viewers that the browser refers to when it needs to handle the appropriate file type.

The other method is that used by the Windows versions of Internet Explorer and by the Windows versions of Netscape Navigator 4 and later. These use the Windows file associations to set up viewers. For instance, by default Windows associates WAV files with the Sound Recorder program. That means if you double-click a WAV file in File Manager, Sound Recorder opens and plays the file. Internet Explorer and Navigator 4 and 4.5 use the same systemwide file-association system to determine which program should be used when it comes across a file type.

The next section gives you a look at installing a viewer in a Windows version of Internet Explorer, which is very similar to what you would do in the Windows version of Netscape Navigator 4 or 4.5. The section after that covers installing a viewer in a Windows version of Netscape Navigator 3, which is similar to the way installation is handled in other, non-Windows versions of Navigator and in some other browsers.

Installing a Viewer in Internet Explorer

When you install a viewer in Internet Explorer, you're not merely modifying Internet Explorer's internal settings; you are modifying the Windows file-association settings. When you click a file type that Internet Explorer doesn't recognize, it opens the dialog box shown in the following figure. (This dialog box is similar to what you saw from Netscape.) Because Explorer doesn't recognize the file type, you have to tell it what to do. Click the **Open It Using an Application on Your Computer** option button, and then click **OK**. Explorer transfers the file and then tries to open it.

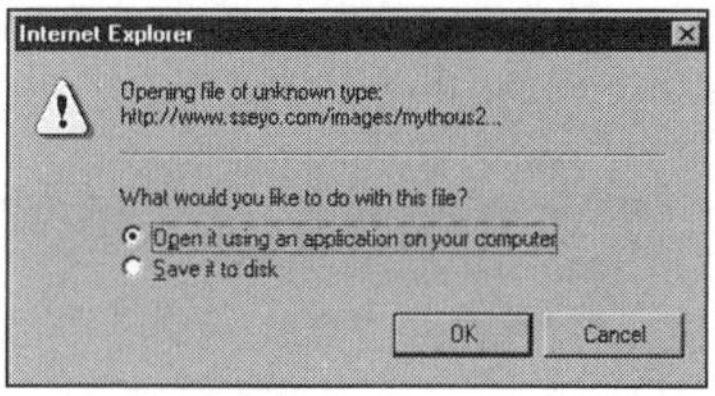

If Explorer doesn't recognize a file, you will see this dialog box.

You'll then see the Open With dialog box, shown next. Type a name for this type of file into the text box at the top. Then, if you can find the viewer you want to use in this list, click it and click **OK**. If you can't find it, click the **Other** button. In the Open dialog box that appears, select the viewer you want to use.

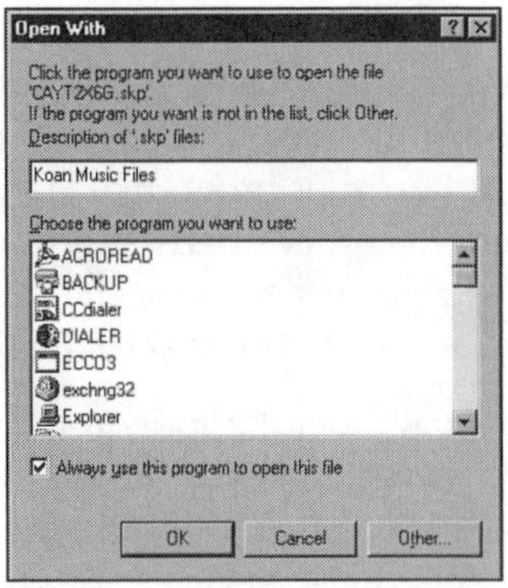

Enter a name for the file type, and then choose the application you want to use as a viewer.

Installing a Viewer in Explorer Beforehand

You can also install an Internet Explorer viewer before you need it. You do this by using the File Types system, which you can access from the Windows Explorer file-management utility or, in some versions of Internet Explorer and in Netscape Navigator 4, from within the browser.

Open Windows Explorer, and then select **View**, **Options** (or **View**, **Folder Options** in some versions), and then click the **File Types** tab. You'll see an Options dialog box similar to that shown in the following figure. (In some versions of Internet Explorer, you'll be able to access this dialog box in the same way, although more recent versions don't allow this. In Netscape Navigator 4 for Windows, select **Edit**, **Preferences**, and then open the **Navigator** category and click the **Applications** subcategory. The Navigator dialog boxes will be slightly different from those shown here, but similar enough for you to be able to follow along.)

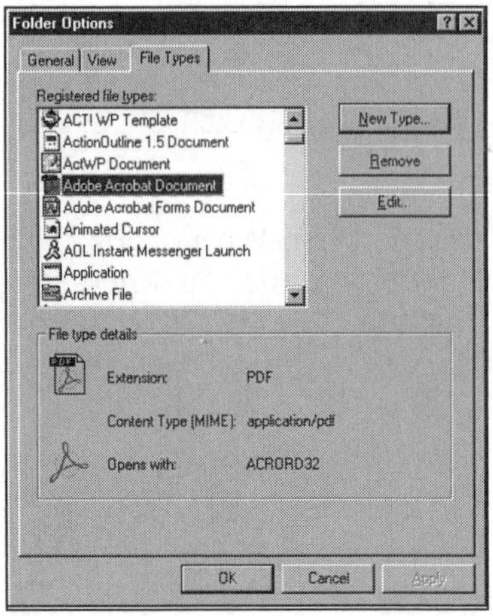

You can add viewers to Internet Explorer by using the Options dialog box.

To add a new viewer, click the **New Type** button, and then fill in all the information in the dialog box that appears. Enter the description (whatever you want to call it), the file extensions used by that file type, and the MIME type. Click the **New** button and type **open** in the first text box you see. Then click the **Browse** button and find the application you want to use as the viewer.

What's MIME?

MIME stands for multipurpose Internet mail extensions. Although originally intended for email transmission of files, MIME is used on the Web to identify file formats. You can find detailed information about MIME and a large list of MIME types at `http://www.cis.ohio-state.edu/hypertext/faq/usenet/mail/mime-faq/top.html` or at `http://home.netscape.com/assist/helper_apps/mime.html`.

Installing a Viewer in Netscape 3

This section explains how to configure a viewer in the Windows version of Netscape Navigator 3. The process is similar in earlier versions of Netscape and even in other browsers. Rather than modifying the list of Windows file associations, you're modifying a list belonging to the browser. (For Netscape 4 and 4.5, go back and read the Internet Explorer instructions; these versions of Netscape use a similar method.)

Suppose you came across a link that looked interesting, and you clicked it. Netscape displayed the Unknown File Type dialog box, shown next. This means that Netscape doesn't recognize the file, so you have to tell it what to do.

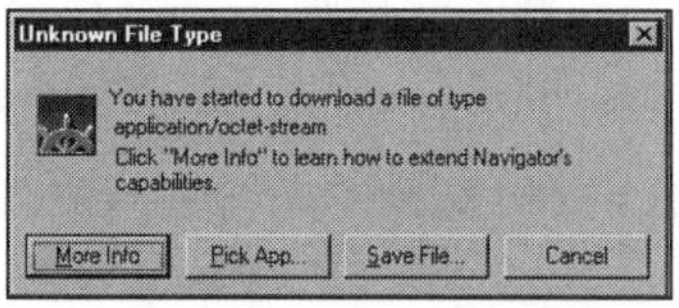

The Unknown File Type dialog box opens if you click a link to a file that Netscape doesn't recognize.

If you want, you can click the **More Info** button. Netscape will open another browser window and display an information document with a link to a page from which, perhaps, you can download a plug-in. Let's assume that you already know there is no plug-in for this particular file type or that for some other reason you want to configure a viewer. Click the **Pick App** button, and you'll see the dialog box in the following figure.

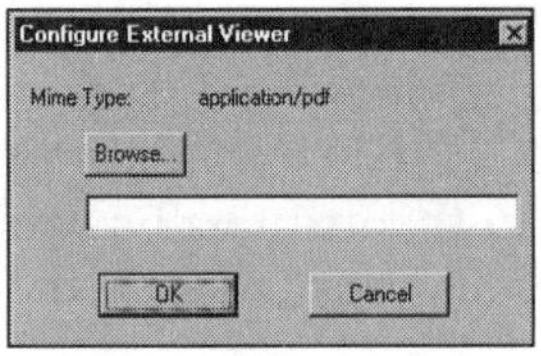

The Configure External Viewer dialog box lets you define which viewer should handle the file type.

Click the **Browse** button and then find the program that you know can handle this type of file. (Remember, you can find viewers at the sites listed in Appendix C.) Double-click the program, and it is placed into the Configure External Viewer dialog box. Then click **OK**. That's it! You've just configured the viewer. The file referenced by the link you clicked will now be transferred to your computer and sent to the program you defined as the viewer. The viewer will then display the file (assuming, of course, that you picked the right viewer).

Setting Up Netscape Navigator Beforehand

You can also set up Netscape Navigator's viewers before you ever get to a site that uses unusual file formats. Choose **Edit**, **Preferences**, and then open the **Navigator** category and click the **Applications** subcategory. Or, if you're using an early version of Navigator, choose **Options**, **General Preferences**, and then click the **Helpers** tab. You'll see the dialog box shown next.

What's That Button For?

In case you're wondering, the Unknown: Prompt User option button is the default setting for formats that haven't been set up with a viewer. If you click a file for which you've configured this setting, Netscape will ask you what to do with the files of this type when they are transferred to your browser.

The big list shows all the different file types (well, most of them; you can add more using the **Create New Type** button). To configure a viewer for one, click it in the list and then click one of the **Actions**. You can tell Netscape to **Save to Disk** if you want, but if you intend to configure a viewer, click **Launch the Application** instead. Then click the **Browse** button to find the application you want to use as the viewer.

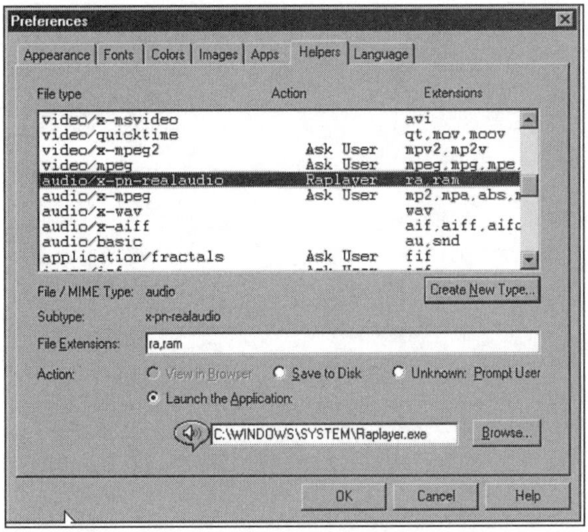

You can preconfigure viewers in Netscape's Preferences dialog box.

The Least You Need to Know

- A browser can handle many file formats: HTML, text, graphics, and sounds of various kinds. If a browser encounters a file format that it can't handle, it tries to pass the file to a viewer or plug-in.
- Viewers and plug-ins are designed to play or display file types that browsers can't handle. The difference between the two is that a plug-in temporarily converts the browser window into a viewer, but a viewer is a completely separate program that opens without changing the browser window in any way.
- There are hundreds of viewers and plug-ins for scores of file types. Most of these file types are rarely used, however.
- Plug-ins are more convenient than viewers are. However, if you find a viewer that has more features than the plug-in, use it.
- If your browser comes across a file type that it doesn't recognize, it asks you what to do. You can then install a plug-in or specify a viewer.

Part 2

There's Plenty More

The Internet is far more than just the Web, although you might not be able to tell that from the media coverage. There's a system called push, for example, which is a sort of Web automation tool. But there are other important systems that have nothing to do with the Web. The Internet has hundreds of thousands of discussion groups (newsgroups and mailing lists); a file library system called FTP, and a once popular menu system known as Gopher. And, of course, there's chat. No, it's not really chat—instead of talking, you type—but many people find it to be a great way to while away an hour or ten. And you'll learn about a system (Voice on the Net) that enables you to make international phone calls for just pennies an hour! You might even use Telnet, a relatively little used system that allows you to log on to computers around the world. Even if you don't use all of the services covered in this part of the book, you're almost certain to find something useful.

Chapter 8

Push Information to Your Desktop

In This Chapter

- Push: Bringing data to your desktop in a scheduled flood
- The push monolith: Microsoft Active Desktop kills off Netscape Netcaster
- Adding channels to your desktop
- Finding more push programs: PointCast, BackWeb, and more

This chapter takes a look at a relatively little used, yet at one time much touted, Internet service, *push* technology. The term push is a misnomer, but nobody asks me to come up with these names; think of push as scheduled pull. People talk of information being "pushed" to your computer, rather than your having to get the information using your Web browser. But a push system is like an automated Web browser—the program retrieves the information for you automatically.

Here's how it works. You install a push program on your computer, and then configure the program to periodically retrieve information. For instance, you can tell the program that you want to see the latest news headlines from CNN every 10 minutes, that you want to check the weather forecast before you leave work each evening, and that you want to see the latest version of the corporate Web site when you come in each morning.

Webcasting

Another term you'll hear related to push systems is *Webcasting*. A company can set up information that it plans to distribute to people using push technology. This is Webcasting, the "broadcasting" of data through push channels. Of course, in the computer business, terms often have multiple meanings! Microsoft uses the term Webcasting to refer to the transmission of streaming video or audio across the Internet, not push.

As long as the program has been started—and you can set up the program to start automatically every time you start your computer—the program will automatically grab information from the Internet for you. Because information arrives on your computer's desktop without your direct intervention, it appears that the information is being pushed to your desktop—thus the term *push*.

Push was supposed to be the big new technology of 1997. It turned into a big flop. Whereas push proponents thought most people would be using push by now, in fact most are not. However, the technology is easily available. It's part of Windows 98, which means millions of people have it available, and for a while it came with Netscape Communicator—millions more are using one of these versions of Communicator. So it *is* in use—it's just nowhere near as popular as it was supposed to become.

There is, however, a *true* push technology that is tremendously popular and becoming more so every day: email publishing. Many thousands of newsletters and bulletins are published via email, and it's a true push system because the publisher sends it out (pushes it out) when it's ready. Your email program doesn't retrieve the information; it waits for it to arrive. Still, email isn't generally thought of as a push technology (as I said, I don't make up all these definitions), so I won't be talking about it in this chapter.

New Productivity Tool, or Great Futzing Opportunity?

The companies making push programs claim that these systems provide a fantastic way to boost productivity. *Scientific American*, after reading some of this corporate fluff, even described push as an "innovation that (might) improve work." I figure that push provides great "futzing" opportunities. The Gartner Group, which did a study of computers and their effect on productivity, defines futzing as the things people do with their computers that waste time, as opposed to things they do that are productive. (Each employee wastes $5,590 of futzing time each year, The Gartner Group claims.) Push programs have been criticized for clogging up networks with scheduled retrievals of information, information that users might not even read (it's so easy to schedule that you might end up getting far more information than you can handle). Anyway, how does reading the latest news headlines or sports scores increase productivity?

Every computer product enhances productivity—or so you'd believe if you believe everything that computer-industry PR departments claim. In fact, very few technologies are clearly productivity boosters, and I personally doubt whether push technology is one of them.

A Lot of Choice, but One Big Player

Although a number of push systems are available, there is now just one big player: Microsoft, of course. Microsoft has built its push technology—Active Desktop and the Internet Explorer Channel Bar—into its browsers and operating system. Not too long ago Netscape was also in the push business, with a product called Netcaster. But they've let Netcaster die. While it was included in earlier versions of Netscape Navigator—Version 4.0 and 4.02—they left it out of Version 4.5. Just goes to show how popular push *didn't* turn out to be, I guess.

This game does have other players, though. PointCast, for example, is the first really popular push program on the Internet. BackWeb and Castanet are two other systems that have received a lot of attention, and there are a number of smaller and less well-known systems.

Microsoft's Active Desktop

Active Desktop has been available for some time; it was included with some versions of Internet Explorer 4 and is still there in Version 5. It's now available to millions more people because it's built into the Windows 98 operating system. Active Desktop provides two ways to add channels: You can specify a Web page, or you can select one of the channels already prepared for you.

To specify a Web page as a channel, open your Display Properties dialog box (right-click on a blank area of the desktop and select **Active Desktop**, **Customize My Desktop**), and you'll see something like the following figure.

You add channels in this dialog box.

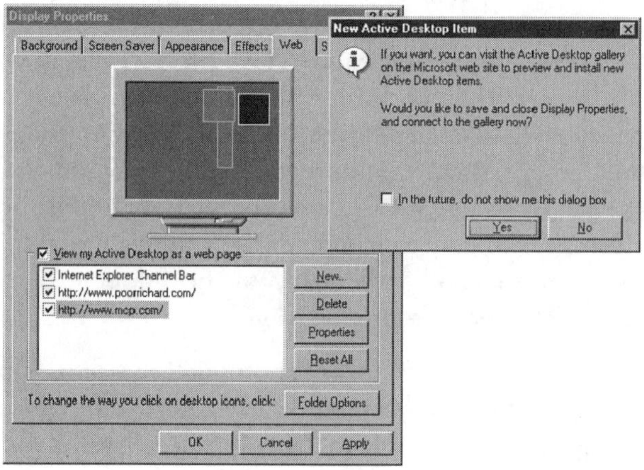

To add a channel, make sure the **View My Active Desktop As a Web Page** check box is checked; then click the **New** button and you'll see a message asking whether you want to visit the Microsoft site and select a channel. Click **No**, and then enter the URL of the Web page you want to add. (What happens next depends on which version of Internet Explorer you're working with. These instructions are for Version 5; other versions may vary slightly.) Click **OK**, and you'll see a box with a **Customize** button. Click the button to start a wizard that helps you set up the channel you've just created. This wizard allows you to enter an update schedule—to specify when you want the system to grab the latest information from the Web site—and also allows you to enter a password, so you can access private Web sites. (I've been saying for years that the major use of push is to get a daily pornographic picture, and I'll bet that's what the password support is for.) If you prefer, you can tell the wizard that you don't want to schedule updates—the page will be updated only when you choose an update by selecting **Synchronize** from the the little triangle button in the top-left corner of the channel window. (Or right-click the desktop, and then choose **Active Desktop**, **Update Now** to update all your channels at once.)

Channels appear on your desktop as sizable windows. (To size the window, drag the bottom-right corner; to move the window, drag the top-left corner.) You can use the window as if it were a normal Internet Explorer window; just click the links to move around. You can use the right-click pop-up menu to access various commands.

Note also that you can define various channel properties; click the little triangle button in the top-left corner of the channel window (the button might not appear until you click on or near the top of the window—move around a little, it can be hard to "grab"), and select **Properties**. You'll then be able to define various settings: You can specify that you want to know when the Web page changes, but not to automatically transfer the new information; specify how many levels to go down through the links in the Web page; ask the system to send an email message to you if the Web page changes; tell the system not to transfer pictures, sound, or video from the page; limit the size of the overall transfer; and so on.

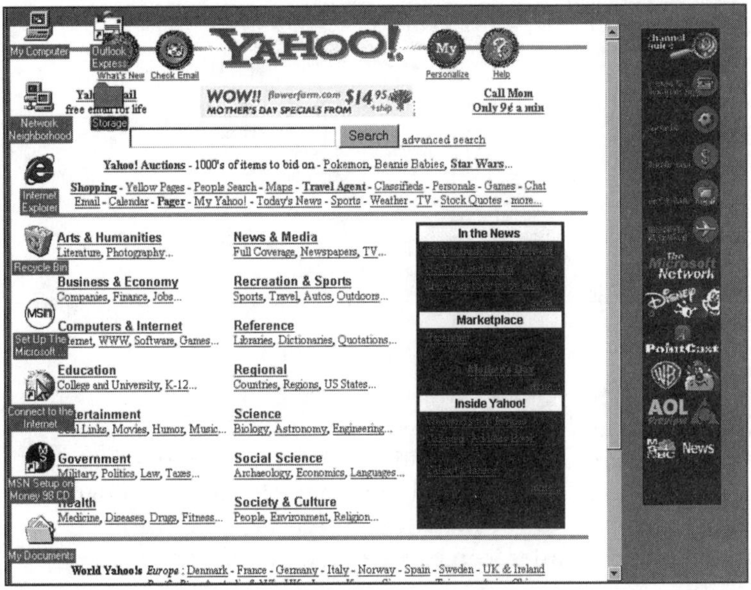

You could create a channel out of your favorite search site (see Chapter 17) onto your desktop, so it's always available. This is Yahoo!, placed onto the Windows 98 desktop.

Using Preconfigured Channels

In the preceding figure, you can see a vertical bar on the right side of the window. This is the Internet Explorer Channel Bar, and it allows you to choose from a wide selection of preconfigured channels. To turn on the Channel Bar, right-click the desktop and select **Active Desktop**, **Customize My Desktop**. In the Display Properties dialog box, check the **Internet Explorer Channel Bar** check box. (Note that you might not be able to see the channel bar if you set up a Web page as a desktop channel that covers the entire screen—depending on the version of software you're using, the channel bar might be obscured.) Click one of the categories, and a window will open displaying a list of options. You'll be able to see a summary of what each channel does, and, if you want, subscribe to the channel. You can see in the following figure one of these preconfigured channels, *The New York Times*. You can add these channels to your system as "active channels." Active channels appear when you click the little **Channels** button in the taskbar (the button that looks like a satellite dish).

This is The New York Times *preconfigured push channel.*

A Quick Look at Netcaster

Millions of users still have Netcaster, the push program included with Netscape Communicator, despite the fact that Netscape has decided to kill it off (Version 4.5 does not have Netcaster). Let's take a quick look at how to work with this program. You can start Netcaster by selecting **Communicator**, **Netcaster** from within Netscape Navigator or using the Netcaster icon or Start menu option.

Netcaster has *channels*; each information source you define is known as a channel, and they're all stored in the My Channels area of the Netcaster *drawer* (Netcaster's "control panel"). You can see a picture of the drawer in the following illustration. Notice the little tab on the left side of the drawer; click it to open or close the drawer. (The drawer, when open, obscures everything underneath it on your computer screen, so you'll have to close it when working in other programs.)

Netscape Netcaster's drawer, the system's "control panel."

What Can You Put in a Channel?

In the early days of push, you could choose from only a predefined set of information channels. These days, some push systems, such as Netcaster and Microsoft Active Desktop, allow you to define any Web page as an information source. You can choose to get your best friend's paintball Web site delivered to you automatically, for instance. You might choose to see the latest driveway at the Driveways of the Rich and Famous site or check on today's Dilbert cartoon. The choice is yours.

There are two ways to add a channel, that is, to tell the program which information sources you want to use. You can select a channel from the predefined set (the ones listed in the Channel Finder area), or you can specify a particular Web site.

Using the Channel Finder

Click the Channel Finder bar to see all the preselected channels. If you don't see a channel that interests you in the Channel Finder, click the **More Channels** bar in the Channel Finder, and a browser window opens with many more channels.

If you'd like more information about a channel that is listed, click that entry, and it will open up to display a logo and an **Add Channel** button. Click that button, and a window opens, displaying information about that channel (as you can see in the following figure). If you decide that you definitely do want this channel, click the **Add Channel** button that you'll see near the top of the window; otherwise, click **Cancel**.

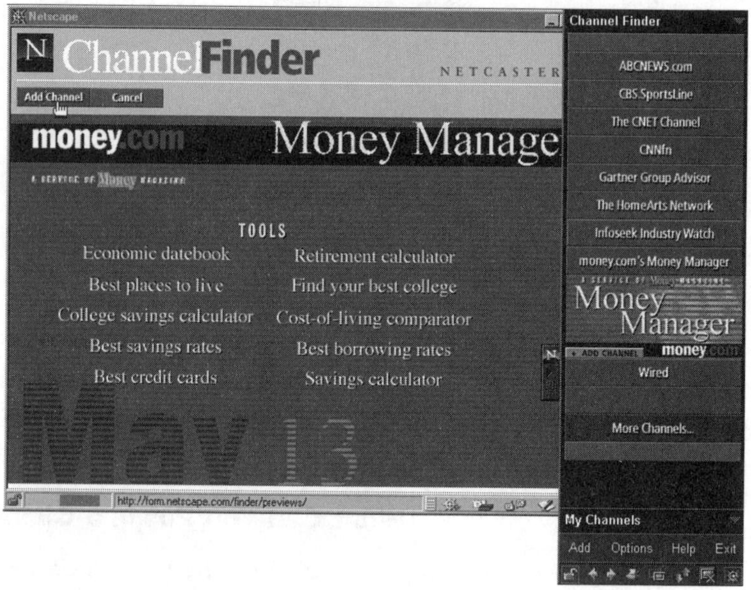

*Click a channel button, and then click **ADD CHANNEL** to add the channel to your collection.*

When you click the **Add Channel** button, a dialog box opens, as you can see in the following figure (you might see a window in which you must register Netcaster first). This box shows you the name of the channel (you can change the name if you want), and the location (the URL) of the Web page. Note that you can also define how often the page is updated, that is, how often information is retrieved from this site. If you clear the **Update This Channel or Site Every** check box, the channel is, in effect, turned off; it will not be updated. Leave the box checked, though, and select an option from the drop-down list box to define how often the channel will be updated, from once every 30 minutes to once a week.

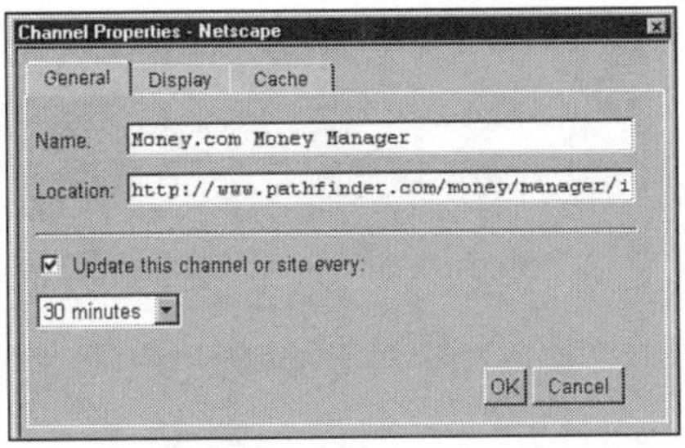

Tell Netcaster how often you want to update the information in this channel.

You now have two ways to display this channel. Click the **Display** tab, and then select either **Default Window** or **Webtop Window** (see the following figure). Default Window is a normal browser window. The Webtop Window is a special window; the information will appear on your computer's desktop, as a sort of desktop wallpaper. (I'll show you the difference in a moment.)

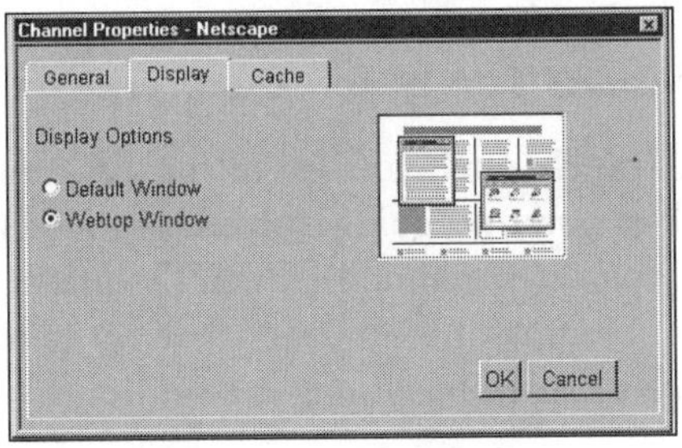

Use a normal browser window, or display the information as desktop wallpaper.

Now click the **Cache** tab to see the information in the following figure. This tab enables you to set the size of Netcaster's special cache, in which it stores channel data. This cache is separate from the cache used by Navigator (see Chapter 5, "More About the Web," for information about browser caches).

The Cache tab also enables you to define how many levels deep the channel should go. For instance, if the channel goes one level deep, it will contain the main page only. If it goes two levels deep, it will contain the main page and all the pages linked to that page. If it goes three levels deep, it will contain the main page, all pages linked to the main page, and all pages linked to *those* pages. Downloading several layers can make a channel take up a *lot* of disk space and take a long time to transfer, but it makes it quicker for you to read the pages. For instance, if you're downloading a news channel, you'll be able to see the headlines on the main page and read the associated story. You'll be able to do that whether online or offline, and the news stories won't have to be transferred across the Web when you're ready to read them; they'll come from the cache.

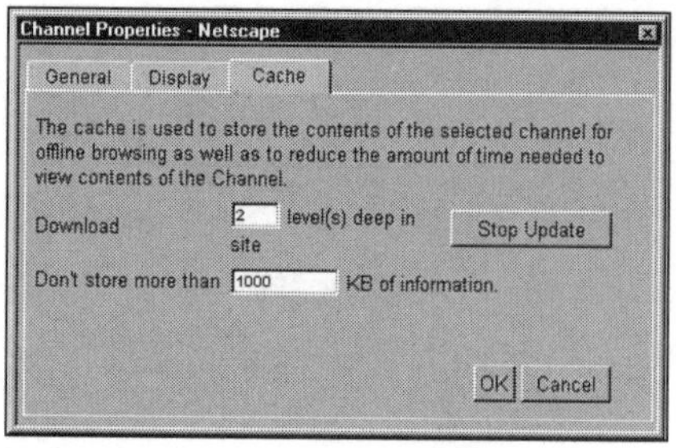

Configure the cache and the number of levels that should be transferred from the site.

Too Many Levels Means Too Much Data Transfer

Be careful with this levels setting. The channels you see in the Channel Finder have been created especially for Netcaster, so going down three levels is probably not a problem. But if you set up your own channels (which I'll discuss next), going down three levels will be a real problem with Web pages that contain a lot of links. Retrieving even as few as two or three levels might take hours.

Notice the Stop Update button, which you can use later to stop a channel transfer (to open a channel's Properties dialog box later, open the My Channels area of the drawer, right-click the channel name, and select **Properties**).

Adding Any Web Page

You can specify any Web page as a channel. In other words, you can have Netcaster automatically retrieve information from whichever of the tens of millions of Web pages are most important to you. Simply click the **Add** button at the bottom of the drawer, and you'll see the Channel Properties dialog box that we used before. You'll use the box in the same way as before, the only difference being that you must provide a name and the location (the URL) of the Web page. That's all there is to it.

Using Your Channels

To work with your channels, click the **My Channels** bar in the drawer; you'll see a list of your channels. Click the channel you want to view, and it will open. If you defined it as a Default Window channel, then a browser window opens. This setting is good if you have a channel from which you often need to begin a Web session. If you defined a channel as a Webtop channel, though, all your windows and icons are replaced with a Webtop window, as you can see in the following figure.

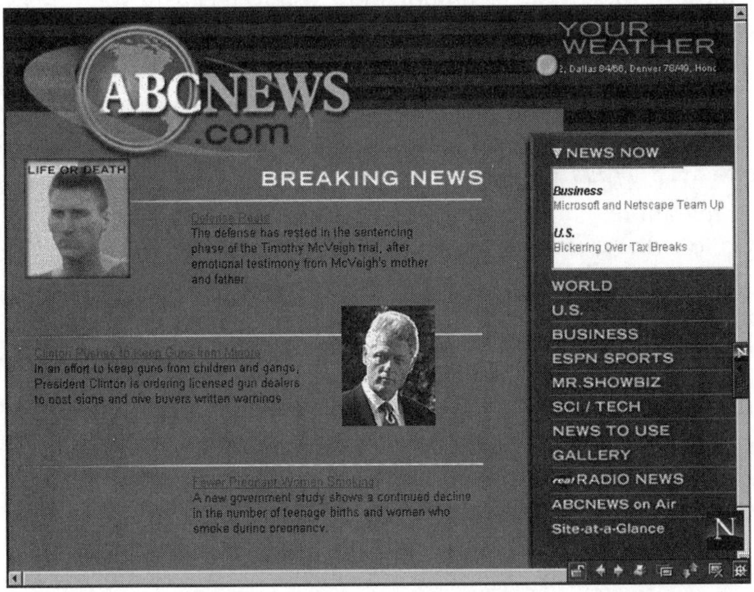

Webtop windows take over your computer desktop.

You can use the Webtop just like a Web page in the browser; it's just that this Web page has taken over your screen, with the exception of the icons you can see in the lower-right part of the screen: the Netcaster tab, the Webtop toolbar, and a Netscape icon.

The Webtop toolbar contains buttons that are used to manage a Webtop session. The buttons display Security information for a page displayed on the Webtop; go Back and Forward through the Webtop "browser's" history list; print the current Webtop page; hide or display the Webtop (in effect displaying or hiding your normal desktop); move the Webtop to the front or back (in front of or behind the normal operating system desktop); close the Webtop; and open a browser window.

Play with these buttons to see their effect. For instance, you can push the Webtop to the back, so the Webtop acts almost like true desktop wallpaper. Open program windows appear above the Webtop, although the program icons that are normally shown on the desktop are not there (at least, that's how it is in the current version of Netcaster; this might change later).

Other Push Systems

As I mentioned earlier, a number of push systems are available. Although the specifics of working with other systems vary, the basic principles remain the same: Pick an information channel, tell the program how often the information should be retrieved, and then sit and wait. Most of these systems do not allow you to pick any Web site as a channel; they generally limit you to preconfigured channels. If you want to try one of these other systems, go to one of the following sites. You'll find software you can download and install, generally free of charge.

- **BackWeb** This program has around 50 channels, from American Singles to ZDNet News. Go to `http://www.backweb.com/`.
- **Castanet** This program has around 40 channels, from MissingKids to WallStreetWeb. Go to `http://www.marimba.com/`.
- **PointCast** Perhaps the best-known of the push programs, this program has around 30 preconfigured channels, including newspapers, magazines, newsletters, and more, from *American Metal Market Cold-Finished Bar Supplement* to *Ekonomicke zpravodajstvi*. Go to `http://www.pointcast.com/`.

I mentioned the push hype early in this chapter. Because companies have discovered that push is *not* the next great publishing medium, things have slowed down in the push world. In some cases, companies have pulled out of push, so some of these push services have fewer channels now than they did a year or so ago. And there are fewer programs than there were in the heyday of push. (Heydays don't last very long on the Internet.)

Just What We Need: More Acronyms!

Microsoft has defined a new data format for push systems, CDF (Channel Data Format). A Web author can use XML (Extended Meta Language) tags to identify portions of a Web page to a push program, defining the best way for the information to be displayed, who the "broadcaster" is, and so on. Any push program that comes to the Web site sniffing for data will see these tags and extract just the information it needs.

CDF has been adopted by some push-technology companies (such as PointCast and BackWeb), but others have said they want nothing to do with it. Not surprisingly, Netscape was one of the companies that has chosen to ignore CDF.

There's another form of push program: the offline browser. An offline browser is a program that automatically retrieves information for you. You tell it which page to retrieve and how many levels to go down through the links, and it gets all the info for you while you're sleeping or at lunch. That in itself is not a push system—it's simply an automatic browser. (They're called offline browsers because after the information has been retrieved, you can log off the Internet and read the Web pages.) But some of these offline browsers also allow you to schedule updates; you could tell the system to check a Web site each day to see whether it has changed, and if it has, to retrieve the new pages. In effect, the program has become a push program. You can find many offline browsers at the software sites mentioned in Appendix C, "All the Software You'll Ever Need."

The Least You Need to Know

- Push programs retrieve information from the Internet for you automatically. You specify the information you want and how often you want it, and the program gets it for you.
- *Push* is a misnomer; these systems are really scheduled pull systems.
- The two big players in the push game are Netscape's Netcaster and Microsoft's Active Desktop. (But Netscape is killing off Netcaster.) There are many others, though, such as BackWeb and PointCast.
- Push systems generally allow you to select preconfigured channels from a list.
- Some push systems—including Netcaster and Active Desktop—allow you to set up any Web page you want as a channel.

Chapter 9

Newsgroups: The Source of All Wisdom

In This Chapter

- What is a newsgroup?
- What can you find in newsgroups?
- Finding out what newsgroups exist
- What is Usenet?
- Choosing a newsreader

In this chapter, I'm going to introduce you to one of the Internet's most dangerous services: newsgroups. Many people find these discussion groups to be addictive. Get involved in a few groups and, if you have an addictive personality, you'll soon find that the rest of your life is falling apart as you spend hours each day swapping messages with people all over the world, on subjects such as bushwalking in Australia, soap operas, very tall women, or very short men.

If you don't have an addictive personality, newsgroups can be interesting, stimulating, and extremely useful. Anyway, being addicted to newsgroups is better than being addicted to booze or drugs. In this chapter, you'll find out what newsgroups are; in the next chapter, you'll find out how to use them.

What's a Newsgroup?

Let me answer the question, "What's a newsgroup?" with another question: Are you familiar with bulletin board systems (BBSs)? Electronic BBSs work much like the corkboard-and-thumbtack type of bulletin board. They're computerized systems for leaving both public and private messages. Other computer users can read your messages, and you can read theirs. There are tens of thousands of small BBSs around the world, each of which has its own area of interest. In addition, many computer companies have BBSs through which their customers get technical support, and many professional associations have BBSs so their members can leave messages for one another and take part in discussions.

An information service such as CompuServe or America Online is essentially a collection of many bulletin boards (called *forums* in CompuServe-speak or *message boards* on AOL). CompuServe has a few thousand such BBSs. Instead of having to remember several thousand telephone numbers (one for each BBS), you can dial one phone number and access any number of BBSs on the service.

As you've already seen, the Internet is a collection of networks hooked together. It's huge, and consequently it has an enormous number of discussion groups. In Internet-speak, these groups are called *newsgroups*, and there are thousands of them on all conceivable subjects. Each Internet service provider subscribes to a selection of newsgroups—perhaps just 5,000 or 10,000, but sometimes as many as 40,000, maybe even more. One service provider I've seen has more than 50,000 newsgroups available.

A New Way to Serve Newsgroups

Some service providers are using a fancy new news server system that allows them to provide tens of thousands of newsgroups, yet use minimal resources. Rather than transfer all the messages in all the newsgroups to the service provider's computers, a list of groups is transferred (most of the actual newsgroup messages are not). It's not until a user actually tries to read messages from a newsgroup that the messages are transferred across the Internet to the service provider, and then from the service provider to the user. This system is known by the delightful phrase, *dynamic sucking feed*.

What do I mean by *subscribe*? These newsgroups are distributed around the Internet by a service called Usenet; consequently, they're often referred to as Usenet groups. Usenet distributes over 30,000 groups (the number keeps changing), but not all service providers get all of the groups. A service provider can choose which groups it wants to receive, in essence *subscribing* to just the ones it wants. Although more than 30,000 internationally distributed newsgroups exist (along with thousands more local groups), most providers get only a few thousand of them.

If your service provider subscribes to a newsgroup, you can read that group's messages and post your own messages to the group. In other words, you can work only with groups to which your service provider has subscribed. You read newsgroup messages by using a *newsreader*, a program that retrieves messages from your service provider's *news server*.

If you've never used a newsgroup (or another system's forum, BBS, or whatever), you might not be aware of the power of such communications. This sort of messaging system brings computer networking to life, and it's not all computer nerds sitting around with nothing better to do. (Check out the Internet's alt.sex newsgroups; these people are not your average introverted propeller-heads!) In my Internet travels, I've found work, made friends, found answers to research questions (much quicker and more cheaply than I could have by going to a library), and read people's "reviews" of tools I can use in my business. I've never found a lover or spouse online, but I know people who have (and, anyway, I'm already married). Just be careful not to get addicted and start spending all your time online.

Public News Servers

If your service provider doesn't subscribe to a newsgroup you want, ask the management to subscribe to it. If they won't, you *might* be able to find and read it at a public news server. Try looking at these sites for information about public servers:

`http://dir.yahoo.com/Computers_and_Internet/Internet/Usenet/Public_Access_Usenet_Sites/` `http://www.serverseekers.com/`

You can also read newsgroups through a Web site, at `http://www.supernews.com/`.

So What's Out There?

You can use newsgroups for fun or for work. You can use them to spend time "talking" with other people who share your interests—whether that happens to be algebra (see the `alt.algebra.help group`) or antique collecting (`rec.antiques`). You can even do serious work online, such as finding a job at a nuclear physics research site (`hepnet.jobs`), tracking down a piece of software for a biology project (`bionet.software`), or finding good stories about what's going on in South Africa for an article you are writing (`za.events`).

The following newsgroups represent just a tiny fraction of what is available:

`alt.ascii-art`. Pictures (such as Spock and the Simpsons) created with ASCII text characters.

`alt.comedy.british.blackadder`. Discussions about Mr. Bean's earlier life.

`alt.missing-kids`. Information about missing kids.

`bit.listserv.down-syn`. Discussions about Down's syndrome.

`misc.forsale`. Lists of goods for sale.

`rec.skydiving`. A group for skydivers.

`sci.anthropology`. A group for people interested in anthropology.

`sci.military`. Discussions on science and the military.

`soc.couples.intercultural`. A group for intercultural couples.

News?

True to its UNIX heritage, the Internet uses the word *news* ambiguously. Often, when you see a reference to news in a message or an Internet document, it refers to the messages left in newsgroups (not, as most people imagine, to journalists' reports on current affairs).

If you are looking for information on just about any subject, the question is not "Is there a newsgroup about this?" The questions you should ask are "What is the newsgroup's name?" and "Does my service provider subscribe to it?"

Can You Read It?

The many newsgroups out there take up a lot of room. A service provider getting the messages of just 3,000 newsgroups might have to set aside tens of megabytes of hard disk space to keep up with it all. So service providers have to decide which ones they will subscribe to. Nobody subscribes to all the world's newsgroups because many are of no interest to most Internet users, and many are not widely distributed. (Some are of regional interest only; some are of interest only to a specific organization.) So system administrators have to pick the ones they want and omit the ones they don't want. Undoubtedly, some system administrators censor newsgroups, omitting those they believe have no place online.

I've given you an idea of what is available in general, but I can't specify what is available to you. You'll have to check with your service provider to find out what they offer. If they don't have what you want, ask them to get it. They have no way of knowing what people want unless someone tells them.

> Check This Out
>
> **I Want to Start One!**
>
> Do you have a subject about which you want to start a newsgroup? Spend some time in the `news.groups` newsgroup to find out about starting a Usenet newsgroup, or talk to your service provider about starting a local newsgroup.

Okay, Gimme a List!

The first thing you might want to do is find out what newsgroups your service provider subscribes to. You can do that by telling your newsreader to obtain a list of groups from the news server; I'll talk more about newsreaders later.

What if you don't find what you are looking for? How can you find out what's available that your provider does not subscribe to? There are lots of places to go these days to track down newsgroups. I like Liszt (`http://www.liszt.com/news/`), which currently lists more than 30,000 newsgroups, and Tile.Net (`http://www.tile.net/`), which you can see in the following figure. Both Liszt and Tile.Net also list thousands of mailing lists (see Chapter 11, "Yet More Discussion Groups: Mailing Lists and Web Forums"); Tile.Net also lists FTP sites (see Chapter 12, "The Giant Software Store: FTP"). You can try the Usenet Info Center (`http://sunsite.unc.edu/usenet-i/`) or the Finding Newsgroups and Mailing Lists page (`http://www.synapse.net/~radio/finding.htm`). You can also search at any Web search site (which you'll learn about in Chapter 17, "Finding Stuff"). For instance, try Yahoo! (`http://dir.yahoo.com/Computers_and_Internet/Internet/Usenet/Newsgroup_Listings/`).

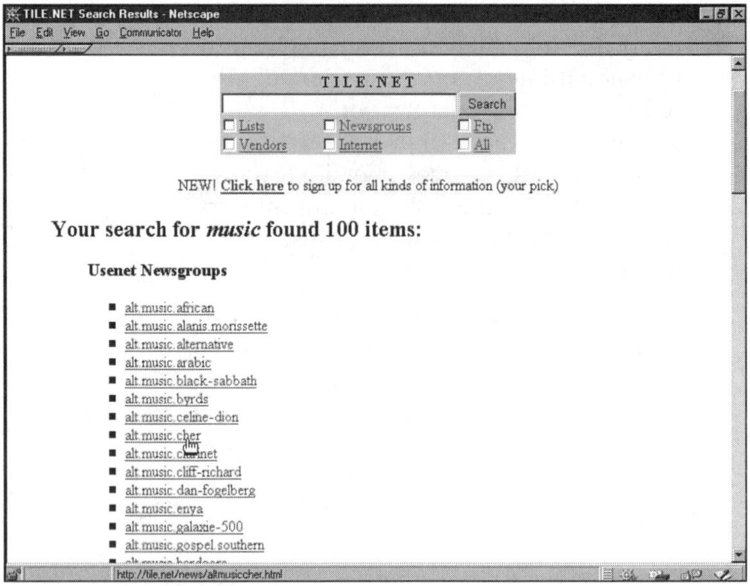

`Tile.Net` *is a good place to find out what's available on Usenet.*

Moderated Groups

As you'll see when you refer to some of the directories of newsgroups, some newsgroups are *moderated*, which means someone reads all the messages and decides which ones to post. The purpose is to keep the newsgroup focused and to prevent the discussions from "going astray." Of course, it might look a little like censorship, depending on what you want to say.

Where Does It All Come From?

Where do all these newsgroups come from? People all over the world create newsgroups on their computers. Any system administrator can create a newsgroup, and many do. Each host has newsgroups of local interest that contain information about the service provider's services, local politics, local events, and so on.

A large number of newsgroups, although not all of them, are part of the Usenet system. Like the Internet, Usenet is a network of networks. No one owns it, and it doesn't own anything itself. It is independent of any network, including the Internet (in fact, it's older than the Internet). Usenet is simply a series of voluntary agreements to swap information.

What's in a Name?

Newsgroup names look much like host addresses: a series of words separated by periods. The reason for this format is that, like host names, newsgroup names are set up in a hierarchical system (although instead of going right-to-left, they go left-to-right). The first name is the top level. These are the primary top-level Usenet groups:

Comp Computer-related subjects.

news Information about newsgroups, including software you can use to read newsgroup messages and information about finding and using newsgroups.

rec Recreational topics, including hobbies, sports, the arts, and so on.

sci Discussions about research in the "hard" sciences, as well as some social sciences.

soc A wide range of social issues, such as discussions about different types of societies and subcultures, as well as sociopolitical subjects.

talk Debates about politics, religion, and anything else that's controversial.

Misc Stuff. Job searches, things for sale, a forum for paramedics. You know, stuff.

Not all newsgroups are true Usenet groups. Many are local groups that Usenet distributes internationally (don't worry about the difference, it doesn't matter). Such newsgroups are part of the alternative newsgroup hierarchies. They have other top-level groups, such as

alt "Alternative" subjects. These are often subjects that many people consider inappropriate, pornographic, or just weird. In some cases, however, the newsgroup is simply interesting reading, but someone created the newsgroup in an "unauthorized" manner to save time and hassle.

bionet Biological subjects.

bit A variety of newsgroups from BITnet.

biz Business subjects, including advertisements.

clari Clarinet's newsgroups from "official" and commercial sources; mainly UPI news stories and various syndicated columns.

courts Newsgroups related to law and lawyers.

de Various German-language newsgroups.

fj Various Japanese-language newsgroups.

gnu The Free Software Foundation's newsgroups.

hepnet Discussions about high energy and nuclear physics.

ieee The Institute of Electrical and Electronics Engineers' newsgroups.

info A collection of mailing lists formed into newsgroups at the University of Illinois.

k12 Discussions about kindergarten through 12th-grade education.

relcom Russian-language newsgroups, mainly distributed in the former Soviet Union.

vmsnet Subjects of interest to VAX/VMS computer users.

You'll see other groups, too, such as the following:

brasil Groups from Brazil (Brazil is spelled with an "s" in Portuguese).

Birmingham Groups from Birmingham, England.

podunk A local interest newsgroup for the town of Podunk.

thisu This university's newsgroup.

Okay, I made up the last two, but you get the idea. You'll run into all sorts of different hierarchies, with new ones appearing all the time. To see a list of virtually all the top-level group names in both Usenet and alternative newsgroups, go to `http://www.magmacom.com/~leisen/master_list.html`.

Reaching the Next Level

The groups listed in the previous section make up the top-level groups. Below each of those groups are groups on another level. For instance, under the alt category is a newsgroup called alt.3d, which contains messages about three-dimensional imaging. It's part of the alt hierarchy because, presumably, it was put together in an unauthorized way. The people who started it didn't want to go through the hassle of setting up a Usenet group, so they created an alt group—where anything goes—instead.

Another alt group is `alt.animals`, where people gather to talk about their favorite beasties. This group serves as a good example of how newsgroups can have more levels. Because animals are such a diverse subject, one newsgroup isn't enough. Instead of posting messages to the `alt.animals` group, you can choose your particular interest. The specific areas include the following:

`alt.animals.dolphins`

`alt.animals.felines.lions`

`alt.animals.felines.lynxes`

`alt.animals.felines.snowleopards`

`alt.animals.horses.icelandic`

`alt.animals.humans`

These are just a few examples of the many newsgroups available. If you're into it, chances are good there's a newsgroup for it.

All areas use the same sort of hierarchical system. For example, under the bionet first level, you can find the genome level, with such newsgroups as `bionet.genome.arabidopsis` (information about the Arabidopsis genome project), `bionet.genome.chrom22` (a discussion of Chromosome 22), and `bionet.genome.chromosomes` (for those interested in the eucaryote chromosomes).

I'm Ready; Let's Read

Now that you know what newsgroups are, you'll probably want to get in and read a few. Newsgroup messages are stored in text files, saved on your service provider's computer system. You'll read the messages using a newsreader to help you filter through all the garbage.

If you are with an online service, you already have a built-in newsreader. These range from the good (MSN's newsreader is pretty capable) to the absolutely awful (CompuServe's was horrible last time I looked; maybe its next software upgrade will fix that). If you are with a service provider, they might give you a newsreader, or it might be already installed on your computer. For example, Netscape Navigator and some versions of Internet Explorer have built-in newsreaders, and Windows 98 comes with Outlook Express (see the following figure), which includes a newsreader. Or you might have one of many other newsreaders, such as WinVN, Gravity, and Free Agent on Windows or NewsWatcher and Nuntius on the Macintosh. Note, though, that there are far fewer newsreaders available now then there used to be. As with other forms of Internet software—push programs and VRML viewers, for instance—there was a sudden "bloom" of software from 1994–1996, followed by a gradual die-off.

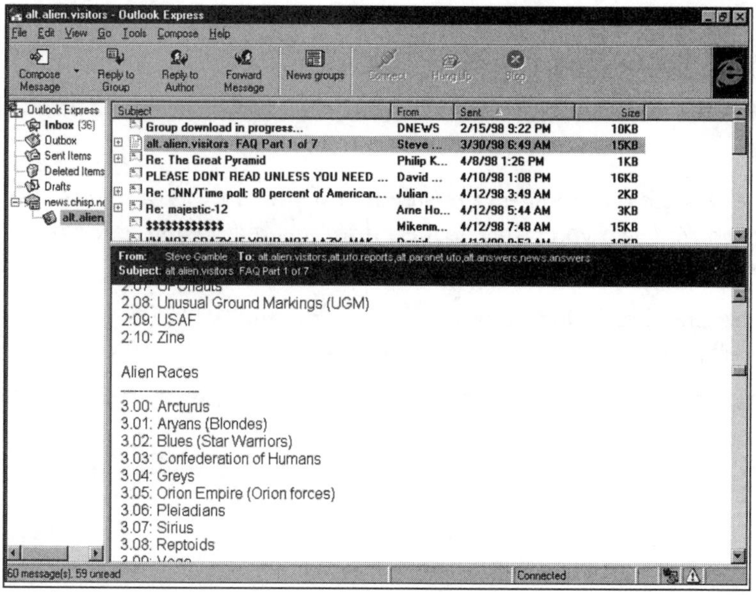

Outlook Express, which is included with Windows 98, displays the list of messages in the top pane and the selected message in the lower pane.

Still Using UNIX?

If you are using a command-line interface, send email to `ciginternet@mcp.com`, with news in the Subject line to receive the newsgroup chapters (Chapters 15 and 16) from the first edition of *The Complete Idiot's Guide to the Internet,* which explain how to use a UNIX-based newsreader.

I'm going to use the Outlook Express newsreader for my examples in the next chapter. If you have something different, the commands you use will vary, but the basic principles will remain the same. Of course, different programs have different features, so you might want to try out a few programs to see what you like (see Appendix C, "All the Software You'll Ever Need," for information about finding software).

The Least You Need to Know

- A newsgroup is an area in which people with similar interests leave public messages, a sort of online public debate or discussion.
- There's a newsgroup on just about every subject you can imagine. If there isn't, there probably will be soon.
- Newsgroup names use a hierarchical system, and each group might have subgroups within it.
- The major online services have built-in newsreaders. If you are with a service provider, it might have given you a newsreader. If for any reason you're looking for a newsreader, try the software "libraries" listed in Appendix C.
- Some available newsreaders include Gravity, Free Agent, and WinVN on Windows or NewsWatcher and Nuntius for the Macintosh.

Chapter 10

Your Daily News Delivery

In This Chapter

- Starting your newsreader
- Reading and responding to messages
- Marking messages as read
- Rot13: encoded messages
- Sending and receiving binary files
- Special newsreader features

This chapter explains how to work in the newsgroups. As I mentioned in the preceding chapter, I'm going to use the Outlook Express newsreader for my examples, but many other newsreader programs are available. Although each program is a little different, they all share certain characteristics. Check your program's documentation for the specific details and to learn about any extra features it includes. Even if you don't have Outlook Express, I suggest that you read this information because it provides a good overview of the functions available in most newsreaders.

If you are using an online service, you might be using that service's system to work in the newsgroups. For instance, in MSN you'll see links or icons all over the place representing collections of newsgroups. Many of MSN's BBSs (the term MSN uses for forums or subject areas) contain icons that represent links to newsgroups. Click the icon to go to the newsgroups. The most recent MSN software uses the Outlook Express newsreader or the Microsoft Internet News newsreader (an earlier version of Outlook Express). You can find information about newsgroups from the main MSN window by selecting the **Communicate** link, then **Internet Center (Newsgroups)**, and then **Newsgroups**. If you're using an old version of the MSN software, you can use the Go To word **Internet** to go to the Internet BBS. In CompuServe, use **GO INTERNET** (or in the new CompuServe 2000, click the large **Internet** button in the toolbar and select **Newsgroups**); in AOL, use the keyword **Internet** to find more information about starting the newsreaders.

A Quick Word on Setup

I want to quickly discuss setup and subscribing. If you are with an online service, there's nothing to set up; it's all done for you. If you are with a service provider, though, you might have to set up the newsreader.

First, your newsreader must know the location of your news server. Ask your service provider for the hostname of the news server (the news server is the system the service provider uses to send messages to your newsreader); the hostname might be `news.big.internet.service.com`, or `news.zip.com`, or something like that. Then check your newsreader's documentation to see where to enter this information.

The other thing you might have to do is subscribe to the newsgroups you are interested in. I've already said that your service provider has to subscribe to newsgroups; this means that the provider ensures the newsgroups are available to its members. However, the term *subscribe* has another meaning in relation to newsgroups. You might also have to subscribe to the newsgroup to ensure that the newsgroup you want to read is available to your newsreader. Not all newsreaders make you subscribe in order to read a newsgroup. For instance, you don't have to worry about subscribing if you use MSN's newsreader or if you are reading newsgroup messages through a newsgroup "gateway" Web site such as Super-news (`http://www.supernews.com/`). Many newsreaders, however, require that you fetch a list of newsgroups from your service provider (the newsreader has a command you'll use to fetch and display the list and might even offer to do so the first time you start the program) and then subscribe to the ones you want to read. Subscribing is no big deal; you simply choose which ones you want. Until you subscribe, though, you can't see the messages.

Pick Your Own Newsreader

Some of the online services have rather weak newsreaders. But if your online service allows you to get to the Internet through a TCP/IP connection, you might be able to install another newsreader, such as Gravity, Free Agent, NewsWatcher, or Nuntius. However, to do so, you might have to connect to one of the public news servers that I mentioned in Chapter 9, "Newsgroups: The Source of All Wisdom." The online services often have special news servers that are not designed to be accessed by TCP/IP; they're designed to be accessed with the service's own program. Check with your service's technical support staff.

Starting and Subscribing

The following figure shows the Outlook Express newsreader, which comes with Windows 98. The first time you use the program a dialog box opens, asking for all the configuration information. Then the Newsgroups dialog box opens (shown in the following figure) and begins grabbing a list of newsgroups from your service provider's news server.

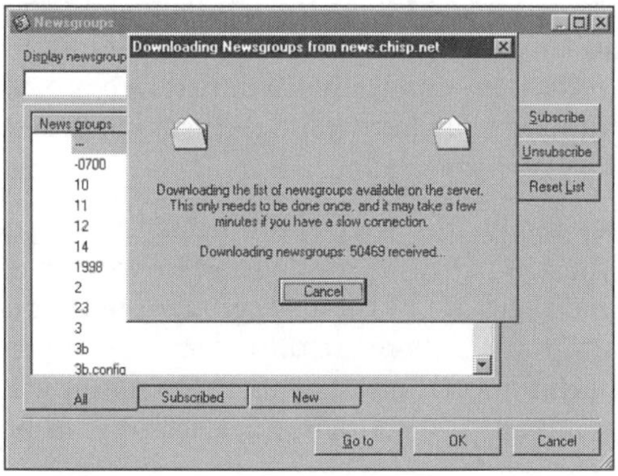

The Outlook Express Newsgroup dialog box, where you can view a list of all the newsgroups your service provider has subscribed to; at the moment, the system is downloading a list of newsgroups from the server.

After you have the list, you can decide which newsgroups you want to read. (Remember that this is a list of only the newsgroups that your service provider has subscribed to, not a full list of all the groups distributed by Usenet. For information about finding newsgroups not included in this list, see Chapter 9.) In Outlook

Express, you click the group you want to read, and then click the **Subscribe** button, or simply double-click the name. (You can also use the text box at the top; type a name or part of a name to move to that part of the list.)

Where Are the Alt. Groups?

If you are with an online service, you might find that you can't initially read the alt. groups and perhaps some others as well. Your online service might regard these groups as a trifle "naughty," in which case you have to apply for permission to read them. Go to your online service's Internet forum or BBS to find out how to activate these groups, or refer to the parental control information.

When you close the dialog box, you'll see a list of the newsgroups you subscribed to in a pane on the left side of the window. You can subscribe to more later by clicking the **Newsgroup** button or by selecting **Tools**, **Newsgroups** to see the dialog box again (to refresh the list, click the **Reset List** button). You can also open the dialog box, click the **New** tab, and then click the **Reset List** button to see a list of newsgroups that your service provider has added since you last collected the list.

Click one of the newsgroups you've subscribed to in the left pane, and the top pane will display a list of messages from that newsgroup (see the next figure). It might take a little while for these messages to transfer, especially if your service provider is using the dynamic sucking feed I mentioned in the last chapter. (If so, you'll see a message header that says `Group download in progress`.)

Many newsgroups are empty—they rarely, if ever, contain messages—so you won't always see message "headers" in the top pane. Most newsreaders will have some kind of indicator showing how many messages are in the newsgroup (see the numbers in parentheses in the following illustration). If there are only a few messages, it's quite possible that all the messages are promotional messages completely unrelated to the subject of the newsgroup, perhaps advertising get-rich-quick schemes or pornographic Web sites.

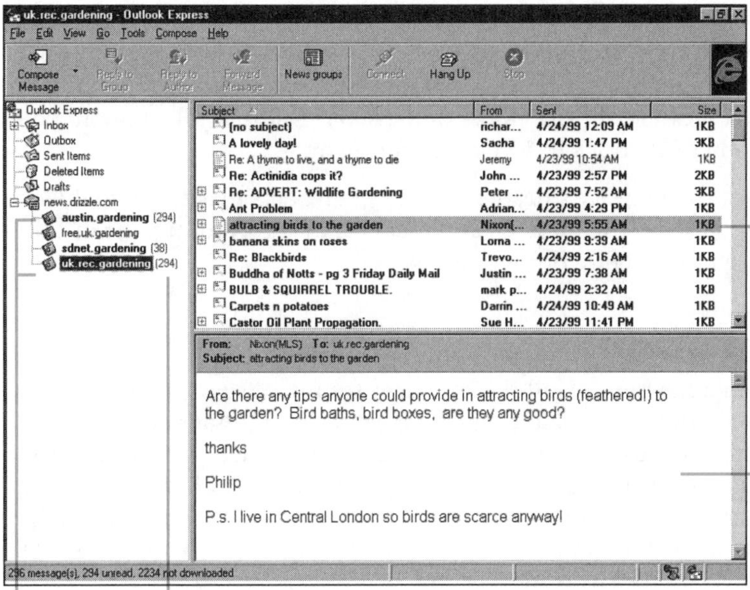

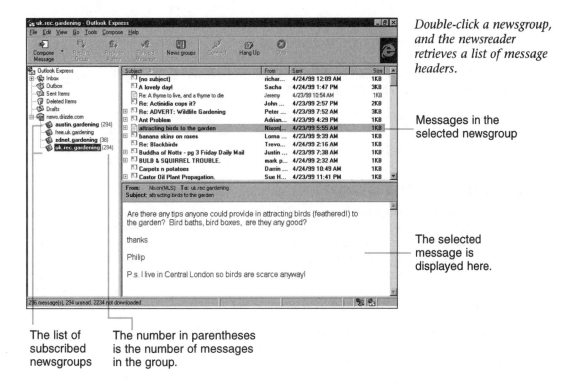

Double-click a newsgroup, and the newsreader retrieves a list of message headers.

Messages in the selected newsgroup

The selected message is displayed here.

The list of subscribed newsgroups

The number in parentheses is the number of messages in the group.

Taking a Look

Notice that some messages are indented below others, and that there's a small - icon next to the messages. This icon indicates that the message is part of a *thread* (known as a *conversation* in some newsreaders). So what's a thread? Suppose you post a message to a newsgroup that isn't a response to anyone; it's just a new message. Then, a little later, someone else reads your message and replies. That message, because it's a reply, is part of the thread you began. Later, someone else sends a response to *that* message, and it becomes part of the thread. (Note, however, that there's generally a long lag time—a day or more—between the time someone sends a message to a newsgroup and the time that message turns up in everyone's newsreader.)

Not All the Messages

You might not see all the messages listed at once. Some newsreaders enable you to specify a number to retrieve each time (in the program's Options or Preferences dialog box). So if the newsgroup is very busy, only a portion of the messages will be listed; you'll have to use another command to retrieve the rest.

If you click the little - icon, the thread closes up, and you see only the message at the beginning of the thread. The icon changes to a + icon. Click the + icon to open up the thread again. (A message that has a - icon but does not have messages indented below it is not part of a message thread.) Most newsreaders (but not all) support threading and many other functions in a very similar manner.

To read a message, click the message's header (some newsreaders make you double-click). The newsreader retrieves the message and places it in the bottom pane of the window, as you can see in the figure on the next page.

The Messages Are Gone!

The first time you open a newsgroup, all the messages from that newsgroup currently held by your service provider are available to you. How long a message stays in the newsgroup depends on how busy that newsgroup is and how much hard disk space the service provider allows for the newsgroup messages. Eventually all messages disappear. You don't necessarily see all the newsgroup's messages the next time you use your newsreader, though. When you return to the newsgroup later, you might see all the messages *except* those marked as read.

Why didn't I just say "all the messages except those that you have read?" Well, the newsreader has no way of knowing which messages you've read—it can't see what you are doing. Instead, it has a way of marking messages that it thinks you've read, and it generally provides you with a way to mark messages as read, even if you haven't read them (in effect, providing a way for you to tell the newsreader that you don't want to see the messages).

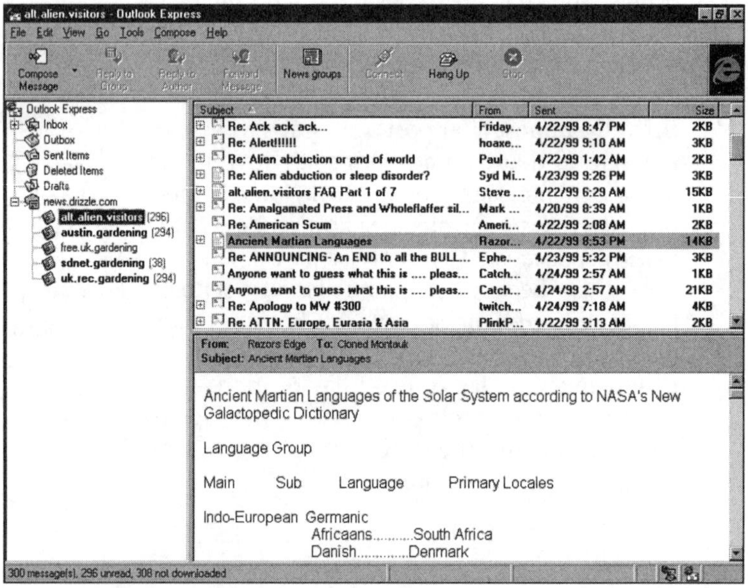

This message is from the `alt.alien.visitors` *newsgroup.*

Marking Your Messages

Most newsreaders mark a message as read when you open the message. Some newsreaders enable you to quickly scan messages without marking them as read. Outlook Express, for instance, has a setting in the Options dialog box labeled **Message Is Read After Being Previewed for x Second(s)**. So you can set this option to, say, 10 seconds, allowing you to read a little bit of a message and move on, leaving the message marked as unread.

In addition, newsreaders often allow you to mark the messages as read even if you have not read them. This capability might come in handy to tell the newsreader that you don't want to see certain messages when you come back to the newsgroup in a later session. Suppose you get a couple of messages into a conversation and realize that it's pure rubbish (you'll find a lot of messages that have virtually no usefulness to anyone!). Mark the entire thread as read, and you won't see the rest of the messages the next time you open the newsgroup window. Or maybe the messages are worthwhile (to someone), but you quickly read all the messages' Subject lines and find that nothing interests you. Mark them all as read so you see only new messages the next time.

You can generally mark messages as read in several other ways as well. Here's what you can do in Outlook Express, for instance:

- Click a message header and select **Edit**, **Mark As Read**.
- Click a message header and select **Edit**, **Mark Thread As Read** to mark the entire thread as read.
- Right-click a message header and select **Mark As Read** or **Mark Thread As Read** from the shortcut menu.
- Choose **Edit**, **Mark All As Read** to mark all the current newsgroup's messages as read.

Different newsreaders handle read messages differently. Some newsreaders remove them from the list, so you see only the unread messages listed. Gravity, an excellent and popular Windows newsreader (`http://www.microplanet.com/`), does this. If you don't want the newsreader to remove the read messages, you can change the view by choosing **Newsgroup**, **Filter Display**, **Read Articles** to see just messages you've read, or **Newsgroup**, **Filter Display**, **All Articles** (or by selecting these from the drop-down list box in the toolbar) to make Gravity show the read message headers in gray text. Other newsreaders might use special icons or gray text to indicate messages that you've read.

Articles

In keeping with the "news" metaphor, newsgroup messages are often known as *articles*.

Outlook Express, on the other hand, displays all the messages, read and unread. But you can select **View**, **Current View**, and then choose an option. Choosing **Unread Messages**, for instance, would make Outlook work like Gravity; it would display only the messages you haven't yet read.

I Want the Message Back!

If you need to bring a message back, your newsreader probably has some kind of command that enables you to do so. For example, Gravity has the **Newsgroup**, **Filter Display**, **Read Articles** command that I just mentioned. But if your service provider no longer holds the message you want to see—that is, if the message has been removed from the service provider's hard disk to make more space for new messages—you're out of luck. So if you think there's a chance you might want a message later, save it using the **File**, **Save As** or equivalent command.

Many newsreaders even have commands for marking messages as unread. Perhaps you've read a message, but want to make sure it appears the next time you open the newsgroup. You can mark it as unread so that it will appear in the list the next time you open the newsgroup. In Outlook Express, for instance, select **Edit**, **Mark As Unread**.

Moving Among the Messages

You'll find a variety of ways to move around in your messages. As you already know, you can double-click the ones you want to view (some newsreaders use a single click). In addition, you'll find commands for moving to the next or previous message, the next or previous thread, and, perhaps, the next or previous unread message or thread. In Outlook Express, these commands are on the View, Next menu.

Many newsreaders also provide a way for you to search for a particular message. Outlook Express has several Find commands in the Edit menu, which allow you to search for a message by the contents of the From line or the Subject line. Outlook Express also enables you to search through the text of the currently selected message. Some other newsreaders have much more sophisticated utilities. In Gravity, for example, select **Search**, **Search** to access a dialog box in which you can search for text in the From or Subject lines or even within the text of the messages; you can also specify whether to search the selected newsgroup or all the subscribed newsgroups. You can even tell Gravity whether to search only those messages already transferred to the newsreader or to search messages still held by the news server.

Saving and Printing

If you run across a message that you think might be useful later, you can save it or print it. Simply marking it as unread isn't good enough because newsgroups eventually drop all messages. So sooner or later it won't be available.

Most newsreaders have a File, Save As (or File, Save) command or toolbar button. Most also have a File, Print command or button. Of course, you can always highlight the text, copy it to the Clipboard, and then paste it into another application, such as a word processor or email program.

Your Turn: Sending and Responding

There are several ways to send messages or respond to messages. For example, you can use any of the techniques listed here in Outlook Express. (Although Outlook Express is typical, and many newsreaders use these same command names, some newsreaders might use different names.)

- You can send a message that isn't a response (that is, you can start a new thread). In Outlook Express, for instance, select **Compose**, **New Message** or click the **Compose Message** toolbar button.
- You can reply to someone else's message (the reply is often known as a follow-up). Choose **Compose**, **Reply to Group** or click the **Reply to Group** button.
- You can reply to someone privately via email (that is, send a message that *doesn't* appear in the newsgroup). Select **Compose**, **Reply to Author** or click the **Reply to Author** button.

- Reply to both the author and the newsgroup at the same time. Select **Compose, Reply to Newsgroup and Author**.
- You can send a copy of the message to someone else. Select **Compose, Forward** or click the **Forward Message** button.

Sending messages to a newsgroup—or via email in response to a message—is much the same as working with an email window. You type the message and then click some kind of **Send** or **Post** button.

What's This Gibberish? Rot13

Now and again, especially in the more contentious newsgroups, you'll run into messages that seem to be gibberish. Everything's messed up, and each word seems to be a jumbled mix of characters, almost as if the message were encrypted. It is.

What you are seeing is *rot13*, a very simple substitution cipher (one in which a character is substituted for another). Rot13 means "rotated 13." In other words, each character in the alphabet is replaced by the character 13 places further along. Instead of A you see N, instead of B you see O, instead of C you see P, and so on. Got it? So to read the message, all you need to do is substitute the correct characters. Easy. (Or *Rnfl*, as I should say.)

For those of you in a hurry, there is an easier way. Most newsreaders have a command that quickly does the rot13 for you. For instance, in Outlook Express, you can select **Edit**, **Unscramble (rot13)**, and, like magic, the message changes into real words. If you don't run across rot13 messages and want to see what rot13 looks like, use the command to take a normal message and convert it to rot13 message (which is what I did for the following figure). How do you create one of these messages to send to a newsgroup? You'll often find a rot13 command in the window in which you create a message. For instance, in Gravity's message composition window, there's an **Options, Scramble (rot13)** command. For some reason, Outlook Express, although it can unscramble messages, doesn't let you use rot13 when sending messages.

You might be wondering why a person would encode a message with a system that is so ridiculously easy to break. People don't rot13 (if you'll excuse my use of the term as a verb) their messages as a security measure that's intended to make them unreadable to anyone who doesn't have the secret key. After all, anyone with a decent newsreader has the key. No, using rot13 is a way of saying "if you read this message, you might be offended; so if you are easily offended, *don't read it*!" Rot13 messages are often crude, lewd, or just plain rude. When a message is encoded with rot13, the reader can decide whether he wants to risk being offended.

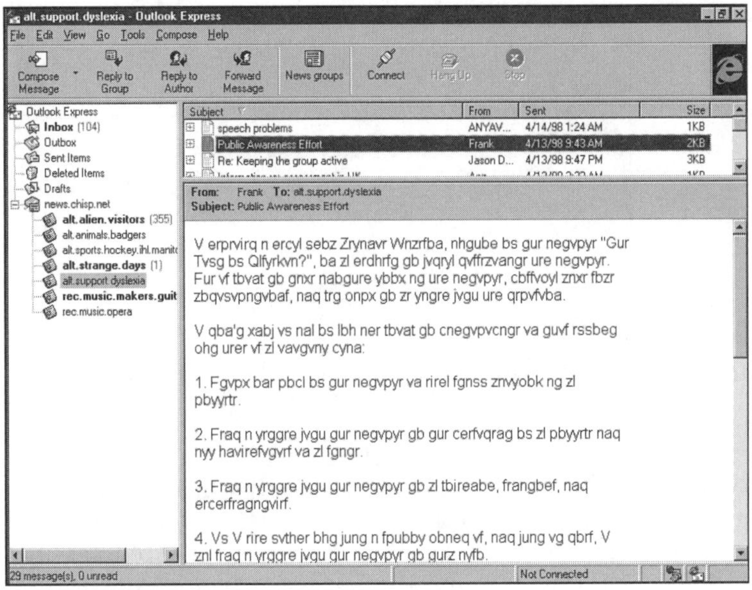

An example of a rot13 message.

Pictures (and Sounds) from Words

The newsgroups contain simple text messages. You can't place a character into a message that is not in the standard text character set. So if you want to send a computer file in a newsgroup message—maybe you want to send a picture, a sound, or a word processing document—you must convert it to text. Some of the newer newsreaders help you do this, either by automating the process of attaching MIME-formatted files to your messages or by uuencoding files and inserting them into your messages. (I discussed this issue in relation to email, back in Chapter 2, "The Premier Internet Tool: Email.") Some newsreaders will even convert such files on-the-fly and display pictures inside the message when they read the newsgroup messages; others will automatically convert the file to its original format.

If you were using Outlook Express, for example, you could follow these steps to send a file:

1. Open the message composition window using the **Compose**, **New Message** command or the **Compose**, **Reply to Newsgroup** command.
2. Choose **Insert**, **File Attachment** or click the **Insert File** toolbar button (the little paper clip). You'll see a typical File Open dialog box, from which you can choose the file you want to send.
3. Select the file and click **OK**. The name of the attached file appears in the bottom pane of the message composition window (see the following figure).
4. Send the message (click the **Post** button or select **File**, **Send Message**). The name of the file appears in the message header when you view the messages in that particular newsgroup.

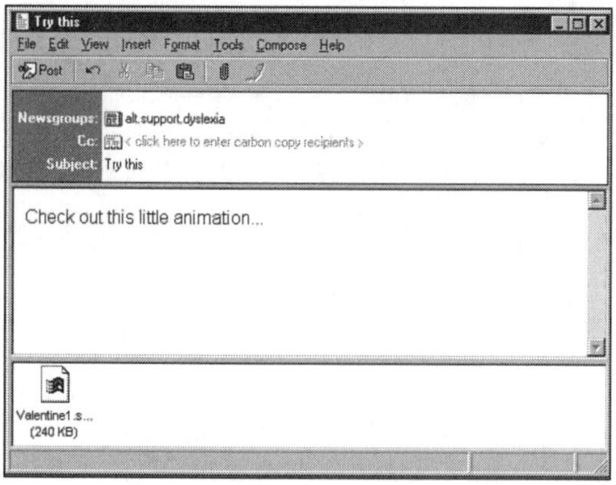

Most newsreaders let you send uuencoded or MIME files to a newsgroup. You can see the file at the bottom of this email composition window.

What method was used to send this message? MIME or uuencode? Outlook Express doesn't make this clear. Some newsreaders let you quickly specify which method to use; Gravity, for instance, enables you to select **uuencode** or **MIME** from a drop-down list box at the top of the window. In Outlook Express, the method of transmission is hidden away. By default, the program uses uuencode when sending to newsgroups (that's the standard method of sending files to newsgroups). If you want to use MIME, you have to go back to the main Outlook Express window, choose **Tools**, **Options**, click the **Send** tab, click the **Settings** button next to **News Sending Format: Plain Text**, and click the **MIME** option button. Convenient, eh? (It doesn't matter too much when sending messages to newsgroups, but Outlook Express uses the same method for email messages, which is very inconvenient because you might want to switch between MIME and uuencode now and again.)

When a message with an attached file is posted to a newsgroup, what do participants of that newsgroup see? If the attached file is an image, as many are, some newsreaders will display the picture inside the message. Others might display the message text, something like that shown in the following figure.

No Built-In Converter?

If you are using a newsreader that doesn't have a built-in conversion system, you can save the message on your hard disk and then use a conversion program such as Wincode (a Windows program that converts uuencode), munpack (a DOS program that converts MIME), or Yet Another Base64 Decoder (a Macintosh program that converts both uuencode and MIME). You can find conversion programs at the software libraries mentioned in Appendix C, "All the Software You'll Ever Need."

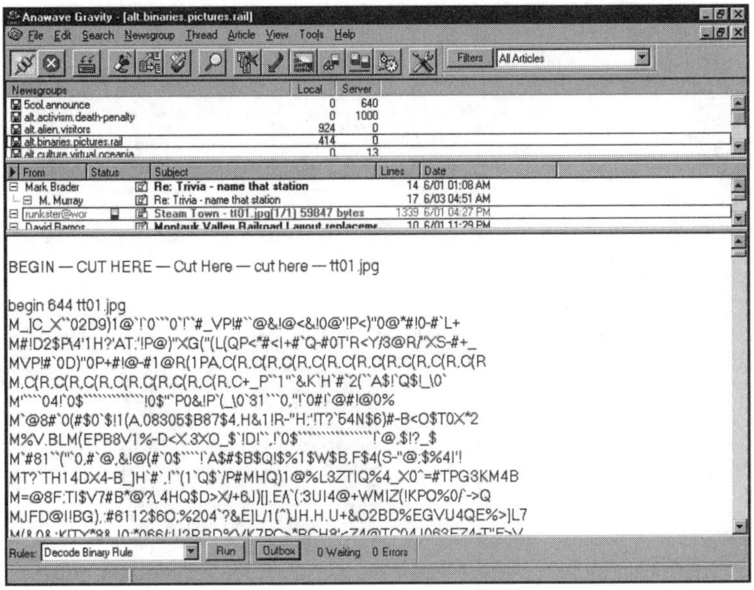

This message contains an attached file. The jumbled text is the file, converted to text. The text must be converted back before you can view the file.

Even if your newsreader doesn't initially display the image within the message, it might be able to convert the image file. In particular, newsreaders can often convert GIF, JPEG, and perhaps BMP files to their original formats. In the case of Gravity, for instance, you can click the **View Image** button or select **Article**, **View**, and Gravity converts the file for you and then places it in a viewer window (as you can see in the following figure). Outlook Express will display the image by default. You can tell it *not* to display images by choosing **Tools**, **Options**, clicking the **Read** tab, and clearing the **Automatically Show Picture Attachments in Messages** check box.

A few newsreaders can even decode several messages together. If someone posts a large picture split into several pieces, for instance (as people often do), the newsreader might automatically retrieve all the pieces and paste them together.

The Fancy Stuff

Some newsreaders have useful extra features. For example, the newsreader might be able to automatically "flag" messages if the header contains a particular word. Or you might be able to set up the newsreader to automatically remove a message if the header contains a particular word. Outlook Express has a filtering system that you can use to automatically throw away some messages, depending on who sent the message or what the subject is, if it's older than a specified time, or if it's longer than a specified length (choose **Tools**, **Newsgroup Filters**). Some other newsreaders have much better filtering systems. Gravity, for instance, can throw the message away, display a special alert message, or save the message in a text file according to what appears in the header or body text.

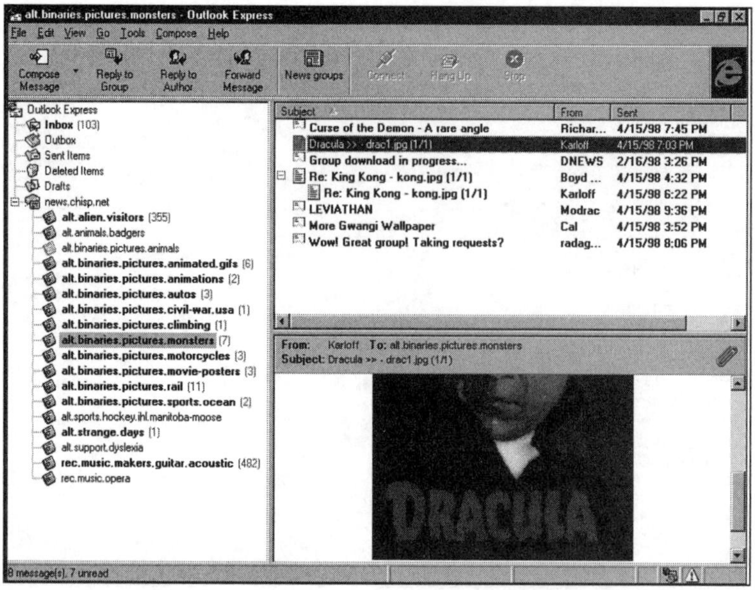

In this case, the message window displays an image that's been inserted into a message.

Many newsreaders display links in the newsgroup messages. You can click e-mail addresses or Web URLs that appear in messages to automatically open the mail window or your browser. Outlook Express can set up a little slide show, displaying one image after another in messages that contain multiple images.

Newsreaders can do a lot of different things, so you might want to experiment to find out what's available in the newsreader you have; if you spend a lot of time in newsgroups, you might want to go searching for the most capable newsreader. (Check out Appendix C for information about finding software.)

A Word of Warning

Newsgroups can be addictive. You can find messages about anything that interests you, angers you, or turns you on. If you are not careful, you can spend half your life in the newsgroups. You sit down in the morning to check your favorite newsgroups, and the next thing you know you haven't bathed, eaten, or picked up the kids from school.

Hang around the newsgroups, and you'll find people who are obviously spending a significant amount of time writing messages. These people are usually independently wealthy (that is, they work for large corporations who don't mind paying them to talk politics over the Internet or who don't know that they are paying them to do so). If you have a job, a family, and a life, be careful!

The Least You Need to Know

- To begin using the newsgroups, start your newsreader, and then download a list of newsgroups from the server. You might also have to subscribe to the groups you want to read; each newsreader does this a little differently.
- A good newsreader lets you view a "thread" or "conversation," which shows how messages relate to one another.
- Rot13 is a special encoding system that stops people from accidentally stumbling across offensive messages. Many newsreaders have a rot13 command that converts the message to normal text.
- You can include binary files in messages using uuencode or MIME.
- Many newsreaders these days can decode uuencode and MIME attachments. If your newsreader doesn't, you'll need a utility such as Wincode or munpack (for Windows and DOS) or Yet Another Base64 Decoder (for the Macintosh). Or you can get a better newsreader.

Chapter 11

Yet More Discussion Groups: Mailing Lists and Web Forums

In This Chapter

- More discussion groups?
- How mailing lists work
- Manual and automated lists
- LISTSERV mailing lists
- Finding lists of interesting groups
- Subscribing to mailing lists
- Working with Web forums

Are you getting enough sleep? Are you socializing, meeting with friends and family? Do you have time to eat and bathe? Yes? Then you're clearly not spending enough time on the Internet. I've already shown you how to work with thousands of newsgroups, which are discussion groups on almost any subject (see Chapter 9, "Newsgroups: The Source of All Wisdom," and Chapter 10, "Your Daily News Delivery"), but obviously that's not enough. So here are thousands more discussion groups: the mailing lists and Web forums.

The difference between mailing lists and Web forums and newsgroups is simply the manner in which messages are distributed. Newsgroups are distributed through a system specifically set up for their distribution, but mailing lists are distributed via email, and Web forums make messages available at a Web site through the use of Web-page forms. How many of these discussion groups exist? Liszt (`http://www.liszt.com/`)

currently indexes over 90,000 mailing lists. L-Soft, the publisher of the well-known LISTSERV mailing-list program, claims there are 76,170 LISTSERV mailing lists, and LISTSERV is just one of many programs used to run these lists. There must be hundreds of thousands of mailing lists. (Because there's no central distribution system, tracking them all is not easy.)

As for Web forums, anyone with a little time and money (or lots of time and a few geek genes) can set up a discussion group at his Web site, so there could be many thousands of these. Again, they're hard to track, but Reference.com (`http://www.reference.com/`) at one time estimated that there were about 25,000 Web forums. (However, Reference.com hasn't updated that estimate in a long time, so who knows what the real figure is.)

How Do Mailing Lists Work?

Each mailing list discussion group has an email address. You begin by subscribing to the group you are interested in. (I'll explain how in a moment.) The email address acts as a mail *reflector*, a system that receives mail and then sends it on to a list of addresses. Every time someone sends a message to a group of which you are a member, you get a copy of the mail. And every time you send a message to a group address, everyone else on the list gets a copy.

In Chapter 10, you learned that you read newsgroups using special programs called newsreaders. However, you don't need any special program to work with a mailing list; all you need is whatever program you use for reading your email. You send email messages to the list in the same way that you send messages to anyone else: You enter the mailing list's address in the To: box of your mail program's Compose window, type your message, and send it. Incoming messages from the mailing list are placed in your Inbox right along with messages from your friends and colleagues.

To find the mailing lists of interest to you, follow these suggestions:

- Use your Web browser to go to the Liszt site (`http://www.liszt.com/`), probably the best directory of mailing lists. You can also try Tile.Net (`http://www.tile.net/`). You can search these lists for a particular name or by subject.
- Go to `http://www.lsoft.com/catalist.html`, where you'll find the Catalist, the "official catalog of LISTSERV lists."They recently listed an index of more than 24,324 public lists, out of a total of 164,708 LISTSERV lists.
- Send an email message to `listserv@listserv.net`. In the message text, type **list global keyword**, where keyword is a word you want to search for within the mailing list names or subjects. For instance, you could type **list global geo** to find lists related to geography. You'll get an email message back listing the matches.
- Search for mailing lists at one of the Web search sites (covered in Chapter 17, "Finding Stuff"), or try the `http://dir.yahoo.com/Computers_and_Internet/Internet/Mailing_Lists/` Web page.

- Go to the `news.announce.newusers` newsgroup. Sometimes you can find a list of mailing lists posted there. (See Chapters 9 and 10 for information about working with newsgroups.)
- Learn by word of mouth. Hang around in some newsgroups and mailing lists, and you'll hear about private mailing lists that you might be able to join by invitation.

Peered Groups

Some LISTSERV mailing lists are *peered*. A peered LISTSERV group is the same as a *moderated* newsgroup: Someone is checking the mail and deciding what stays and what gets trashed.

The Types of Lists

There are two basic types of mailing lists:

- Manually administered
- Automated

Some very small mailing lists are set up to be administered by a person who will add your name to the list. Such lists are often private, with subscription by invitation only. Other lists use special mailing list programs to automatically add your name to the list when you subscribe. These are often, although not always, public lists that are open to anyone.

One of the most common and best known forms of automated lists is the LISTSERV list. These lists are named after the LISTSERV mailing list program and were generally distributed through the Internet by the BITnet computer network. These days the LISTSERV program is widely used outside the BITnet network.

There are other mailing list programs, too; Majordomo is one of the most common. But you don't need any fancy mailing list software to set up a small mailing list; it's quite easy to set up a manually administered mailing list. Some mailing lists are run from UNIX Internet accounts using a few simple utilities to make the work easier. For instance, a UNIX user can set up a forwarding utility to automatically forward incoming email to a list of email addresses.

Using a LISTSERV Group

Many people think that mailing lists and LISTSERV groups are one and the same. Not quite. Although LISTSERV groups are a type of mailing list (perhaps the largest category), not all mailing lists are LISTSERV groups. The term *LISTSERV* refers to one popular mailserver program; mailing lists administered by the LISTSERV program are known as LISTSERV groups, LISTSERV lists, or just LISTSERVs. LISTSERV began way back in 1986, and ran across the BITnet network. However, most LISTSERV groups are now based on the Internet. There are well over 135,000 LISTSERV groups, covering subjects such as those listed in the following table.

A Sampling of LISTSERV Groups

Mailing List	Description
ACMEPET-L@ACMEPETMAIL.COM	AcmePet's Weekly Newsletter
AFNS@AFPRODUCTS.EASE.LSOFT.COM	Air Force News Service
AUSPGRIS@LISTS.DPI.QLD.GOV.AU	Australian Plant Genetic Resource Information System list
AUSSIE-AGTEACH-NET@LISTS.DPI.QLD.GOV.AU	The Aussie Agriculture Teacher's Discussion List
AUSTVGUIDE@YOUR.ABC.NET.AU	Australia TV Program Schedules
BIG@NETFINITY2.STOCKINVESTOR.COM	Stockinvestor Newletter
BOSUENET@LISTSERV.HEANET.IE	Botswana Students Union Eire
BURPEENEWS@DISPATCH.GARDEN.ORG	A gardening newsletter from Burpee and the National Gardening Association
BVNEWSLETTER@MAILSERV.DIGITALCITY.COM	Black Voices Newsletter
CALIGUS@LISTSERV.HEANET.IE	Biology and management in the control of lice on fish farms' project
CELTIC-L@LISTSERV.HEANET.IE	CELTIC-L - The Celtic Culture List.
CHRISTIANITY-ONLINE@LISTSERV.AOL.COM	Christianity Online Connection newsletter
COLOCARD-FR@BLIZZARD.SNOW.COM	Colorado Card - Front Range
COMPUTERWORLD_DAILY@LISTSERV.COMPUTERWORLD.COM	Computerworld Daily Mailing List
CSMS-G@CSMS.EDU.MN	Computer Science & Management School of Mongolia
CYBERGRRL-WEBNEWS@LISTS.CGIM.COM	CyberGRRL! Webnews
DIETCITY@PEACH.EASE.LSOFT.COM	The resource for diet and nutrition information on the Web!
DIX-NEUF@LISTSERV.LIV.AC.UK	19th Century French Studies
DOCOMO@ML.SOFTWARE.NE.JP	NTT DoCoMo Weekly news Magazine in Japansese
EDONLINE@TVISIONS.COM	The Journal of Electronic Defense Listserv
EMIGRANT@LISTSERV.IOL.IE	The Irish Emigrant - weekly newsletter for the Irish abroad
FBN@LISTSERV.AOL.COM	Fly-Fishing Broadcast Network

Mailing List	Description
I-ADVERTISING@GUAVA.EASE.LSOFT.COM	The Internet Advertising Discussion List
IBN-L@LISTSERV.HEANET.IE	Irish Bird Network
KOSOVO-L@FIDO.ORG.YU	Kosovo crisis: discussions and articles (Yugoslavian list)
MAIG@LISTSERV.CYBERHQ.NET.MY	The Malaysian Astronomy Interest Group
MICRONLINK@MICRON.NET	The Micron Electronics, Inc. Product Announcement List
MICROSOFT_SECURITY@ANNOUNCE.MICROSOFT.COM	Microsoft Product Security Notification Service
MOMSONLINE@LISTSERV.AOL.COM	Moms Online Main Mailing List
MSN-UK-NEWS@ANNOUNCE.MICROSOFT.COM	MSN Update: Your Guide to What's Happening on msn.co.uk
MW-WOD@LISTSERV.WEBSTER.M-W.COM	Merriam-Webster's Word of the Day
POSTMITA@LISTSERV.NIC.IT	Postmasters of Italian Domains
SAFONLINENEWS@AFPRODUCTS.EASE.LSOFT.COM	U.S. Air Force Online News—The Air Force Corporate Newspaper
SCTB11@IDEFIX.SPC.ORG.NC	Eleventh Meeting of the Standing Committee on Tuna and Billfish
SOPHIA@LISTSERV.LIV.AC.UK	Ancient Philosophy
SS-HURRICANE@MAILSERV.DIGITALCITY.COM	Sun-Sentinel Hurricane Advisory
TASTING@PEACH.EASE.LSOFT.COM	Wine Tasting's List
TELECOMMAGAZINE@TVISIONS.COM	The Telecommunications Magazine Listserv
TVGUIDE@LISTSERV.TVGUIDE.COM	TV Guide Online Insider
VBHOWTO@LISTSERV.XTRAS.COM	The Weekly Source of Tips and Tools for the Visual Basic Developer
VOICES-L@ORACLE.WIZARDS.COM	Voices in My Head List
WWF-L@LISTSERV.AOL.COM	World Wrestling Federation Newsletter
YOUTH-TECH@LISTSERV.AOL.COM	A Weekly Newsletter for the Kids & Teens Technology Community

Does this list give you an idea of the wild, wacky, and well-worth-reading mailing lists available to you? (I'm planning to check out the Voices in My Head list.) And this tiny portion of what's out there just includes the LISTSERV groups; the many non-LISTSERV groups cover similarly eclectic subject matters.

The LISTSERV Address

A LISTSERV address consists of three parts: the group name, the LISTSERV site, and (usually) .bitnet. For instance, the address of the group College Activism/Information List is `actnow-l@brownvm.bitnet`. Actnow-l is the name of the group, and brownvm is the name of the site. (As you can see in the previous table, some of these LISTSERV groups, such as `SLAVERY@UHUPVM1.UH.EDU`, don't have the .bitnet bit at the end.) A site is a computer that has the LISTSERV program, and it handles one or more LISTSERV groups. A site might have dozens of groups; The brownvm site, for instance, also maintains the ACH-EC-L, AFRICA-L, and AGING-L forums, among a few dozen more.

Let's Do It: Subscribing

When you've found a LISTSERV group to which you want to subscribe, you must send an email message to the LISTSERV site (not to the newsgroup) asking to subscribe to the list. Don't worry, you are not going to have to pay anything; the vast majority of mailing lists are completely free. Send a message with the following text in the body (not the subject) of the message:

SUBSCRIBE *group firstname lastname*

For instance, if I wanted to subscribe to the actnow-l list at the brownvm LISTSERV site, I would send a message to `listserv@brownvm.bitnet`, and in the body of the message, I'd write **SUBSCRIBE actnow-l Peter Kent**. As you can see in the following figure, you send the message to `listserv@`*`sitename`* (in this case, to `listserv@brownvm.bitnet`), and the SUBSCRIBE message contains only the name of the group (not the entire group address).

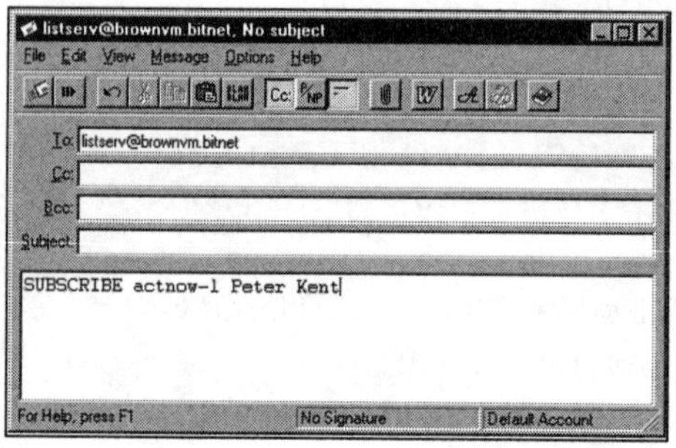

This is all it takes to subscribe to a LISTSERV mailing list. (This is the AK-Mail email program.)

Don't Forget These Details

Note that you might have to put something in the Subject line; some email programs won't let you send email unless you include a subject. In such a case, just type something (a space or 1, for instance) in the Subject line. If your email program automatically inserts a signature (information such as your name, street address, and so on that is inserted at the end of the message), turn off the signature before sending the message, or you'll get error messages back from the LISTSERV site.

You might (or might not) receive some kind of confirmation message from the group. Such a message tells you that you have subscribed and provides background information about the group and the different commands you can use. You might receive a message telling you how to confirm your subscription. If so, follow the instructions in the message. You might also receive instructions about working with the mailing list; read these instructions carefully, as they will contain important information.

After you've subscribed, you can either sit back and wait for the messages to arrive, or you can send your own messages. To send messages, address mail to the full group address (to `actnow-l@brownvm.bitnet`, for example).

Enough Already! Unsubscribing

When you're tired of receiving all these messages (and the volume might be overwhelming), you'll have to unsubscribe, which you do by sending another message to the LISTSERV address. You still send the message to `listserv@`*`sitename`* (such as `listserv@brownvm.bitnet`), but this time, type **SIGNOFF *groupname*** (**SIGNOFF actnow-l**, for instance) in the body of the message.

The next figure shows the SIGNOFF message you use to unsubscribe. Again, make sure you address it to `listserv@`*`sitename`*, not to the group name. Make sure the group name—but not the entire group address—appears after SIGNOFF.

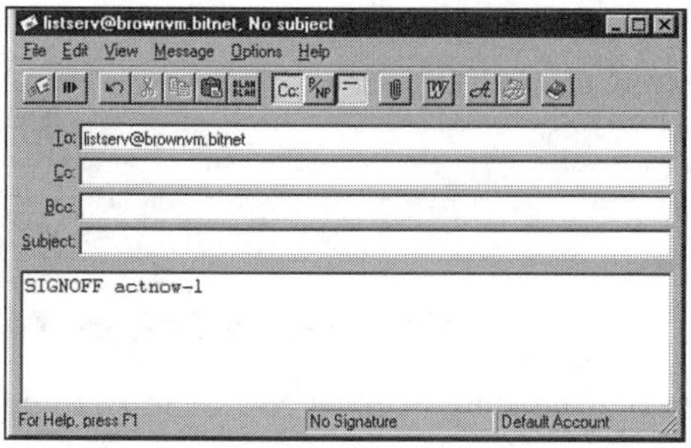

Unsubscribing to a LISTSERV mailing list is also easy.

Message Digests

To make your mailing lists easier to handle, get message digests. With message digests, you'll receive one large message at the end of the day that contains all the messages the mailing list has received during the day instead of receiving dozens of messages throughout the day. To request message digests, send a message to the LISTSERV server at `listserv@`*`sitename`* and type the message **set *listname* digest** (such as **set actnow-l digest**).

The message you receive at the end of the day has a list of subjects at the top. You can use your email program's Find command (or save the message in a text file and use your word processor's Find command) to quickly get to the messages that interest you. If you want to turn off the digest, use the command **set *listname* nodig**. Note, however, that not all mailing lists can provide message digests.

Getting Fancy with LISTSERV

You can do a few neat things with LISTSERV. By sending email messages to the LISTSERV site, you can tell the LISTSERV software how you want to handle your messages. You can ask LISTSERV to send you an acknowledgment each time you send a message (by default, most groups won't do this). You can find information about another group member, or you can tell LISTSERV not to provide information about you to other users. You can tell LISTSERV to stop sending you messages temporarily (perhaps when you go on vacation), or you can tell it to send only the message subjects instead of the entire messages. You can request a specific message, and you can even search the archives for old messages.

When you first subscribe to a mailing list, it's a good idea to send the **info** command to the `listserv@sitename` address (not the newsgroup). Put the word **info** in the body of the message. A document containing important information about working with the list will be returned to you.

Remember This!

Remember that when you want to send a message to be read by other group members, you must address it to the `groupname@sitename`. For all other purposes (to subscribe, unsubscribe, change user options, get more information, and so on), send the message to `listserv@sitename`. Send these messages to the group itself, and you might get complaints. But hey, you wouldn't be alone. Many of us (me included, several times) forget to change the address and send these commands to the wrong address! These days, some LISTSERV servers can recognize a message that contains commands, intercept it before it gets to the mailing list group, and send it back to you.

You can also combine commands in one message. For instance, you can send an email message to `listserv@sitename` with these lines in the body of the message:

list

query *groupname*

info ?

This message tells LISTSERV to send you a list of the groups handled by this site (**list**), to tell you which options you have set (**query *groupname***), and to send you a list of information guides (**info ?**). It's a good idea to use this last command to find out about user documentation the list has available, and then to use the **info *document-name*** command to have specific documents sent to you. (At some sites, sending email to the LISTSERV address with the message **INFO REFCARD** will get you a document outlining the commands.)

Using Majordomo

Another very popular mailing-list program is Majordomo. Subscribing to a Majordomo list is similar to working with LISTSERV. To subscribe, send a message to `majordomo@`*`sitename`*. For instance, `majordomo@usa.net`, `majordomo@big.host.com`, and so on. In the body of the message, type **subscribe group *firstname last-name***.

The same as with LISTSERV, eh? When you unsubscribe, though, you'll use a different command. Instead of SIGNOFF, use:

unsubscribe group

Finally, when sending messages to the group, remember to send them to *`group@sitename`*.

Majordomo might be set up differently, though. You might have to send your subscription message to *`listname`*`-request@`*`hostname`*. For instance, if the list is called goodbeer, and it's at the `bighost.com` hostname, you would send your subscription request to `goodbeer-request@bighost.com`. After you've subscribed, you can send your correspondence to the list to `goodbeer@bighost.com`.

Mailing-List Programs

There are many mailing list programs. They all work in a similar manner, but with a few variations. In some cases, for instance, you don't have to provide your name, just enter a **subscribe group** command. Or maybe the command will be **join group**. Also, some mailing list programs require that you place the command in the Subject line, not the body of the message.

Using Manually Administered Lists

Some lists are administered manually. That means there is no computer running the list; instead, some person reads the subscription requests and adds people to the list manually. Such a mailing list can be administered in many ways. You might send email to the person who administers the list and say, "Hey, add me to the list please." Often, however, there's a special address associated with the list. You might have to send your subscription message to `listname-request@`*`hostname`* (just as you would for some of the Majordomo lists).

Handling Mailing List Correspondence

Working with a mailing list is quite simple. When a message arrives, you find it in your email inbox along with all your normal email. If you read a message to which you want to reply, use the reply function of your email program (see Chapter 2, "The Premier Internet Tool: Email" for more information), and the new message is addressed to the correct place. At least, in most cases, it is addressed correctly. Check the return address that your email program enters for you. With some mailing lists, you'll find that the return address in the header of the message you received is not the address to which you are supposed to send messages—rather, it's the address of the person who sent the message to the group. I find this rather irritating, but many groups work this way. You might be able to use a **Reply to All** command (not all mail programs have this, but many do) to send a message to the originator *and* to the list. Otherwise, you'll have to type the list address into the To box in your mail composition window. To send a message about a new subject, write a new message, address it to the mailing list address, and send it.

Beware of Replies

On the other hand, there's a very good reason to set up a mailing list so the reply automatically goes to the sender instead of the list. The single most common and embarrassing mistake made on mailing lists is to send a private message to the mailing list. This is not just a "newbie" mistake, by the way; even in mailing lists full of long-term Internet geeks, people accidentally post private messages publicly. If a mailing list is set up with a Reply To address that returns mail to the list, be very careful!

In some ways, working with mailing lists is not as convenient as working with newsgroups. The newsgroup programs have a lot of features for dealing with discussions. Of course, your email program will almost certainly let you print and save messages just as a newsgroup program would. What's often missing, though, are the threading functions that you get in newsgroup messages (which enable you to quickly see which messages are part of a series of responses). Some mail programs have these—Netscape's Messenger, part of the Communicator suite of programs, does—but most do not. You might also find that messages are sent to you out of order, in which case you might end up reading a response to a message before you read the original message. This is another reason you might want to use the message digest (discussed earlier) to get the messages in the most convenient form possible.

Filtering Tools

Learn how to use your mail program's filtering tools. That way you can quickly direct incoming mail from mailing lists into the appropriate folders and even automatically delete messages that you're not interested in.

Using the Web Forums

Web forums are discussion groups associated with a particular Web site. They're often technical support forums, forums set up by a company to help provide information to their customers, but you might run into forums about many subjects and for many purposes.

Finding Web forums is a little difficult right now; they're the sort of thing you run into, rather than go looking for. Reference.com (`http://www.reference.com/`) tracks a few Web forums, but it doesn't provide a list of them—perhaps it will soon. You could search for **"web forum"** at AltaVista (see Chapter 17), and you'll find thousands, although in a very disorganized listing. I haven't yet been able to track down a good Web forum directory.

To use a Web forum, click the appropriate links at a Web site. You'll use forums to read messages and to respond to them; you can see an example in the following figure.

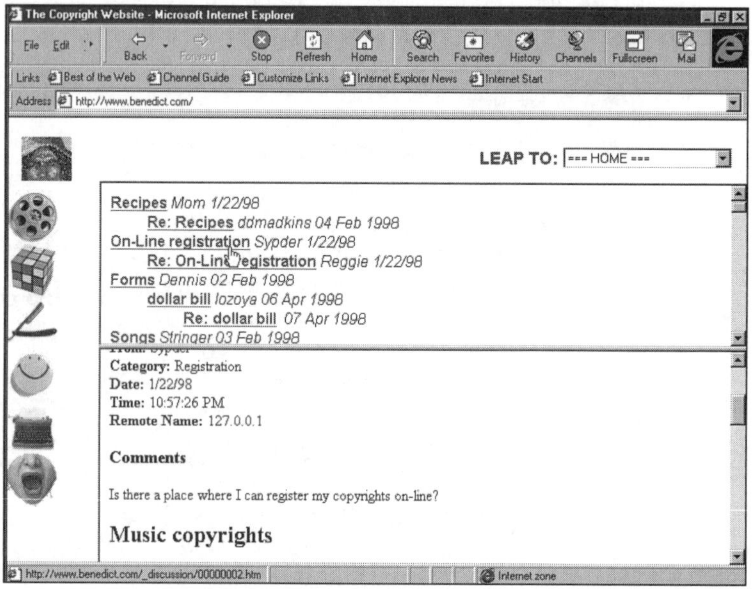

One of perhaps 25,000 Web forums—in this case, a copyright discussion group.

The Least You Need to Know

- A mailing list is a discussion group in which messages are exchanged through the email system.
- Mailing lists might be administered manually or run by a program such as LISTSERV or Majordomo.
- Subscribe to a LISTSERV group by including the command **subscribe *groupname firstname lastname*** in the body of a message and sending the message to `listserv@`*`sitename`*.
- To unsubscribe from a LISTSERV list, send the command **SIGNOFF *groupname*** in the body of a message.
- To subscribe to a Majordomo list, you normally send a message saying **SUBSCRIBE *groupname firstname lastname*** in the body. The message goes to the Majordomo address (such as `majordomo@bighost`), not the list name address. Some Majordomos might be set up differently, though.
- To unsubscribe from a Majordomo list, use the **UNSUBSCRIBE** command (not SIGNOFF).
- To subscribe to a manually administered list, write to the person running the list and ask to join. Or you might need to send an email to *`listname`*`-request@`*`hostname`*.
- When you join a list, send a message with the **info** command in the body to find out important information about working with the list.
- Thousands of Web forums are available, but they're hard to track down. Search for **"web forum"** at AltaVista.

Chapter 12

The Giant Software Store: FTP

In This Chapter

- What is FTP?
- FTP might be difficult, but it *can* be easy
- FTPing with your Web browser
- Clues that will help you find files
- FTPing with true FTP programs
- Dealing with compressed files
- Protecting yourself from viruses

The Internet is a vast computer library. Virtually any type of computer file imaginable is available somewhere on the Internet. You'll find freeware (programs you can use for free) and shareware (programs you must pay a small fee to use) and almost all types of files: music, pictures, video, 3D images, and many types of hypertext documents. You'll probably find every file type you can possibly name on the Internet. Where are these files? You can download plenty of files from the World Wide Web (as explained in Chapters 4-7), but another system predates the Web: FTP.

To give you a little bit of history, FTP is one of those quaint old UNIX-geek terms. It stands for *file transfer protocol*, and it's an old UNIX system for transferring files from one computer to another. FTP is the original core of the Internet: The whole purpose

Using the Command Line?

Command-line users can refer to Chapters 18 and 19 of the first edition of *The Complete Idiot's Guide to the Internet* for more information. Send email to `ciginternet@mcp.com` with allftp in the Subject line to have the chapters mailed to you. See Appendix E, "The Email Responder," for more information on using the mail responder.

Tracking Down a File with Archie

What if you know the file you want, but you have no idea where to look for it? A quick way to track down a file that's stored somewhere on an Internet FTP site is to use Archie, which you'll read about later in this chapter.

of the Internet was to allow the transfer of computer files between research institutions. Even email came later; it was reportedly slipped into the Internet by geeks who didn't keep the bureaucrats fully apprised. (The geeks feared that the managers would think email would be misused; from what I've seen of electronic communications, the managers would have been right!)

The FTP sites spread all over the Internet contain millions of computer files (over 100 million). Although some of these sites are private, many are open to the public. With FTP, you might discover a fascinating file on a computer in Austria (or Australia, or Alabama, or Anywhere). You might have checked it out because someone told you where it was, because you saw it mentioned in an Internet directory of some kind, or because you saw a message in a newsgroup about it. You might have even found the file at a Web site and chosen to use FTP to transfer it—I'll explain why you might want to do that under "It's the Real Thing: Using a Genuine FTP Program," later in this chapter. The file could be a public domain or shareware program, a document containing information you want for some research you're working on, a picture, a book you want to read, or just about anything else.

Suppose then that you're searching for a certain file. You might be told to "FTP to such and such a computer to find this file." That simply means "use the FTP system to grab the file." In some cases, you might have specific permission to get onto another computer and grab files. A researcher, for instance, might have been given permission to access files on a computer owned by an organization involved in the same sort of research—another university or government department, perhaps. (I have private FTP directories on various publishers' FTP sites, so I can upload Web pages, or chapters for a book, or whatever.) To get into a directory that requires special permission, you need to use a login name and a password.

In other cases, though, you'll just be rooting around on other systems without specific permission. Some systems are open to the public; anyone can get on and grab files that the system administrator has decided should be publicly accessible. This type of access is known as *anonymous FTP* because you don't need a unique login name to get onto the computer; you log in as anonymous and enter your email address for the password. If you are working at the UNIX command line, as many unfortunate people still do, you have to type this information. If you use anything else, you are using a program that will enter this information for you.

Different Flavors of FTP

FTP was originally a command-line program in which you had to type commands at a prompt and press the Enter key. Information would then scroll past on your screen, perhaps too fast for you to read (unless you knew the secret command to make it slow down or stop). You'd have to read this information and then type another command. Although UNIX geeks get some sort of strange masochistic pleasure out of that sort of thing, real people found early FTP to be a painful experience—and most people avoided it.

In the early 1990s (a year or two before the Internet boom), FTP became automated to some extent. This automation made it possible to get to some FTP sites using *Gopher*, a system that's covered in Chapter 16, "Gopher and Telnet—Still Alive, but Barely." With Gopher, you selected files from a menu system instead of by typing commands. Yet even this system was inconvenient for a number of reasons, the most important being that you could access only FTP sites for which some kindly Gopher author had created menus.

Next came graphical FTP programs. Most of these graphical FTP programs let you see lists of files and use your mouse to carry out the operations. Using FTP with these systems was a pleasure; all of a sudden FTP became easy.

Of the many graphical FTP programs available, the best I've seen are CuteFTP and WS_FTP (Windows shareware programs) and Fetch and NetFinder (Macintosh shareware programs); see Appendix C, "All the Software You'll Ever Need," for information about finding all these programs. Another FTP program is Anarchie, a Macintosh shareware program that melds FTP with Archie (we'll be looking at Archie later in this chapter). Many others are available, particularly for Windows.

Finally, FTP was incorporated into Web browsers. You can now go to an FTP site using your Web browser. Because the FTP site appears as a document with links in it, you can click a link to view the contents of a directory, to read a text file, or to transfer a computer file to your computer.

This chapter focuses on running FTP sessions with a Web browser, for a couple of reasons. First, it's a very easy way to work with FTP. Second, you probably already have a Web browser. However, there are some very good reasons for getting hold of a true FTP program; I'll discuss this issue toward the end of this chapter.

Hitting the FTP Trail

To work through an FTP example, let's go to `ftp://ftp.dartmouth.edu/`. This site is where you can find the Macintosh Fetch FTP program. (If you prefer to visit another FTP site, you can follow along and do so; the principles are the same. You can find a list of FTP sites to play with at `http://tile.net/ftp-list/`.)

What's in a Name?

Take a minute to analyze a site name. The `ftp://` part tells your browser that you want to go to an FTP site. The FTP site name (or hostname), `ftp.dartmouth.edu`, identifies the computer that contains the files you are after. That name might be followed by a directory name. I haven't given you a directory name in this example, but I could have told you to go to `ftp.dartmouth.edu/pub/software/mac`. The `/pub/software/mac` bit tells the browser which directory it must change to find the files you want.

Name or Number

The FTP site or hostname could be a name (such as `leo.nmc.edu`) or a number (such as `192.88.242.239`). If it's a number, or if the name doesn't begin with `ftp.`, you *must* precede it with `ftp://`.

To start, open your Web browser, then click inside the **Address** or **Location** text box, type `ftp://ftp.dartmouth.edu` (or `ftp://` and the address of another site you want to visit), and press **Enter**. In most browsers these days, you can omit `ftp://` as long as the FTP site name begins with ftp. In other words, instead of typing `ftp://ftp. dartmouth. edu`, you can generally get away with typing only `ftp.dartmouth.edu`.

In a few moments, with luck, you'll see something like the screen shown in the following figure. Without luck, you'll probably get a message telling you that you cannot connect to the FTP site. If that happens, check to see whether you typed the name correctly. If you did, you'll have to wait and try again later; the site might be closed, or it might be very busy. Notice, by the way, that you didn't have to enter the anonymous login name or your email address as a password. The browser handled all that for you.

Incidentally, there's another way to get to an FTP site. Many Web authors create links from their Web pages to FTP sites. Click the link, and you'll go to that site. Try visiting `http://tile.net/ftp-list/`, and you'll see what I mean.

Files and Links: What's All This?

What can you see at the FTP site? Each file and directory is shown as a link. Depending on the browser you are using, you might see information about the file or directory (see the following figure). You might see a description of each item (*file* or *directory*, for instance) and the file size, so you'll know how big a file is before you transfer it. You'll often see the file date and little icons that represent the directory or file type. The following figure shows both files and directories.

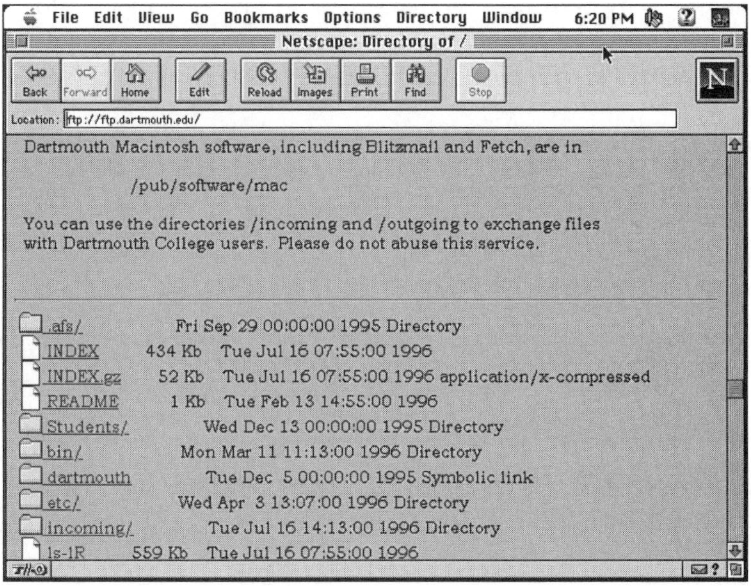

If you've used command-line FTP, you'll love working in a browser. This is the Macintosh version of Netscape Navigator.

Private FTP Sites

To enter a private FTP site, you have to enter a login ID and a password. You can often enter the FTP site information in the format `ftp://username:password@hostname/directory/`. For example, if you enter **`ftp://joeb:1234tyu@ftp.sherwoodforest.com/t1/home/joeb`**, your browser connects to the `ftp. sherwoodforest.com` FTP site and displays the /t1/home/joeb directory; it uses the username joeb and the password 1234tyu to gain access. However, in some browsers, using that method causes the browser to save your password in a drop-down list box associated with the Location text box. Therefore, if you want to be really safe, use the format `ftp://username@hostname/directory`. When the browser connects to the FTP site, it opens a dialog box into which you can type your password.

Click a directory link to make the browser display another Web document that shows the contents of that directory. In most browsers, you'll also find a link back to the parent directory: In Netscape, you'll see an "Up to a higher level directory" link, for instance. The following figure shows what you will find if you click the **pub** link at the `ftp.dartmouth.edu` site. Why pub? Because that's the name commonly used for the directory that holds publicly available files. You can see that there are a couple of files in this directory and many more subdirectories (the subdirectories are the little folders).

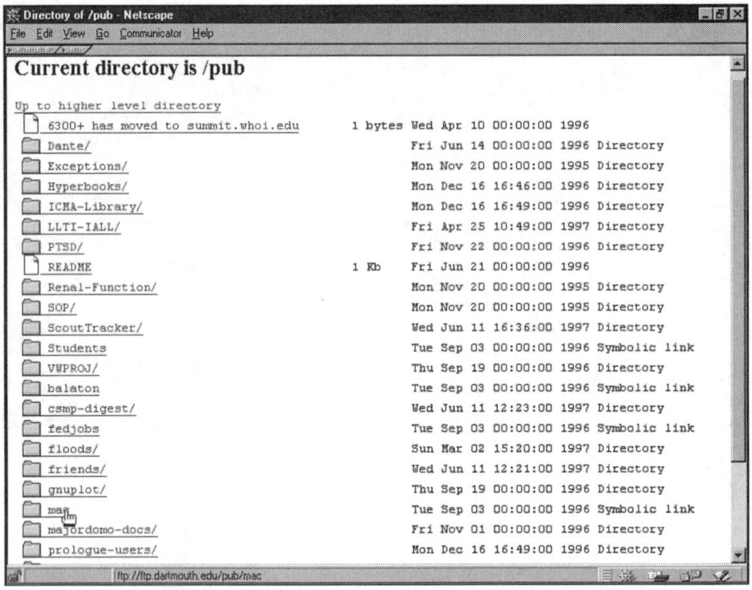

The contents of the pub directory at the FTP site. This time you're looking at a Windows version of Netscape.

What happens when you click a link to a file? The same thing that would happen if you did so from a true Web document. If the browser can display or play the file type, it will. If it can't, it will try to send it to the associated application. If there is no associated application, it will ask you what to do with it, allowing you to save it on the hard disk. This process all works in the same way as it does when you are at a Web site—the browser looks at the file type and acts accordingly. (See Chapter 7, "Web Multimedia," for more information.)

Finding the Pot o' Gold

Now that you're in, you want to find the file that you know is somewhere on this system. (In my example, you're looking for Fetch, the Macintosh FTP program.) Finding files at an FTP site is often a little difficult. There are no conventions for how such sites should be set up, so you often have to dig through directories that look like they might contain what you want, until you find what you want.

When you first get to an FTP site, look for files called INDEX, OO-INDEX, README, DIRECTORY, and so on. These files often contain information that will help you find what you need. The more organized sites even contain text files with full indexes of their contents or at least lists of the directories and the types of files you'll find. Click one of these files to transfer the document to your Web browser, read the file (all Web browsers can display text files), and then click the **Back** button to return to the directory.

You'll often find that directories have names that describe their contents: slip will probably contain SLIP software, mac will have Macintosh software, xwindow will have X Window software, windows will have Microsoft Windows software, gif will contain GIF-format graphics, and so on. If you know what you are looking for, you can often figure out what the directory names mean. In the example, you knew where to go because when you first arrived at the site you saw a message saying that Fetch was in /pub/software/mac. So you clicked **pub**, and then **software**, and then **mac**.

It Looks a Little Strange

You'll often find full FTP site and path information, which takes you straight to the directory you want (such as `ftp.dartmouth.edu/pub/software/mac`). If you're used to working in DOS and Windows, FTP site directory names might seem strange for two reasons. First, a forward slash (/) instead of a backslash (\) separates the directories in the path. The DOS world uses a backslash (\), but the UNIX world uses the forward slash character (/) instead—and most Internet host computers still run on UNIX, so the forward slash has become a convention. Second, the directory names are often long. In DOS and Windows 3.1, you can't have directories with more than 12 characters in the name (including a period and an extension). In Windows 95, 98, and NT, however, you can. These more recent operating systems and UNIX computers allow long file and directory names. (Even if you're using Windows 3.1 or perhaps even a DOS browser, you can still enter long filenames into your browser—you just can't create files with long names on your system.)

Getting the File

When you find the file you want, click it, and save it in the same way you would save a file from a Web document (see Chapter 5, "More About the Web"). The following figure shows Fetch being saved from FTP.

Many files on FTP sites are *compressed*. That is, a special program has been used to "squeeze" the information into a smaller area. You can't use a file in its compressed state, but if you store it and transmit it in that state, you'll save disk space and transmission time. You can read more about these compressed formats in Chapter 15, "What on Earth Are All Those File Types?" In this example, you are transferring an HQX file that contains a SIT file. A program such as StuffIt Expander can extract the SIT file (a compressed file) from within the BinHex HQX file (a common format for transferring Macintosh files across the Internet).

You can save files from FTP sites with a few clicks.

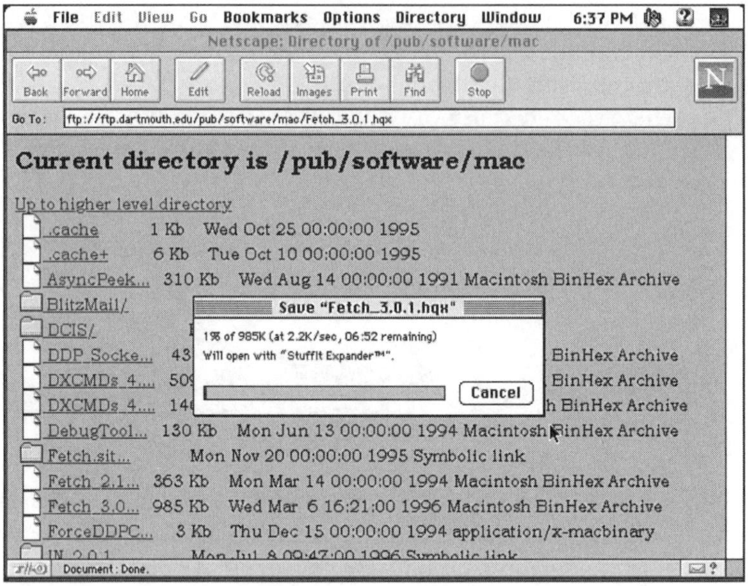

Same Name, Different Extension

While digging around in an FTP site, you might notice that files often have the same name except for the last few characters; you might find THISDOC.TXT and THISDOC.ZIP, for instance. The first file is a simple ASCII text file, and the second is a ZIP file, which (you'll probably notice) is much smaller than the first. If you know you can decompress the file after you have it, download the compressed version; doing so will save you transfer time.

It's the Real Thing: Using a Genuine FTP Program

There are some very good reasons for using a genuine FTP program instead of making do with your Web browser. First, you might run into FTP sites that don't work well through a Web browser. Some browsers simply don't like some FTP servers. Also, if you need to upload files to an FTP site, you might have problems; more recent browsers, such as Netscape Navigator 3 and 4, allow you to do this, but many other browsers don't. (In Navigator, you can drag files from, for example, Windows Explorer and drop them onto the FTP site displayed in the browser window to automatically upload those files.)

Another reason for getting hold of a true FTP program—a reason that's little understood yet very important—is that some good FTP programs (such as CuteFTP) can resume interrupted transfers. For instance, suppose you've almost finished transferring the latest version of your favorite Web browser, which could easily be 15MB (add an MB to that figure for every month that passes), when the transfer stops. Why it stops is not important; perhaps your two-year-old rugrat just reached up and pressed that big red button on the front of your computer. Perhaps your service provider's system just died. Maybe lightning struck the power lines somewhere, and the power went out. Whatever the reason, if you're using a Web browser to transfer that file, you'll have to start all over again. If you were using a good FTP program, though, you could reconnect, go back to the FTP site, and begin the transfer again, but all that the program would need to do would be to transfer the missing part of the file, not all the stuff that had already transferred.

Now, I've heard it said that the Internet represents in some ways a giant step *backward* in technology. Well, okay, I've said it myself a few times. Resumed transfers is one of those cases in which the technology being used on the Internet is way behind what has been used *off* the Internet for years. (Online help is another case.) This technology is just finding its way to the Internet, but for the moment Web browsers cannot resume interrupted downloads. Some FTP programs, although not all, can. (Note that not all FTP servers can resume interrupted transfers, so this feature won't work all the time.)

If you transfer a lot of files across the Internet, in particular large files, you should use a true FTP program. Not only can you use the FTP program when you are working in an actual FTP site, you can also use it at other times. In many cases, when you think you're transferring from a Web site, the file is really coming from an FTP site. For example, the following illustration shows Shareware.com, a large shareware library. Notice that underneath the links to the download files you can see little labels that tell you where each file is stored—`ftp.tas.gov.au`, for instance. In this case, you can quickly see that the file is coming from an FTP site. However, most Web pages won't be this convenient. You can still figure out if the file is coming from an FTP site, though; point at the link, and in the status bar you'll see the URL of the file—in this case, `ftp://ftp.tas.gov.au/pub/simtelnet/win95/music/cd2mp31u.zip`.

You can quickly copy this information from the link by using the browser's pop-up menu (in a Windows browser, right-click on the link and choose something such as **Copy Link Location**; in a Macintosh browser, you'll probably be able to hold the mouse button down for a moment to open the pop-up menu). Then you can paste the information into your FTP program and use that program to download the file.

If that's not enough, here are two more reasons to use a real FTP program. It's often quicker and easier to connect to a site using an FTP program than a Web browser, and you can also set an FTP program to keep trying automatically every few minutes. So if the site's busy, the FTP program can keep trying until it gets through. You also might run into cases in which the browser FTP features are not enough. For those times, you need to get a real FTP program.

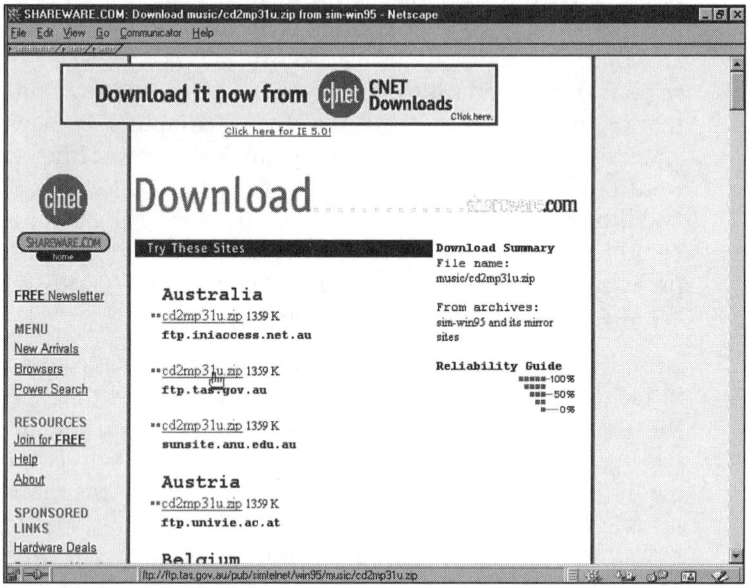

Yes, it's a Web page, but the files the page links to are stored at an FTP site, as you can see by pointing at a link and looking at the status bar.

Which and Where

There are lots of good FTP programs. If you use the Macintosh, try Fetch or Anarchie. For Windows, try WS_FTP or CuteFTP (my personal favorite). Many good Windows FTP programs are available as freeware or shareware on the Internet. See Appendix C for ideas on where to look for the software you want. (Remember, you need a program that will allow you to resume interrupted downloads, which means you'll probably have to pay the registration fee!)

When you get an FTP program, go through that old familiar routine: Read the documentation carefully to be sure you understand how to use it. (FTP programs are generally fairly easy to deal with.) To give you an idea of how FTP programs work, let's take a quick look at CuteFTP. CuteFTP is very easy to use. If you've ever used UNIX FTP, you know that using it is like eating soup with a fork—not particularly satisfying. CuteFTP, on the other hand, is what FTP should be. You have all the commands at your fingertips, plus a library of FTP sites to select from. No more mistyping FTP hostnames!

Installing CuteFTP is simple. Just run the installation program. Then start CuteFTP by going through the Windows 95 Start menu or double-clicking CuteFTP's Program Manager icon. CuteFTP has two ways to connect to an FTP site: You can add an entry to the Site Manager (press **F4** to open it, and then click **Add Site**) or use Quick Connect (**Ctrl+C**). Use the Site Manager for FTP sites you expect to visit again (they'll be stored in the Site Manager); use Quick Connect if you *don't* expect to be back.

For instance, in the following figure you can see the FTP Site Edit box, the one that opens when you add a site to Site Manager. Enter the following information:

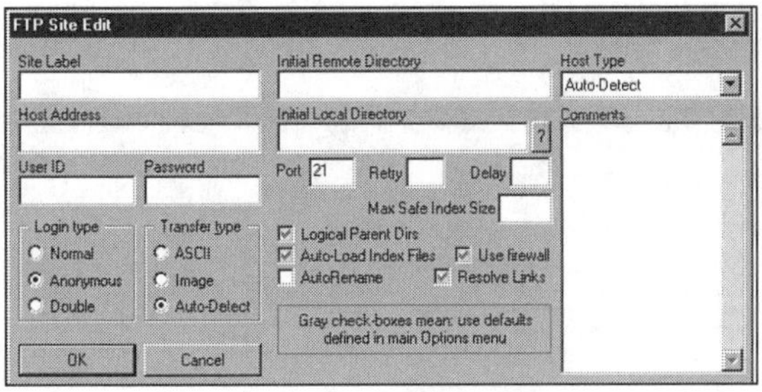

Adding FTP site information to the Site Manager.

1. Type a **Site Label** (anything that helps you remember what the site contains). This name appears in the Site Manager.
2. Enter the FTP site **Host Address**.
3. If you are going to an "anonymous" FTP site, leave the **Anonymous** option button selected. You need to enter only a **User ID** and **Password** if you're going to a private FTP site.
4. If you know which directory you want to go to when you get to the FTP site, enter it in the **Initial Remote Directory** text box.

5. You can also enter the **Initial Local Directory**, the directory on your computer that should be displayed and into which transferred files will be placed. You can always select this later, though.
6. You can ignore most of the other settings; they're almost always okay or represent advanced features.
7. Click the **OK** button to save the information.
8. In the Site Manager, click the new entry, and then click **Connect** to begin the session.

When you click **Connect**, CuteFTP tries to connect to the FTP site. After it connects, you'll see the FTP site's directories listed on the right and the directories on your computer's hard disk listed on the left (see the following figure). You can move around in the directories by double-clicking folders or by right-clicking somewhere in the right pane and selecting **Change Directory** from the pop-up menu (that feature is handy, because if you know where you want to go it's a lot quicker to type it in than to go through each directory in the path to get there).

FTP transfers made easy: Just drag the files you want onto the directory on your hard disk.

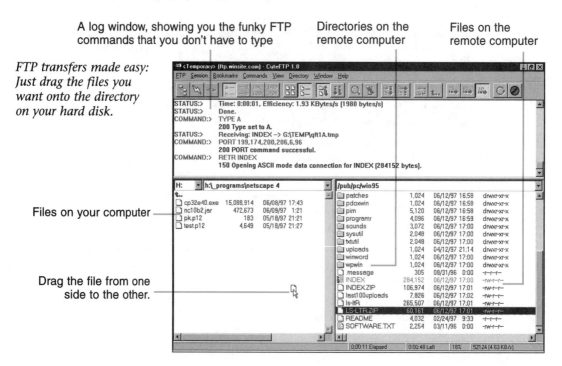

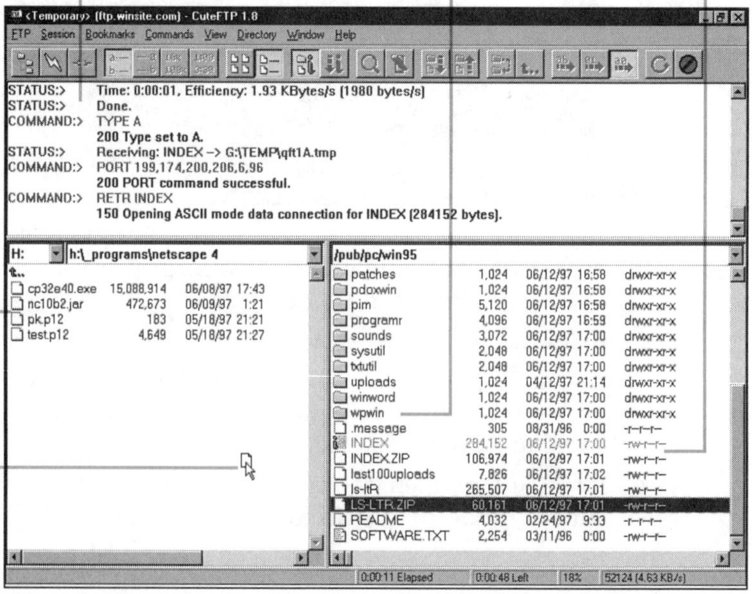

To read an index file, right-click the file and select **View**. To transfer a file to your system, just drag it from one side to the other (or if you prefer using menus, right-click and choose **Download**).

ASCII Versus Binary

Notice the little ab, 01, and a0 buttons on the right side of the toolbar? These buttons control whether the files are transferred as ASCII (the ab button), as Binary (the 01 button), or whether the program should decide the better way to transfer them (the a0 button). Make sure you select the correct one before transferring a file. Select **ASCII** for files you know to be ASCII text files; select **Binary** for anything else. Remember, word processing files are not ASCII; they're binary; they contain special codes that are used to define the character formatting. You can tell the program to automatically determine a file's transfer type by using the **FTP**, **Settings**, **Text File Extensions** menu option.

It's Alive! Viruses and Other Nasties

If you haven't been in a cave for the past six or seven years, you've probably heard about computer viruses. A *virus* is a computer program that can reproduce itself and even convince unknowing users to help spread it. It spreads far and wide and can do incredible amounts of damage.

As is true of biological viruses, the effects of a virus on your system can range from nearly unnoticeable to fatal. A virus can do something as harmless as display a Christmas tree on your screen, or it can destroy everything on your hard disk. Viruses are real, but the threat is overstated. It's wise to take certain precautions, though, to ensure that you don't transfer viruses from FTP sites—or Web sites, for that matter—to your computer system. We'll be talking more about viruses in Chapter 18, "Staying Safe on the Internet."

Where Now?

Although there are thousands of FTP sites all over the world, FTP generally is either a service of last resort—people go to the Web first and use FTP only if they know exactly where to go to get what they are looking for—or a service that is linked to Web pages. Perhaps you've read in a newsgroup message or a magazine article that a particular file is available at a particular FTP site. You can go directly to the site to find it, but most people don't go looking for things at FTP sites. The Web sites are far more convenient starting points.

However, you might want to see the `http://tile.net/ftp-list/` Web site, the TILE.NET/FTP Reference to Anonymous Sites, or perhaps the Monster FTP Sites list (`http://hoohoo.ncsa.uiuc.edu/ftp/`), where you can find thousands of FTP sites. If you are searching for a particular file and can't find it at the sources mentioned in Appendix C, you might want to try Archie, a friendly (but slow) little fellow who'll help you dig around in FTP.

Searching FTP Sites

If you're looking for a particular file at an FTP site, how can you possibly find it? In a moment, we'll look at Archie, an FTP-search system that's been around for some time. But there's an alternative to Archie, which might in fact be easier to use. The Lycos search system (a Web-search system that we'll look at in Chapter 17) has a database of more than 100 million FTP files. It seems to be a very fast system.

Visit `http://ftpsearch.lycos.com/`. You'll find four different ways to search for FTP files. You can simply enter a word into a very simple search form. You can use the Advanced form or the Normal form (which seems to be somewhere between the basic and Advanced forms). And then there's the "original" form, which is more complicated, and seems to be similar to an Archie search, which we'll look at next.

For Aspiring Geeks: Archie Searches

Designed by a few guys at McGill University in Canada, Archie is a system that indexes anonymous FTP sites (that is, public FTP sites), listing the files that are available at each site. Archie lists millions of files at FTP sites throughout the world and provides a very useful way to find out where to go to grab a file in which you are interested. There's just one problem: Archie's extremely busy these days and can be very slow.

There are several methods for connecting to Archie:

- You can use Archie through the *command line*. This method is unwieldy and difficult, though, and you *don't* want to do it this way if you can help it! If you absolutely can't help it, send email to `ciginternet@mcp.com` with Archie in the Subject line to receive the Archie chapter from the first edition of *The Complete Idiot's Guide to the Internet*. (See Appendix E for more information about working with Email Responder.)
- You can use your Web browser to go to an Archie *gateway*, a Web page containing a form that will help you search an Archie index. You enter information into the form, the information is sent to the Archie server, and the response from the server appears in another Web page.
- You can use a special Archie client program, such as WS_Archie (Windows) or Anarchie (Macintosh).
- You can use email to send questions to an Archie server.

Archie on the Web

You need to use a "gateway" to an Archie client, of which there are dozens on the Web. Open your Web browser and go to `http://web.nexor.co.uk/archie.html` to find a list. Just in case that Web site's busy, try one of these Archie sites:

`http://www.lerc.nasa.gov/archieplex/`

`http://www.gh.cs.su.oz.au/Utils/archieplexform.html`

`http://src.doc.ic.ac.uk/archieplexform.html`

Archie?

What does Archie mean? It's not an acronym (unlike Veronica and Jughead, whom you'll meet in Chapter 16). Instead, it comes from the word *archive* (as in file archive). Remove the *v* and what do you have? Archie.

Most Archie sites offer both forms and non-forms search methods. Internet Explorer and Netscape Navigator are forms-capable browsers, which means that they can display forms components such as text boxes, command buttons, option buttons, and so on. If you are using one of these browsers or another forms-capable browser, select the forms search. (Most browsers can work with forms these days.)

Searching Archie

The following figure shows an example of an Archie form, one at Imperial College in London (located at `http://src.doc.ic.ac.uk/archieplexform.html`). The simplest way to search is to type a filename or part of a filename into the What Would You Like to Search For? text box and press **Enter** (or click the **Start Search** button). For instance, if you want to find the WS_Archie program you're going to look at later in this chapter, type **wsarchie** and press **Enter**. Why not **WS_ARCHIE**? Because even though the program name is WS_Archie, the file you need is called WSARCHIE.ZIP or WSARCHIE.EXE. Of course, there's no way for you to know that if I hadn't told you. If you are using a Macintosh, you might search for **anarchie** (as shown).

Different Gateways, Different Options

Archie forms vary. Each Archie gateway is a little different, so if you use a different one from the one you're about to look at, you might find that the options vary slightly, although they should be very similar.

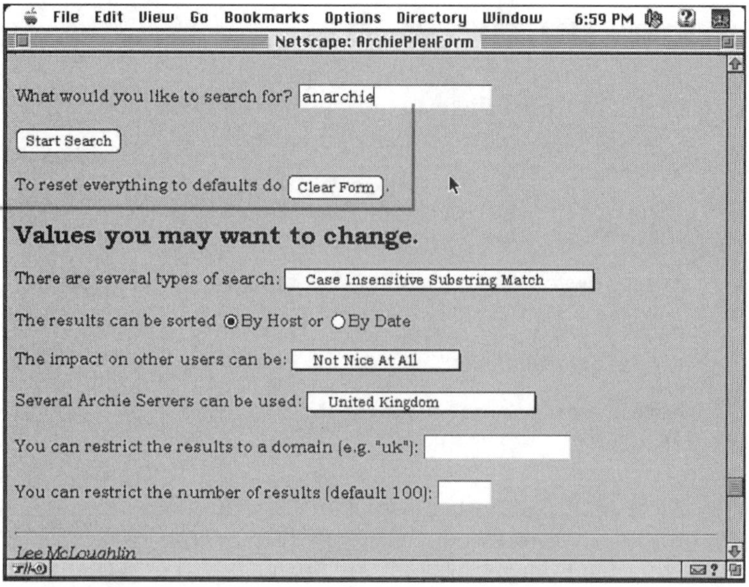

Archie gateways provide a link from the Web to Archie servers around the world.

Type the name of the file that you're looking for.

Archie searches are frequently very slow; often they don't work because the Archie server you selected is busy. (I'll show you how to choose another server in a moment.) If you are lucky, though, you'll eventually see a screen showing what the Archie server found, with links to the file you are looking for. It might show many links, because the file you want—and perhaps files with similar names—might be held on many different FTP sites.

Search the Document

Remember that you can use your browser's Find function to search the list of files after it's onscreen (in both Internet Explorer and Netscape, it's **Edit**, **Find** or **Ctrl+F**). Suppose you want to download an EXE file (a self-extracting archive) instead of a ZIP file. Search for **.exe** to go directly to the file you need.

Archie's Options

Below the text box where you type what you want to search for are more options you can use to narrow your search. Here's what you'll find:

- **Search type** There are four types of searches, which I'll explain in a moment.
- **Sort by** The list of files that is returned to you might be sorted by file date or according to the host containing the file. The file-date search is a good idea, as it will help you pick the latest version of the file.
- **Impact on other users** You can tell Archie that you are not in a hurry (so other users can go first) or that you want the results right away. Difficult choice, huh?
- **Archie servers** You can select which Archie server you want to use from a list. If you find that the Archie server you tried is busy, or if it can't find what you want, try another one. You might want to try servers in countries in which the people are currently asleep; obviously those servers are likely to be less busy at night than during the day.
- **Restrict the results to a domain** You can tell the Archie server that you want to see files only in a particular domain (a particular host-computer type) such as UK (FTP sites in the United Kingdom), COM (commercial FTP sites), EDU (educational FTP sites), and so on.
- **Number of results** You can tell the Archie server how many results you want to see.

The Search Types

Before you begin searching for a filename, you should determine which type of search you want to use. You have the following choices:

- **Exact or Exact Match** You must type the exact name of the file for which you are looking.
- **Regex or Regular Expression Match** You will type a UNIX regular expression. That means that Archie will regard some of the characters in the word you type as wild cards. If you don't understand regular expressions, avoid this type of search altogether. (Everyone except UNIX geeks should probably avoid this option.)
- **Sub or Case Insensitive Substring Match** This tells Archie to search among filenames for whatever you type. That is, it will look for all names that match what you type, as well as all names that *include* the characters you type. If you are searching for "wsarch," for example, Archie finds "wsarch" and "wsarchie." Also, when you use a sub search, you don't need to worry about the case of the characters; Archie finds both "wsarch" and "WSARCH."

- **Subcase or Case Sensitive Substring Match** This is like the sub search, except that you need to enter the case of the word correctly. If you enter "wsarch," Archie finds "wsarch" but not "WSARCH." You should generally avoid this type of search.

More often than not, you'll want to use the sub search (Case Insensitive Substring Match), and you'll probably find that sub has been set up as the default. It takes a little longer than the other types, but it's most likely to find what you are looking for. Understand, however, that filenames are not always set in stone. With thousands of people posting millions of files on thousands of computers, filenames sometimes get changed a little. If you have trouble finding something, try a variety of possible combinations.

Hardcore Archie

There are two more ways to use Archie: You can get an Archie client program—a program such as WS_Archie (Windows) or Anarchie (Macintosh)—or you can use email. Few people will use these methods; to be quite honest, few people ever use Archie, even through a Web page. Still, if you want an Archie client, look at one of the software libraries mentioned in Appendix C. If you want to use Archie by mail—a *very* geeky option, and often very slow, too—send email to one of these addresses:

```
archie@dogbert.rutgers.edu

archie@archie.tu-darmstadt.de

archie@archie.sogang.ac.kr
```

Type **help** on the first line of the body of the message, and send it off. In response, you'll get a file that explains how to use the system. You can also send a message to any of these addresses with the word **servers** on the first line to get a list of all the available Archie servers.

The Least You Need to Know

- FTP stands for file transfer protocol and refers to a system of file libraries.
- Anonymous FTP refers to a system that allows the public to transfer files.
- Start an FTP session in your Web browser using the format `ftp://hostname` in the Address text box (replacing *hostname* with the appropriate URL) and pressing **Enter**.
- Each directory and file at an FTP site is represented by a link; click the link to view the directory or transfer the file.
- If your browser can't connect to a particular site, or if you want the capability to resume interrupted downloads, get a true FTP program, such as CuteFTP (Windows) or Fetch (Macintosh).
- Protect yourself against viruses, but don't be paranoid. They're not as common as the antivirus companies want you to think.
- If you're having problems finding a particular file at the Web file archives, try searching Lycos' FTP Search, or use Archie.

Chapter 13

Yak, Yak, Yak: Chatting in Cyberspace

In This Chapter

- What are chat and talk?
- Chat sessions and public auditoriums
- Using the online service chat rooms
- Using a graphical chat program
- Working with IRC (Internet Relay Chat)
- Real uses for chat

One of the most important—yet least discussed—systems in cyberspace is chat. It's important because its immense popularity has been a significant factor in the growth of online services (not so much the Internet as a whole). It is, perhaps, the least discussed because the fact is that many people use the chat systems as a way to talk about sex and even to contact potential sexual partners. In this chapter, you'll take a look at chatting in cyberspace, using a variety of different chat systems, both Internet based and online-service systems. You'll also learn that there's plenty more than sex-related chat.

Chatting and Talking

What is chat? Here's what it's *not:* a system that allows you to talk out loud to people across the Internet or an online service. That sort of system does exist (see Chapter

14, "Internet Conferences: Voice on the Net, Whiteboards, and More"), but a chat system does not use voice; it uses the typed word. Communications are carried out by typing messages.

What's the difference between chat and email, then? With email, you send a message and then go away and do something else. You come back later—maybe later that day, maybe later that week—to see whether you have a response. Chat is quite different: It takes place in *real time*, to use a geek term. (What other kind of time is there but real time, one wonders.) In other words, you type a message, and the other party in the chat session sees the message almost instantly. He can then respond right away, and you see the response right away. It's just like, yes, a chat—only you are typing instead of talking.

Chat Can Have Voice

The problem with the Internet is that you make a statement today, and tomorrow it's wrong. Right now the use of voice in chat sessions is rare. Voice *is* being added to chat, though, and you can expect chat sessions to gradually come to resemble the real thing, as people type less and talk more. However, as wonderful as that might sound, it presents a problem. Many chat users are working at big companies, sitting in their little cubicles, typing away and looking busy. Their bosses might think they are working hard, but they are actually gabbing away in one chat system or another, and voices would just give away the game!

There's also an Internet system known as *talk*, which also isn't talking. Talk is a system in which one person can "call" another on the Internet and, after a connection has been made, can type messages to the other person. It's very similar to chat after the two parties are connected, but the manner in which you connect is different. With chat, you have to go to a chat "room" to chat with people; with talk, you simply open the talk program, enter the email address of the person you want to connect to, and click a button to call that person (who might not be available, of course).

To further complicate the issue, some Voice on the Net programs (discussed in Chapter 14) incorporate these talk programs, but they sometimes call them *chat* systems! For instance, Netscape Communicator's Conference program (known as CoolTalk in earlier versions of Netscape Navigator) has a little program that you can use to type messages to another person, but it's called the Chat tool. The name *talk* seems to be disappearing from the Internet vernacular, being replaced by chat for all forms of *chat* and *talk*.

Chat is one of those "love it or hate it" kind of things. Many people just love it; they even find it addictive, spending hours online each night. Personally, I can do without it. It's an awkward way to communicate. I can type faster than most people, yet I still find chat rather clunky. I've been the guest in chat question-and-answer sessions in both MSN and CompuServe and at a Web site called TalkCity, and quite frankly my experiences with chat sessions have not exactly been the high points of my life. The sessions tended to be chaotic at worst, simply slow at best. You run into too many people trying to ask questions at once (some chat systems are not designed to allow someone to control the flow of questions very well), lots of typos, long pauses while you wait for people to type and they wait for you, and so on. I'm no chat fan, but chat certainly appeals to millions of people.

Sex?

Should I be talking about sex in this book? My editors have suggested that I avoid sexual subjects for fear of offending people. Chat, however, is a case in which it's hard to avoid the sexual. Certainly many people go to chat rooms for nonsexual purposes. But be warned that many (possibly most?) are there to meet members of the opposite sex (or the same sex in some cases) for sexual purposes.

Two Types of Sessions

Chat sessions are categorized into two types: private and group. Generally, what happens is that you join a *chat room*, in which a lot of people are talking (okay, typing) at once. Then someone might invite you to a private room, where just the two of you can talk without the babble of the public room. These private rooms are often used for cybersex sessions, although, of course, they can also be used for more innocent purposes, such as catching up on the latest news with your brother-in-law in Paris, discussing a project with a colleague, or talking about a good scuba-diving spot in Mexico.

Public chat rooms are often used as a type of auditorium or lecture hall. A famous or knowledgeable person responds to questions from the crowd. Michael Jackson and Buzz Aldrin, for instance, have been guest "speakers" in chat forums, as have many other world-famous people.

Score One for the Online Services

I'm going to mostly discuss the online services in this chapter because they generally have the most popular, and in some ways the best, chat systems. Chat has been extremely important to the growth of the online services, so they've made an effort to provide good chat services. Chat on the Internet, though, is still relatively little used and in many ways not as sophisticated. (That's changing as many new chat programs designed for the Internet, often running through the Web, are being introduced.)

If you use CompuServe or AOL, you can get to the chat rooms by using the GO or keyword **chat**. Most forums have conference rooms for chatting, too, but they are often empty. If you use The Microsoft Network, you'll find chat rooms scattered all over the place; almost every forum (or BBS as they're known in MSN-speak) has a chat room. Click the chat link and either Microsoft Chat will open, or, in a few cases, a simple chat program appears inside the Web page. (The latest MSN system is based on Web pages displayed inside Internet Explorer.) If you're still using the older software, you can go to a Chat BBS by opening the **Communicate** menu and selecting **Chat Central**.

If you have Windows 98, you'll find that the Microsoft Chat program is available from the Start menu: **Start**, **Programs**, **Internet Explorer**, **Microsoft Chat**. This program is currently set up to work with a couple of chat servers: `chat.msn.com` is available only to Microsoft Network members, but `publicchat.msn.com` is open to anyone, even nonmembers—if you can connect to the Internet, you can open Microsoft Chat and connect to this chat server.

Using Internet Relay Chat (IRC) on the Internet is a little more complicated than using the online services. I cover IRC later in this chapter.

Chatting in AOL

In AOL, click the **People** button, and then select **People Connection** from the menu that opens (if you're not using the latest version of the software, you might have to use the keyword **chat**, or click the **People Connection** button in the Welcome window). You'll go straight to a chat window (see the next figure). Use the **List Chats** button to see all the available chat rooms. There are about a dozen categories and hundreds of individual rooms.

AOL's system enables you to create private rooms so that you and your friends (or family or colleagues) can use that room without interference. If you want to talk to only one person, you just double-click the person's name in the People Here box and click the **Message** button. If the person responds, you get your own private message window for just the two of you. You can see in the following figure that this message box has special buttons that allow you to modify the text format.

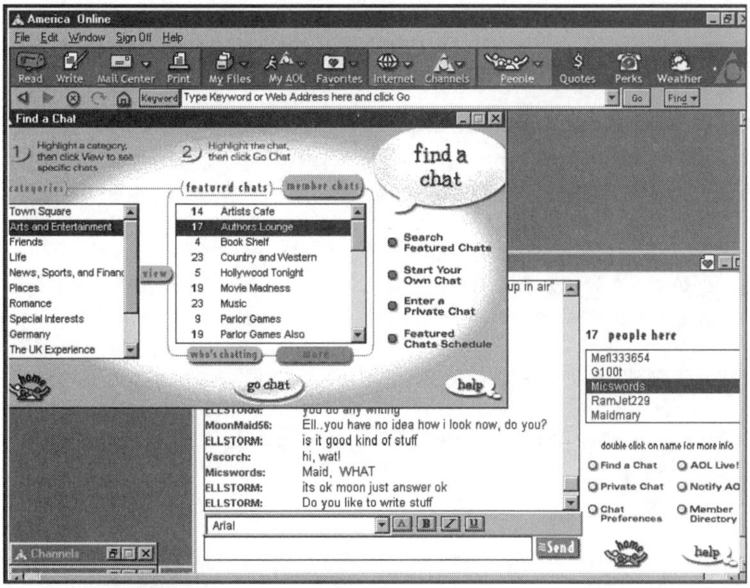

AOL's chat room system: lots of glitz, very busy.

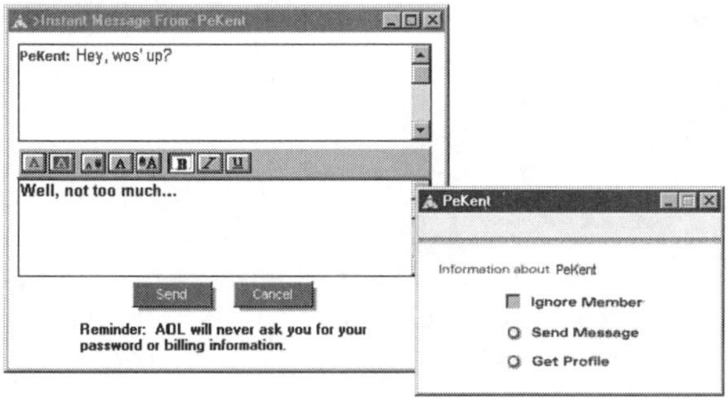

AOL provides you with a little message window in which you can carry on private conversations.

CompuServe's Chat Rooms

To use a CompuServe chat room, you can go to just about any forum or to the Chat forum, where you'll find loads of chat sessions. Most forums have a number of conference rooms, but unless some kind of presentation has been scheduled, they might all be empty. You can be sure to find people to chat with in the Chat forum, though (**GO CHAT**, or click the big **Chat** button in the main menu).

CompuServe's chat system has been completely revamped, and the old CB radio analogy has completely gone (CompuServe used to call their chat system a CB system, after the Citizens' Band radio systems that were so popular in the 1970s). You'll start by picking a chat category (General Chat, Adult Chat, Conferences and Special Events, and so on). Then click the **Chat** button to see a list of chat rooms.

Double-click a room to open the chat window, or click a room and then click the **Participate** or **Observe** button to take part in the chat room's discussion or just "listen in." (See the following figure.)

The list of rooms shows you how many people are in each room; this might be helpful if you want to pick a quiet one or get right into the action. As you can see in the figure, you can "listen" by reading other people's messages. Whenever you want to jump in, you can type your own message in the lower panel of the window; press **Enter** to send the message, or click the **Send** button. You can invite people to private rooms, too; click the **Who's Here** button to see a list of members, and then click the person you want to speak with and click **Private Chat**.

CompuServe's chat system.

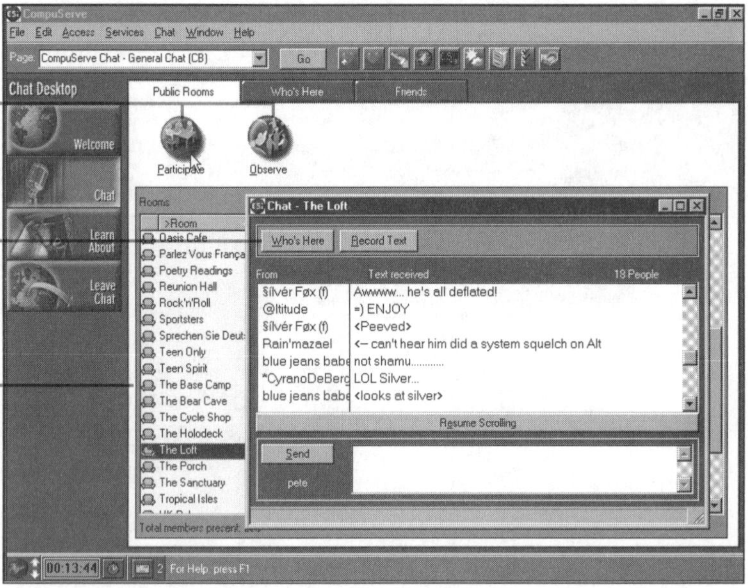
Click one of these buttons to join or listen in.
Use this button to see a list of the people in the session.
Click here to select a room.

Microsoft Chat and MSN

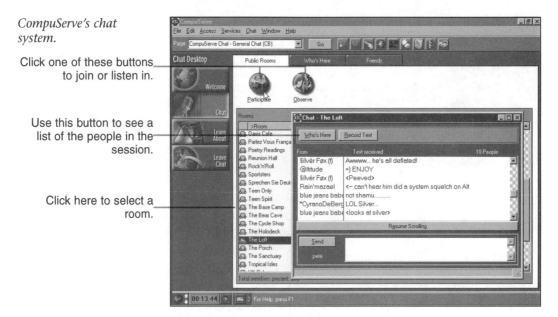

Microsoft Network uses a program called Microsoft Chat. Microsoft has included this program in Windows 98 as well, so even if you don't have an MSN account, you can still use Microsoft Chat.

To open Microsoft Chat, select **Start**, **Programs**, **Internet Explorer**, **Microsoft Chat**. You'll see a dialog box that lets you select the server you want to work with. If you're an MSN member, you can use either of the servers (there are currently only two). If you're not an MSN member, select `publicchat.msn.com`; although this chat server is hosted by MSN, anyone can enter its chat rooms. When you select **OK**, you'll see a list of rooms. Just double-click the one you want to enter. If you're an MSN member, you can also enter a chat room directly from one of MSN's forums; lots of chat rooms are scattered around, and clicking a link will open Microsoft Chat.

MSN's chat system used to be rather weak; it simply didn't have all the features available on other online system chat rooms. However, the latest version of Microsoft Chat is very good, providing all sorts of useful features. You can send files and sounds, include links to Web sites and email addresses (recipients just have to click a link to activate it), hold private conversations with chat room members, and so on. If you want to set up a private chat you can do that, too; you have to create a room, and then invite the person to that room. It's not quite as convenient as, say, AOL, in which you can invite someone to a room and the room is automatically created if the invitee accepts. But still, Microsoft Chat has a number of handy features; you can make your new room invisible to all but those you invite, make the room accessible by invitation only, and even define an access password.

Microsoft Chat has two chat modes: text and Comic Chat. Comic Chat is a type of chat system that uses **avatars** (which we'll look at under "Pick Your Avatar," later in this chapter), which are little pictures that represent participants. Both systems use the same basic program, but anyone can choose to view the chat in text or Comic Chat mode. You can see an example of the text mode in the following figure; I've included a picture of Comic Chat mode later in this chapter.

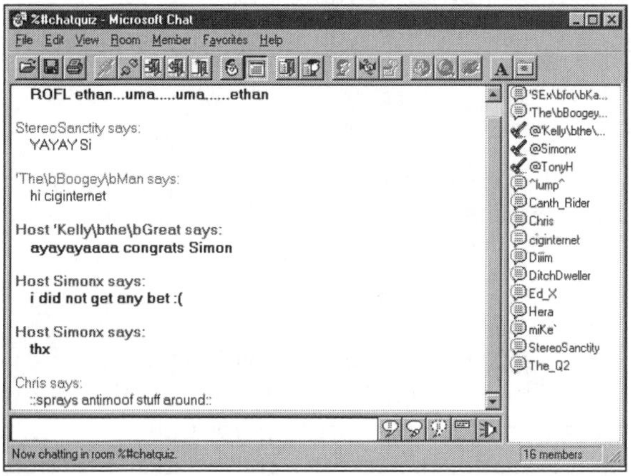

MSN's chat system can work in two modes: text only and Comic Chat. You can see the Comic Chat mode later in this chapter.

Commands to Look For

Although the details for using each chat system differ, a number of features are similar in most systems. For example, these features are generally similar (even though the names might vary):

- Who or People Here shows a list of people currently participating in the chat session.
- Invite enables you to invite a participant in the current chat to a private chat room. (On AOL, you send the person an Instant Message.)

- Ignore or Squelch enables you to tell the program to stop displaying messages from a particular user. This command is very useful for shutting up obnoxious chat-room members. (You'll find a lot of them!) It's also a good tool for "tuning out" conversations you don't want to hear.
- Profile allows you to view information about a particular participant, including whatever information that person decided to make public. Some systems allow more information than others, but the information might include a person's email address, interests, real name, and even phone number and address in some systems (although most participants choose *not* to include this information).
- Change Profile or Handle gives you access to the place where you'll change your own information. Some systems let you change your profile from within the Chat program, but on others you might have to select a menu option or command elsewhere.
- Record or Log or Capture usually lets you record a session. (Of course, in most cases you'll want to forget the drivel—oh, there I go again!)
- Preferences enables you to set up how the system works: whether to tell you when people enter or leave the room, for example.
- Kick or Ban are available on some systems if you set up the chat room yourself. Kick allows you to remove someone from the chat room; Ban stops the person from getting back in.

No matter which chat system you use, read the documentation carefully so you can figure out exactly how to get the most out of it.

Pick Your Avatar

The latest thing in chat is the use of graphical systems in which you select an *avatar*, an image that represents you in the chat session. The first figure on the following page shows a room with several avatars, each representing a real-life person, in Club Chat. Selecting an avatar is a simple matter of clicking a button in the top-left portion of the window, and then choosing from a drop-down list box. Then you can type a message in the text box at the bottom and click the **Send** button. You can also choose from a small selection of sounds ("Aaaah," "Joy," "Doh," and other such intellectual utterings).

So far I've heard mixed reactions to these graphical chat systems. Some people say they are awful; some say they're nothing special; some say it's just stuff to get in the way of the chat. Others really like them. Experiment and decide for yourself.

The major online services have avatar chats. For example, Microsoft Network's Comic Chat is a form of avatar chat (see the second figure on the following page). Other avatar chats are available on the Web. Try one of these sites, which have links to a number of chat sites that use avatars:

The Palace (`http://www.palacespace.com/`)

WorldCHAT (`http://www.worlds.net/`)

Although you can reach these sites on the Web, you have to download a special Chat program and then reconnect using that program.

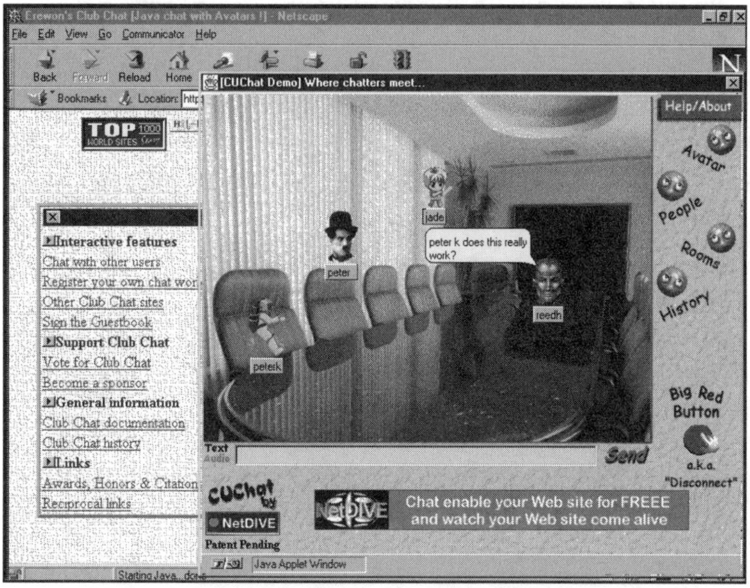

Playing with avatars in Club Chat.

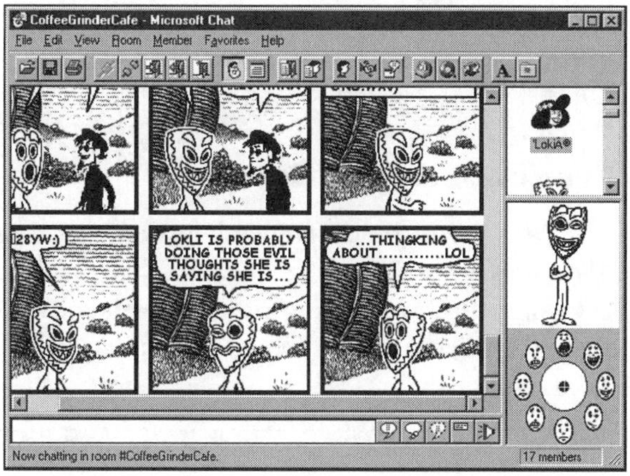

MSN's Comic Chat in action. You can pick your own avatar and even change the avatar's expressions by clicking the box in the lower-right corner.

They're Everywhere!

These avatar chats are now sprouting on the Internet like weeds in my backyard. The Palace software, for instance, allows people to set up their own chats at their own Web sites—and many people have done so already. For more information, see the Palace site (`http://www.palacespace.com/`) or look at Yahoo!'s 3D Worlds information (`http://www.yahoo.com/Recreation/Games/Internet_Games/Virtual_Worlds/3D_Worlds/`).

Web Chat's Coming Up Fast

Most chat participants are still using chat systems running on the online services, but it might not always be that way. Hundreds, perhaps thousands, of Web-based chat systems have sprung up and in some cases are quite good. There are chat sites set up for celebrity "visits," education-related issues, gay chat, skateboarding chat, and more. If you're a chat fan and have been hiding out in the online service chat rooms, perhaps it's time to take a look at the World Wide Web and see what's available. (Here's a good place to start: `http://www.yahoo.com/Computers_and_Internet/Internet/World_Wide_Web/Chat/`.)

Chat Versus Discussion Group

There's a little confusion on the Web about the difference between chat rooms and discussion groups. Some Web sites advertising "chat" actually have Web forums (see Chapter 11, "Yet More Discussion Groups: Mailing Lists and Web Forums"). If the discussion isn't "real time"—you type something, someone immediately responds, you type back—then it's not chat.

Web chat systems vary from the very clunky—your message is displayed within a Web page, which must be constantly rewritten to see the conversation—to the very good. The better sites, such as TalkCity (`http://www.talkcity.com/`), have their own chat programs that you must download before you enter the chat room. These are true chat systems, with the same sort of features as the chat rooms in the online services. You can see an example of the Talk City chat program in the following figure.

Internet Relay Chat: Productivity Sinkhole?

I'll admit I haven't spent a lot of time in Internet Relay Chat (IRC). That's mainly because what few visits I have made have been so uninspiring that I can't think of a good reason to return. But there I go again, slamming a chat system. Many thousands of people really *do* like IRC, so let's take a look at how to use it.

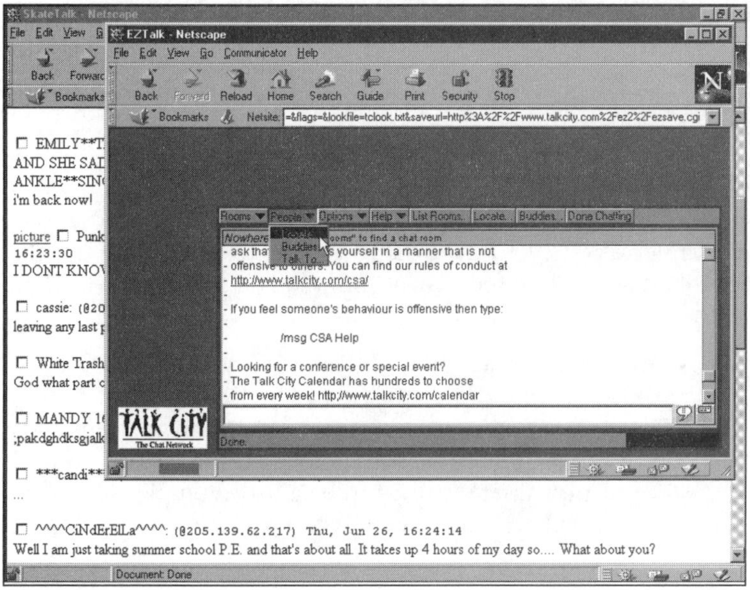

Talk City, one of the Web's more sophisticated chat sites. In the background, you can see a more primitive Web-page type chat system.

Command-Line User?

If you don't have a graphical user interface, you cannot use the fancy IRC programs, of course. You'll have to use a command-line interface to IRC, which is very awkward, but thousands of other people have managed, and you can, too. For help doing this, you can get the IRC chapter from my out-of-print book *The Complete Idiot's Next Step with the Internet* by sending email to `ciginternet@mcp.com` and putting the word **irc** in the Subject line (leave the message body blank). For more information, see Appendix E, "The Email Responder."

Step 1: Get the Software

The first thing you'll need is an IRC *client program*. That's the program you'll use to send and receive IRC communications. If you are using a Macintosh, try Ircle, a well-known IRC program for that operating system. On Windows, you might try mIRC or PIRCH.

Go to the software archives I discuss in Appendix C, "All the Software You'll Ever Need," and download a copy of some kind of IRC program. Then follow the documentation's instructions to set up the program and spend some time reading everything there is to read. Unfortunately, IRC can be a little complicated, if only because it has so many features.

Nicknames

Your nickname is the name by which you will be identified in the chat sessions. Notice that you can remain anonymous in a chat session by entering incorrect information into the Real Name and Email Address boxes.

Step 2: Connect to a Server

The next thing you have to do is connect to an IRC server somewhere. IRC servers are programs run on someone's computer out on the Internet and act as "conduits," carrying information between IRC participants. These servers are the equivalent of the online services' chat forums. At a server, you'll find hundreds of IRC channels that you can choose from.

Find the command that you must use to connect to a server. With mIRC, for instance, the dialog box in the following figure opens automatically when you start the program. You can get back to it later (to select a different server, for example) by choosing **File**, **Setup**.

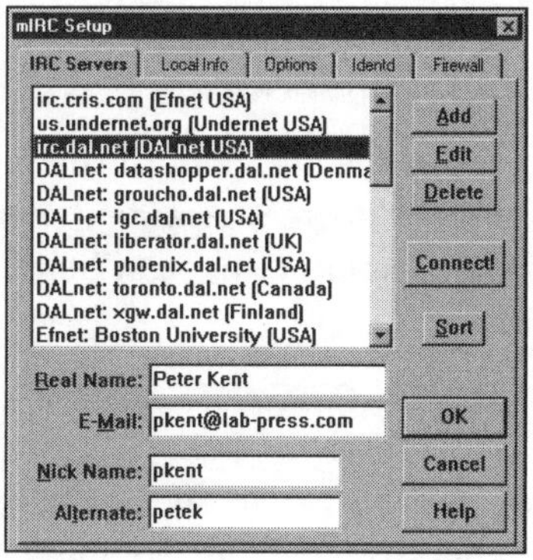

Here's where you choose a server to connect to and enter your personal information in mIRC.

Select the server you want to use, click the **Connect** button, and away you go. You're connected to the server, and a dialog box appears, listing some of the channels (see the next figure). This listing is by no means all the channels; most servers have hundreds. This box holds a list of the ones you are interested in (actually it's initially a list of channels that the programmer thought you might like to start with, but you can add more). To get into one of these channels, double-click it.

If you'd like to see a complete listing of all the channels, close the dialog box, type **/list** in the text box at the bottom of the main window (which is where you type your messages and any IRC commands), and press **Enter**.

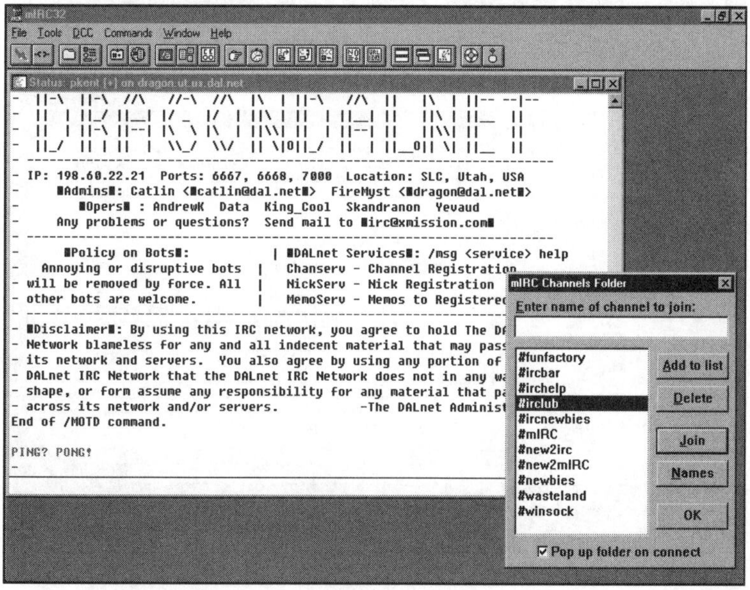

You've connected, and you're ready to join a channel.

Know the Commands

IRC commands begin with a slash (/), and there are loads of them. Most IRC programs hide the commands from you to some degree, providing menu commands instead, but they don't replace all of them. Some things can be done only by using the original typed IRC command.

In mIRC, the **/list** command opens a window in which all the channels are listed. This window might take a while to open because there are so many channels. As you can see in the title bar in the first figure on the following page, this server has 744 channels! If you want to enter one of these channels, all you have to do is double-click it.

After you are in a channel, just start typing; it's much like chatting in any other chat system. In the second figure on the following page, you can see a chat in progress. As usual, you type your message in the little box at the bottom, and you view what's going on in the big panel. The participants are listed on the right side. You can invite one to a private chat by double-clicking a name. You can right-click to see a pop-up menu with a series of commands such as Whois (which displays information about the user in another window).

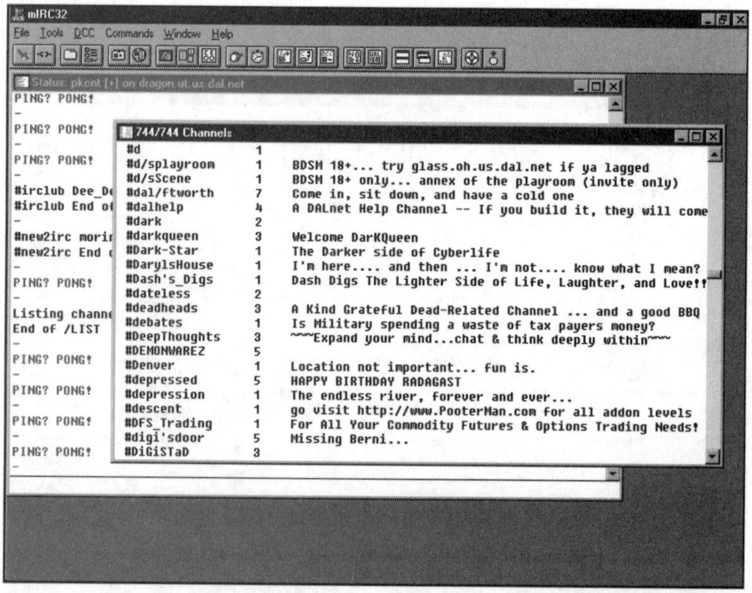

mIRC's channel listing: Are 744 channels enough for you?

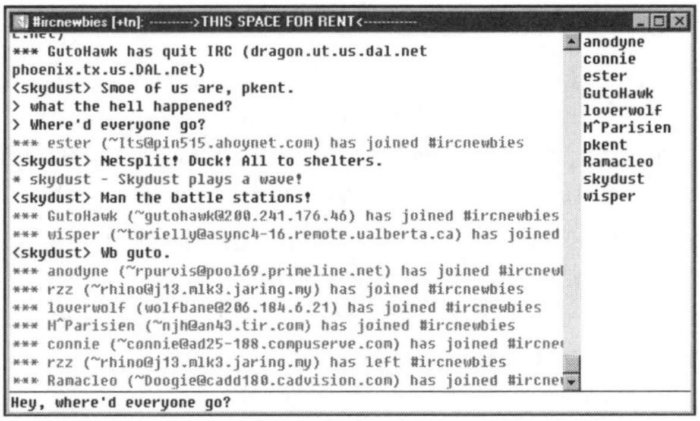

Here's where you chat in mIRC.

There's a lot to learn about IRC. IRC programs are a little complicated because IRC has so many features. For example, you can transmit computer files to other users; people often send pictures to one another. You can also add a special program that reads (with a voice, that is) incoming messages from other chat members, and you can ban, kick, and ignore users (if you open a channel, you have some control over who you let in) and plenty more.

Spend some time playing around with the program you choose to see what it can do, and read the documentation or help files carefully. It's complicated stuff, but after you learn what one program can do, you can pick up how to use one of the others very quickly.

How Many Conversations Can You Keep Going?

IRC is almost a game. People get into multiple chat sessions at once. They chat in the main window, and then they have a few private chat sessions in other windows. That's why it takes them so long to respond sometimes!

What Is It Good For? Real Uses for Chat

It could be argued that chat systems are a complete waste of perfectly good electrons. (*I* wouldn't claim that, of course, but I'm sure many people would.) The chat is often little better than gibberish. "Hey, dude, how goes it? ...Cool man, you?...Yeah, doing well; you chatted with that babe CoolChick, yet?...No, she cute?" Blah...blah...blah. This is neither educational nor particularly interesting.

I should note that not all chats are quite so inane. Chats allow people of like interests to get together in cyberspace, reaching across continents to discuss issues that interest them in a way that would be prohibitively expensive using any other technology. (I've proposed a stupidity tax to make the totally stupid chats prohibitively expensive once again.)

There are other worthwhile uses, too. This list points out a few such scenarios:

- Technical support can be given using chat rooms. This use will become more important as more software is distributed across the Internet. For instance, a small company that, in the past, might have provided support only within the United States can now provide support to the entire world by using chat.
- Companies can use chat systems for keeping in touch. An international company with salespeople throughout the world can arrange weekly "meetings" in a chat room. Families can do the same so that they can keep in touch even when they're separated by thousands of miles.
- Groups that are planning international trips might want to try chat rooms. For instance, if a scout group is traveling to another country to spend the summer with another group, a chat room could provide a way for the leaders to "get together" beforehand to iron out final details.
- Colleges can use chat. Many colleges already provide courses over the Internet, using the Web to post lessons and using email to send in completed assignments. In addition, teachers can use chat to talk with students, regardless of the geographic distance between them.

However, having said all that, chat might eventually be superseded by what's known as Voice on the Net, a system that allows you to place "phone calls" across the Internet and even have conference calls (see Chapter 14). International phone rates have dropped tremendously in the last couple of years, making connecting by typing less attractive than it used to be.

What About Talk?

I mentioned *talk* earlier in this chapter, and then pretty much ignored it. Talk, you'll remember, is a system that allows two people to get together and chat privately online; no need to go to a chat site, you just open your talk program and begin typing.

In the UNIX world—and in the early days, the Internet was firmly entrenched in the UNIX world—talk is widely available and frequently used. (There are two popular UNIX talk programs, imaginatively named *talk* and *ntalk*.) But very few Internet users have installed talk on their Windows or Macintosh systems—in fact, most have no idea what this system is.

You can still find talk programs, though. In fact, talk seems to be undergoing a renaissance, as a number of good talk programs have been introduced recently and promoted by large companies. America Online recently launched *AOL Instant Messenger*, a talk system that allows any Internet user to talk with any other Internet user. AOL members already have Instant Messenger installed (as long as they're using the latest AOL software). Other Internet users can download the software from the AOL Web site (`http://www.aol.com/`).

Yahoo! has a similar program, called *Yahoo! Pager*. You'll need a Yahoo! email account to use this system, but the account is free. (Yahoo! is apparently attempting to justify its $5.4 billion market capitalization by launching services and programs that used to be created by shareware programmers working in basements.) You can download this system from `http://pager.yahoo.com/pager/` (you can see Yahoo! Pager in the following illustration). Remember, though, that whatever system you choose, the people you want to talk to have to use the same system.

Other talk programs are available; you can find them in the software sites mentioned in Appendix C. I used to recommend that people try out a few and see which they prefer, and then tell their friends to download the same one. But it's probably a good idea to work with one of the major systems, such as AOL Instant Messenger or Yahoo! Pager, because they're now in wide use.

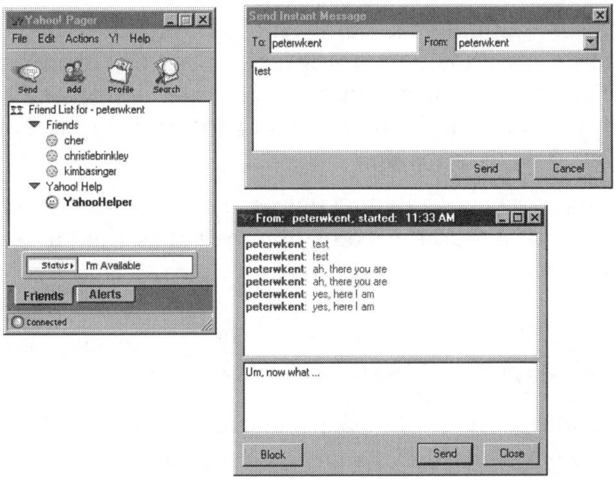

Yahoo! Pager allows you to send a message to one of your friends; when the friend receives the message, a chat window opens and you can continue in a chat session. I don't have any friends, so I'm talking to myself in this illustration.

ICQ (Figure It Out)

ICQ is a talk phenomenon in its own right. Started by a small group of Israeli programmers, in 1998 ICQ was bought by AOL for $287 million, with productivity bonuses that might push the deal over $400 million. It certainly is a great program, but it's far more than just a talk or chat program. It does allow both talk and chat—you can have private or public communication sessions. But it also allows you to send notes that will pop up on people's screens, send files—simply drag a file and drop it onto the recipient's name, and away it goes—launch other programs when files arrive, tell people to telephone you, and so on.

It's a fantastic "collaboration tool," an ideal program for when you're working with people and need to be in constant contact, yet they're somewhere else. You can create a sort of virtual office, with people spread around the world, and constantly share information and ideas. You can even see whether your colleagues are available, as you can set an indicator to show whether you're out for lunch, currently at your computer, or whatever.

It works like this. When you get an ICQ account, you add other ICQ users to your list—you'll add the ICQ accounts of the other people you plan to work with, for instance. Then you'll see little indicators in the ICQ window showing that status of these other ICQ accounts. Sally might have set her ICQ program to show that she's Away; Fred might have set his to show Extended Away; John might have set his to Occupied (Urgent Messages), so he doesn't want to be disturbed by trivia, but he's there if you really need him; Gill might not have logged on yet, so she's shown as Offline, and so on.

So you can see exactly who's available, and what you can do. By clicking on their names and selecting procedures, you can send them messages, initiate a chat (or talk) session, transfer files to them, send notes asking them to call you, and various other things. In fact, there are so many features in this thing that the company even publishes a book explaining how to use it all—this is no dumb chat program.

The product's free, too. (I haven't quite figured out what sort of productivity bonuses you can have when the product doesn't cost anything, and there's no advertising being sold on the system.) You can download it from `http://www.icq.com/` (a horribly complicated Web site, by the way; they're throwing *way* too much information at you at one go). A great system, well worth a look.

Oh, before we leave this chapter—have you figured out what ICQ stands for? Say the letters slowly, then try them fast. Listen to the words that the letters seem to represent, and you'll figure it out.

The Least You Need to Know

- A *chat* system allows participants to take part in public discussions or to move to private "rooms" if they prefer. A *talk* system is a direct link between participants in a conversation, without the need for a public chat room.
- Neither chat nor talk uses voices; you type messages and send them to and from.
- Chat sessions are often very crude and sexually orientated; if you're easily offended, pick your chat room carefully.
- All the online services have popular chat systems. Many Web sites have chat rooms, too.
- If you want to use Internet Relay Chat, you'll have to download an IRC program from a shareware site and then connect across the Internet to a server.
- For a really high-powered chat system that will do just about anything, try ICQ: `http://www.icq.com/`.
- You can use chat rooms to keep in touch with friends, family, or colleagues or to meet new people.

Chapter 14

Internet Conferences: Voice on the Net, Whiteboards, and More

In This Chapter

- International calls for 5 cents a minute
- Getting phone software
- Connecting to a "server" and finding someone to talk to
- Text transmission, whiteboards, conferencing, and more
- Connecting to domestic phone systems from the Internet
- Videoconferencing and other weird stuff

You've already seen a few ways that the Internet allows you to communicate with friends, family, and colleagues. You can use email (Chapter 2, "The Premier Internet Tool: Email"), and you can use chat and talk (Chapter 13, "Yak, Yak, Yak: Chatting in Cyberspace"). But these systems are a little clunky. Most people alive today grew up in the telephone age; we're used to picking up a phone and *talking* to people. And although Internet programmers like to use cute names such as chat and talk, the fact is that these programs *don't* use real chat and don't use real talk; they use typing.

So now I have some good news for you (and some bad news). The good news is that there *is* a system that allows you to really talk across the Internet. The bad news? There's a good chance you'll never use it (at least not anytime soon) because of its disadvantages.

A year or two ago talking on the Internet—known as VON, or Voice on the Net—was set to be the Next Big Thing. But as we've seen elsewhere in this book, Next Big

Things sometimes don't work out (see Chapter 8, "Push Information to Your Desktop," for instance; Push seems to have given up trying to be big). I'm embarrassed to admit that I called it the next big thing, even though I was aware of the problems. Still, VON *is* available, and some people do use it—and little by little it does appear to be turning into something big—so let's take a closer look.

The Incredible Potential of Voice on the Net

A few years ago, I wrote a book with my brother. Because he's in England and I'm in the U.S., I knew we'd be spending a lot of time on the phone—and that worried me. If I had to pay 80 cents a minute, my phone bill was going to skyrocket. So I decided to look into Voice on the Net.

I figured that if I could communicate across the Internet rather than using the phone, I'd save a fortune. With an online service charging $19.95 for unlimited access, my calls would be essentially free. (Internet access in England is much more expensive, but, hey, that's his problem.) Even if I used a service in which I was paying by the hour, it would probably, at that time, have been around $1.00 an hour, less than 2 cents a minute.

Can you see the potential now? Do you have relatives in Russia, Australia, or France? You can cut your costs to the bone, or you can spend the same amount of money but talk for a much longer time than you ever really wanted to. Similarly, if you run a business with offices around the world, you can connect the offices' networks to the Internet, get everyone a sound card and a mike, and spend the money you save on a new Mercedes.

But it gets even better. Imagine that someone created a special program that would allow phone calls across the Internet to be connected to real phone lines. A computer hooked up to the phone lines in, say, London could accept Internet calls from anywhere in the world, connect them to the phone system, and allow Internet users to make *domestic* calls within the United Kingdom. Such a system already exists, although perhaps the theory's better than the reality; we'll look at this sort of service a little later in this chapter.

Internet phones can carry more than just voice. They can also carry text and even doodles; some even allow you to transfer computer files at the same time you speak. So while you are talking to someone, you can be transmitting the text of a memo or sketching something or sending a photograph. Internet phones are a very powerful tool you're going to be seeing a lot of very soon.

The Downside

That's the theory. Now for the facts. I never did use VON to communicate with my brother while working on that book; the disadvantages outweighed the advantages. The phone companies are in no imminent danger of going out of business.

First, many people don't have computers. Fewer still have the sort of equipment required to use a VON system (you'll learn about the hardware requirements in a moment). Even fewer people want to call someone who *also* has the necessary equipment. Then consider these other problems:

- The calls don't provide high-quality sound. You will *not* hear a pin dropping at the other end of one of these lines!
- They are inconvenient. Because few people spend all day connected to the Internet, you'd have to arrange a call in many cases. (Still, in the early days of the telephone, that's just what people did. They arranged a time to go to the drugstore and rent time on the phone, and their relatives on the other side of the country, or the world, did the same. In many parts of the world, that's still how people use telephones.)
- Currently there are still a few compatibility problems; you have to make sure you're both using compatible software, and there are several different transmission systems.

Can You Hold Back Technology?

Although the phone companies will not be going out of business anytime soon, some are still worried enough to try to ban Internet phones or force companies providing VON services to follow the same rules as true telecommunications companies. They reason, quite logically perhaps, that if a company provides international phone service, it doesn't matter whether it's over the Internet or through a phone company—the rules should be the same. At one point, a small group of telecommunications companies tried to get the use of Internet phones banned.

They've given up on that. Apart from the fact that this is similar to a group of horse-drawn carriage manufacturers trying to ban the newfangled automobile, it's hard to see how you can ban this kind of technology. Even if you ban it in the United States, foreign companies will still sell it across the Internet. If we're going to do that, perhaps we should ban international credit card transactions or close our cyberborders. (For more discussion on this issue, see Chapter 24, "The Future of the Internet.") More recently, the phone companies have encouraged the courts to force companies that are routing phone calls across the Internet to play by the same rules as the established long-distance companies (and there's a good chance they'll succeed).

Here's another problem for Internet phone calls. The price for long-distance telephone calls has been dropping precipitously for several years and seems likely to continue. I used to pay 80 cents a minute to call from the United States to the United Kingdom, but now I pay 16 cents, any time of day or night. And pressure seems to be lower still, with companies advertising rates around 10 cents a minute on weekends. With prices this low, VON systems are going to have to improve dramatically before many people will use them.

In 1996, it appeared that the use of VON software was about to increase exponentially, because the major online services claimed that they were about to provide it to their subscribers. They didn't. Perhaps when America Online locked up entirely under the stress of millions of new users, it realized that allowing people to transmit *voice* across the network wasn't such a good idea. (Transmitting a voice signal is what could be regarded as a "high bandwidth" process; that is, it uses up a lot of network time.) If it had trouble transmitting everyone's email and files and chat sessions, what would happen when eight million people started *talking*? So, for the moment, the VON revolution is on hold partly because the online services are not prepared to provide it to their users. But consider this; as more people start using fast Internet connections—cable and ADSL—all of a sudden VON becomes much more attractive again, because quality will increase. And a number of changes in technology are making VON more attractive.

Do You Have the Hardware You Need?

Full-Duplex Versus Half-Duplex

If you have a full-duplex card, both you and the other person can talk at the same time. The card can record your voice at the same time it's playing incoming sounds. If you have only a half-duplex card, you'll have to take turns talking (like people talking over the radio in those old war movies: "Joe, you there? Over").

The idea of working with VON might sound interesting, but there's a small hurdle you have to leap first. Do you have the right equipment?

To even consider using Internet phones, you'll need a fairly new computer. Not necessarily top of the line, but not an old piece of junk, either. If you have a PC, it generally has to be a 486 or better (requirements vary depending on the software you are using). If you have a Macintosh, you'll probably need a Quadra, Performa, or Power PC (some of these programs run only on the Power PC). On any platform, you'll also need a reasonable amount of RAM—probably a bare minimum of 8MB, preferably 16MB or more. But as I always say, you can never have too much money, too much time off, or too much RAM.

Next, you'll need a connection to the Internet, and it should be either a fast network connection (the ideal, of course) or a dial-in direct connection (SLIP or PPP). If you have a dial-in connection, you'll want at least a 28,800bps modem; but your calls will undoubtedly sound better with a 33,600bps modem or faster.

You need a sound card, of course. Be sure that it's a 16-bit card or better and that it also allows you to record (some don't). Ideally, you need a *full-duplex* card. Check the card's specifications (on the box) when you buy it to see whether it's full-duplex. You also need a microphone and speakers or perhaps a headset. Most new computers come with all the equipment you need. But if your computer is three or four years old, you might not have what you need.

Finally, you need the software. That's easy enough to come by, but the big catch is that you have software that uses the same system for transmitting the voice signals as the software used by the person you want to call. That shouldn't be a problem anymore; early in 1998, the H.323 protocol was finally accepted as the industry standard for VON, so pretty much all VON programs should be able to communicate with all other VON programs.

Which Program Should I Use?

Some of the top products are Internet Phone (Vocaltec), Netscape Communicator Conference (previously known as Netscape CoolTalk), and NetMeeting (Microsoft). Internet Phone and NetMeeting have reputations as being a couple of the best products. Conference is important because it's included with Netscape Communicator, so millions of people have it available (although relatively few use it, and Netscape has dropped the product from recent versions of Communicator—if you don't already have it, you won't be able to download it from Netscape anymore). Follow these directions to get your hands on one or all these products:

- **Internet Phone** From an Israeli company called VocalTec, the Internet Phone is available for download from `http://www.vocaltec.com/`.
- **Net2Phone** As with Internet Phone, this product can be used to call not only other Internet-connected PCs, but real phones around the world: `http://www.net2phone.com/`.
- **NetMeeting** Microsoft's Internet phone system is built into Windows 98 and some versions of Internet Explorer. You can download it from the Microsoft site at `http://www.microsoft.com/netmeeting/`.

You can find other products by going to Yahoo! and searching for **internet voice** (see Chapter 17). Or go to the Voice on the Net page at `http://www.von.com/`. Many such products are available as shareware, commercial products, and give-it-away-ware. You'll find WebPhone (NetSpeak), FreeTel, DigiPhone (Third Planet Publishing),

PowWow (Tribal Voice), and others. However, note that this is another area of Internet software that is actually shrinking, as companies stop developing products thanks to the overwhelming lack of interest in VON on the part of general public. One of the top products, TeleVox, is no longer supported by the manufacturer, for instance.

Working with Your Phone Program

Let's take a look at how to work with one of these VON systems. I'll assume that you have your sound card and microphone properly installed—that's one can of worms I'm *not* crawling into! I'll also assume that you've installed some sort of phone program and have run through the setup (so it already has all your personal information that it needs, such as your name, Internet email address, and so on).

Give-It-Away-Ware?

The Internet is full of stuff that is simply given away. Some VON products are free; some are not. NetMeeting comes with Windows 98 or can be downloaded from the Microsoft site. Internet Phone and Net2Phone are not free, although you can get free demo versions.

The next question is, to quote Ghostbusters, *Who ya gonna call?* Yes, I know, you were so excited about the idea of making phone calls on the Internet that you went ahead and installed everything you need. But you haven't quite persuaded your siblings or your mad Aunt Edna to do the same. So you have *nobody* to call. Don't worry; you'll find someone.

All the software companies have set up servers to which you can connect to find someone else who, just like you, is all dressed up with nowhere to go. For instance, if you are using VocalTec's Internet Phone, you'll automatically connect to a server when you start the program. This system is based on "chat rooms"—hundreds of them. (You can create your own room, so the actual number fluctuates.) These chat rooms are not like the chat rooms we looked at in Chapter 13. Rather, they are places where people can "congregate" and then choose to "pair off" in voice conversations. You can create your own private chat room at a predefined time, for instance, to meet friends or colleagues.

Porn Raises Its Ugly Head

These phone servers have turned into yet another sex channel. Many of the chat rooms at the VocalTec Global OnLine Directory are set up for people who want to get involved in cybersex, enhanced with voice and video.

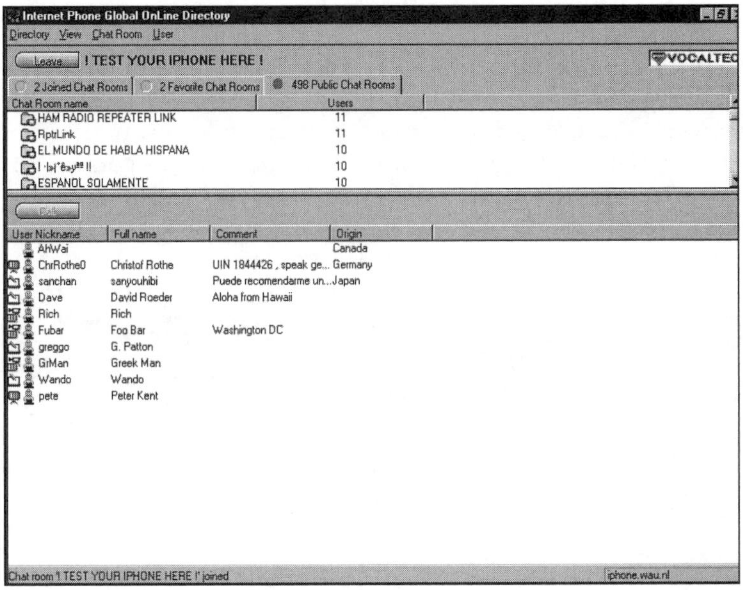

VocalTec's Global OnLine Directory helps you find other Internet Phone users.

To connect to someone in a chat room, click a name and then click the **Call** button. Go ahead; don't be shy. Of course, someone else might try to connect to you first; you'll hear a beep to inform you that someone is trying to call you. You might have the program set up to accept all incoming calls automatically (in Internet Phone, you do that by using the **Phone**, **AutoAnswer** command), or you might have to click a button to accept a call.

Internet Phone at work; you can quickly connect with someone in a chat room and begin talking. (If you're using video, the large picture panel will show the other person.)

The Conference Server

These Internet phone servers all work differently. Conference has a directory available on a Web site; just click the **Web Phonebook** button in the Conference window, or select **Communicator**, **Web Phonebook** (you can see an example of this directory in the following figure). Find the person you want to talk to and click his name. The Conference installation program automatically configures CoolTalk as a Netscape Navigator viewer (see Chapter 7, "Web Multimedia"), so when you click a name in the Web page, Conference opens and tries to contact the other person.

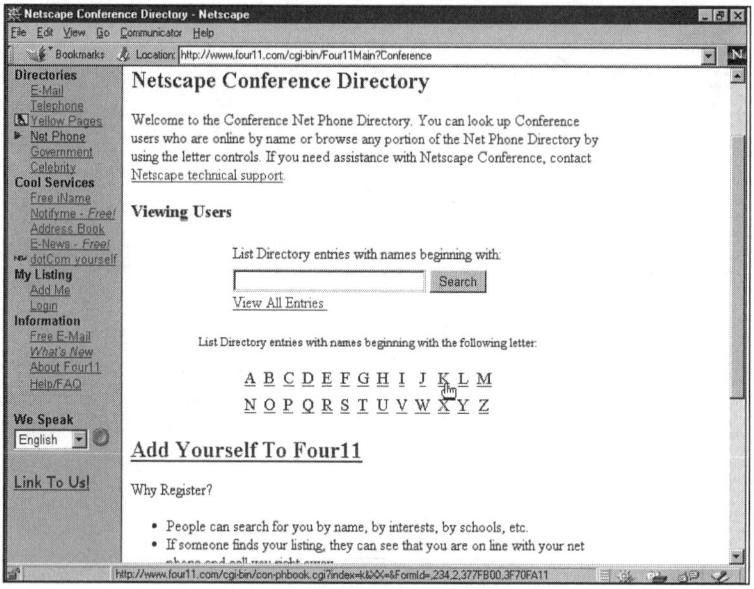

Netscape Conference's Web directory.

Now You Get to Talk

Some of these servers enable you to create new "rooms." You can create private rooms and use these as sort of meeting rooms for your friends and colleagues. Or perhaps you have to just click a person and then a **Call** button or something similar to connect to that person. You'll have to read the program's documentation to figure this out; there are as many different ways to connect as there are programs.

When you are talking, you might find that the sound is a bit warbly. That's okay, though. You might be speaking with someone on the other side of the world for a tiny fraction of what you'd pay your friendly phone company. What do you want? Low cost *and* quality?

If you are both using full-duplex modems, you can probably just talk as if you are on the phone. Otherwise, you might have to take turns speaking, clicking a button to turn your mike on and off. (The button is the equivalent of saying "over.")

Nothing Better to Do?

Connect to one of these servers (not the Conference one, but one of the servers with people connected) and just wait. Every now and then you'll get a call. It's a kind of magical mystery phone session, not knowing who's going to call next. Where does he live? What does she do? Can she get her microphone working? What's the chance he'll be able to hear you?

Your Address Is Not Always the Same

Most dial-in users don't have permanent TCP/IP host addresses. When you connect to your service provider, you are assigned a temporary host address, so the next time you connect you might get a different address. That means it's often difficult to configure voice programs to call other users directly.

If a computer is connected to a network and has a permanent TCP/IP address, then everything's fine; the TCP/IP address is used as the "telephone number." If a computer gets a different address each time it connects, you have to use one of several possible methods. For instance, you can use the phone servers' private rooms as meeting places by arranging to call someone at a particular time and using the room as a way to make the connection.

With some systems, you might also be able to connect by using an email address. The program looks up the email address in an online directory, and then finds the corresponding TCP/IP number and uses that to connect. Netscape Conference can use this system, for instance; each time you start Conference, it connects to the directory and "registers" your email address so it will be available to any callers.

The Bells and Whistles

Internet phone products offer more than just voice connections. You might want to look for some of the following features in an Internet phone system:

- **An answering machine** Some products, such as Conference, have built-in answering machines. If someone tries to contact you while you are not there, your "answering machine" takes a message. Of course, this feature works only if your computer is online. Although it's very useful for people with permanent network connections, it's not nearly as useful for people who dial into a service provider (although a lot of us these days leave our computers permanently connected to the Internet across the telephone line, which irritates the phone companies to no end).

- **Type-while-you-talk capability** This feature can be very handy. You can send text messages at the same time you are talking. For example, you can send small memos or copy parts of an email message you're discussing. If you are working on a project with the other person, you might find it convenient to send to-do lists or schedules back and forth. Authors working together can send materials to each other, programmers can send bits of the code they are discussing, and so on. The following figure shows one system in which you can write as you talk.
- **Image transmission** Related to the business-card feature and to the whiteboard feature (discussed in a moment) is the capability to send a picture while you're talking. If you haven't seen Aunt Natasha in Siberia for a while, she can send a picture of the kids while you are chatting.
- **Conferencing** Why speak to just one person when you can talk to a whole crowd? Some of these programs let you set up conferences, so a whole bunch of you can gab at once. (If you think VON is clunky with one person talking, wait until you try talking to several people at the same time.)

Conference's "Chat" window lets you type messages while you talk.

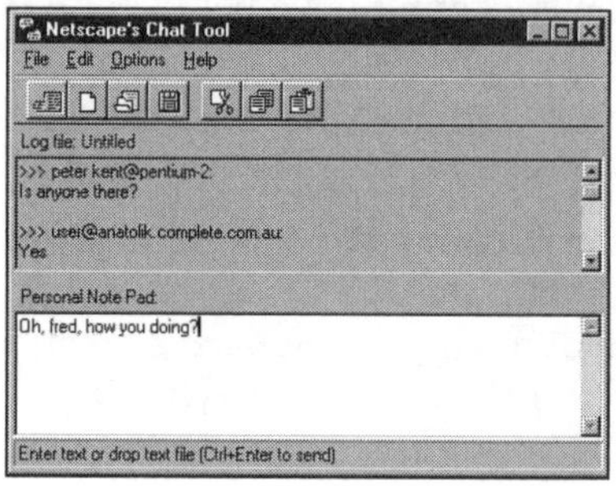

- **Group Web surfing** Only a few programs have this odd feature. The people connected via the program, in some cases a whole bunch of people, can go on group Web surfs together. When one person clicks a Web link, the other participants' Web browsers update to show the new page. This feature is in Netscape Conference and PowWow (`http://www.tribal.com/`).
- **Web-page indicator** You can automatically add an icon to your Web page showing whether you are online and able to accept calls (another neat PowWow feature).
- **Whiteboards** A whiteboard is one of those big white chalkboard-type things you see in conference rooms. A whiteboard feature functions similarly to the type-while-you-talk feature previously mentioned. Instead of typing something, though, you are using a sort of doodle pad. You can sketch something, and it's transmitted to the person at the other end. You can even use this feature to send pictures; you can open the file in the whiteboard so the person at the other end can see it. Conference's whiteboard appears in the next figure.

- **Change your voice** TeleVox has a VoiceFonts feature that enables you to completely change the way your voice sounds during a phone conversation. Neat feature. On the other hand, TeleVox is no longer available, and I haven't seen another product with this feature (although if you have a really slow computer and a really slow connection, your voice is going to sound weird, anyway!).
- **Connecting voice to your Web page** You can put links in your Web pages that, when clicked, open the user's Voice program so he can talk with you. This feature is for real geeks who rarely leave their computers. (You *do* have Web pages, don't you? See Chapter 20, "Setting Up Your Own Web Site," to find out how to create them.)

Unfortunately, it's not a perfect world, so not all voice programs have all these neat features. You'll just have to find the features that are most important to you and go with the program that has those features.

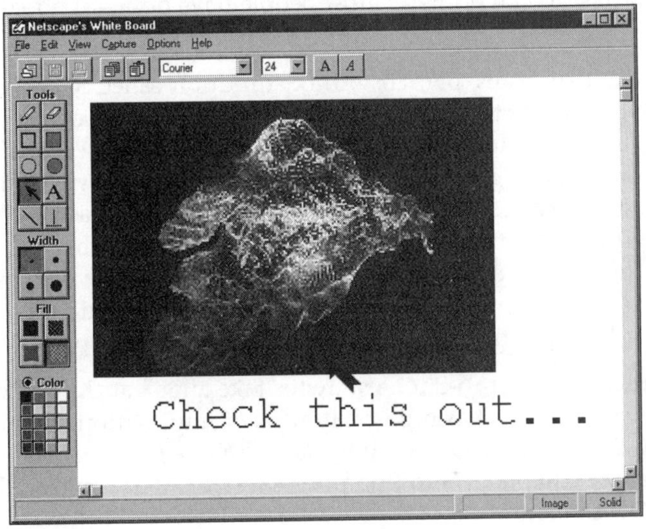

A whiteboard feature lets you send a picture while talking.

Internet-to-Phone Connections

One of the most intriguing uses of Internet conferences is the capability to connect to a computer across the Internet and route onto the local phone service. So you might connect across the Internet from New York to Sydney and be connected to the Australian phone system, which means you can make international calls at very low rates. A number of these services are available already because the VON software publishers, wanting to make their products as useful as possible, have provided them. Net2Phone, for instance (`http://www.net2phone.com/`), and Vocaltec (`http://www.vocaltec.com/`) both provide this service for users of their programs. Some of these services take it one step further. They provide long-distance service from any phone across the Internet. Call from your home phone, and the call is routed across the Internet, for instance. (Rates will be higher to use your own phone than if you're using a computer.)

The problem is, at least from the point of view of the VON software companies, that since VON first appeared on the Internet, real-world phone rates have dropped. For instance, with Net2Phone I could call the United Kingdom for 10 cents a minute. But MCI will let me use a real phone for 10 cents a minute—only 9 cents on Sundays. Net2Phone charges $1.20 to call Afghanistan (comparable to some long-distance companies—I've seen $1.17—although much less than MCI), 34 cents to call Brazil (one phone company I looked at charges 41 cents), and 10 cents to call France (one company I found charges only 8 cents a minute). In some cases, VON services will be worthwhile; if you need to spend a lot of time on the phone to a country that is in a very expensive call area, you might want to look into using one of these VON services. And if you're making calls from countries other than the United States (U.S. rates are very low compared to other countries), then using one of these services might be a good idea. Otherwise, I suspect you'll do what most people have done—ignored VON.

There is another way to make these calls, perhaps. An organization called Free World Dialup II (`http://www.pulver.com/fwd/`) is dedicated to providing free access to phone systems around the world. (Note, however, that Free World Dialup I faded away, so this is the second attempt to get this going, and the Web site doesn't provide information on how to use the service.) This organization says that it has a handful of gateways spread around the world, from Athens to Hong Kong, but it's hard to see how this system can grow, because so many problems are involved. Why would anyone give away free access to a phone system, especially in a country in which the phone company charges for local phone calls (and that's most countries)?

For more information on these Internet-to-Phone systems, take a look at the Voice on the Net page (`http://www.von.com/`). It has links to all sorts of information about Internet-to-Phone products and projects. Or search for *long distance phone* at your favorite Web search engine (see Chapter 17) to find phone services that could well be cheaper and easier than VON services.

Video and Other Weird Stuff

The next step is to add video to the "phone" conversations. The phone companies have been talking about a true video phone for 40 years, but it took the Internet to bring it about. Video has already been added to some of these VON products. As you saw earlier, VocalTec's Internet Phone has a video window.

Mind you, this step is a much bigger one than putting voice on the Internet. Voice is fairly simple. There is not too much data involved in transmitting sounds, relatively speaking. The problem with video, though, is bandwidth. The term *bandwidth* refers to the amount of information that can be transmitted across a connection. A 28,800bps connection has greater bandwidth than does a 14,400bps connection, for instance. Video images contain a lot of information, and you want the information right away. After all, video makes sense only if it's in motion. So a number of compromises have to be made. The images are small, are low-resolution, and have few individual images each second. Thus, video transmitted across the Internet can often be blurry and shaky. Unless you really need it, you might find that the novelty soon wears off.

Personally, I don't think video on the Internet will catch on for a few more years—not until very high-speed connections are cheap and widely available. You also need a fast computer, of course. For now, video is limited to companies with network connections or the few individuals lucky enough to have cable or ADSL connections. However, that hasn't stopped a variety of companies from selling video software for use on the Internet. (And guess what's the real growth area for video on the Internet? Live sex shows and cybersex, of course!)

These products are generally thought of as video-conferencing products, but the principle is the same: real time communications across the Internet between two or more people. Go back to the Voice on the Net site (`http://www.von.com/`), and you'll find information about this, too.

The best-known product is Cu-SeeMe ("see you, see me," get it? Yeah, yeah). This product is so well known in the computer business that it's becoming a generic term, in the same way that *Hoover* is a generic term for vacuum cleaners. You can see a demo of this product at work at `http://www.wpine.com/`.

Other telecommunications systems will be added to the Internet soon. How about getting your faxes and voice mail connected to your email system? If you live in the United States but do business in the United Kingdom, you can have a phone line set up in London. Your customers can call and leave voice mail for you or can fax you at that number, and your messages can then be compressed and attached to an email message that is sent to you! You can have a number in New York, London, or Atlanta, or you can have a U.S. toll-free number. You'll even get the graphics in your faxes sent to you. See JFAX at `http://www.jfax.net/` for more information about this. And keep your eyes open for other weird and wonderful telecommunications/Internet hybrid services.

The Least You Need to Know

- You can connect to other users and actually talk on the Internet at a fraction of the cost of long-distance or international calls.
- New Internet-to-phone system servers are being set up, which will enable you to connect across the world on the Internet, and then call someone using another country's domestic phone system.
- The phone software is plentiful and often cheap or even free. Check out the Web site `http://www.von.com/` for sources.
- Most companies have set up servers to which you can connect and find someone to talk to; test the system before you make the rest of your family use it.
- Some companies now provide Internet-to-Phone connections, allowing you to make calls across the Internet and connect to a real phone.
- Many useful features are available in some products. You can send text or pictures while you talk, talk to a group of people, or even go on group Web trips.
- Video phones are available, but they require fast connections to the Internet to work well.

Chapter 15

What on Earth Are All Those File Types?

In This Chapter

- About the directory (folder) system
- Picking a download directory
- File extensions and file types
- File types you'll run into
- What are compressed files?
- Working with compressed and archive files
- Avoiding viruses

It's possible to work with a computer for years without really understanding directories and file types. I know people who simply save files from their word processor (the only program they ever use) "on the disk." *Where on the disk?* Well, you know, on the hard disk. *Yes, but where? Which directory?* Well, you know, where the program saves the files.

You can get away with this lack of knowledge if you use only one program and don't use it too much. But if you plan to spend any time on the Internet and plan to make the most of your time there, you'll need to understand a bit more about files and directories. You'll come across a plethora of file types, and it helps if you understand what you are looking at.

About Download Directories

I don't want to spend a lot of time explaining what a directory is. This is very basic computing stuff, and if you don't understand it, you should probably read an introduction to computing (such as *The Complete Idiot's Guide to PCs* by Joe Kraynak). However, I'll quickly explain it, and that might be enough.

You can think of a directory as an area on your hard disk that stores computer files. You might think of it as a file folder in a filing cabinet. The hard disk is the filing cabinet, holding dozens, maybe hundreds, of folders (directories). In some graphical user interfaces, such as recent versions of Microsoft Windows and the Macintosh, directories are actually called *folders*. (But I've been using the term *directory* too long to give it up now.)

If you look inside a filing cabinet and open a file folder, what do you find? Documents—those are the individual files. You might also find another folder within the first folder. That's a *subdirectory*. So directories can contain files and other directories, and those directories can contain more files and more directories (more subdirectories), and so on. Therefore, you have what is known as the directory tree. (The following figure shows what this "tree" looks like.) The point of this system is to help you organize your files. It's not uncommon for today's computers to have thousands of files, tens of thousands even. If you don't organize this lot logically, you'll end up with a mess that will make the Gordian knot look simple.

Directories Are Not Areas of the Hard Disk!

Before you email me saying that a directory is *not* an area on your hard disk, let me say *I know that!* It just *appears* to be an area on your hard disk. Computer files are spread across the disk in an apparently illogical and disorganized manner—a piece of a file here, a piece there. The directory system is a visual way to organize the files to make the hard disk easier to use.

The disk says, "I have a directory here that contains these files." But that's a lie, because the files are scattered all over the place. But it doesn't matter. It's rather like a child who *swears* that he has tidied up his room, that his socks are in the dresser and his shoes are in the closet. They're not, of course; everything's scattered over the floor. But you really don't want to look inside because it will just upset you. So you accept it and think in terms of where things *should be* within the room, without wanting to see the truth. Don't worry about the technical details; directories contain files, and that's all you need to know.

Folders within folders within folders make up the directory tree, shown here in the Norton File Manager program.

A *download directory* is a directory into which you download a file. Let's say that you are using your Web browser to download a shareware program from one of the libraries listed in Appendix C, "All the Software You'll Ever Need." Where is that file saved? By definition, it's downloaded into the download directory. What is the download directory named? It might be called DOWNLOAD, but it could be anything; the download directory is whichever directory you tell the program to put the file in.

The directory chosen by the browser as the download directory is not always the best place to put the file. In many cases, it's a lousy choice. Internet Explorer, for instance, wants to place downloaded files on the Windows *desktop*. (In Windows 95, 98, and NT, the desktop is a special subdirectory of the WINDOWS or WINNT directory; anything placed inside that directory will appear on the desktop, which is the area of your computer screen that is visible when all the programs have been closed.) That's often a bad place to put it; if you download a lot of things, your desktop will soon be as cluttered as my office. (And believe me, that's not good.) Of course, you can always move the file to another directory later, but in that case, why not put it where you want it in the first place?

Also, many of the files that you will download are archive files; these files are sort of file "containers." Although an archive file is a single file, it has other files within it, perhaps hundreds of them. When you extract those files, they are generally placed in the same directory. After you extract those files, you no longer have one easily recognized file on your desktop (or in whichever download directory the program chose). You now have dozens or more new files there. Do this with several download files, and you'll soon become confused; which file came from which archive?

Pick a Download Directory Sensibly

When you download files from the Web, FTP, Gopher, your online service, or wherever, think sensibly about where you place the files. Many users create a special directory called *download*. Some programs even do this automatically: Many FTP programs, for instance, create a directory called *download* to be used as the default location for downloaded files. You can place all the downloaded files directly into that directory. Later you can decide what you want to do with each file.

I prefer to go one step further. When I download a file, I think about where I'll eventually want the file. For instance, if it's a document file related to a book I'm working on, I save it directly into one of the directories I've created to hold the book. If it's a program file, I'll have to create a directory to hold the program at some point, so why not create a directory for the program right now and download the file directly into that directory? (Depending on which operating system and program you are using, you might be able to create the directory while you are telling the program where to save the file; or you might have to use some kind of file-management program to create the directory and *then* save the file.)

Learn about directories. Be sure you understand how to find your way around the directory tree (or folder system, as it's known in some operating systems). And be sure you save files in such a manner that you can find them when you need them.

Hidden File Extensions

Windows 95, 98, and NT4 hide the file extensions from you. I think this is particularly stupid, but then, Microsoft didn't ask me before deciding to do this. To see file extensions in Windows 95 and Windows NT, open Windows Explorer and select **View, Options**. Then, under the **View** tab, clear the check box labeled **Hide MS-DOS File Extensions for File Types That Are Registered**. In Windows 98, select **View, Folder Options**. Then, under the **View** tab, clear the check box labeled **Hide File Extensions for Known File Types**.

A Cornucopia of File Formats

Many computer users don't understand the concept of file formats because they never really see any files. They open their word processors, do some work, and then save the file. They might notice that when they give the file a name, the program adds a few letters such as .doc or .wpd at the end, but they don't think much about it. If you're going to be playing on the Net, though, you need to understand just a little about file formats because you'll have to pick and choose the ones you want.

All computer files have one thing in common: They all save information in the form of zeros and ones. The difference between a file created by one word processor and another, or between a file created by a word processor and one created by a graphics program, is in what those zeros and ones *mean*. Just as two languages can use the same basic sounds and string them together to create different words, different programs use the zeros and ones to mean different things. One program uses zeros and ones to create words, another to create sounds, another to create pictures, and so on.

The File Extension

How, then, can computer programs identify one file from another? They can often look for a familiar sequence of zeros and ones at the beginning of a file; if they find it, they know they have the right file. But there's also something called a *file extension* that identifies files, and it has the added advantage of being visible to mere mortals. A file extension is a piece of text at the end of a filename, preceded by a period, that is used to identify the file type. For example, look at this sample filename:

```
THISDOC.TXT
```

The extension is the .txt bit. This extension means the file is a plain text file; any program that can read what is known as ASCII text can open this file and read it.

Different Extensions, Same Format

Some files are identified by two or more file extensions. For instance, the .jpeg extension is often used on UNIX computers to identify a form of graphics file commonly used on the Web. But because Windows 3.1 and DOS can't display four-character extensions, this type of file is often seen with the .jpg extension, different extension, but the same file format. You'll also find HTM and HTML files, TXT and TEXT files, and AIF and AIFF files (sound files).

Now, in most operating systems (including DOS and Windows), file extensions are three characters long; on some operating systems, extensions are three or four characters. Normally, each file has only one file extension. Some operating systems, such as UNIX and Windows 98, for example, allow multiple extensions and extensions with more than three characters, such as THISDOC.NEWONE.TEXT. However, this sort of thing is becoming rare on the Internet these days, and you generally run into only simple three- and four-character extensions.

Macintosh files, by the way, don't require a file extension; rather, an identifier is built into the file, visible to the computer but not to the computer operator. However, note that Macintosh files stored on the Internet often *do* have an extension—.hqx or .sea, for instance. This extension is to make them readily identifiable as Macintosh files by human beings. (I find it amusing that the Mac's programmers, for all the talk of making their computers easy to use, didn't realize how important file extensions are to mere humans.)

You might be thinking that there are probably three or four file formats you need to know about. No, not quite. Try four or five dozen. Table 15.1 gives you a list to get you started.

Table 15.1 File Formats You Should Know

File Format	Type of File It Identifies
ARC	A PKARC file (a DOS compression file).
AU, AIF, AIFF, AIFC, SND	Sound files often used on Macintosh and UNIX systems; Netscape and Internet Explorer can play these sounds.
AVI	Video for Windows.
BMP, PCX	Common bitmap graphics formats.
DOC	Microsoft Word files, from Word for the Macintosh, Word for Windows, and Windows WordPad.
EPS	A PostScript image.
EXE	A program file or a self-extracting archive file.
FLC, FLI, AAS	Autodesk Animator files.
GIF	Graphics files often found in Web pages.
.gzip and .gz	UNIX compressed files.
HLP	Windows Help files.
HTM, HTML	The basic Web document format.
HQX	A BinHex file, a format often used to archive Macintosh files. Programs such as StuffIt Expander can open these files.
JPG, JPEG, JPE	JPEG graphics files, also often found in Web pages.
JFIF, PJPEG, PJP	A few more variations of the JPEG file format.
MID, RMI	MIDI (Musical Instrument Digital Interface) sounds.
MMM	Microsoft Multimedia Movie Player files.
MOV, QT	The QuickTime video format.
MP2	An MPEG audio format.
MP3	A music format that has the music business terrified. It's CD quality, yet takes up only around 1MB for each minute of sound. MP3 files can also include images (CD cover art, for instance), lyrics, artists' bios, and so on.
MPEG, MPG, MPE, M1V	The MPEG (Moving Pictures Experts Group) video formats.

File Format	Type of File It Identifies
PDF	The Portable Document Format, an Adobe Acrobat hypertext file. This format is becoming a very popular means of distributing electronic documents.
.pit	The Macintosh Packit archive format.
PS	A PostScript document.
RAM, RA	RealAudio. This sound format plays while it's being transmitted. Click a link to a RealAudio file, and it begins playing within a few seconds (you don't have to wait until the entire file is transferred).
RTF	Rich Text Format. These word processing files work in a variety of Windows word processors.
.sea	A Macintosh self-extracting archive.
SGML	A document format.
.shar	A UNIX shell archive file.
SIT	The Macintosh StuffIt archive format.
TAR	A UNIX tar archive file.
TIF	A common graphics format.
TSP	TrueSpeech, a sound format similar to RealAudio.
TTF	Windows TrueType font files.
TXT, TEXT	A text file.
WAV	The standard Windows "wave" sound format.
WPD	A WordPerfect document file.
WRI	Windows Write word processing files.
WRL	A VRML (Virtual Reality Modeling Language) 3D object.
XBM	Another graphics file that can be displayed by Web browsers (although it's not used very often these days).
XDM	The StreamWorks WebTV and WebRadio format. This is similar to RealAudio, but it allows the real-time playing of video in addition to sound.
XLS	A Microsoft Excel spreadsheet file.
Z	A UNIX compressed file.
z	A UNIX packed file.
ZIP	A PKZIP archive file (a DOS and Windows compression file), used by many Windows (and even some Macintosh) compression utilities.
.zoo	A zoo210 archive format available on various systems.

Is that all? By no means! Netscape currently claims that it has 176 plug-ins. Although many of these duplicate the functions of other plug-ins, handling the same file types, this number still represents a lot of different file formats. There are all sorts of file formats out there; to be honest, though, you'll run across only a few of them. You might never even run across some of the ones I included in the table; for instance, the .ARC format, which used to be very common in the shareware world, is now quite rare.

File Compression Basics

As you can see from the preceding table, a number of these file formats are archive or compressed formats. These are files containing other files within them. You can use a special program to extract those files; or in the case of a "self-extracting archive," the file can automatically extract the files within it.

Is It Possible?

This is similar to Dr. Who's Tardis, which has much more space *inside* than would be allowed within a box of that size according to normal physics. And, no, I don't plan to explain how it's done. Suffice it to say that, thanks to a little magic and nifty computing tricks, these programs make files smaller.

Why do people bother to put files inside archive files? Or even, in some cases, a single file within an archive file? Two reasons. First, the programs that create these files often compress the files being placed inside, so the single file is much smaller than the combined size of all the files inside. You can reduce files to as little as 2% of their normal size, depending on the type of file and the program you use (although 40% to 75% is probably a more normal range). Bitmap graphics, for instance, often compress to a very small size; program files and Windows Help files can't be compressed so far. If you want to transfer a file across the Internet, it's a lot quicker to transfer a compressed file than an uncompressed file.

The other reason to use these systems is that you can place files inside another file as a sort of packaging or container. If a shareware program has, say, 20 different files that it needs in order to run, it's better to wrap all these into one file than to expect people to transfer all 20 files one at a time.

Archive Versus Compressed

What's the difference between an archive file and a compressed file? They're often the same thing, and people (including me) tend to use the terms interchangeably. Originally, however, an archive file was a file that stored lots of other files: It archived them. An archive file doesn't have to be a compressed file; it's just a convenient place to put files that you are not using. A compressed file must, of course, be compressed. These days, archive files are usually—although not always—compressed files, and compressed files are often used for archiving files. So there's not a lot of difference between the two anymore. There's one notable exception, though. The .tar files you might run across, UNIX tape archive files, are *not* compressed. However, .tar archive files are often compressed using the .gzip format (you'll see something such as filename.tar.gz).

Which Format?

Most compressed DOS and Windows files are in ZIP format, a format often created by a program called PKZIP (but the file format is not owned by anyone, so other programs create ZIP files, too). There are other compressed formats, though; you might also see ARJ (created by a program called ARJ) and LZH (created by LHARC) now and again, but probably not very often. PKZIP won the compression war.

In the UNIX world, .Z, .gz, and .tar files are common archive formats. On the Macintosh, you'll find .sit (StuffIt) and .pit (Packit) compressed formats, as well as .hqx (BinHex) archive files. This table gives you a quick rundown of the archive formats you'll see.

Table 15.2 Common Compressed and Archive File Formats

Extension	Program That Compressed or Archived It
.arc	DOS, PKARC (an older method, predating PKZIP and rarely seen these days)
.exe	A DOS or Windows self-extracting archive
.gz	Usually a UNIX gzip compressed file (although there are versions of gzip for other operating systems, they're rarely used)

continues

Extension	Program That Compressed or Archived It
.hqx	Macintosh BinHex
.pit	Macintosh Packit
.sea	A Macintosh self-extracting archive
.shar	UNIX shell archive
.sit	Macintosh StuffIt
.tar	UNIX tape archive
.Z	UNIX compress
.z	UNIX pack
.zip	PKZIP, WinZip, and many others
.zoo	zoo210 (available on various systems)

It goes without saying (but I'll say it anyway, just in case) that if you see a file with an extension that is common on an operating system other than yours, it might contain files that won't be good on your system. Macintosh and UNIX software won't run on Windows, for instance. However, that's not always true. The file might contain text files, for instance, which can be read on any system. So there are cross-platform utilities; for example, some Macintosh utilities can uncompress archive files, such as ZIP files, that are not common in the Macintosh world, and some ZIP utilities running in Windows can extract files from .gz and .tar files. For instance, some versions of Stuffit Expander, a Macintosh utility, can open ZIP files, and WinZip, a Windows program, can open .gz and .tar files.

Those Self-Extracting Archives

Various programs, such as PKZIP and ARJ, can create files that can be executed (run) to extract the archived files automatically. These files, called self-extracting archives, are very useful for sending a compressed file to someone when you're not sure whether he has the program to decompress the file (or would know how to use it). For instance, PKZIP can create a file with an .exe extension; you can run such a file directly from the DOS prompt just by typing its name and pressing **Enter** or by double-clicking the file in the Windows Explorer file-management program. When you do so, all the compressed files pop out. In the Macintosh world, .sea (self-extracting archive) files do the same thing. Double-click a .sea file, and the contents are automatically extracted.

In the Meantime

How can you download and extract one of these compression utilities from a shareware library before you have a program that will extract an archive file? Don't worry; the programmers thought of that! These utilities are generally stored in self-extracting format, so you can download them and automatically extract them by running the file.

If you find a file in two formats, ZIP and EXE for instance, you might want to take the EXE format. The EXE files are not much larger than the ZIP files, and you don't need to worry about finding a program to extract the files. If you take a ZIP file, you must have a program that can read the ZIP file and extract the archived files from within. You might already have such a program. Some Windows file-management programs, for instance, can work with ZIP files. Otherwise, you'll need a program that can extract from the compressed format. See Appendix C for information about file libraries where you can download freeware and shareware that will do the job.

Your Computer Can Get Sick, Too

Downloading all these computer files can lead to problems: computer viruses. File viruses hide out in program files and copy themselves to other program files when someone runs that program. Viruses and other malevolent computer bugs are real, and they do real damage. Now and then you'll even hear of service providers having to close down temporarily after their systems become infected.

Unfortunately, security on the Internet is lax. The major online services have strict regulations about virus checks. Members generally cannot post directly to public areas, for instance; they post to an area in which the file can be checked for viruses before it's available to the public. But on the Internet it's up to each system administrator (and there are hundreds of thousands of them) to keep his own system clean. If just one administrator does a bad job, a virus can get through and be carried by FTP, the Web, or email all over the world. The large shareware archives are probably quite careful, but there are tens of thousands of places to download software on the Internet, and some of those are probably a little careless.

Techno Talk

Viruses Under the Microscope

The term *virus* has become a catchall for a variety of digital organisms, such as

- Bacteria, which reproduce and do no direct damage except using up disk space and memory.
- Rabbits, which get their name because they reproduce very quickly.
- Trojan horses, which are damaging programs embedded in otherwise useful programs.
- Bombs, which are programs that just sit and wait for a particular date or event (at which time they wreak destruction); these are often left deep inside programs by disgruntled employees.
- Worms, which are programs that copy themselves from one computer to another, independent of other executable files, and clog the computers by taking over memory and disk space.

However, having said all that, I also must say that the virus threat is overstated—probably by companies selling antivirus software. We've reached a stage where almost any confusing computer problem is blamed on computer viruses, and technical support lines are using it as an excuse not to talk with people. "Your computer can't read your hard disk? You've been downloading files from the Internet? You must have a virus!" Most computer users have never been "hit" by a computer virus. Many who think they have probably haven't; a lot of problems are blamed on viruses these days. So don't get overly worried about it. Take some sensible precautions, and you'll be okay.

Tips for Safe Computing

If you are just working with basic ASCII text email and perhaps FTPing documents, you're okay. The problem of viruses arises when you transfer programs, including self-extracting archive files, or files that contain mini "programs." (For instance, many word processing files can now contain macros, special little programs that might run when you open the file.)

If you do plan to transfer programs, perhaps the best advice is to get a good antivirus program. They're available for all computer types. Each time you transmit an executable file, use your antivirus program to check it. (Some programs can even be installed as browser "plug-ins," so they automatically check files that you download through your browser.) Also, be sure you keep good backups of your data. Although backups can also become infected with viruses, if a virus hits, at least you can reload your backup data and use an antivirus program to clean the files (and some backup programs check for viruses while backing up).

Rule of Thumb

Here's a rule of thumb to figure out if a file is dangerous: "If it does something, it can carry a virus; if it has things done to it, it's safe." Only files that can carry out actions (such as script files, program files, and word processing files from the fancy word processors—such as Word for Windows—that have built-in macro systems) can pose a threat. If a file can't do anything—it just sits waiting until a program displays or plays it—it's safe. Pictures and sounds, for instance, might offend you personally, but they won't do your computer any harm. (Can self-extracting archives carry viruses? Absolutely. They're programs, and they run—you don't know that they're self-extracting archives until they've extracted, after all.)

The Least You Need to Know

- Don't transfer files to your computer without thinking about *where* on your hard disk they should be. Create a download directory in a sensible place.
- Files are identified by the file extension, typically a three-character (sometimes four-character) "code" preceded by a period.
- Compressed and archive files are files containing other files within. They provide a convenient way to distribute files across the Internet.
- Self-extracting archives are files that don't require a special utility to extract the files from within. Just run the file, and the files within are extracted.
- Viruses are real, but the threat is exaggerated. Use an antivirus program, and then relax.
- The virus rule of thumb is this: "If it does something, it can carry a virus; if it has things done to it, it's safe."

Chapter 16

Gopher and Telnet—Still Alive, but Barely

In This Chapter

- Why bother with Gopher?
- Finding your way around Gopherspace
- Saving text documents and computer files
- Using Jughead and Veronica to search Gopherspace
- Working with Telnet
- IBM tn3270 Telnet sites
- MUDs, MOOs, and other role-playing games

This chapter examines two systems that many people use, but which most have no idea exist: Gopher and Telnet. These two systems still have their uses, even if they lack the glamour of the World Wide Web.

Digging Through the Internet with Gopher

The World Wide Web is what's "hot" on the Internet right now. Most of the growth in the Internet is occurring on the Web, and it's supposedly doubling in size every few weeks. True, that's another of those dubious Internet statistics, but regardless of the actual figures, it's certainly growing fast.

However, the Web is quite new. At the end of 1993, even well into 1994, the World Wide Web was a sideshow on the Internet. Few people knew how to use it, and fewer still bothered. It wasn't hard to use, but there wasn't much incentive. For most Internet users, there was no way to display pictures, listen to sounds, play video, or do any of the neat things you learned to do earlier in this book. It wasn't just that the Web was primarily text and little else; it was because the software simply wasn't available. (It wasn't until the fourth quarter of 1994, soon after Netscape Navigator was released, that the Web boom really began.)

You might be wondering how Internet users got around back in the distant past (okay, five or six years ago). What was the hot "navigation" system on the Internet in the days before Web? The answer is *Gopher*.

If you never used the Internet in the old command-line days, if Netscape Navigator and Internet Explorer and the other graphical user interface systems that abound are your only taste of the Internet, then you don't know how difficult the Internet could be. (Many people still use the Internet through a command-line interface—that is, typing complicated commands to get things done.) Many people who tried to use the Internet a few years ago were so turned off by the experience that they went away and never came back. FTP (which you learned about in Chapter 12, "The Giant Software Store: FTP") was extremely difficult. Telnet was pretty clunky—and still is. Email was just about bearable. All in all, the Internet was *not* a user-friendly place.

Command-Line Users

If you are one of the unfortunate souls still using the command-line interface, send an email message to ciginternet@mcp.com and put the word **gopher** in the subject line. In return, you'll get the Gopher chapter from the first edition of *The Complete Idiot's Guide to the Internet*. This chapter explains how to use Gopher if you're working from a dumb terminal (dumb being the operative word, one might say).

Let There Be Gopher

Then along came Gopher. This tool was a revolution in simplicity, providing a nice menu system from which users could select options. Instead of remembering a variety of rather obscure and arcane commands to find what they needed, users could use the arrow keys to select options from the menu. Those options could take the user to other menus or to documents of some kind.

The Gopher system is, in some ways, similar to the World Wide Web. It's a worldwide network of menu systems. Options in the menus are linked to menus or other documents all over the world. These Gopher menus made the Internet much easier to use and much more accessible to people who weren't long-term cybergeeks.

For a while, Gopher looked like the future of the Internet—at least to a number of people who invested time and money in Internet software. A variety of "graphical point-and-click" Gopher programs were published commercially and were distributed as shareware and freeware. You might have heard of WinGopher, for instance, an excellent Windows program for navigating through the Gopher system. Today, however, you'll have a hard time finding any Gopher programs at the software archives listed in Appendix C, "All the Software You'll Ever Need."

Then along came the Web. Or rather, along came the graphical Web browsers, which all of a sudden made the Web not only easy to use, but exciting, too. Interest in Gopher subsided rapidly, and everyone rushed off to learn how to create Web documents. Where did that leave Gopher? Still alive and well (although ignored by most Internet users), for a couple of good reasons. First, there were already many Gopher systems set up, and a large number of them remain. (They might not have been updated in several years, but the information's often still there.) Second, there are still millions of Internet users who don't have access to graphical Web browsers, and for them Gopher is the easiest tool available.

A lot of interesting information is stored on Gopher servers around the world. Fortunately, you can get to it with your Web browser. That's right: your Web browser might be designed to work on the World Wide Web, but you can also use it to access Gopher.

Enough History, What Is Gopher?

The Gopher system is based on hundreds of Gopher *servers* (computers that contain the menus) and millions of Gopher *clients* (computers that are running the Gopher menu software that accesses the server's menus). Gopher servers are generally public, so any client can access the information from any server.

Gopher?

Why is it called Gopher? First, it was originally developed at the University of Minnesota, home of the Golden Gophers. Second, "gofer" is slang for someone who "goes fer" things—and Gopher's job is to "go fer" files and stuff. Third, the system digs its way through the Internet, just as a gopher digs through a burrow.

Your Web browser is, in effect, a Gopher client. Working with Gopher through your Web browser works extremely well. Unlike FTP, which works well most (but not all) of the time, your browser will handle Gopher sites just fine *all* the time. (There are a *few* things you can do with a true Gopher program that you can't do with a Web browser, such as see details about a menu option, but few people will miss these features.)

Gopher It!

How do you get to a Gopher server? You can start a Gopher session in two ways: by clicking a link in a Web document that some kindly Web author has provided or by typing the `gopher://` URL into the Address text box and pressing **Enter**. For instance, typing `gopher://wiretap.spies.com/` will take you to Internet Wiretap Gopher server, which you can see in the following figure. (You can also go to a Web page at `http://wiretap.spies.com/`, but don't think that the wiretap archives have been placed onto the Web itself. When you click a link on this Web page, it takes you to the Gopher server. However, it looks as though Wiretap will eventually be converted to Web pages.)

The Internet Wiretap Gopher is worth a visit; you'll find loads of interesting documents here.

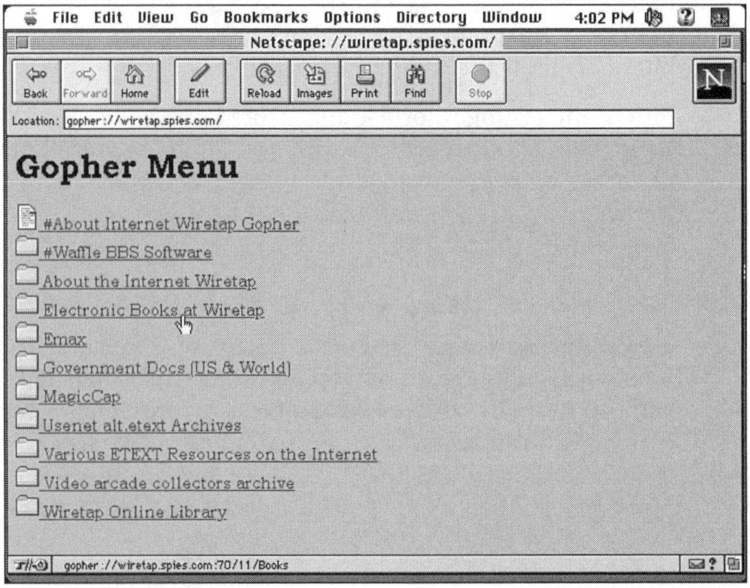

By the way, if you are using Internet Explorer or Netscape (and probably a number of other browsers), you can often ignore the `gopher://` bit. If the gopher address starts with the word *gopher*, you can type the address and forget the `gopher://` part. For instance, you can type `gopher.micro.umn.edu/` instead of `gopher://gopher.micro.umn.edu/`.

Where Can I Start?

For a list of links to Gopher servers, go to `gopher://gopher.micro.umn.edu:70/11/Other%20Gopher%20and%20Information%20Servers`. If that's too complicated to type, go to `http://www.w3.org/History/19921103-hypertext/hypertext/DataSources/ByAccess.html` or `http://www.ncsa.uiuc.edu/SDG/Software/Mosaic/MetaIndex.html`.

How, then, do you use a Gopher server with a Web browser? The Gopher menu options are represented by links; click the link to select that option. If the option leads to another menu, that menu appears in the window. If the option leads to a file of some kind, the file is transferred in the normal way, and your browser displays it or plays it (if it can). Files are treated just the same as they would be if you were working on a Web site.

Most of the documents at Gopher sites are text documents. But as you'll remember from the Web chapters, Web browsers can display text documents within their own windows. Of course, you won't find any links to other documents within these text documents—they're not true Web documents, after all. So when you finish reading the text file, click the **Back** toolbar button to return to the Gopher menu you were just viewing. In the following figure, you can see a text document that I ran across at the Wiretap site. I selected the **Electronic Books at Wiretap** menu option and then the **Aesop: Fables, Paperless Edition** link.

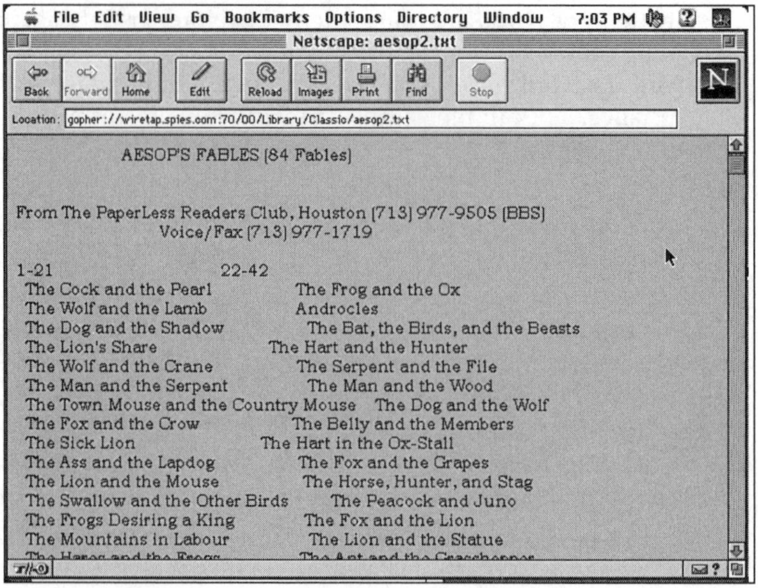

Aesop's fables from the Wiretap site.

Searching Gopher Menus

Some Gopher menus are very long. The original Gopher system had a special / command that allowed you to search a menu. In a browser, you can use the Find command. In Internet Explorer or Netscape, select **Edit**, **Find**.

Archie's Friends, Veronica and Jughead

Gopher servers have two types of search tools: Veronica (Very Easy Rodent-Oriented Netwide Index to Computerized Archives) and Jughead (Jonzy's Universal Gopher Hierarchy Excavation And Display). Do these acronyms mean much? No, but *you* try to create an acronym from a cartoon character's name!

Veronica lets you search Gopher servers all over the world. Jughead lets you search just the Gopher server you are currently working with (not all Gopher servers have Jugheads). If you want to search Gopherspace—the giant system of Gopher menus that spreads across the Internet—or a particular server, find a Veronica or Jughead menu option somewhere.

Cartoon Characters

Why Veronica and Jughead? They are characters in the famous Archie comic strip. Remember Archie, the FTP search system you learned about in Chapter 12? Archie arrived on the Internet first. Then the people who created the Gopher search systems figured Archie needed company, so they named their systems Veronica and Jughead.

For instance, at the `gopher://gopher.cc.utah.edu/` site, you'll find menu options that say "Search Titles in Gopherspace Using Veronica" and "Search Menu Titles Using Jughead." You might have to dig around to find these options on some sites; sometimes they are several levels down the menu system. (I couldn't find Veronica or Jughead at the Wiretap site.) Although many sites don't have Jughead, virtually all have a link to Veronica. These systems are fairly easy to use; it's just a matter of typing keywords and pressing **Enter**. Look around for a link to a help file if you need more information.

Telnet: Inviting Yourself onto Other Systems

Millions of computers are connected to the Internet, and some contain pretty interesting stuff. Wouldn't it be great if you could "reach out" and get onto those computers (well, some of them) to take a look at the games and databases and programs on computers around the world? Well, you can. At least, you can get onto computers whose administrators want you to get on them, and a surprisingly high number do. A special program called Telnet enables you to turn your computer into a Telnet client to access data and programs on some Telnet server.

Many Internet users have private Telnet accounts. A researcher, for example, might have several computers that he regularly works on, and he might have been given a special login name and password by the administrators of those computers. But many computers also allow "strangers" into their systems. (Some days it seems that just about everyone on the Internet is pretty strange, of course, but I'm referring to people that the computer administrators have never met.) This access is completely voluntary, depending on the goodwill of the people who own or operate a particular computer. If a Telnet server is open to the public, anyone can get on the system and see what's available.

Step 1: Find a Telnet Program

First, you'll need a Telnet program. The selection and quality of Telnet programs are among the weakest features of the Internet. There are wonderful Web browsers, and excellent email and FTP programs, but the Telnet programs I've run across all seem a bit weak.

Part of the problem is that there's a limit to how much a Telnet program can help you. When Telnetting, your computer becomes a terminal of the computer you've just connected to, so it has to follow that computer's rules. Because the thousands of systems out there on the Internet each use slightly different menu systems, command systems, and so on, creating a great Telnet program is difficult. All the average Telnet program does is provide a window into which you can type commands and in which responses will appear. Also, because Telnet isn't a terribly exciting subject (when was the last time you saw a *Time* or *Newsweek* article on the wonders of Telnet?) and not much used, relatively speaking, it's been ignored by most software developers.

I know what you're thinking. You're thinking, "He'll probably explain how to use Telnet through the browser, and then how to use a real Telnet program." Well, you're wrong. You *can't* Telnet through your browser. Although you can *start* a Telnet program from your browser, the browser can't *run* the session. At least, none of the most popular browsers have built-in Telnet capabilities. So if you want to use Telnet, you'll need a Telnet program.

You might already have one. If you are working with CompuServe, you'll find a Telnet program built into the CompuServe software (GO TELNET). AOL does not currently have a built-in Telnet program, but you can use the keyword **telnet** to find information about Telnet as well as a library of Telnet programs you can download. (You might have to upgrade your AOL software to the latest version to be able to use one of these Telnet programs.) MSN does not have a built-in Telnet program, either, but you probably have Microsoft Telnet, which is usually installed when you install your Windows 95 or 98 Internet software. If you're using Windows 95, 98, or Windows NT, open the **Start** menu, select **Run**, type **telnet**, and press **Enter**. You might find that Microsoft Telnet opens. If you are with an Internet service provider, you might have received a Telnet program with the software the provider gave you—but there's a good chance you didn't.

A Java Telnet Application

Maybe you *can* use Telnet through your browser. A new Java Telnet application (you can find it at `http://www.first.gmd.de/persons/leo/java/Telnet/`) will run within your browser. However, this application is intended for a Web author who wants to incorporate a Telnet site into his or her Web site.

If you have to find your own Telnet program, you can do so at the software archives listed in Appendix C, "All the Software You'll Ever Need." You might use something such as CRT for Windows or NetTerm for Windows; if you are a Macintosh user, try NCSA Telnet or dataComet. Of course, you might not want to bother tracking down Telnet software until you find a need for it, and many people never do. If you need to access library catalogs, though, you might need Telnet, as many such systems are available via Telnet.

Making the Connection

You have a number of choices of how to begin a Telnet session:

- In your Web browser, click a **telnet://** link. In Web documents, you'll sometimes run across links that use the `telnet://` URL (not very often, though we'll look at a site that has many such links later in this chapter). When you click the link, your Telnet program opens and starts the session with the referenced Telnet site. (If this doesn't work, you'll have to tell your Web browser which Telnet program to use; you enter that in the browser's Options or Preferences.)
- If your Web browser is open, you can also start a Telnet session by typing `telnet://` followed by a Telnet host address and pressing **Enter**. For instance, if you type `telnet://pac.carl.org` into Internet Explorer's Address text box and press **Enter**, Windows Telnet launches and connects to the Denver Public Library's site. (Type **PAC** and press **Enter** to log on.)
- In Windows 95, 98, or NT, you can also open the Windows **Start** menu, click **Run**, type `telnet://`*`hostname`* (such as `telnet://pac.carl.org`), and press **Enter**. The Telnet program starts automatically.

A Telnet site name looks something like this: `pac.carl.org`, `freenet.sfn.saskatoon.sk.ca`, `fdabbs.fda.gov`, or sometimes a number, such as `150.148.8.48`. If you are opening a Telnet site from within your Telnet program, you'll enter the Telnet site or hostname into the appropriate dialog box. For instance, to get a Telnet program to connect to a Telnet site, you might have to select **File**, **Connect** (or something similar), enter the Telnet site, and press **Enter**. If you are using CompuServe, use the **TELNET GO** word, choose **Access a Specific Site**, type the Telnet hostname, and press **Enter**. You can see CompuServe's Telnet window in the following figure.

*CompuServe has a built-in Telnet window that you can access using the **TELNET GO** word.*

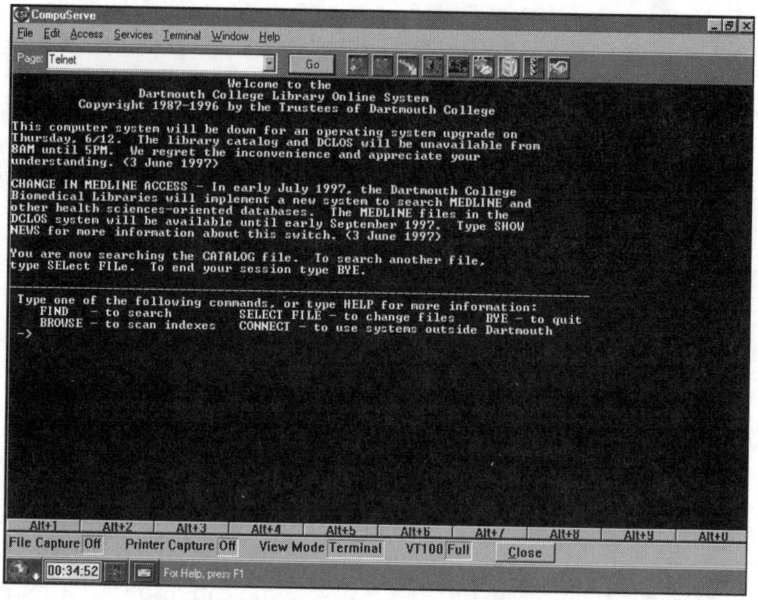

HYTELNET: Your Guide to the World of Telnet

To get a taste of what's available in the world of Telnet, take a look at HYTELNET, the Telnet directory. This directory used to be available only through Telnet, but now you can view the directory at a World Wide Web site, which is much more convenient. (No wonder nobody uses Telnet anymore—even the Telnet aficionados use the Web because it's more convenient!) Open your Web browser and go to `http://www.lights.com/hytelnet/` or `http://www.cc.ukans.edu/hytelnet html/START.TXT.html`. HYTELNET is very out-of-date and might even disappear soon (the owner has been promising to kill it or replace it with something else for some time now).

More Directories

Your online service might also list interesting Telnet sites. For instance, in CompuServe use **GO TELNET**, and then select **List of Sites** or **Telnet Site Descriptions**. You can also try `http://www.w3.org/History/19921103-hypertext/hypertext/DataSources/ByAccess.html` and `http://www.ncsa.uiuc.edu/SDG/Software/Mosaic/MetaIndex.html`, or search for the word "telnet" at Web search sites; see Chapter 17, "Finding Stuff."

From HYTELNET, you can launch Telnet sessions on computers all over the world. Find the Telnet site you're interested in, and you'll see information about what the resource is and how to use it. For instance, the next figure shows information about the NASA/IPAC Extragalactic Database Telnet site, where you can find information about all sorts of extragalactic stuff—galaxies, quasars, and infrared and radio sources, for instance. This page shows the Telnet address (`ned.ipac.caltech.edu`) and the login name you must use to log in once connected (`ned`). It also shows a list of commands you can use once connected. Note that it also has a link; the Telnet addresses are links that you can click to launch your Telnet program and begin the Telnet session.

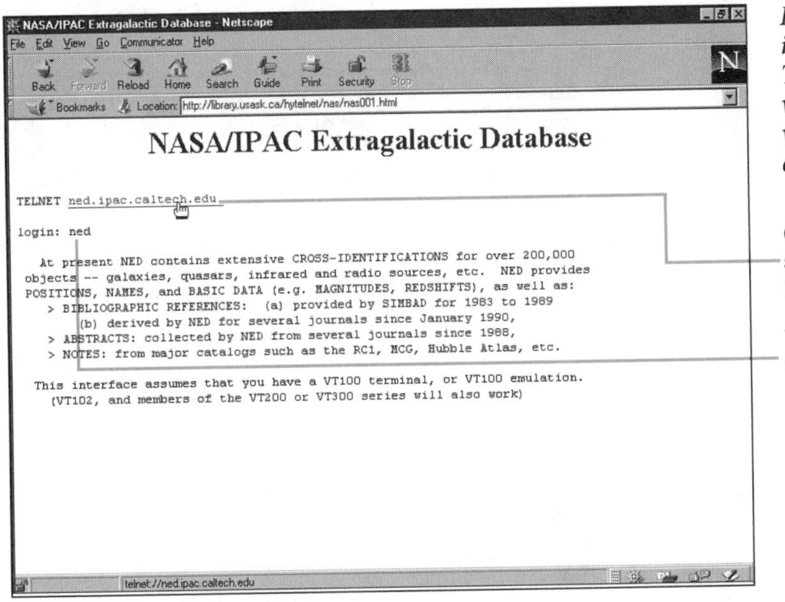

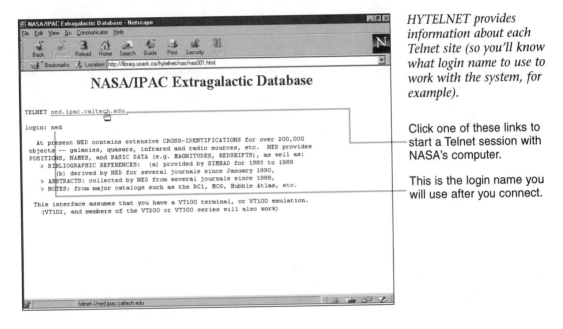

HYTELNET provides information about each Telnet site (so you'll know what login name to use to work with the system, for example).

You're In. Now What?

After your Telnet program has connected to the Telnet site, you might have to log in. To do so, you'll need to know the account name you should use. HYTELNET describes Telnet sites, including the required account names. When you find a Telnet site described in a book or magazine, the account name is often included. In some cases, you *won't* have to log in; the computer will let you right in without asking for further information. In other cases, the introductory screen you see when you first connect might tell you what to use. The site shown in the following figure (Saskatoon Free-Net) explains how to log on.

When you connect to a Telnet session, you often have to identify the type of computer terminal you are using. Of course, you are using a PC, but your Telnet program can *emulate* (pretend to be) a standard terminal program. By default, it's probably set to emulate a VT-100 terminal, which is good because the VT-100 setting works in most cases you'll run into. If you run into a site that doesn't like the VT-100 setting—perhaps the text on your screen isn't displayed properly during the session—you can try changing the emulation. But you don't always have many choices.

You can log on to the Saskatoon Free-Net as a guest.

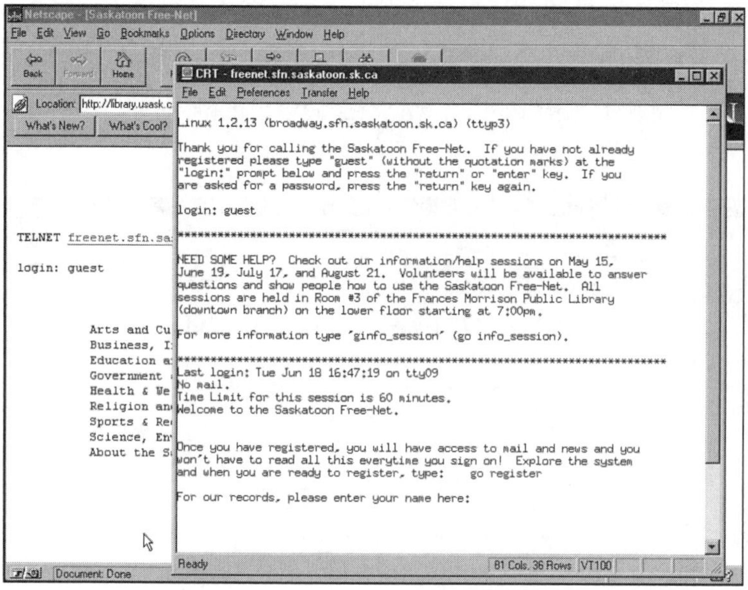

Terminal Emulations

When you connect to a Telnet site, you are, in effect, turning your computer into a *dumb terminal*. The programs at the Telnet site will run on that site's computer, not yours. All you are using your computer for is to send text commands to the Telnet site and to view the results. That's just what a computer "terminal" does. But there are many types of terminals. Your Telnet program is pretending to be a computer terminal, but it has to be told which one to imitate (or *emulate*, in computer jargon). The VT-100 terminal is one of the most common types, and it is recognized by most Telnet sites.

Working in a Telnet Session

Every Telnet system is different. Your Telnet program functions as a means of transferring what you type on your computer to the computer you are connected to and for that computer to send text back to you. In effect, you've turned your computer into a dumb terminal connected to another computer, so you have to follow the rules of that system. What you see depends on what sort of system is set up on that computer. It might be a series of menus from which you select options, or it might be a prompt at which you type. Each system varies.

Let me warn you about one thing: Telnet can be very slow sometimes. On occasion, you might type something and not see what you have typed for several seconds or even several minutes. It depends on the amount of network traffic going that way as well as the number of people working on that machine at that time. If you find a particular task to be too slow, you should probably try again later. If that Telnet site is always slow, maybe you can find another site with the same services.

I'm not going to go into much more detail about Telnet, because quite frankly most of you won't use it. Those of you who do should get to know your Telnet program. Read the documentation carefully and learn the ways the program can help you. Note that Telnet programs vary from the absolutely awful to the quite reasonable; you're unlikely to find a really good one, though. Telnet is not an easy system to use; if you like the Web, you just might hate Telnet.

Telnet's Ugly Sister: tn3270

Some Telnet sites are on IBM mainframes running "3270" software. If you try to Telnet to a site and find that the connection is instantly closed (even before you get to the login prompt), that particular site *might* be a 3270 site (although there's no guarantee of it).

On the other hand, if you log in and see something similar to this

```
VM/XA SP ONLINE-PRESS ENTER KEY TO BEGIN SESSION
```

or this

```
VM/ESA ONLINE-PRESS BREAK KEY TO BEGIN SESSION
```

you've definitely reached a 3270 site. Or if you see boxes being drawn using Xs, you've probably reached a 3270 site. Your Telnet program probably won't be able to handle a tn3270 session. You're welcome to try it and see, but there's a good chance it won't.

These 3270 sessions are not that common, so you might never run into them. But if you really have to use a tn3270 site, you'll need to find a tn3270 emulator. You might try QWS3270 (a Windows tn3270 emulator), dataComet (a Macintosh program that can run both Telnet and tn3270 sessions), or tn3270 (a Mac tn3270 program). There's also a Netscape Navigator plug-in called WebTerm (`http://www.wpine.com/webterm/`). See Appendix C for information on software sites where you can find these programs. If you have Netscape Communicator Professional (an old version of Communicator), you already have a tn3270 program, IBM Host-On-Demand, which you can open from the Communicator menu. (Netscape seems to have lost interest in IBM Host-On-Demand—it's apparently no longer available.)

MUDs, MOOs, and MUCKs

Although Telnet is not very popular among the general Internet population, there's a subculture that loves it: the role-playing games community. These people play games known by such bizarre names as MUDs (Multiuser Dimensions or maybe Multiuser Dungeons), MOOs, MUCKs, Tiny MUDs, Teeny MUDs, UnterMUDs, and so on. In these games, you type responses to a program running in a Telnet session. The program might describe where you are: you're in a room with a door on the West wall, a window on the East wall, and steps going down. You then tell it what to do: you might type **door** to go through the door. If this sounds exciting, these games are for you. (If it doesn't, you're not alone.)

If you are interested, check out one or more of the following options:

- Try `gopher://gopher.micro.umn.edu`. When you get to the Gopher menu, choose **Fun & Games** and then **Games**.
- Visit The MUD Connection: `http://www.mudconnect.com/`.
- Try searching for MUD at Yahoo! or another search site (see Chapter 17, "Finding Stuff").
- If you use AOL, you can find quite a bit of information about MUDs using the **telnet** keyword.

Although these games have predominantly been Telnet games in the past, they are now moving onto the Web. In addition, there are special client/server programs designed for role-playing games.

I'm told that these games are extremely addictive—apparently people log on and get stuck for days at a time. Personally, I don't see the excitement. But then again, I don't understand why some people become addicted to collecting string or hubcaps. Who am I to judge?

The Least You Need to Know

- Gopher is a text-based menu system, a real boon to Internet users working with text-based software.
- You can easily work with Gopher through a Web browser, traveling through Gopherspace by clicking menu options.
- To save a text document or file, click the link. Your browser will treat it the same way it treats any file on the World Wide Web.
- Jughead and Veronica help you search for information in Gopherspace.
- Telnet is little used, but much loved by those who use it. You might already have a Telnet program; if not, you can find one in the software libraries mentioned in Appendix C.
- Try the HYTELNET site (`http://www.lights.com/hytelnet/`); it has links to hundreds of Telnet sites.
- When you connect to a Telnet site, you might have to enter a login name and password; HYTELNET tells you what to use.
- After you are in a Telnet site, you are on your own. Each Telnet site has its own rules.

Part 3

Getting Things Done

Now that you've learned how to use the Internet's services, it's time to learn some important general information about working on the Net. This place is so huge, you might have trouble finding what you need; I'll show you where to look. You'll also need to learn how to stay safe on the Internet. You've heard about the problems that go along with using credit cards on the Internet, about kids finding pornography, and so on—we'll examine the truth and the lies.

In addition to covering all those issues, I'll answer all sorts of questions I've heard from Internet users, from how to get rich on the Internet to whether using your credit card online is safe. I'll also tell you about a couple of dozen ways that people use the Internet. Maybe you'll find something worth pursuing, or you'll think of an idea of your own. And you'll even find out where the Internet is going in the future.

Chapter 17

Finding Stuff

In This Chapter

- Finding people
- Searching the Internet with search engines
- Using Internet directories
- Searching newsgroups
- Other Internet services

By now you must have realized that the Internet is rather large: tens of millions of users, millions of files in FTP sites, millions and millions of Web pages, Telnet sites, Gopher servers, newsgroups, mailing lists—this thing is huge. How on earth are you ever going to find your way around?

Finding what you need on the Internet is surprisingly easy these days. Dozens of services are available to help you find your way around. That's what this chapter is about: finding what you need and where you need to go.

Finding People

The most complicated search task is finding people on the Internet. There are millions of Internet users and no single Internet directory. Unlike the online services, which have directories you can search to find someone you want to contact, there's no one place to search on the Internet. But that's not so surprising. After all, there's no single directory for the world's telephone system, and the Internet is comparable—it's thousands of connected networks that span the world. So how are you going to find someone?

Still Working at a Command Line?

If you are using the command-line interface, send an email message to `ciginternet@mcp.com` and type **`who`** in the Subject line of the message (leave the body blank). In return, you'll receive the chapters on finding people from the first edition of *The Complete Idiot's Guide to the Internet*. For more information, see Appendix E, "The Email Responder."

Quite frankly, the easiest way to find someone's email address is to talk to that person or talk to (or email) a mutual acquaintance. You can spend hours looking for someone in the Internet's various directories. If you know of someone else who might have the information, or know the person's telephone number, you can save yourself some time and trouble by tracking down the email address that way. If you can't contact the person directly, or can't think of someone else who knows the person you're after, you'll have to dig a little deeper.

Directories, Directories, and More Directories

There are a lot of directories on the Web. (No, I don't mean directories on a computer's hard disk this time; now when I say *directories*, I mean it as in the telephone directory or directory assistance.) A good place to start is at your browser's people search page. For instance, if you're using Netscape Navigator 4.51, select the **People** button from the Personal toolbar (select **View**, **Show**, **Personal Toolbar**). In Netscape Navigator 4, click the **Guide** button and select **People** from the drop-down menu. In Navigator 3, click the **People** button in the Directory Buttons bar. If you're not using that browser, you can go directly to Netscape's People page (`http://home.netscape. com/netcenter/whitepages.html`). Each time you go to this page, Netscape displays the Netscape People Finder. The following figure shows the Netscape People Finder.

Another good directory to use is Yahoo! People Search (go to `http://www.yahoo.com/search/people/`), which you can see in the second figure on the following page. This directory of people on the Internet is surprisingly good. I searched for my own name and found myself, along with about 90 other Peter Kents. (I hadn't realized there were so many of us.) You can search for a name and, using the advanced settings, narrow the search by including a city and state, or you can search for a telephone number. Note, however, that these directories are often quite out-of-date. I found a couple of old listings for myself; one of the email addresses had not worked for about three years.

If you don't find the person you need in Yahoo! People Search, don't worry; there's still a chance you'll find him. Yahoo!'s `http://dir.yahoo.com/Reference/Phone_Numbers_and_Addresses/Email_Addresses/` page has links to dozens more directories; when I looked a moment ago, I found links to almost 150 different directories, some of which had links to dozens more, including directories at colleges, celebrity directories, many regional directories, and so on.

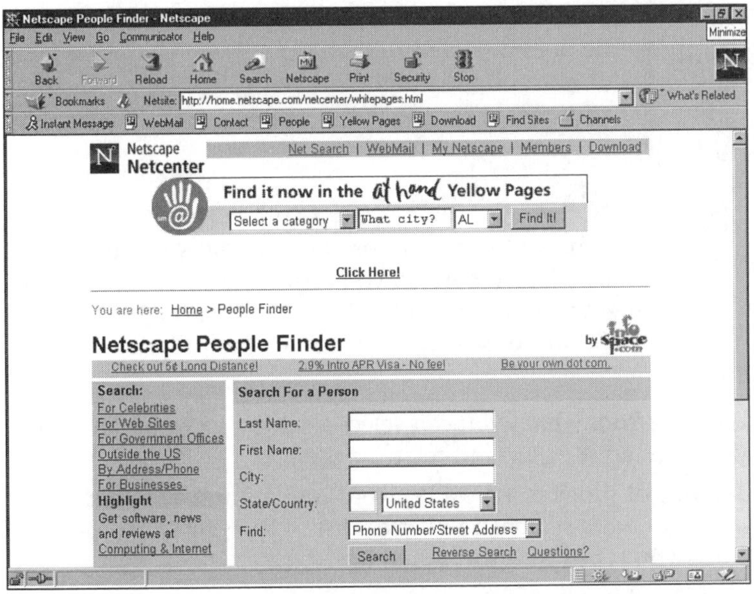

Netscape's People Finder form.

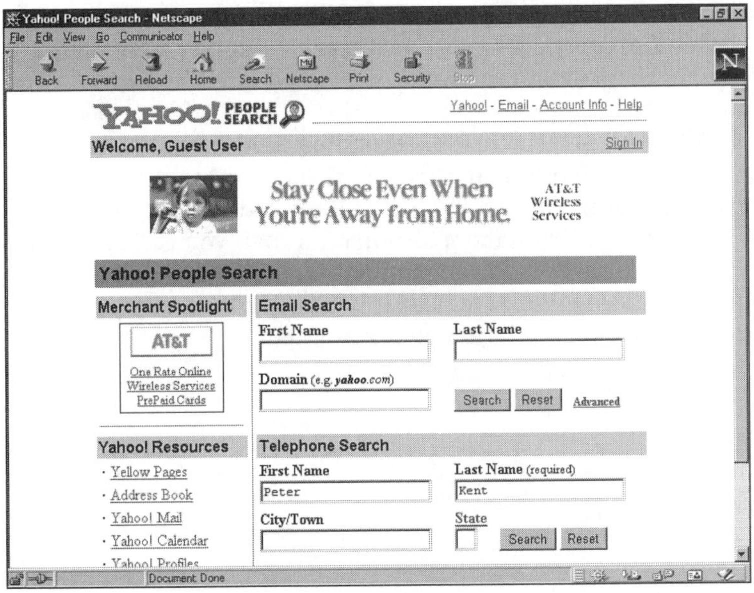

The Yahoo! People Search form.

Other Search Engines, Too

Yahoo! is not the only *search engine* you can use to find directories. We'll look at more search engines later in this chapter, and many of them will have links to directories you can use to find people, too.

I'm not going to go into more detail about these directories. A year or two ago, it was quite difficult to find people on the Internet (when I searched for myself for the first edition of this book, I had a lot of trouble finding myself—and I knew where I was!). These days there are so many directories of people that, with a bit of time and trouble, you have a good chance of finding the person you need (even if he doesn't have Internet access—you can often track down a phone number more easily than an email address).

Using the Search Sites

You want to find information about something or other. Where do you start? The best place is probably at the Web search sites. There are dozens of these sites, and I'm always surprised what I can turn up in just a few minutes of searching. There are basically three ways to use these search sites:

- You can view a directory from which you can select a subject category and subcategories; then you'll see a list of links to related pages.
- You can search an index of subjects; type a keyword into a form, and then click a **Search** button to carry out a search. You'll see a list of links to Web pages related to the subjects you typed into the search form.
- You can search an index of pages. Some search engines let you search for words within Web pages. AltaVista, for example, once claimed that it had an index of most of the words on 30 million Web pages, at over a million Web sites! (That was a few years ago, and AltaVista doesn't state a specific number anymore.) You'll see a list of pages that contain the words you typed into the form.

Which type of search should you use? The first or second method should normally be your first choice. Services such as AltaVista are very useful, but because they don't categorize the pages—they search for words within the pages instead of searching the subjects of the pages—they often give you more information than you can ever handle. The other services categorize pages (and sometimes even describe or review pages), so they are generally easier to use. Save places such as AltaVista for "plan B," when you can't find what you're looking for on your first attempt.

Finding the Search Sites

Getting started is easy. Most Web browsers these days have a button that takes you straight to a search page of some kind (generally a form that lets you search a choice of search sites). For example, both Netscape and Internet Explorer have a Search button.

The Best?

Which is the best Web search site? There is no "best." Even though I really like Yahoo!, I sometimes use others. Each one is different and works in a different way, which means each one will give you a different result. Try a few and see which you like, or check to see how others rate them.

Here are a few search sites you can use. I've started with Yahoo! because that's where I prefer to start. Of course, after you've used a few search sites, you might find that you have a different preference.

- **Yahoo!** `http://www.yahoo.com`
- **Lycos** `http://www.lycos.com/`
- **Infoseek** `http://infoseek.com/`
- **HotBot** `http://www.hotbot.com/`
- **AltaVista** `http://www.altavista.digital.com/`
- **GO2NET** `http://www.goto.net/`

What's the difference between a Web directory and a Search engine? A directory provides categorized lists of Web pages from which you can select a category, and then a subcategory, and then another subcategory, and so on until you find the site you want. A search engine lets you use a program with which you'll search a database of Web pages. With a search engine, you type a keyword and click a **Search** button or press **Enter**. The search engine then searches the database for you. Some sites such as Yahoo! contain both directories and search engines.

Browser Tip

Here's a quick way to search for something: Search directly from your browser's Location text box. If you're using Netscape Navigator, enter two words into the Location box. For instance, if you want to search for information about hiking in Iceland, type **iceland hiking**. (If you just want to search for one word, enter it twice, as in **iceland iceland**.) Press **Enter**, and Netscape picks a search engine for you from its selection (Infoseek, Excite, and Lycos) and sends the search keywords to the search engine. If you're using Internet Explorer, type **find** followed by the word you want to search for: **find iceland**, for instance.

Netscape Navigator 4.5 takes this whole thing one step further (I can't say I like this system). Type a single word into the location bar and press Enter, and Navigator will probably do an Internet Keyword "Smart Browse" search (this is configured in the **Preferences** box: select **Edit**, **Preferences**, and click on **Smart Browsing** under the **Navigator** category). It will search for that word through the Netscape Netcenter directory. Considering the way in which the browsers used to work—entering a single word would search for the .com domain of that word—this new system is a real disruption to the whole domain system.

How Do I Use the Search Engines?

Internet *search engines* enable you to search a database. Take a quick look at Infoseek (`http://www.infoseek.com/`) in the following figure as an example. Start by typing a search term into the text box. You can type as little as a single word, but you might want to get fancy—in which case you should read the instructions. You'll find a link at Infoseek, probably labeled Tips or Huh?, that takes you to a document that describes exactly what you can type. Read this document; it gives you many suggestions and hints for using the search engine. (Most search engines have a link such as this to background information.)

As you will learn in the information document, you can enter these types of things at Infoseek:

- Words between quotation marks. Entering words this way tells Infoseek to find the words in the exact order you type them: "the here and now."

- Proper names. Be sure these names are capitalized correctly: Colorado, England, or Gore, for instance.
- Words separated by hyphens. Entering words this way tells Infoseek to find both words as long as they are close together in the document: diving-scuba, for instance.
- Words in brackets. Entering words this way tells Infoseek to find the search words if they appear together, but not necessarily in the order in which you've entered them: `[diving scuba]`, for example.

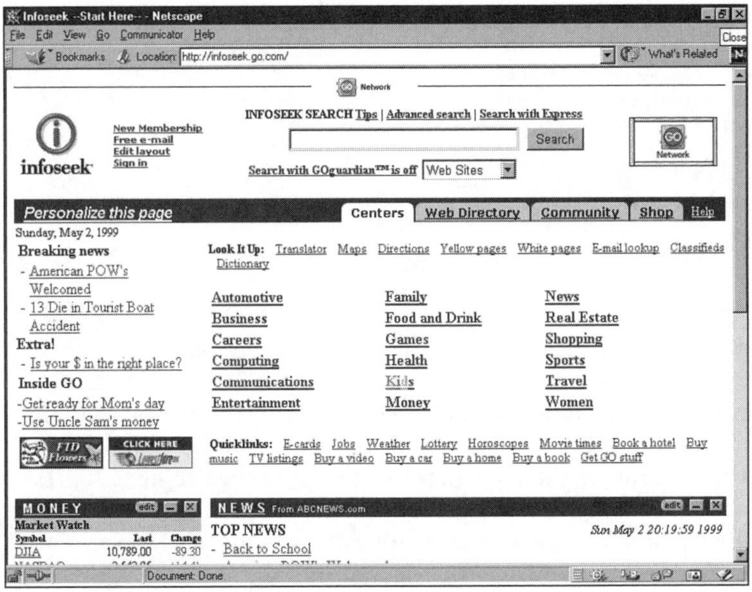

Infoseek, a Web search engine.

Each search engine is a little different and allows you to use different sorts of search terms. You can always search by entering a single word, but the more you know about each search engine, the more efficiently you can search.

When you first go to a search engine, look around for some kind of link to a Help document. When you finish reading the Help information, click the **Back** button to return to the Infoseek page with the text box. Enter the word or phrase you want to search for, and then press **Enter** or click the **Search** button. Your browser sends the information to Infoseek, and with a little luck you'll see a result page shortly thereafter (see the following figure). Of course, you might see a message telling you that the search engine is busy. If so, try again in a few moments.

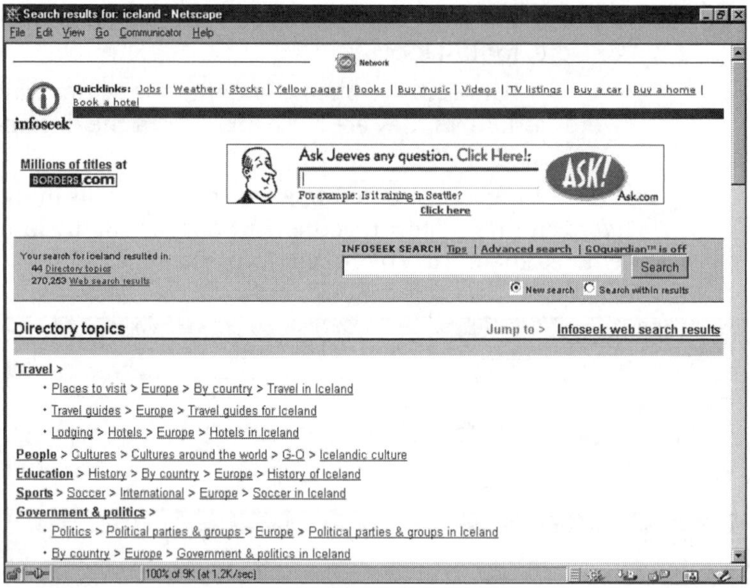

Infoseek found a few links to Icelandic subjects for me.

As you can see in the figure, when I searched for "iceland," Infoseek found 44 directory topics and 270,253 links to Web sites that contain information about Iceland. The document I'm viewing doesn't show me all the links, of course. It shows me the first 5 directory topics and a jump to Infoseek Web Search Results link to the first 10 and provides a link at the bottom of the page that I can click to see the next 10. It found links to topics such as *Travel in Iceland, Travel Guides to Iceland, Hotels in Iceland, Icelandic Culture,* and plenty more. If one of these links interests me, all I have to do is click the link and away I go, over the North Atlantic and into Iceland.

Browsing the Internet Directories

For a sample of Internet directories, take a look at Yahoo!. Go to `http://www.yahoo.com/`. Yahoo! has a search engine, so you can type a word into the text box if you want, but notice the category links: Arts & Humanities, Education, Health, Social Science, and so on. Each of these links points deeper into the Yahoo! system, a level lower down in the hierarchical system of document categories. To see how this system works, click **Recreation & Sports**, and you see a document from Yahoo! with a list of more categories: Amusement and Theme Parks@, Aviation, Fitness@, Motorcycles@, and so on.

The @ sign at the end of some of these categories indicates that this entry is a sort of cross-reference: you will be crossing over to another category if you select this link. For instance, click **Fitness@**, and you'll see a page from the Home:Health category. This page also contains links to other fitness-related categories, from aerobics, to Health Clubs, Organizations to Web Directories.

You'll also notice that some links are shown with bold text and numbers in parentheses after them, such as **Aerobics (10)**, and links that are not bolded, such as Just Move. The bold links take you farther down the hierarchy, displaying another document that contains more links. The number in parentheses after the link shows how many links you'll find in that document. The regular text links are links across the Internet to Web documents that contain the information you're looking for.

Finding Specific Stuff

Now that you've seen how to search for general stuff, you're ready to learn about searching for specific stuff. Instead of going to a general search site, you can go to one of many sites that help you find specific things. For example, you might want a site where you can search for Web pages related to animals (`http://www.animalworldwide.com/`), boat stuff (`http://boatingyellowpages.com/`), or kid stuff (`http://www.yahooligans.com/`). You can find scores of these specialized search sites, with information about everything from lawyers to pets. A good place to find them is at `http://www.yahoo.com/Computers_and_Internet/Internet/World_Wide_Web/Searching_the_Web/Web_Directories/`. You can also find them at any of the other big search sites.

Just Tell Me in English

The latest thing in search engines is *natural-language searching*. The problem with most search engines is that they're not particularly friendly. They expect you to ask a question in just the right way. But hang on a minute; haven't we all seen *Star Trek* and *2001: A Space Odyssey*? Aren't we supposed to *talk* to these stupid computers in plain English?

In theory, a natural-language search engine enables you to ask a question in plain English: *Where can I find pictures of rabbits*?, for instance, or *How do I find cheap airline tickets*? In practice...well, they work pretty well although, as with most computer programs, far from perfectly. The best known of these systems is Ask Jeeves (`http://www.ask.com/`). This system responds with a number of things—first, it asks a number of questions, and if one of the questions is close to your question and you click on the Ask button next to it, you'll probably find the information you want. It also provides links to pages that it found through several other search systems—WebCrawler, Infoseek, Excite, Yahoo!, and AltaVista. When asked *Where can I find pictures of rabbits*?, it responded with, *Where can I see pictures of rabbits?, Where can I find a concise encyclopedia article on rabbits?, Where can I find information about rabbits as pets?, How can I determine the sex of my rabbit?*, and *Where can I search an online database of images?* All pretty good matches. Use common words (such as picture and rabbit) and there's a good chance you'll get some useful information. On the other hand, you never know. I tried *tell me the best way to employ a clinometer* and it actually found a page that explains how to build a clinometer for measuring tree heights, in addition to links to companies that make these instruments.

Finding Out What People Are Saying

Are people talking about you (do you hear voices in your head?)? If you want to know what people are saying about you on the Internet, you can search newsgroup messages for particular words. You can search for your own name to find out what your friends—or enemies—are saying about you, or you can search for a subject if you are researching a particular topic.

There are a number of places you can search newsgroups. One of the best is DejaNews (`http://www.dejanews.com/`). Or try Yahoo!; go to `http://www.yahoo.com`. Select the **Advance Search** link located to the right of the search button. Then click the **Usenet** option button and enter your keywords. (Another alternative is to go to Infoseek and select **Newsgroups** from the drop-down list box before you search.) When the search site carries out the search, it displays a page of links to the matching messages. Click a link to read the message. Another great place to search is `http://www.reference.com/`, which helps you search newsgroups, mailing lists, and Web forums.

Set a Bookmark to Repeat the Search Later

Here's a handy little trick. If you've just done a search about a subject that you think you'll want to check back on later—to see what new information has appeared on the Internet—bookmark the search. I don't mean the search site, but the search itself. Go to the search site, carry out the search, and when you get the page displaying the search results, bookmark that page. The next time you want to search, all you have to do is select that bookmark. Your browser automatically sends the search statement to the search engine, which carries out the search and displays the result. (This trick works on most, although not all, search sites.)

FTP, Gopher, Telnet, and More

No, you are not finished. You can search for much, much more. Go back to the earlier chapters on FTP, Gopher, Telnet, newsgroups, and mailing lists, and you'll see that I gave you information about how to find things on those services. For instance, you can use Archie to search FTP sites, and you can use Tile.Net and other similar services to find mailing lists and newsgroups related to subjects that interest you. You can also use Jughead and Veronica to search Gopherspace. If you don't find what you need at any of the Web sites you learned about in this chapter, spend a little time searching the other services.

The Least You Need to Know

- There is no single directory of Internet users, so the easiest way to find someone is often to ask a mutual acquaintance.
- There are now lots of good directories. You might have to search a few, but there's a good chance that eventually you'll find the person you're looking for.
- A search engine is a program that searches for a word you enter.
- You can search indexes of keywords describing the contents of Web pages, or you can search the full text of the Web pages (millions of words in millions of pages).
- A directory is a categorized listing of Web links. Choose a category, then a subcategory, then another subcategory, and so on until you find what you want.
- Natural-language searches allow you to ask a plain-English question...and you'll often get a good answer, too.
- Services such as DejaNews, Yahoo!, and Infoseek let you search newsgroup messages. The result is a list of matching messages. Click a link to read a message.
- You can set a bookmark on a page that displays search results; to repeat the search quickly at a later date, all you have to do is select that bookmark.

Chapter 18

Staying Safe on the Internet

In This Chapter

- Keeping kids "safe"
- Protecting your email
- The identity problem
- Internet addiction
- Protecting your credit card
- Keeping out of trouble with your boss or spouse

There are many dangers on the Internet—most of them imagined or exaggerated. We're led to believe that our children will become corrupted or be kidnapped, our credit cards will be stolen, and we'll be arrested for copyright infringement. Although some of these dangers are real, keep in mind that you're sitting in front of a computer at the end of a long cable. Just how dangerous can that be? If you use a little common sense, it's not dangerous at all.

Your Kid Is Learning About Sex from Strangers

Sex, sex, sex. That's all some people can think of. The media's so obsessed with sex that sometimes the only thing that our journalists seem to notice are stories with a little spice in them. Consequently, the press has spent a lot of time over the past couple of years talking about how the Internet is awash in pornography. Well, it isn't.

I'll admit that there are pornographic images on the Internet, but in general you won't just trip over pornography. If you decide to take a look at the `alt.binaries.pictures.erotica.pornstar` newsgroup, for instance, just what do you expect to find?! You can hardly claim to be offended if you choose to enter such a locale. In some cases, the publicly accessible sex-related Web sites are quite "soft." Take a look at the *Hustler* or *Playboy* sites, and then run down to your local magazine store and take a look at them there. You'll find that the bookstore version is far more explicit than the Web version. (Believe me, I've done this little experiment—but only in the interest of research, you understand.)

You Can Do Your Own Research

Because this is a family book, I'm not going to go much further on this topic. If you care to research the subject of sex on the Internet further, just go to the search engines (see Chapter 17, "Finding Stuff") and search for "sex." (But don't carry out this experiment and then blame me if you're offended by something you find!)

On the other hand, some very explicit stuff is available on the Internet. Since I wrote the third edition of this book in 1996, Web sites seem to have become more explicit. In 1996, the Computer Decency Act was holding people back—much of the really explicit stuff was hidden away on private Web sites. To get in you had to subscribe by providing a credit card number. Since then the Computer Decency Act has been struck down by the courts. There are still many private sites, but quite a lot of very smutty stuff is available at the free Web sites. Furthermore, some porn sites use email messages to bring in new customers; they send these messages to just about any email address they can find, so some of the recipients are children. A number of newsgroups carry extremely explicit sexual images and, in a few cases, images of violent sex. (Even though most things don't particularly shock me, I have to admit that I've been disgusted by one or two things I've seen in newsgroups.)

Although the press would have you believe it's hard to get to the Smithsonian Web site or to read a newsgroup about cooking without somehow stumbling across some atrocious pornographic image, this is far from the truth. You have to go looking for this stuff. The chance that you'll stumble across it is about as good as the chance that you'll run into Queen Elizabeth on your next trip to the supermarket. Unless, that is, you make a spelling mistake. Type **whitehouse.com** into a Web browser instead of

whitehouse.gov, type **sharware.com** instead of **shareware.com**, or **nassa.com** instead of **nasa.com** (which doesn't exist anyway—it should be `www.nasa.gov`), and you'll end up at a porn site. So when you make your fingers do the walking, walk slowly and carefully.

Don't Expect the Government to Help

If you have kids, you already know that they can be a big bundle of problems. The Internet is just one more thing to be concerned about. Still, you signed up for the job, and it's your responsibility.

Many people have suggested that somehow it's the government's responsibility to look after kids. (These are often the same people who talk about "getting the government off our backs" when it comes to other issues.) A few years ago, the U.S. Congress passed the Computer Decency Act (CDA), which bans certain forms of talk and images from the Internet. This law definitely had an effect, and pornography was, for a while, harder to find on the Internet. But the CDA was a sloppily written piece of overreaction; it could be construed to ban all sorts of genuine public discourse, such as discussions about abortion. Consequently, the law was judged unconstitutional by a federal court in Philadelphia and later overturned by the U.S. Supreme Court.

The court in Philadelphia wrote that "Those responsible for minors undertake the primary obligation to prevent their exposure to such material." Hey, isn't that what I said? (I originally wrote most of this *before* the law was struck down. Looks like there could be a judicial career waiting for me!)

The bottom line is that the Computer Decency Act is history. Even if it's replaced by something else (various U.S. states are trying a variety of clumsy experiments), remember that the Internet is an international system. How is the U.S. government going to regulate Swedish, Finnish, Dutch, or Japanese Web sites? It's not. So what are you going to do to keep your kids safe?

It's Up to You; Get a Nanny

If you want to protect your kids, I suggest you spend more time with them at the computer or get a nanny. You can't afford a nanny, you say? Of course, you can. Lots of programs are available to help you restrict access to "inappropriate" sites. Programs such as Net Nanny (I'm not endorsing this one in particular; I just used it so I could put "Nanny" in the heading) contain a list of sites that are to be blocked; you can add sites from your own hate-that-site list, or you can periodically download updates from the Internet. Using these programs, you can block anything you want, not just pornography. As the Net Nanny site says, you can "screen and block anything you don't want running on your PC, such as bomb-making formulas, designer drugs, hate literature, Neo-Nazi teachings, car theft tips—whatever you're concerned about."

You can find Net Nanny at http://www.netnanny.com/. To find other such programs, search for the word **"blocking"** at Yahoo! or some other Web search site (or go directly to http://www.yahoo.com/Business_and_Economy/Companies/Computers/Software/Internet/Blocking_and_Filtering/Titles/). You'll find programs such as SurfWatch, CyberPatrol, CYBERSitter, NetShepherd, TattleTale, Bess the Internet Retriever, and Snag. (I'm serious, all these are names of real programs!) If you use an online service, you'll also find that it probably offers some way of filtering out areas you don't want your kids to get to. America Online has had such filtering tools for a long time. MSN enables you to block the Internet's alt. newsgroups and other "adult" areas.

You'll also soon find blocking tools built into most Web browsers. Internet Explorer already has blocking tools. To use them, choose **View**, **Internet Options** and click the **Ratings** or **Security** tab. You'll find an area in which you can turn a filtering system on and off. This system is based on the Recreational Software Advisory Council's ratings (although you can add other systems when they become available), and you can turn it on and off using a password. You can set it up to completely block certain sites or to allow access with a password (just in case you don't practice what you preach!). The following figure shows a site that's blocked except for password entry.

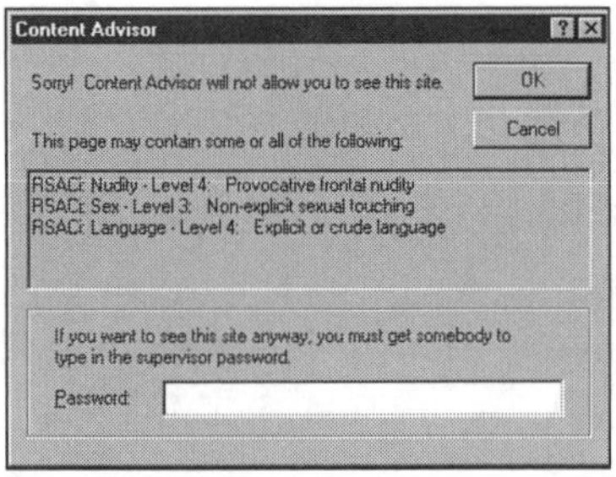

With Internet Explorer's Ratings turned on, your kids can't get in—but you can.

I've heard people criticize these blocking programs for two reasons: 1) because they're not perfect (of course, they're not) and 2) because they're an affront to the concept of free speech. Personally, I believe they are very useful and effective. I believe in supervising my kids, and these programs provide a supervision tool for a new era. They also provide a way for concerned parents to keep their kids away from sites they object to without locking people up and forcing adults to read nothing more than sixth-grade materials on the Web.

From a personal viewpoint (it's *my* book, after all), this whole sex-on-the-Internet is a whole lot of fuss about almost nothing. Sure, clean up the Internet—but what are you going to do about the schoolyard? Schools are hotbeds of filthy language and talk about sex, sprinkled with the occasional pornographic magazine and actual sex. I have the perfect solution, though. I call it "chemical supervision," and it entails giving kids drugs to reduce certain hormonal levels. Remember, you heard it here first.

The Internet Content Rating Association (ICRA)

In May of 1999, a group of major Internet companies met in London to form an international organization to protect children (and, note, free speech) on the Internet. The companies included Microsoft, AOL Europe, Bertelsmann Foundation, British Telecom, Cable & Wireless, Demon Internet (UK), EuroISPA, IBM, Internet Watch Foundation, Software & Information Industry Association, and T-Online Germany. These companies have decided to push a Web-site rating system based on the RSACi (Recreational Software Advisory Council on the Internet) system that is embedded into Internet Explorer (but not, at present, in Netscape Navigator).

Your Private Email Turned Up in the *National Enquirer*

Email can get you in a lot of trouble. It got Oliver North in hot water, and ordinary people have lost their jobs or been sued over things they've said in email. Several things can go wrong when you use email:

- The recipient might pass the email on to someone else.
- The message can be saved on a backup system and read by someone other than the recipient later.
- Someone could spy on you and read your email looking for incriminating comments.

The most likely scenario is that the recipient intentionally or thoughtlessly passes on your message to someone who you didn't count on seeing it. The second problem—that the message could be copied to a backup system—is what got Oliver North (and others) into trouble. Okay, you can't expect Oliver North to understand this stuff. But it's even got Microsoft in trouble! Microsoft email messages have been used in their recent problems with the Justice Department. Even if you delete a message and the recipient deletes the message, it might still exist somewhere on the network if the system administrator happened to do a backup before it was deleted. So if you are ever the subject of some kind of investigation, that message could be revived. A message goes from your computer, to your service provider's computer, to the recipient's service provider's computer, to the recipient's computer—at least four places from which it could be copied.

Finally, someone might be out to get you. Internet email is basic text, and a knowledgeable hacker with access to your service provider's system (or the recipient's service provider's system) can grab your messages and read them.

What do you do, then? The simplest solution is to avoid putting things in email that you would be embarrassed to have others read. The more complicated solution is to encrypt your email. A number of encryption programs are available that scramble your message using a public-key encryption system, and, as discussed in Chapter 3, "Advanced Email: HTML and Encryption," encryption systems are now being incorporated into email programs. Figure out how they work, and use them.

Digital Signatures

You can also use public-key encryption systems to digitally sign documents. When you encrypt a message with the private key, it can be decrypted only with your public key. After all, your public key is public. But if it can be decrypted with your public key, it *must* have come from your private key. Therefore, it must have come from you.

If you don't have an email program with built-in encryption, you can find an add-on system. A good way to start is to search for the word **"encryption"** at any of the Web search sites (or try `http://www.yahoo.com/msn/Computers_and_Internet/Security_and_Encryption/`). There's a problem with these systems, though. Right now, they're complicated to use (the systems built into email programs are generally much simpler). PGP, for instance, can be very complicated; if you want to use it, I suggest that you get one of the "front-end" programs that make it easier to use, such as WinPGP. In addition, because few people use encryption anyway, if you want to use it, you'll have to arrange to use it first. Remember also that even if you encrypt your mail messages, they're not completely secure; you're still trusting the recipient not to pass on the decrypted message to someone else.

Prince Charming Is a Toad!

I'm not sure why I should have to explain this, but when you meet someone online, *you don't know who that person is!* Something about electronic communications makes people quickly feel as though they know the person with whom they are communicating, but they don't!

There are two problems here. First, cyberspace is not the real world. People communicate in a different way online. As another author told me recently, "I know people who seem to be real jerks online, but who are really nice people offline. And I've met people who seemed to be great online, but were complete jerks offline."

Then there's the misrepresentation problem. Some people flat out lie. A man who claims to be single might be married. A woman who claims to look like Michelle Pfeiffer might really look like Roseanne Barr. A 35-year-old movie executive who graduated from Harvard might actually be a 21-year-old unemployed graduate of Podunk Bartending School. It's easy to lie online when nobody can see you. Couple that with a natural tendency to feel like you know the people you meet online, and you have trouble.

Not everyone lies online, though. As my friend Phyllis Phlegar wrote in *Love Online* (Addison Wesley), "Even though some individuals choose to be deceptive, many others see the online world as the ultimate place in which to be totally honest, because they feel safe enough to do so." (Phyllis met her husband online.) She also recognizes the dangers: "As long as the person or people you are talking to can't trace you, free-flowing communication between strangers is very safe." But if you're not careful and you give out information that can be used to trace you, Prince Charming might turn out to be the Prince of Darkness. And if you do choose to meet someone in person after meeting that person online, be cautious.

Internet Stalkers

Internet stalkers are for real. People have been murdered, raped, and variously assaulted by people they've met online. But remember, they can't get to you unless you provide them the information to reach you. Getting into trouble is unlikely, but it can happen, so use some common sense. If you really have to meet someone you've run into online, for instance, do so in a way that you can leave if you decide your offline impression of the person doesn't match your online impression.

She's a He, and I'm Embarrassed!

Chapter 13, "Yak, Yak, Yak: Chatting in Cyberspace," covers chat systems, which are great places to meet people. For many, they're a great place to meet people of the opposite sex (or of whichever sex you are interested in meeting). But keep in mind that sometimes people are not of the sex that they claim to be. I don't pretend to understand this, but some people evidently get a kick out of masquerading as a member of the opposite sex. Usually men masquerade as women, which could be construed as the ultimate compliment to womanhood or could simply be blamed on the perversity of men. Either way, there's a lot of it around, as the saying goes. (I recently heard chat systems described as being full of "14-year-old boys chatting with other 14-year-old boys claiming to be 21-year-old women." True, it's an exaggeration, but it illustrates the point well.) So if you hook up with someone online, bear in mind that she (or he) might not be quite who he (or she) says (s)he is.

Profiles

If you are a member of an online service, be careful about what you put in your profile. Most services allow you to list information about yourself—information that is available to other members. Omit your address, phone number, and any other identifying information!

You Logged On Last Night, and You're Still Online This Morning

The Internet can be addictive. I think three particular danger areas stand out: the chat systems, the Web, and the discussion groups (mailing lists and newsgroups). Apparently, chat is extremely addictive for some people. I've heard stories of people getting stuck online for hours at a time, until early in the morning—or early in the morning after that. I know of people who've met people online, spent hundreds of hours chatting, and finally abandoned their spouses for their new "loves."

The Web is not quite so compelling, but it's a distraction, nonetheless. There's just so much out there. If you go on a voyage of discovery, you *will* find something interesting. Start following the links, and next thing you know you've been online for hours. Discussion groups are also a problem. You can get so involved in the ongoing "conversations" that you can end up spending half your day just reading and responding.

What's the answer to Net addiction? The same as it is for any other addiction: self-discipline, along with some support. It also helps if you have a life in the real world that you enjoy. Fear probably helps, too (such as the fear of losing your job or kids). If you need help, why not spend a bit more time online? Do a search for "**addiction**," and you'll find Web sites set up to help you beat your addiction. You might also take the Internet Addiction survey at The Center for On-Line Addiction (`http://netaddiction.com/`) to see whether you really have a problem.

Just Because You're Paranoid Doesn't Mean Someone Isn't Saying Nasty Things About You

A little while ago, someone started saying rather unpleasant things about me in a mailing list. What she didn't tell people was that she had a sort of vendetta going against me and had for some time. (No, I'm not getting into details.) Anyway, I saw her comments in one mailing list and was struck by a thought: There are tens of thousands of internationally distributed newsgroups and thousands more mailing lists! What else is she saying? And where?!

There's a way to find out what's being said about you (or someone or something else) in newsgroups and Web pages. This is something that might be very useful for anyone who is in the public eye in any way (or for people involved in feuds).

To see what's being said about you in a Web page, search AltaVista; this service lets you use a search engine that indexes all the words in a page, instead of just categorizing Web pages (Chapter 17 explains how to use search engines). To search a newsgroup, though, you'll need a program such as DejaNews (`http://www.dejanews.com/`). In DejaNews, you type a name or word you want to search for, and the service searches thousands of newsgroups at once and shows you a list of matches (see the following figure). Click the message you are interested in to find out exactly what people are saying about you. (You can also search DejaNews from some of the other search engines, which have links to it.)

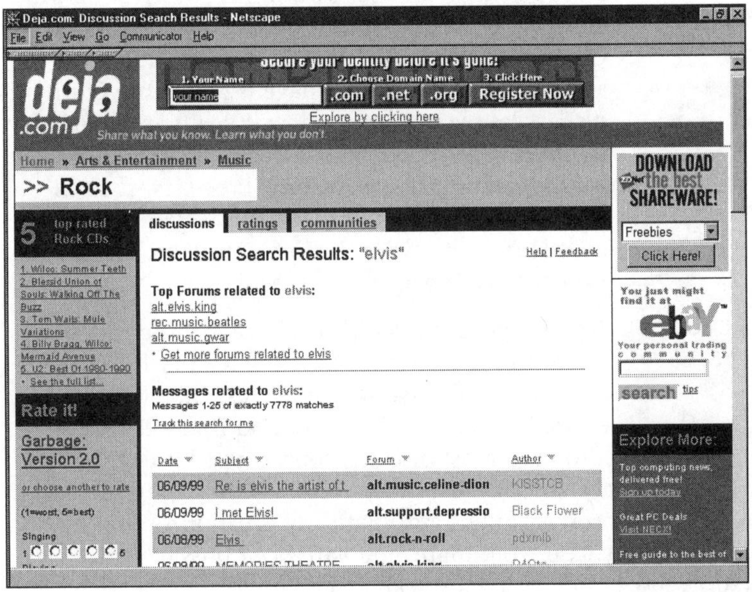

DejaNews provides a great way to search newsgroup messages. (Looks like Elvis has been busy.)

When I did this little search on my own name, I was surprised at what I found. I discovered information about a science-fiction conference at which I was to be a guest, and I found messages in which people recommended a book I'd written about PGP. I also discovered that there's a stunt man called Peter Kent (I found that in alt.cult-movies).

DejaNews is not the only such service; you can find a list of these services at http://dir.yahoo.com/Computers_and_Internet/Internet/Usenet/Searching_and_Filtering/. How about mailing lists? Reference.com (http://www.reference.com/) indexes many mailing lists and some Web forums (and newsgroups). You can even set up a service that searches automatically for you once a week or so, and then emails you the result.

I Was "Researching" at Hustler Online, and Now I'm Unemployed

This title is more than a joke. Some people really have been fired for viewing "inappropriate" Web sites during work hours. This seems quite unfair to me; companies give people Web browsers, often unnecessarily. They provide a temptation, and then fire the people who succumb!

It's Bugged!

Your boss can spy on your Internet activities using special software programs, regardless of whether you clear the cache and history list. So maybe you'd better just get back to work.

Of course, you can avoid such problems by staying away from the sites in the first place. But if you must go there, practice safe surfing by clearing the cache when you finish! (I discussed the cache in Chapter 5, "More About the Web.") When you visit a site, a copy of the Web page is saved on your hard disk in case you want to view it again at a later time. In effect, this creates a history of where you've been. And speaking of history, some browsers (such as Internet Explorer and Netscape Navigator 4) have excellent multisession history lists, which will also list every Web page you've seen!

To cover your tracks, clear the cache to remove the offending pages. Then clear the history list (either clear it completely, or remove just the offending entries). Netscape Navigator and Internet Explorer also keep a list of URLs you've typed into the Location bar, so if someone starts typing, say, www.4work.com at your computer, before the URL is completed the browser might automatically finish it for you by typing www.4adultsonly.com! (In any case, you might not want your boss to know that you've been visiting 4work.com, either—it's a job search site.)

I Think Kevin Mitnick Stole My Credit Card Number!

Here's another Internet myth: Shopping on the Internet is dangerous because your credit card number can be stolen. The second part of the myth is correct. Yes, your number can be stolen. But the first part is nonsense. Using your credit card on the Internet is not unsafe. Let me give you a couple of reasons.

First, credit card number theft is quite rare on the Internet. It can be done, but only by a computer geek who really knows what he's doing. But why bother? Credit card numbers are not very valuable because it's so easy to steal them in the real world. For example, a little while ago I handed over my credit card to a supermarket clerk and then started bagging my groceries. The clerk put my card down while I wasn't looking. The woman behind me in the line moved forward and set her bag down on the counter. When I went to look for my card, it was gone. It wasn't until I (politely) asked her to move her bag that I found the card underneath. From the look on her face, I'm sure she knew where it was.

This sort of theft is very common. When you give your card to a waiter, a grocery-store clerk, or someone at a mail-order company, you don't think twice about it. But for some reason, people are paranoid about theft on the Internet. Banks know better, though. Internet-business author Jill Ellsworth found that credit card companies regard Internet transactions as safer than real-world transactions.

The second reason is that both Netscape and Internet Explorer, the two most used browsers, have built-in data encryption. Many Web sites now use special Web servers that also have built-in encryption. When a credit card number is sent from one of these browsers to one of these secure servers, the data is encrypted and is therefore unusable. The following figure shows how several Web browsers indicate a secure Web site. Notice the little padlock in the lower-right or lower-left corner of the window? Both Internet Explorer and Netscape Navigator 4 use a locked padlock to indicate that a site is secure. Netscape 2 and 3 displays a key image in the lower-left corner for the same purpose; if the key is broken, the site is not secure. Navigator 4 also puts a yellow line around the padlock toolbar icon.

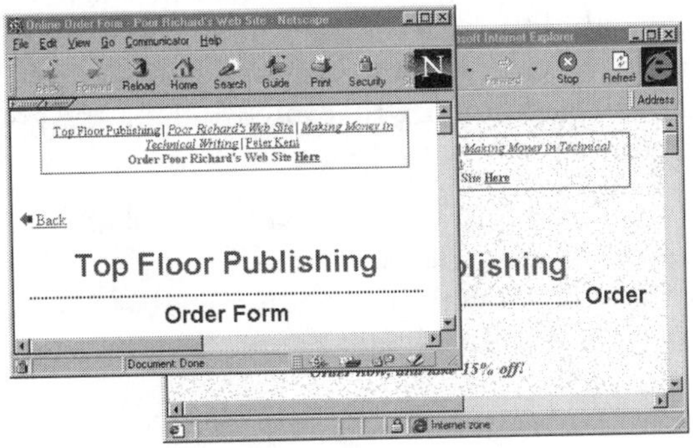

When you see a locked padlock or a key in the status bar, you can send your credit card number without worry.

As for Kevin Mitnick, cyberthief extraordinaire, there's a lot of confusion about what he did. He broke into systems and stole information en masse. (He didn't steal individual numbers as they flew across the Internet.) No matter how you pass your credit card number to a vendor, the most dangerous time is *after* they've received the number—and there's little you can do about that.

My Wife Found My Messages in alt.sex.wanted

A lot of people are saying a lot of odd things on the Internet. Undoubtedly, each day thousands of people with very poor judgment make millions of statements that could get them in trouble. This little problem has long been recognized. And for some time now there's been an (almost) perfect way around it: You post messages anonymously.

One way to do that is to configure your email or newsgroup program with incorrect information (with another name and email address, for instance). When you send the message, the header contains that incorrect information instead of the true data. That tactic will fool most list members, but it's not completely safe; the header also contains information that allows the message to be tracked by a system administrator (or the police), and in any case falsifying the header in your email is likely to upset people and might even be illegal soon.

A better method is to sign up for a free email account on the Web. A lot of companies now provide such email accounts (you can find a list at `http://www.yahoo.com/Business_and_Economy/Companies/Internet_Services/Email_Providers/Free_Email/`; Yahoo! even gives away email accounts). Why do they do this? So they can sell advertising. Anyway, many of these systems allow you to sign up for an account anonymously. Sure, you have to provide information about yourself, but it doesn't have to be real.

To use email, you log on to your Internet account through whatever service provider or online service you happen to use. Then you go to the mail system's Web site and log on to your mail account. You can now send and read your email. Each message that goes out is sent from the Web site, not from your service provider or online service. So there's nothing in the header that directly identifies you.

How safe is this email service? Someone reading your message won't be able to find you without the help of the system administrators at the email service and your service provider or online service. So this service is pretty safe for day-to-day anonymity, but perhaps not so safe if you are doing something that might offend the government or police of the country in which those services are found.

Another method is to use an anonymous remailer, a system that posts the messages for you, stripping out all information that can be used to track you down. In other words, you send the message to the remailer with information about which newsgroup or person it should be posted to, and the remailer sends the message on, sans identity.

You can find these services by searching for remailers at a search site (or go to a list of remailers at `http://www.cs.berkeley.edu/~raph/remailer-list.html` or Yahoo!'s Anonymous Remailers page: `http://www.yahoo.com/Computers_and_Internet/Security_and_Encryption/Anonymous_Mailers/`). But note that these systems are not perfect. They depend on the reliability of the person running the service and, in some cases, on that person's willingness to go to prison. If the police come knocking at his door, the administrator might just hand over his records. (This has happened; at least one anonymous remailer has handed over information.) Another problem with remailers is that they go one way only. You can send, but not receive.

Another Problem

Who runs the anonymous remailers? If you were a smart computer cop, wouldn't it occur to you to set up your own anonymous remailer? It already has occurred to various police forces, so you can't be absolutely sure that the anonymous remailer you are using isn't merely a trick to track down people saying things that they "shouldn't" say.

Nothing's completely safe. Even using a genuine anonymous remailer can leave you at risk; your email could be intercepted between your computer and the remailer, for instance. As the *Frequently Asked Questions About Anonymous Remailers* document (`http://www.cs.berkeley.edu/~raph/remailer-faq.html`) says, "Hard-core privacy people do not trust individual remailers...[they] write programs that send their messages through several remailers...only the first remailer knows their real address, and the first remailer cannot know the final destination of the email message."

I "Borrowed" a Picture, and Now They're Suing Me!

As you've seen throughout this book, grabbing things from the Internet is as easy as stealing from a baby—but there's none of the guilt. It's so easy and so guilt-free that many Internet users have come to believe in a sort of "finder's keepers" copyright morality. If it's there, and if you can take it, you can use it.

The law says otherwise, though. Here's a quick summary of copyright law: If you created it, it belongs to you (or to your boss if he paid you to create it). You can put it anywhere you want, but unless you sign a contract giving away rights to it, you still own the copyright. You don't have to register copyright, either.

Check This Out

Can I Take It for Personal Use?

In most cases, you probably can. When you connect to a Web site, all the things that are transferred to your computer end up in the cache anyway. However, some enthusiastic copyright lawyers claim that the use of a cache is in itself illegal, that even storing images and text on your hard drive goes against copyright law.

Copyright law is quite complicated, however, and this summary misses many essential details. The important thing to understand is that it *doesn't* belong to you if you didn't create it! Unless something has been placed on the Internet with a notice explicitly stating that you can take and use it, you can take it for personal use, but you can't use it publicly. You can't steal pictures to use at your Web site, for instance. (Even if there is a notice stating that the item is in the public domain, it might not be. After all, how do you know that the person giving it away created it?)

Copyright law even extends to newsgroups and mailing lists. You can't just steal someone's poetry, story, ruminations, or whatever from a message and distribute it in any way you want. It doesn't belong to you. Of course, if you are concerned that your work will be taken from a newsgroup or mailing list and distributed, don't put it there!

I Downloaded a File, and Now My Computer's Queasy

Yes, you know what I'm talking about: computer viruses. These nasty little programs get loose in your computer and do things they shouldn't, such as wipe out your hard drive or destroy the directory information that allows your computer to find files on the drive.

First, my role as contrarian dictates that I inform you that much of the fuss about viruses is greatly exaggerated. When something goes wrong with a computer, a virus usually gets the blame. An example of how the virus threat is exaggerated is the famous Good Times virus. This virus never existed; it was a myth from the start. The story was that an email message containing a virus was being passed around the Internet. The story was obviously wrong because a plain email message without a file attached cannot contain a virus.

Only files that "do things" can contain viruses. That includes program files, as well as document files created by programs that have macro languages. For instance, a variety of Word for Windows and Excel macro viruses just appeared in the past few years (what took them so long?). If a file can do nothing by itself—if it has to have another program to do something to it—it can't carry a virus. A plain text file (including text messages) can't do anything, and GIF or JPG image files cannot cause harm. (I'm just waiting for the next big hoax: Someone will start a rumor that there's an image file used at many Web sites that contains a virus and that all you have to do is load the page with the image to infect your computer.)

Yes, viruses do exist. Yes, you should protect yourself. There are many good antivirus programs around, so if you plan to download software from the Web (not just images and documents from applications other than advanced word processors), you should get one. But no, it's not worth losing sleep over.

I've Been Browsing, and Now They're Coming to Get Me

If you browse around on the Web, can you be identified? Well, not easily. In most cases, a Web-site owner cannot track a visitor back to a particular computer. But still, a lot of people are very concerned about privacy and the fact that perhaps, just perhaps, they are identifiable.

One problem is trust. To a great degree, the Internet is based on trust, although perhaps misguided. For instance, let's consider cookies for a moment. These are little bits of information saved in text files on your computer's hard drive. Your account name at a Web site might be saved in a cookie, for instance, so the next time you arrive at the site your account name is automatically entered into a log-in form. Now, there's a lot of nonsense spoken about cookies, and about how Web sites can steal information from them. They can't—a site can retrieve only a cookie that it set on your hard drive itself. But consider this. If you download a piece of shareware, that program could, without your ever realizing it, read your cookies, and transmit the information across the Internet. Of course, it could read much more—it could look for Quicken and Microsoft Money files and transmit them, too (although Microsoft has the perfect solution—make their files so huge it would take forever to transfer them).

So a lot of what we do on the Internet is based on trust, trust that the programs we're using aren't out to steal information, for instance. We also assume that we won't be tracked back from a Web site to our computer. But such tracking is possible. Not by most Web-site owners, but certainly by governments and police agencies. There is a digital trail left when you wander around the Internet. It's a trail that's split into pieces, and parts of the trail are available to different people and companies. But if you have enough influence, you might be able to persuade everyone along the trail to provide you with the information you need.

There are people, of course, who don't have such a high degree of trust, and so there are now a number of systems in development that will make it possible to surf the Web anonymously. For instance, there's a program called Freedom, from a Canadian company called Zer0-Knowledge Systems (`http://www.zeroknowledge.com/`). This system allows you to create various different "digital identities," and to transmit information through their server. The system works with the Web, and with newsgroups. "For example," they say, "if you like to debate politics online you can designate one pseudonym as your 'politics' pseudonym. Use it when you post in political newsgroups, surf activist web sites, email your political contacts, and chat in political chat rooms. No one can trace it back to your real self."

There's also a service called Anonymizer (`www.anonymizer.com`). Visit this site, enter a URL into a form at the site, and the service will grab the page for you and forward it to you. Is there really a call for such services? Well, Anonymizer claims to have "anonymized" over 158 million Web pages so far!

The Least You Need to Know

- Yes, there's sex on the Internet, but not as much as the press claims. Get a filtering and blocking program if you want to keep the kids away.
- Email can easily be stolen or forwarded. Don't write anything that you could be embarrassed by later.
- People on the Internet sometimes lie (just like in the real world). They might not be who they say they are (or even the sex they claim to be).
- Internet addiction? Snap out of it! (Or go online and get some help.)
- You can search thousands of newsgroups at once, with systems such as DejaNews, to see what people are saying about you.
- Your boss can find out which Web sites you are visiting, so watch out!
- Credit card transactions made on the Internet are safer than those made in the real world.
- Anonymous email accounts can protect your identity in email and newsgroups.
- You don't own what you find on the Internet; it's copyright protected.
- Viruses are relatively few and far between; but it's a good idea to protect yourself with an antivirus program.

Chapter 19

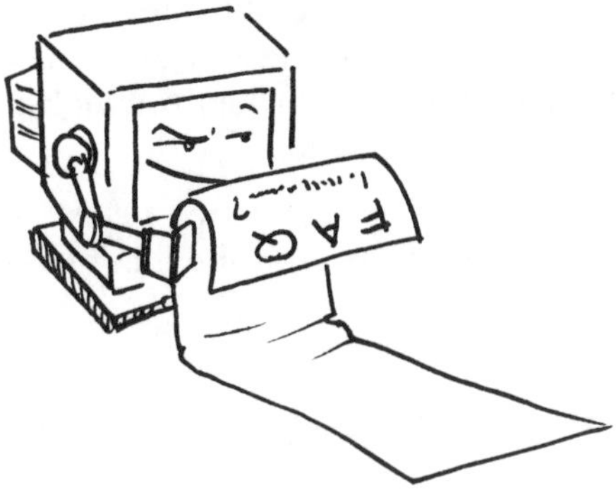

21 Questions: The Complete Internet FAQ

In This Chapter

- Shell accounts, finger, and Winsocks
- Changing your password
- Why some programs won't run in Windows
- Can you sell fish on the Internet?
- Slowdowns and connection problems
- Staying anonymous and much more

In this chapter, you will find answers to some questions you might have and a few problems you might run into—everything from the meaning of certain terms to solutions for certain problems.

1. What's a Shell Account?

You might remember me telling you (back in Chapter 1, "The Internet: What's It All About?") that a few years ago most people dialing into a service provider were using dial-in terminal accounts. These are often known as *shell* accounts. If you have a TCP/IP account with a service provider, you probably also have a shell account. Or if you sign up with a Web-hosting company to host your Web site (see Chapter 20, "Setting Up Your Own Web Site"), you'll probably get a shell account, too.

So you have a choice: You can connect to the Internet via the fancy graphical software, or you can connect using the bland command-line interface. Why bother with the command line when you can have the splashy graphics? The answer to the next question will provide an example of why you would want to, and when you look at the finger command later in this chapter, you'll see another example.

Most service providers give you a free shell account when you sign up for a PPP account. Others have the nerve to charge extra for the privilege. You shouldn't have to pay extra for it.

2. How Do I Change My Password If I'm Using a PPP Connection?

The fact that this is even a problem strikes me as a little strange. Many service providers don't provide a convenient way for you to change your password with a dial-in direct connection, yet they'll tell you that you should change your password frequently for security's sake. They *could* provide a Web form, but most don't. Many Web-hosting companies don't provide a password either. So how *do* you change your password?

Not a Good Sign

Some major service providers don't let you change your password at all. You have to call and ask them to do it for you, which is a *very* bad way to go about it!

If you are with an online service such as MSN, AOL, or CompuServe, the main program probably has some kind of password menu option. But if you are with a service provider, you might have to connect to their system with a terminal program. You need to get to the menu system used by people who are not fortunate enough to have a dial-in direct account. Find a menu option that says "Account Assistance" or something similar, and then look for one that says something like "Change Password."

But how do you get to the menu you need to change your password? One way is to connect using a simple serial-communications program (such as Windows 3.1's Terminal or Windows 95's HyperTerminal) or any commercial or shareware terminal program. You dial the phone number for your shell account and then log in, but you'll have to ask your service provider for information because the login instructions might be different. If you want more information about this procedure, you should see the first edition of this book; send email to `ciginternet@mcp.com`, type the word **first** in the Subject line, and leave the body of the message blank. You'll get Chapter 7 in an email response message. (For more information about using the email responder, see Appendix E, "The Email Responder.")

The other way is to connect to the Internet in the manner you usually employ and then open a Telnet program (see Chapter 16, "Gopher and Telnet—Still Alive, but Barely"). Connect to your service provider through Telnet, log on to your shell account, and then go to the change-password menu option. Call and ask your service provider which Telnet address to use.

3. What's a Winsock?

Winsock is short for "Windows sockets," and it's the program used by Microsoft Windows to act as an interface between TCP/IP programs running on the computer and the Internet itself. Just as a printer needs a printer driver to interface between the programs and the printer, the Internet needs a driver to interface between the programs and the Internet. In the Windows world, that driver is known as a Winsock. If you have a Macintosh, you don't have a Winsock, of course, but you still need TCP/IP software.

If you use Windows 3.1, you have to acquire a Winsock program separately—it doesn't come with the operating system. Most service providers and online services now include Winsock with the software they provide you (you can install it yourself if need be; one of the most commonly used ones is Trumpet Winsock, which you can find at many software archives; see Appendix C, "All the Software You'll Ever Need").

In Windows 95, 98, and NT, Winsock is built in, so you don't need to get a separate program. (However, you might need an advanced degree in networking to figure out how to use it.) The easiest way to handle all this is to get an installation program from a service provider or an online service that installs and configures the Winsock for you.

4. Why Won't Netscape Run in Windows 95?

This problem is not quite as common as it used to be, but it's still around; in fact, it got me just the other day. Suppose you are using Windows 95 and have connected to an Internet service provider that gave you Windows software to install. Then you go to the Netscape Web site to download the latest version of that navigator, or maybe you download the latest version of Internet Explorer. Which version do you pick? Why, the 32-bit version, of course, the one designed for Windows 95, 98, and NT. You install the program, and try it—but it doesn't work. What's going on?

The problem might be that, although you are using Windows 95 (what's known as a 32-bit operating system), the Winsock program you are using is a 16-bit program. Remember, the Winsock is the "driver" that connects your programs to the Internet. The Winsock is installed when you install the software needed to dial into the Internet. To run a 32-bit program (such as the Windows 95 versions of Netscape or Internet Explorer), you must use a 32-bit Winsock!

A year or two ago, many services were still providing 16-bit Winsocks, even though millions of people had Windows 95. Although most online services and service providers are now providing 32-bit Winsocks, some of the more inept services are still working with 16-bit Winsocks. If your service provider is still using an old 16-bit program, your only options are to stick with 16-bit programs (those created for Windows 3.1) or to convince the service provider to help you set up Windows 95's, 98's, or NT's Dial-Up Networking software. Or, if they won't help, find a service provider that will.

Anytime you run a 16-bit Winsock, you are stuck with 16-bit Internet programs. If you are trying to install a 32-bit Windows program and can't get it to work, start by checking to see whether you have a Winsock designed for Windows 95 or NT.

5. Why Won't My Browser Display This or That or the Other?

When you buy a TV, you expect to be able to use it to watch any program on any channel you have available. You don't expect to see error messages telling you something in a program can't be displayed or messages saying that if you want to see a particular program you'll have to install the *Jerry Springer* plug-in.

That's not the way it works on the Web. Browsers behave differently. Some browsers won't work with JavaScript or Java (or you might have turned off these things in your program preferences). Old browsers can't display frames and can't work with plug-ins—or if you have a recent browser, maybe you haven't installed the plug-in that a particular site requires.

You can avoid some of these problems, but by no means all, by working with the most up-to-date version of Netscape Navigator. You can get away with using the most recent version of Internet Explorer, too, although it's likely that it won't be quite as up-to-date as Netscape Navigator. But whichever browser you choose, there will *always* be certain features that won't work properly.

6. Can You Sell Fish on the Internet?

This is a real question that someone asked me during a radio show interview. (The question came from a fisherman in Alaska who was looking for new markets.) And I don't have the definitive answer. All I can say is, "maybe." But you'd better have a really good plan!

I don't know how you can go about selling fish, but I do know that you can sell various kinds of stuff—real stuff, not other Internet services. The editors took a poll and told me they'd seen salad dressing, teddy bears, model horses, live horses, legal services, picture-scanning devices, Internet tutoring, and real estate for sale. There are also books, CDs, and videos—as well as hot sauce, pizza, and a newsletter for writers of children's stories, and all sorts of other stuff. Of course, all these people are not necessarily making money doing this, but some most certainly are.

CDnow sold 16 million dollars' worth of music CDs in 1997, around $50 million in 1998, for instance, and that company was started by 24-year-old twin brothers (see *The CDnow Story: Rags to Riches on the Internet*, by Jason Olim, Matthew Olim, and Peter Kent, Top Floor Publishing). More modest successes abound. I know a small publisher selling more than $30,000 worth of books a year through his Web site; a company that sells a remote control "flying saucer" (it's actually a helium balloon) gets a significant portion of its income from the Web; and a fantasy-sports software company finds many new customers on the Internet. My own Web site (`http://poorrichard.com/`) is most definitely making a profit, and sales are growing. If you want to know more about making money on the Internet, see Chapter 21, "Making Money on the Internet."

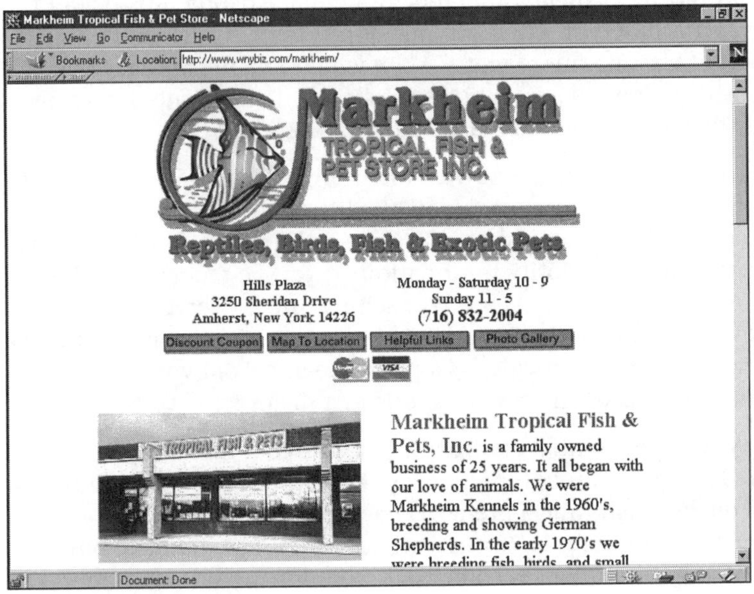

Maybe you can sell fish on the Internet.

7. If I Have a Fast Modem, Why Are Transfers So Slow?

You've just installed a fancy new 56Kbps modem, the very latest in modem technology you've been told, and still some Web sites are about as speedy as molasses on a cool day in Iceland. What's going on here? Your information has to pass through many computer systems, along lots of lines; hey, it might be coming from halfway across the world, after all.

Think of this transfer across the Internet as a relay race. The information you want is passed from person to person, maybe dozens of times, between the Web site and you. The last person in the chain is that speedy 56Kbps modem you bought. But when you look at the others involved in the race, you see that some are as athletic as Roseanne, and others are as fast as your grandmother. Still others might be very fast, but they've got other jobs to do, too. They are involved in hundreds of relay races at the same time! If you are at a very popular Web site, for instance, hundreds of other people just like you are trying to get information at the same time, and that relay runner might be having serious problems keeping up. (In any case, your 56Kbps modem almost certainly isn't operating at 56Kbps—see Appendix D, "Finding Internet Access and the Right Equipment.") I know I've told you that the Internet is a bunch of telephone wires connected to one another, but the truth is that it often operates like millions of bottlenecks strung together on a long piece of string.

If it's any consolation (and it probably isn't), it's not just you having problems; millions of other people are sitting at their computers in Alberta, Arizona, Austria, and other places beginning with different letters, saying, "I just bought this 56Kbps modem. Why did I bother wasting my money?" Why would anyone bother to get a fast modem? Because with a slow one, you'll be even slower. The Internet isn't slow all the time, so the faster your modem, the faster data transfers will be.

Another reason that your traffic might be slow is something called *differentiated service levels* or *preferential packets*. Information sent across the Internet is sent in small packets of data, each packet containing the address that's needed to get it to where it has to go. The packet can also include priority information. There are reports that the companies owning the Internet backbones are now selling priority service to major corporations. (A backbone is a major line on the Internet; you might think of the line from your computer to your service provider as a path, the line from your service provider to the backbone as a road, and the backbone as a major freeway.)

If a backbone company sells preferential treatment, it means that information going to or from the preferred site goes through right away. Any other packets of information have to wait in a queue. Each time a preferred packet arrives, that packet goes to the front of the queue. Mid-afternoon in North America is often a very busy time on the Internet anyway; corporate employees come back from lunch and log onto the Dilbert site or perhaps even do some work. But if those employees are getting preferential treatment, then it's even slower for the rest of us. So if your packet is sitting in a queue on a backbone on the other side of the country, it doesn't matter how fast your modem is—the packet can't get to you!

8. What's the Difference Between Yahoo! and Netscape Navigator?

If you've read this far, you should understand the difference. But I've heard this question a few times now—or rather, I've heard statements that made it clear that the speaker didn't understand the difference—so I thought I should cover it. Statements such as "Oh, you've got Yahoo! on your computer, too." Or "I know how to start Yahoo!, but I'm not sure how to get to my company's Web site."

Netscape Navigator (or Internet Explorer) is a program running on your computer. Yahoo! is a Web page. The confusion arises because many people have Yahoo! (or Netcenter, or some other search page) set as their home page—the page that is displayed whenever the browser starts.

What appears in the center of the browser is not part of the browser; it's something that somebody has published on the Web. It's available to anyone, who has access to the Internet, so don't think you're special because you've got it.

9. Why Isn't Anyone Reading My Web Page?

I guess you heard the nonsense that "A Web page is a billboard that can be seen by millions," and you believed it. Let me put it this way: There are 250 million people in the United States, but if you put up a *real* billboard in the United States, will 250 million people see it? I won't bother answering that.

The Web is not a highway, and your page is not a billboard. If you want people to come to your Web page, you have to promote it. Don't believe all that "If you want people to come to your Web site, it has to be compelling" nonsense either. A Web page has to serve a purpose; if it serves its purpose well and is well promoted, it can do well (even if it doesn't use Java to display some pointless animation).

10. How Can I Remain Anonymous on the Internet?

Many people are concerned with keeping their privacy and anonymity on the Internet. In particular, women who like to spend time in chat rooms often feel the need to put up a protective wall between themselves and other members. If a relationship develops with someone online, they want to be in control of how much information about themselves they allow others to discover.

There are some basic strategies you can use to maintain your anonymity on the Internet:

- Get an account with an online service or service provider and obtain an account name that is nothing like your own name. If your name is Jane Doe, use an account name such as *HipChick* or *SusanSmith*.
- Many online services enable you to enter information about yourself, also known as a profile, that others can view (in chat rooms, for instance). If you are with an online service, be sure your profile is empty.
- If you are with a service provider, ask your provider to disable finger for your account. (Finger is a service that other Internet users can employ to find information about you—see the next section.)
- After you are on the Internet, be careful not to leave identifying information when you're leaving messages in newsgroups, working with mailing lists, and so on.

Although these strategies won't ensure full anonymity, they work pretty well in most cases. To find out who HipChick or SusanSmith is, someone would have to persuade your service provider to divulge information. That's not impossible, but in most cases, it's unlikely (unless you're doing something to incite the interest of the police or the FBI).

You can also get a free email account from Juno, Yahoo!, Hotmail, or many other companies. When you fill in the form identifying yourself, dissemble (the word used to be lie, I believe, but politicians thought that word too coarse). See Chapter 18, "Staying Safe on the Internet," for more information on staying safe and anonymous.

11. What's Finger?

With the finger UNIX command, you can retrieve information about other people on the Internet if you have just a little bit of information. You can use this command in either of two ways:

- Log on to your shell account and get to the command line (you should find a menu option somewhere that will take you there; ask your service provider if you can't find it). At the command line, type **finger** and press **Enter** to run the command.
- Install a finger client, a program that allows you to run finger from within your graphical user interface—from Windows or the Macintosh, for instance. (See Appendix C for a list of software archives.)

Some You Win, Some You Lose

Many service providers completely disable finger requests. Others disable certain types of requests. For instance, if you were to try a command such as `finger smith@big.net`, some service providers would send a list of all the account holders called Smith, but some providers simply wouldn't respond.

Suppose you've seen the `HipChick@big.net` email address and want to find out about HipChick. You use the finger command `finger HipChick@big.net` and press **Enter**. A request for information is sent to big.net. You *might* get such information as the account holder's real name, which is why I told you to make sure finger is disabled if you want to remain anonymous!

12. Can Someone Forge My Email?

A year or two ago I saw a message in a mailing list from someone complaining that an email message to the list was forged. Someone else had sent a message using this person's email address. Another member of the list wrote a message telling her that she should be more careful. He said (a little bluntly) that if she left her computer unattended, she should expect trouble. Thinking I'd play a little game, I sent a forged message to the list in *his* name. (No, I didn't know him, and I definitely didn't have access to his computer.) "That'll teach him," I thought, "He should be more careful."

It's very easy to forge email messages—so easy, in fact, that I'm surprised it doesn't happen more often. (It probably happens more often to people who spend a lot of time in newsgroups, mailing lists, and chat rooms—where it's easy to get into fights—than to people who use other services.) A person can forge a message simply by entering incorrect configuration information into a mail program or, better still, the mail program of a public Web browser. However, before you run out and play tricks on people, I should warn you that this mail can still be traced to some degree. (It might be difficult, though, for anyone other than a police officer with a warrant to get the service providers to do the tracing for him.)

How can you avoid this problem? There's not much you can do except keep your head down and stay out of "flame wars" (which I'll discuss next). You *could* digitally sign all your messages, as discussed in Chapter 3, although that might be overkill.

13. What's a Flame?

I've heard it said that the Internet will lead to world peace. As people use the Net to communicate with others around the world, a new era of understanding will come to pass...blah, blah, blah. The same was said about the telegraph and the television, but so far, there hasn't been much of a peace spin-off from those technologies! But what makes me sure that the Internet will not lead to world peace (and might lead to world war) is the prevalence of flame wars in mailing lists and newsgroups.

A *flame* is a message that is intended as an assault on another person, an ad hominem attack. Such messages are common and lead to flame wars, as the victim responds and others get in on the act. In some discussion groups, flame wars are almost the purpose of the group. You'll find that the Internet is no haven of peace and goodwill—and I haven't even mentioned the obnoxious behavior of many in chat rooms.

14. I'm Leaving My Service Provider. How Can I Keep My Email Address?

I currently have three Internet accounts. Over the past few years, I've had dozens of accounts, and that means I've had dozens of email addresses. Although this is unusual, it's certainly not unusual for people to have a handful of accounts as they search for the best one. Unfortunately, keeping your friends and colleagues up-to-date on your email address is a real hassle. If only there were a way to keep the same address, even when you changed providers.

There just might be. You can register your own domain name. You can do this through a number of places, such as Network Solutions (`http://www.networksolutions.com/`), and Register.com (`http://www.register.com/`). At the time of writing it costs $70 for the first two years and $35 a year after that to keep the domain name, but prices are going to drop soon, because domain registration has just been opened up to competition. Many service providers will register a domain for you, but they might charge you an additional fee to do so.

After you have your own domain name, you can set up a mail service (search for **email service** at a search site such as Yahoo!) and assign the domain name to that service. Then all your email addressed to that domain will be sent to the service, which will store it in your POP (Post Office Protocol) account. You'll use a mail program to download your mail from there. (When you register a domain name, you have to already have chosen a service, because the email service provider has to set up its computers to recognize the name.) If you plan to set up a Web site with a Web-hosting company, then you can register the domain to that company's servers, and you'll get your email there (see Chapter 20).

After you are using an email service or getting email through a Web-hosting company, it doesn't matter which service provider or online service you use to get onto the Internet. You can change from one company to another as many times as you like, and you'll still be able to get to your mail through the email provider or hosting company. And if you ever decide to move your domain name to a different email provider or hosting company? Then find the new company and transfer your domain to it. Whether you change email providers, hosting companies, or Internet service providers, you can always keep your email address. Email services start at around $5 a month, and even Web-hosting accounts are available for less than $10 a month.

Another way to keep your email address is to sign up with a free or low-cost email service. A number of these are around now (search at `http://www.yahoo.com/` for **free email service**). These services are usually free because they sell advertising that is shown when you get your mail. If you don't mind that, though, this is a good way to get and keep an email address, regardless of how many times you change your service provider. One of these companies (MailBank: `http://mailbank.com/`) has bought up thousands of domain names based on people's last names, so for $5 a year you can have an address that uses your last name as the domain name: john@kent.org, fred@smithmail.com, and so on.

15. Why Can't I Get Through to That Site?

You'll often find that you cannot connect to sites that you've used before or that you've seen or heard mentioned somewhere. You might find Web pages that you can't connect to, FTP sites that don't seem to work, and Telnet sites that seem to be out of commission. Why?

The first thing you should check is your spelling and case; if you type one wrong character or type something uppercase when it should be lowercase (or vice versa), you won't connect. (The following figure shows the dialog box Netscape Navigator displays when you've typed the name incorrectly.) Another possibility is that the service you are trying to connect to might just be very busy, with hundreds of other people trying to connect. Depending on the software you are using, you might see a message to that effect. Or it could be that the service is temporarily disconnected; the computer that holds the service might have broken or might have been disconnected for service. Finally, the service might not be there anymore.

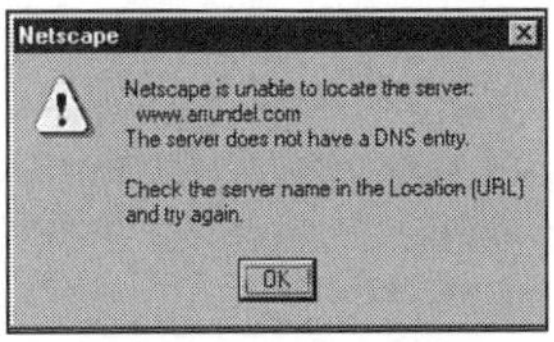

Oops! I mistyped the URL, and my browser can't find the host.

Trying again a few times often helps; you'll be surprised just how often you can get through to an apparently dead site just by trying again a few moments later. Also note that some software is a little buggy. For instance, some browsers seem to hang up and appear unable to transfer data from a site at times; but canceling the transfer and starting again often jump-starts the process.

Don't Place the Blame Too Quickly

Often it's your service provider, not the site you are trying to connect to, that's having problems. Try connecting to a variety of sites, and if you can't get through to any, it's probably a problem with your connection to the service provider or with the provider's system. Try disconnecting and logging back on.

Remove the Period

When you type a URL, don't type a period at the end. You might find URLs in books and magazines that appear to end with a period because they are used at the ends of sentences. But real URLs don't end with periods.

16. Why Won't This URL Work?

URLs are a special case because even if they don't seem to work, you might be able to modify them and get them to work. First, be sure you are using the correct case. If a word in the URL was shown as uppercase, don't type lowercase (if the URL doesn't work with some words uppercase, though, you might try lowercase).

Second, be sure you are using the correct file extension if there is one. If the URL ends in .htm, be sure you are not typing .html, for instance. If the URL still doesn't work, start removing portions of the URL. Suppose you have this URL:

```
http://www.big.net/public/software/macintosh/internet/listing.html
```

You've tried using both `listing.html` and `listing.htm` at the end, and neither seems to work. Drop `listing.html` and try again. You might get a document with links to something you can use. If you still don't get anything, remove the `internet/` part (in other words, you are now typing just `http://www.big.net/public/software/macintosh/`). If that doesn't work, remove the next part, macintosh/. Continue in this manner, removing piece after piece, and in most cases, you'll eventually find something useful.

17. Why Do So Many People Hate AOL?

It's an unfortunate truth that America Online members have a bad reputation on the Internet. You might run across rude messages in which people insult AOL members or treat them as if they are the scum of the earth. Here's what happened. AOL, like all the online services, decided that it had better get Internet access in a hurry. So it started adding Internet services, and it added newsgroup access quite early. All of a sudden, about a gazillion AOL members flooded onto the Internet in a rush that would have had the bulls at Pamplona running in the opposite direction. Millions of AOL members overwhelmed these discussion groups with questions such as "How do you download files from this group?" and "Where are the pornographic pictures?" Of all the online services' members, AOL's members were probably the least computer-literate. (AOL had targeted the "family" market, while CompuServe, for instance, had been a geek service for years.)

The Internet had been, until just a few months before, a secret kept from most of the world. All of a sudden, it was as busy as a shopping mall on a Saturday afternoon, and every bit as cultured. And there was an obvious scapegoat: all those people with @aol.com email addresses! Unfortunately, you might still run across anti-AOL bias on the Internet.

18. My Download Crashed, So I Have to Start Again. Why?

Most online services use file-transfer systems that can "recover" if the transfer is interrupted. For instance, if you are halfway through downloading a file from CompuServe when your three-year-old kid decides he wants to see what happens when he presses the big red button on the front of your computer, all is not lost. After you reboot the computer and reconnect to CompuServe, you can begin the file transfer again. But you don't have to transfer the whole thing; instead the transfer begins in the middle.

However, that usually won't work on the World Wide Web. (In some cases it will work—in most cases it won't. It all depends on the type of utility the site is using for transfering files.) You often can resume interrupted downloads at FTP sites, though, with some FTP programs, which is one reason that FTP can be so useful (see Chapter 12, "The Giant Software Store: FTP"). If you prefer to use your Web browser for transferring files, though, you'll have to keep your kid away from the computer (or try covering the button with a piece of card).

19. Where Do I Find...?

You're in the wrong chapter; see Chapter 17, "Finding Stuff."

20. Are .com and .net Interchangeable?

What's the difference between .com, .net, and .org? Often not much, except that .com is often assumed. These are known as TLDs, Top Level Domains. A .com domain is supposed to be a commercial domain. A .net domain is in some way Internet-related—Internet service providers often have .net domains—and an .org domain is supposed to be some kind of organization, such as a charity or professional organization. But partly because browsers were set up to work with .com as the default (if you type a single word into a browser you might find that the browser tries to go to *thatword*.com—type `cat`, for instance, and it might try to go to cat.com), .com has become the domain to get. So even if a service provider has a .net domain, it probably also has a .com domain, too. `http://www.earthlink.com/` and `http://www.earthlink.net/` will both get you to the same place.

That's not to say you can interchange .com and .net, or .org for that matter. If you're given a URL that ends in .net, you need to use .net, because .com might not work. However, more and more companies are registering matching domain names—.com, .net, and .org. The registration authorities are encouraging this, perhaps as a way to make more money. It certainly negates the whole purpose of having different TLDs.

21. Is It Safe to Make a Credit-Card Transaction over the Internet?

Yes. Don't believe all the nonsense about the dangers of transmitting a credit-card number across the Internet; it's perfectly safe. There might be a problem after it gets to where it's going, of course, but the chance of it being stolen en route are pretty small. I heard recently that there are no known cases of credit-card numbers being stolen "on-the-fly," which means all the fuss about credit-card security over the last few years has been one monumental case of making a mountain out of a molehill.

Just One More Question...

You're going to come away from this book with lots of questions because the Internet is big, there are many different ways to connect to it, and there's a huge amount of strange stuff out there. I hope this book has helped you start, but I know you'll have many more questions.

After you are on your own, what do you do? Try these suggestions:

- **Get the FAQs** FAQ means "frequently asked questions," and it refers to a document with questions and answers about a particular subject. Many newsgroups and mailing lists have FAQs explaining how to use them, for example, and Web sites often have FAQ pages. Look for these FAQs and read them!
- **Continue your reading** I've written about a dozen Internet books and need to sell them, so continue buying (and reading) them. Well, okay, there are other writers putting out Internet books, too (you might have noticed a few). To become a real cybergeek, you'll need to learn much more. So check out a few of these books.
- **Read the documentation** There are literally thousands of Internet programs, and each is a little different. Be sure you read all the documentation that comes with your programs so you know how to get the most out of them.
- **Ask your service provider!** I've said it before, and I'll say it again: If your service provider won't help you, get another service provider! The Internet is too complicated to travel around without help. Now and again you'll have to ask your service provider's staff for information. Don't be scared to ask—and don't be scared to find another provider if the first one won't or can't answer your questions

The Least You Need to Know

- A shell account is a dial-in terminal account. You might have a free shell account, and you might need to use your shell account to change your password.
- Getting rich on the Internet is a lot harder than it's been made out to be.
- You might have a fast modem, but if the Internet is busy, things will still move slowly.
- Use an email service if you want to be able to switch between service providers without changing your email address each time.
- You can be anonymous on the Internet if you are careful.
- If your service provider won't answer your questions, you need another service provider!

Chapter 20

Setting Up Your Own Web Site

In This Chapter

- Your 10-minute Web page
- Setting a page as your home page
- Why create your own Web pages?
- All about HTML
- Adding links
- Creating a hierarchy of pages linked to the home page
- Shortcuts to grabbing links
- Where can you put your Web site?

A few years ago, I would never have considered putting a chapter about creating Web pages in an introduction to the Internet. But times change. Many newcomers to the Internet are setting up Web sites—in fact, many people get onto the Internet *so* they can set up a Web site.

Luckily, setting up a basic Web site is very easy. A Web site is just a collection of Web pages, and creating a single Web page is quite simple—so simple that I'm betting I can teach you to create a simple Web page in, oh, one chapter. No, I take that back! I'll bet you can create a very simple customized Web page in about 10 minutes. I'll cheat a little, though, by giving you a template, in which you can fill in the "blanks."

My Fill-In-the-Blanks Web Page

I've created a Web page for you; you can get it from the email responder. Send an email message to ciginternet@mcp.com with **ownweb** in the Subject line of the message. (For more information about using the mail responder, see Appendix E, "The Email Responder.") When you receive the message, save it as a text file with the HTM extension. Then open the file in a text editor, such as SimpleText (on the Macintosh) or Notepad (in Windows). Or, instead of saving the message in a text file, copy the text from the email message and paste it into a text editor or word processing document. Remove all the text *before* the <HTML> text. (*Don't* remove the <HTML> part; just remove all the text prior to it.) Also remove any text that appears after </BODY>, near the bottom of the message.

If you use a word processor instead of a text editor, you'll have to remember to save the file as a text file instead of as a normal word processing file when you finish working with it. As you'll learn later in this chapter, Web pages are simple text files. In many cases, using a word processor is not a great idea because word processors often automatically insert special characters such as curly quotation marks and em dashes, and other characters that can't be converted to plain text. Therefore, you're better off using a text editor.

For the impatient among you, those who don't want to wait for the mail to arrive (although it'll probably only take a few seconds), I've included the text from the sample file here. You can type the following lines into your text editor if you want, but you must be sure you type them exactly the same as they appear here:

```
<HTML>
<HEAD>
<TITLE>My Very Own Web Page—Replace if You Want</TITLE>
</HEAD>
<BODY>
<H1>Replace This Title With Whatever You Want</H1>
Put whatever text you want here.<P>
This is another paragraph; use whatever text you want.
<H2>First Subcategory: Replace this With Whatever Title You Want</H2>
<A HREF="http://www.mcp.com">The Macmillan Web Site</A><P>
<A HREF="url_here">Another link: replace this text</A><P>
<A HREF="url_here">Another link: replace this text</A><P>
<A HREF="url_here">Another link: replace this text</A><P>
<A HREF="url_here">Another link: replace this text</A>
<H2>Second Subcategory: Replace this With Whatever Title You Want</H2>
Put more text and links here.
<H2>Third Subcategory: Replace this With Whatever Title You Want</H2>
Put more text and links here.
<H2>Fourth Subcategory: Replace this With Whatever Title You Want</H2>
Put more text and links here.
</BODY>
</HTML>
```

The following figure shows you what this file looks like when displayed in a Web browser. For now, don't worry if you don't *understand* what is going on here; you're trying to break a speed record, not actually learn right now. In a few moments, I'll explain how this whole Web-creation thing works.

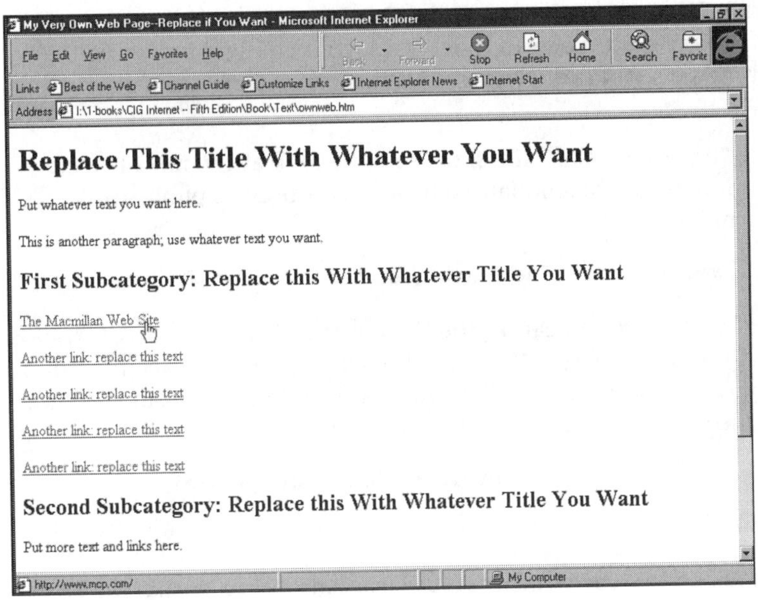

This is what the Web page template looks like in a Web browser.

First, I want you to replace some things. You can start with the text between the <TITLE> and </TITLE> *tags*. Whatever text you type between those tags will appear in the browser's title bar (as you can see in the figure), so replace the text that's there by typing your name, or **My Home Page**, or whatever you want. When you finish doing that, replace the text between the <H1> and </H1> tags. The text you type here will be a heading—the top-level heading, as a matter of fact. You can use the same text that you entered as the title if you want (that's what Web authors often do).

What's a Tag?

Text that has a less-than symbol (<) in front of it and a greater-than symbol (>) after it is known as a *tag*. The tags tell your Web browser how to display the text in an HTML file.

Now, save your work, but don't close the text file. Use your Web browser to open the file; you can double-click the file in Windows File Manager or Windows Explorer, or use the browser's **File**, **Open** command. You can see the changes you've made.

Next, add some text to the file if you want. Replace the text immediately below the `<H1></H1>` heading, or remove it if you don't want it. (Notice, by the way, that you must end each paragraph with the `<P>` tag.) After that, replace the next headings with names of categories that describe the sort of links you want in your page. If you have favorite music sites that you visit, you might make the first heading Music. Another heading might be Financial, and another might be Goofing Around. It's your page. Use whatever categories you want. You can quickly see your changes by saving the file and clicking the browser's **Reload** (Netscape Navigator) or **Refresh** (Internet Explorer) button.

Before you change the "Another link..." lines, take a close look at the links I've created. The first one is a link to the Macmillan Web site. (This book is published by Que, a division of Macmillan.)

```
<A HREF="http://www.mcp.com">The Macmillan Web Site</A><P>
```

The words *The Macmillan Web Site* appear on the Web page as the actual link text; you can see those words in the figure. The URL for the linked page goes between the quotation marks, as in `"http://www.mcp.com"`. Keeping that in mind, go ahead and modify the links I've provided. For instance, you might change this:

```
<A HREF="url_here">Another link: replace this text</A><P>
```

to this:

```
<A HREF="http://www.iuma.com">Internet Underground Music Archive</A><P>
```

Be Careful

Be sure that you don't remove any of the < or > symbols. If you do, it can really mess up your page.

Replace all the generic links with links to Web sites you like to visit. As a shortcut, you can copy a link, paste it a few times below each category heading, and then modify each of the copied links so that they point to more Web sites. When you finish making your changes, save the page and click the browser's **Reload** or **Refresh** button. Right before your very eyes, you'll see your brand-new 10-minute Web page. Didn't I tell you it was easy?

Make It Your Home Page

After you've created a home page, you need to tell your browser to use it as the home page. In Internet Explorer, begin by displaying your new page in the browser window. Then, in Internet Explorer 5, select **Tools**, **Internet Options**, and click the **Use Current** button to set the page in the browser as the home page. (In Explorer 3, choose **View**, **Options** and click the **Start and Search Pages** tab; in Explorer 4, it's the **Navigator** tab, or maybe the **General** tab! Then you might have to choose **Start Page** from the Page drop-down list box.

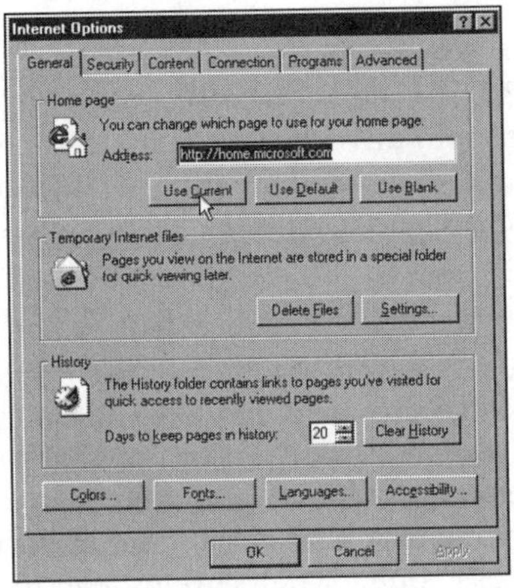

In Internet Explorer, you can click the Use Current button to select the currently displayed page as the home page.

To make your Web page the home page in Netscape Navigator 4 and 4.5, load the page into the browser, and then choose **Edit**, **Preferences**, click the **Navigator** category, and click the **Use Current Page** button. In Navigator 3, choose **Options**, **General Preferences**, and click the **Appearance** tab. Look for the **Browser Starts With** text box. You have to type the path and filename of the page you want to open. (For instance, in Windows 95, you would type `c:\program files\netscape\communicator\ownweb.htm` for a file named OWNWEB.HTM that's in the \PROGRAM FILES\NETSCAPE\COMMUNICATOR\ directory on drive C:.) Then click the **OK** button.

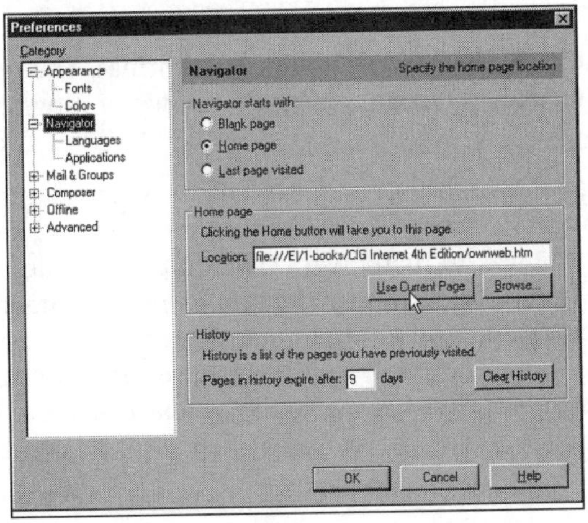

Setting the home page in Netscape Navigator 4.5 is similar to doing so in Internet Explorer (and much easier than in Netscape Navigator 3).

The next time you start your browser, you'll see your very own home page. And the next time you click the **Home** button, up pops your home page.

Your Web Page: What's It Good For?

Why bother creating your own page? There are a few reasons. First, telling your browser to view a home page on your hard drive will speed up loading the program. Most browsers these days are configured to use a home page at the browser publisher's Web site, but it's much quicker to load from a "local" drive than to transfer a page from across the Internet. If that were the only reason, though, you could just copy an HTML document from the Web somewhere and put it on your hard drive.

The second reason has to do with the fact that everyone uses the Internet in a different way. The home page someone else has created won't have all the links you want and will contain plenty of links that you don't want. So you might as well customize your home page to work the way you want it to work and include links to sites you want to go to. You can also create a home page that has a series of documents linked to it (such as one for work, one for music, one for newsgroups, and so on).

Another reason (if you still need coaxing) is that you might want to put information about yourself or your business on the World Wide Web. You're not limited to creating a Web page for your own use and saving it on your hard drive. You can create a Web page that the world can read by saving it on your service provider's system so that it's available to the Internet at large.

HTML Basics

You've already seen how simple Web authoring can be. Now you're going to learn a bit more theory about *HTML* (Hypertext Markup Language). HTML is the language of the Web, and all those <xxx> tags you looked at are HTML tags.

HTML files are not very complicated. They're in a simple text format. The nice thing about a simple text file is that it's widely recognized by thousands of programs and many types of computers.

It's important to understand that although text editors (such as Notepad and SimpleText) create text files, word processors do not. A word processor is like an advanced text editor. It formats the text in many ways that simple text files cannot. It adds character formatting (italic, bold, underline, and so on), special characters (curly quotation marks, copyright symbols, em and en dashes, and many others), and formats paragraph spacing, for example. That's why you have to be careful when creating HTML files in a word processor; you must save the file as text instead of in the word processor's file format.

HTML files are text files that have been specially designed to be read by Web browsers. They use the same characters as any other text file, but they use a special convention that all Web browsers understand. That convention is this: "If you see anything in brackets such as these < >, you know it's a special code." When Web browsers are rendering the HTML document into normal text so that they can display the document on the screen, they look for these brackets and follow the instructions inside them.

You've already created a Web page, so you know what tags look like. But take a minute to go back and examine the tags you used.

- <TITLE> </TITLE> The text between these tags is the title of the document. You won't see this text in the document; it's simply an identifier that the browsers use. For instance, Netscape and Internet Explorer would put the text in the title bar. In addition, this title is used in bookmark and history lists, and if you've put the page out on the Web, the title might be used by Web search sites (see Chapter 17, "Finding Stuff") to help them index or categorize your site.
- <H1> </H1> These particular tags mark the first-level heading. You can include up to six levels using the tags <H2> </H2>, <H3> </H3>, <H4> </H4>, <H5> </H5>, and <H6> </H6>. Experiment with these tags in your own Web page.
- <P> This tag is used at the end of a paragraph. Simply typing a carriage return in your HTML file will *not* create a new paragraph in the final document that appears in the browser. You must use the <P> tag instead. Without the tag, the paragraphs will run together.

> Check This Out
>
> **Rendering**
>
> This term is used to describe the action carried out by the browser when it looks at the HTML codes and formats the text according to the instructions within those codes. It strips the codes from the text and displays the resulting text in the browser.

> Check This Out
>
> **Does It Have to Be Uppercase?**
>
> Don't worry about the case of the tags. You can type <title>, <TITLE>, <Title>, <TItlE>, or <TiTlE>—whatever tickles your fancy.

Notice that, in most cases, tags are paired. There's an opening and a closing tag, and the closing tag is the same as the opening tag with the exception of the forward slash after the left angle bracket. <H1> and </H1> form a pair, for instance. The <P> tag is one exception to this. You need only the <P> tag, and it appears after the paragraph.

Finally, there's an *anchor* tag, which is used to create a link:

```
<A HREF="http://www.mcp.com">The Macmillan Web Site</A><P>
```

Anchors

The <A HREF="url"> tags are often called anchors. For this reason, many people refer to the actual links in the Web documents as anchors.

Notice that the URL is included within the angle brackets and within quotation marks. A *link tag* (a tag that you use to create a hypertext link in your document) consists of <A, followed by a space, followed by HREF=". After that tag, you enter the URL. You've looked at URLs before; these are the same URLs that you can use to tell a browser to go to a particular Web site. At the end of the URL, you add ">, followed by whatever text you want. (That text is going to appear on the finished Web page as the link text.) Following the text, you use the closing tag </A>. In the preceding example, I also used the <P> tag to start a new paragraph; I wanted to be sure that the link would appear on its own line.

<P> and </P>

You've already learned that the <P> tag doesn't have to have a matching code to make a pair. Actually, you can use <P> and </P> as a pair if you want. <P> marks the beginning of a paragraph, and </P> marks the end. However, this is not necessary, and few Web authors do so unless they want to add certain "attributes" to the <P> tag—but that's further into HTML than we'll go in this book.

A Word About Paragraphs

Web browsers don't deal with paragraphs in the same way that word processors do. If the browser finds several spaces, including blank lines, it will compress all the space into a single paragraph unless it sees the <P> tag somewhere. When it finds the <P> tag, it ends that paragraph and starts a new one below it, generally leaving a blank line between the two. If for some reason you want to move text down to the next line but you don't want a blank line between the two lines of text, you can use the <BR> tag instead of <P>. The <BR> tag inserts a line break without starting a new paragraph.

Don't Stop at One: Multiple Pages

You can easily create a hierarchy of documents. Why not have a document that appears when you open the browser, with a table of contents linked to several other documents? In each of those documents, you can then have links related to a particular subject.

Say you want to set up a document for the music sites you are interested in. Call it RNR.HTM, or MUSIC.HTM, or whatever you want. Create that document in the same way you did the first one, and put it in the same directory. You can then create a link from your home page to the rock n' roll document, like this:

```
<A HREF="RNR.HTM">Rock n' Roll</A>
```

Although RNR.HTM is a filename, you can use it in place of the URL. In fact, RNR.HTM is a URL: it's what's known as a *relative URL*. This link tells a Web browser to look for the RNR.HTM file. Although it doesn't tell the browser where to look for the file, the browser makes a basic assumption. Because the URL doesn't include the hostname or directory, the only place the browser can look is in the same directory as the original file. (And that's just fine because you are going to place the RNR.HTM file in the same directory, right?)

This is really simple, isn't it? You create a home page (called HOME.HTM) with links to any number of other documents in the same directory. You might have links to sites for rock n' roll, art, music, conspiracy theories, or whatever sort of information you are interested in and can find on the Web. Then you fill up those documents with more links to all those interesting sites. Whad'ya know? You're a Web publisher!

Finding URLs

There are shortcuts to creating the links in your home page. Who wants to type all those URLs, after all? One way to grab the URLs is to visit the Web page you are interested in and copy the text from the Location or Address text box at the top of the browser window. To do that, you can highlight the text, and then press **Ctrl+C** or select **Edit**, **Copy**. (Most browsers have some method for copying the URL.) Then you can just paste it into your home page.

You can also grab URLs from links on a document. Right-click a link to see a pop-up menu (if you're using a Macintosh, try clicking and holding the mouse button down for a second or two). Click the **Copy Shortcut** option in Internet Explorer, or click the **Copy Link Location** option in Netscape.

You can also grab information from the bookmark list or, in some cases, the history list. In Internet Explorer, you can open Favorites (that's the name it uses for its bookmark system). Choose **Favorites**, **Organize Favorites** (or **Favorites**, **Open Favorites Folder** in earlier versions), right-click an item, and choose **Properties**. Then click the **Internet Shortcut** tab and copy the URL from the **Target URL** text box.

In Netscape, you can open the Bookmarks window (**Window**, **Bookmarks** or perhaps **Communicator**, **Bookmarks**, **Edit Bookmarks**) and do much the same thing. Right-click an item, select **Properties**, and then copy the URL from the box that appears. (Or click the item and select **Edit**, **Properties**.) You can also choose **File**, **Save As** to save the entire bookmark system in an HTML file. Then you can open that file in a text editor and pick and choose which URLs you want.

Publishing on the Web

If you want to publish on the Web—that is, take the pages you have created and make them available to anyone on the Web—you have a two-step process to go through. First, you create the page. But then you have to place it somewhere that is accessible to the Internet. It has to be put on a Web server.

Most online services and Internet service providers allow their subscribers to post their own Web pages. Some of these services even allow each subscriber to post a megabyte or two, sometimes as much as 10MB, of Web pages, graphics, and so on. Check with your service to find out how much data you can post and where to put it. But a service provider isn't the only place to put a Web site. You have a variety of additional choices:

- **On your own Web server** You can buy your own Web server (you need a computer, connection hardware, and Web-server software), connect it to the Internet, and place your Web site on that server. This is what I call the "open your wallet" method. It's expensive and complicated, and few people should try it.
- **At a free-page Web site** There are organizations and individuals who provide free Web space to anyone who asks. See `http://www.yahoo.com/Business_and_Economy/Companies/Internet_Services/Web_Services/Free_Web_Pages/`.
- **At a cybermall** You can sign up with a Web mall. In general, however, Web malls tend to be expensive and often not very high quality.
- **At a Web store** A number of stores allow companies to place pages in the Web store. For instance, a number of book sites sell space to small publishers.
- **At a Web host's site in a subdirectory or subdomain** A Web host is a company that sells space on its Web server to companies that want a Web site. The cheapest way to do this is to use the hosting company's URL and have your Web site as a subdirectory: `http://www.verybigwebhost.com/yoursite`, for instance.

Getting a Domain Name

Go to Network Solutions (`http://www.networksolutions.com/`) or Register.com (`http://www.register.com`) to register a .com, .net, .org, or .edu domain name. For other domains, try a commercial service such as AllDomains: `http://www.alldomains.com/`.

- **At a Web host's site as a virtual host** You place your Web pages on a Web host's server, but you use your own domain name: `http://www.yoursite.com/`.

Finding a Web Host

A free Web site, or the space available at an online service or service provider is fine for most people. But if you're serious about setting up a Web site for a small to medium company or for some kind of club or organization, you'll probably want to use a Web-hosting company, for several reasons:

- You need your own domain name. It will be easier for your clients or members to remember, easier to get listed at Yahoo! (the single most important search site on the Internet; they have a bias against sites placed in a subdirectory of an online service or service provider), and you won't have to change your Web site's URL each time you move your Web site. Most online services or service providers won't let you use your own domain name with your basic Internet access account.
- Most online services and service providers don't provide the sort of services that a Web site needs, such as the capability to run scripts (the things that make Web forms work).

Where can you find a low-cost hosting company? A good place to start is Budgetweb at `http://www.budgetweb.com/`. This large directory of Web-hosting companies has prices that start as low as $9 a month (I pay around $30 a month for my Web site; if you pay too little, you might end up with an unreliable service, of course).

There's a problem, though. Selecting a hosting company can be rather complicated. There are so many things to consider, you shouldn't choose one until you understand what you're looking for. I'll provide a little help, though. At my Web site, you'll find a free report called *20 Questions to Ask a Web-Hosting Company* (`http://www.poorrichard.com/freeinfo/special_reports.htm`), which should give you enough information to get started.

Posting Your Web Pages

After you have a Web site, how do you get the pages from your computer to the Web site? Generally, you'll have to use FTP, which you learned about in Chapter 12, "The Giant Software Store: FTP." This system enables you to transfer files from your computer to another computer on the Internet. Some of the online services use a different system, though; check with your online service for more information.

If you're using an HTML authoring program, though, you might have a transfer utility built in. These programs are like word processors for HTML. You type your text, format the text using normal word processing tools, and the programs create the HTML for you. Many of these tools are available, and they can greatly simplify Web creation. See `http://www.yahoo.com/Computers_and_Internet/Software/Internet/World_Wide_Web/HTML_Editors/` for links to some of these programs.

Using Web Templates

Now that you've learned a little about HTML, I guess I should tell you that you might not need to know anything about HTML. Many Internet service providers have templates you can use to create your Web pages. In other words, you can go to a service provider's Web site, and follow through a series of forms in which you enter your information, pick colors and backgrounds, upload images, and so on. All the HTML coding is done for you, and the page is automatically posted at the service provider's Web site. Check at your service provider's Web site to see whether such templates are available to you.

There are even sites that provide these sorts of tools for free. You get a free Web site, and you get templates to help you build the pages. To find services such as these, visit a search site such as Yahoo! and search for free Web sites. Tripod (`http://www.tripod.com/`) and GeoCities (`http://www.geocities.com/`) are two of the biggest such sites.

The Least You Need to Know

- Creating a home page is very simple; you can use the template provided to create one in as few as 10 minutes.
- Enclose HTML tags within brackets < >.
- In most cases, you need an opening tag and a closing tag, such as `<TITLE>My Home Page</TITLE>`.
- You use tags to tell your browser which text you want displayed as titles, headings, links, and so on.
- To create a link, type `<A HREF="URL">Your Link Text</A>`, replacing URL and Your Link Text with those you want to use.
- If you use a filename in place of the URL in the link, the browser will look in the same directory as the current document.
- You can replace your browser's default home page with your new one.
- After you've created a page, you can post it at your service provider's site so the whole world can see it!
- There are other ways to post your site on the Web, though, from free sites to Web-hosting companies. Most businesses, clubs, and organizations should use a hosting company.

Chapter 21

Making Money on the Internet

In This Chapter

- Ways to make money on the Internet
- Is the Internet for every business?
- How much will using the Internet for business cost?
- Bringing people to your Web site
- Using email as a marketing tool

Want to make money on the Internet? Oh, that's easy. First, start a business selling some kind of Internet service or software. Run it for a few months on a shoestring, and then go public. It doesn't matter what the intrinsic value of the company is—as long as it has the word "Internet" attached to it somehow, you'll get rich.

A couple of years ago I thought perhaps that this Internet-investment hype was beginning to die out, but it appears to be alive and well. Internet IPOs (Initial Public Offerings) are still hot, and companies with little intrinsic value have huge market caps (that is, market capitalization, the total value of their stock). Amazon.com, for instance, as I write, is worth over $22 billion. Barnes and Noble, on the other hand, a company that actually makes money, and sells many times more books than Amazon.com, is worth only $2.3 billion. Is Amazon.com really worth ten times Barnes and Noble? Almost certainly not…except for the fact that enough people think it is, and so, for the moment, it is. But then, there was a time when tulips were being traded in Holland for vast sums. Eventually, it came to an end.

Is the end on the way for Internet stocks? Probably not for a while. But there are rumblings in the wings. As Andy Grove, the chairman of Intel, said not too long ago, "It remains to be seen whether the Internet companies that have essentially infinite access to capital will be able to grow up to be self-sufficient institutions and adjust to a future when money won't be free." Translation #1: These companies might not be worth what people are paying for them. Translation #2: When the investment money runs out, these companies might be in trouble.

There's Another Way

Not so long ago, the only people making money on the Internet were people selling Internet services: software companies, service providers, hardware manufacturers, and so on. It seemed that almost nobody was making money on the Internet unless they were selling goods or services to people who wanted to make money on the Internet, sort of like an author making lots of money by selling get-rich-quick schemes to people who'd never get rich. In fact, the high failure rate of Internet businesses was a joke among Internet insiders. A few years ago, when I told an executive at a major Internet software company that I wanted to write a book about companies that have figured out how to make money on the Internet, he said, "Is anyone making money? I mean, we are, but is anyone else?"

These days it's easy to find companies that are succeeding. Many companies, including small one-person businesses, are taking orders online or using the Internet to successfully promote their business. I've spoken with a small publishing company selling $3,000 worth of books at their Web site each month, a small gaming-software publisher that finds a "significant" proportion of its new customers on the Web, and a two-man business selling toys online—and selling lots of them. *I* make money on the Internet, too. I sell enough books at my Web site (`http://www.topfloor.com/`) to make far more than just pin money! I also know of a new business that started a mailing list discussion group. This business doesn't sell anything online, but the owner told me the mailing list became such a great promotional tool that it was the single most important factor in the business's growth and success.

I do a lot of radio interviews, and the most common question I hear is, "Can you really make money on the Internet?" My response is, "Yes, but you probably won't." Yes, because many people are doing it. You probably won't, because most people aren't doing it right. To point you in the right direction, this chapter will give you a few guidelines for using the Internet as a business tool.

Do You Have a Product?

A lot of people have rushed into business on the Internet with the idea that as long as they have something—anything—to sell, they can make money. The Internet is paved with gold, so it's just a matter of kneeling down and digging it up. Many people who've never run a business before see the Internet as such a great opportunity that they'd better get in fast. Never mind that they don't know the first thing about selling, or filling orders, or managing a business. They want to get in, and they want to get in now.

But Internet users are not stupid—at least, no more stupid than anyone else. If you're selling garbage, you'll have a hard sell. The first step in going into business on the Internet is the same as going into business in real life: You've got to have a product or service people want to buy.

Can a Web Site Help Every Business?

There's so much hype on the Internet (remove the hype and it would collapse within hours) that many people now believe that every business should have, must have, a Web site. But in many cases a Web site won't do a lot of good. Don't expect a sudden rush of sales just because you have a couple of Web pages.

Take, for instance, the case of a small local plumbing business. Will setting up a Web site be worth the time and hassle (and believe me, it can take a lot of both), not to mention money (it doesn't have to take much money, though)? Probably not. Few people will search the Web looking for a plumbing company; they're more likely to look in the Yellow Pages (and even if they do look online, they'll probably use the online Yellow Page systems, such as Yahoo!'s Yellow Pages or Zip2, which won't take them to a company's Web site). Spending a lot of money on a Web site probably won't be cost-effective.

However, maybe a plumbing company *can* use a Web site. Let's say this company sells plumbing supplies and perhaps even has a plumbing supply catalog that it sends to independent plumbers. In this case, it makes sense for the company to have a Web site. The company's market might be nationwide, and the Web can become one more channel for reaching customers.

There's another very low-cost way that a Web site might help a small company. As radio-show host Tom King has suggested, a Web site can be used as what he called an "electronic business card" for businesses that are out and about providing services. The plumbing company could put its URL on the sides of the vans, in large letters: `http://UnplugQuick.com/`, or whatever. In effect, the vans become links to a little catalog of the company's services on the Web.

Some people will remember the URL they've seen on the side of the truck and might go to the site rather than look in the Yellow Pages. Such a business card site isn't intended to attract visitors or do much more than provide a way for someone who's seen the URL to find the company's phone number, mailing address, information about services, perhaps a map showing where to find the company, and so on. Most people who see the URL won't visit the site, but a small Web site can be so cheap that it can still be affordable and worth using to catch the few who will. That's one of the nice things about the Web—you can experiment at a very low cost.

How Cheap?

Web sites can be very affordable, especially if you're willing to do the work yourself. Here's a quick breakdown of costs for a very basic "business-card" Web site:

Domain name registration	$70
Web site hosting	$9 to $20 per month
Good HTML authoring program	$50 to $100, or perhaps free
Your time	???

Let's have a quick look at these items.

Domain Name Registration

To do any business Web site properly, you need your own domain name. That's the first part of a Web site. For instance, I have the domain name `poorrichard.com`, so my Web-site domain is `http://PoorRichard.com/` or `http://www.PoorRichard.com/`.

Your own domain name sounds better, more professional, and it's generally shorter and easier for your visitors to remember. If you move the Web site from one host to another, you can keep the domain name. It's also easier to get your own domain name registered on Yahoo!, the most important search system on the Web (it has a bias against Web sites that are subdomains of other domain names, such as `http://www.bigbiz.com/PoorRichard`).

Registering a .com domain name—the .com is a commercial domain—will cost $70 for the first two years and $35 each year after that, although prices will probably drop soon thanks to a new competitive market for domain names. You can register at `http://www.networksolutions.com/` or `http://www.register.com/`, and probably lots of other places pretty soon. (You might pay more, though, if you choose to pay to have your domain "parked" while you're looking for a Web-hosting company.) Assuming you pay $70, the cost of your domain over the first two years is $2.92 a month.

Web Site Hosting

We discussed Web hosting in Chapter 20, "Setting Up Your Own Web Site." You can host a very simple Web site, using your own domain name, for as little as $9 or $10 a month. You might pay more if you want extra services, perhaps $15 a month. I pay around $30 a month, but I have a big site with a lot of services, so I pay a little more.

HTML Authoring Program

In Chapter 20, you saw how to create Web pages. You can create a very simple "business-card" Web site doing the HTML yourself. But you can also buy an HTML-authoring program, or even use shareware or freeware, and create things very quickly that would be quite complicated if you had to learn all the HTML. A good HTML authoring program costs around $50 to $100. That's $2.08 to $4.16 a month over the first two-year period you'll own your domain name.

You might even be able to get away with paying nothing. If you use Netscape Communicator, for example, you have a program called Netscape Composer. It's not a full-featured authoring program, but it will do all the basics. There are many other free HTML programs around, too.

Your Time

This one's tricky. It depends how you value your time. You'll have to spend some time finding a hosting company and learning how to use the HTML program. How long? Hard to say. You might end up spending five hours looking for a hosting company, perhaps less if you're not very choosy (remember to see my free report, *20 Things to Ask a Web-Hosting Company* at `http://www.PoorRichard.com/freeinfo/special_reports.htm`). Then perhaps another five hours really getting to know your HTML authoring program. Within 10 hours, perhaps a lot less, you could have a decent little site up and running.

So what's the total cost? Depending on your choices, around $5 to $7 a month for the domain and authoring program over the first two years, plus whatever you decide to pay for hosting, which probably is $9 to $20 a month. Not a huge investment. Note, however, that this amount is for a simple business-card type site. The more complicated you get, the more you'll end up paying, although the real cost might be in terms of the time you put into the site.

There's No Such Thing As an Internet Business

There is, however, such a thing as a business that uses the Internet as a business tool. It's important to remember this, because ultimately, if you're in business on the Internet, you're still in business. And that can be lots of hard work. If you're selling products on the Internet, most of the work might be done *off* the Internet, for example. Creating the products, processing orders (which, for many small businesses, might be done offline), fulfilling orders, and addressing customer service problems are all issues that you must deal with. It's important to remember that if you're going to set up a business on the Internet, you are still setting up a real business, and you need to understand all the real-world concerns that entails.

Search Engines Are Not Enough

You've probably heard that a Web site is a billboard on the information superhighway. This Internet mantra has been kept alive by the Web design companies that want your business. Guess what? It's not true.

You can see a billboard as you drive by on the freeway. A Web site just sits there in the darkness of cyberspace, waiting for someone to visit. It's not a matter of "build it and they will come." If you don't *bring* visitors to the site somehow, nobody will see it. There are many ways to bring visitors to the site, the most obvious being using search engines. But there are problems with that method.

There are millions of Web sites on the Internet, all vying for business. And there seem to be thousands of businesses claiming that they can put you right at the top of the search engines' lists. These companies create special coding, which will be read by any search engines that look at the Web pages in your site. This coding, known as META tags, is designed to push your Web site to the top of its category at the search engines. Be a little wary of these claims, though.

First, it's going to cost you, perhaps 25 cents or more for every person who comes to your Web site thanks to a listing created by a search optimization company. But cost might not be too much of a problem, because the company might not send much traffic your way; one company told me that on average it sends around 25 people a day to a Web site using its service—not exactly a flood.

Results from search engine optimization don't work well for a few reasons. First, you can't fool Yahoo!, the single most important search site; entries are added to Yahoo! by real human beings, not a computer program, so they don't care about META tags. As for the other search sites, they're constantly modifying the way they index pages, trying to stop these companies from fooling them into putting Web pages high into their lists. Finally, there's an awful lot of competition; we can't all be at the top of a list.

It's important to get your Web site registered at the major search sites: Yahoo!, Excite, AltaVista, HotBot, Netscape's new Netsite, Lycos, and so on. Visit each site and find a registration link. The number one tip for good site registrations is to be sure the title tag in the page you are registering is descriptive of the page, including keywords that people are likely to use when looking for pages like yours. But relying on search sites is not enough; you need more ways to bring people to your site.

Why Would Anyone Come to Your Site?

First, consider why anyone would want to come to your site. The billboard idea doesn't work; setting up a Web site and waiting for people to arrive doesn't work. But "make it useful, let people know about it, and then they'll come" really does work. If your site is useful, and you do your best to let people know about it, they will visit.

Think about your Web site. Ask yourself, "Why would anyone come to my site? If it wasn't *my* site, would I visit?" If you can't answer the first question, and the answer to the second is no, then you've got a problem.

Don't Forget the Real World

If you're already in business, you already have ways to tell people about your Web site: your business cards; the side of your car, van, or truck; your letterhead; your print, radio, and TV ads. Let people know about your Web site and give them a reason to visit. If you're not in business yet, but plan to launch an Internet business, you'll ignore the real world at your peril. Notice that all the large Web businesses advertise in the real world. They do that because they know they can't ignore the real world and focus solely on Internet promotions.

Don't forget to use the press, too. If you have a Web site of interest to horse lovers, be sure the horse magazines know about it; if your site is aimed at sailors, send a press release to the sailing magazines, and so on.

Look for Partnerships

Here's something else all the large Internet companies already do. They look for partnerships with other Web sites. For instance, do a search for some kind of music subject at Yahoo!, and you're likely to see a CDnow logo pop up along with the list of Web sites. CDnow paid a lot of money for that partnership, of course, but partnerships can start at a very low level. Ask people to link to your Web site; if someone has a list of links, a directory to useful resources, perhaps your site should be in the directory.

Offer to give away products at someone's Web site. I've done book giveaways to promote new books. Web site owners are often happy to do this, because they feel it adds value to their site. You'll need a form at your Web site (which is a little out of the scope of this chapter, but simple feedback forms are often easy to install, or at least cheap to have installed for you). People who want to win the product can then register their email address with you. You can then use the list to announce the winners and gently plug the product, too. I've used this method to build my Poor Richard's Web Site News newsletter (`http://www.PoorRichard.com/newsltr/`). When people signed up for a free copy of one of my books, I asked whether they wanted a free subscription to my newsletter, too—and most did. Look carefully for ways to work with other sites; they're often very powerful ways to bring people to your site.

Use Mailing Lists and Newsgroups (Carefully!)

You can also promote your site in discussion groups, but do so very carefully. Don't go into these groups and simply advertise your site. But if group members would find your site interesting, you can mention that. For instance, a law site might mention articles of interest to writers and publishers in the writing and publishing discussion groups; a horse site might announce schedules of competitions in horse show groups; and so on. The discussion groups provide a great way to reach people, as long as you're careful not to annoy them with obnoxious advertising.

Don't Forget Email

It's easy, with all the hype about the Web, to forget the power of email. But email publishing is very popular and very effective. Even many successful Web sites use email as a promotion. For instance, the CDnow site (`http://www.cdnow.com/`) has a periodic, customizable newsletter that's free for the asking—and more than 800,000 people have asked! You can select particular types of music, and CDnow will send you announcements about those genres. This fantastic marketing tool is really low cost, next to nothing when compared to the cost of doing a real-world mailing to that many people.

Your mailing list is unlikely to be that large, at least for a while. But it's still worth building. Consider creating bulletins, newsletters, and product announcements. Don't turn every one into an ad; be sure there's something of value in every message you send out. But don't ignore the value of contacting people via email, either.

Read My Special Reports

I've barely scratched the surface here; there's an awful lot to learn if you want to set up business on the Internet. Visit my site for free reports on the subject, and hey, why not sign up for my free newsletter, too? You can find details at `http://www.PoorRichard.com/`.

The Least You Need to Know

- Thousands of people are making money on the Internet; you can too, perhaps, but only if you know the ropes.
- Think carefully about if and how a Web site can help your business. Depending on what you're trying to do, you might find the cost doesn't outweigh the benefits.
- Web sites can be very cheap. A simple "business-card" site might cost between $14 and $30 a month.
- A Web site is not a billboard. You have to bring people to your site somehow, and that takes work.
- Register with the search engines, but don't get hung up about them; you can't rely on them to bring in all your business.
- Look for other ways to bring in visitors. Give people a reason to visit your site, and then get the word out about the site every way you can think of.
- Don't forget to use email; it's an essential marketing tool.

Chapter 22

Ideas

In This Chapter

- What use is the Internet?
- Using the Internet for business and pleasure
- Finding information online
- Music and culture
- What else do you want to do?

Throughout this book, I've explained many of the services the Internet can provide. But you might now be wondering "What good are these things?" Unfortunately, until you get onto the Internet, get hooked, and forget that you have responsibilities out in the "real" world, it's difficult to understand what the Internet can do for you. (Imagine, for a moment, the Neanderthal thawed out of the ice and introduced to modern technology: "Okay, so I can use this soap stuff to remove the smell from my armpits, right? What for?") This chapter gives you a quick rundown on just a few of the ways in which ordinary (and some not-so-ordinary) folks are incorporating cyberspace into their daily lives.

Keeping in Touch

The world has shrunk over the past few years—at least for those of us in cyberspace. I hadn't spoken with my sister in a decade or two, but now that she's online I hear from her every week or two (every day or two if her computer's acting up). My brother lives a continent away, but I hear from him frequently via email. An old school friend and I planned a trip to Iceland, using email to swap lists of things we'll need. Just recently I've received email from several people I'd worked with a decade ago in another life. Email is a wonderful system—sort of like the U.S. mail on amphetamines.

Meeting Your Peers

Many people use the Internet as a way to keep in touch with their peers. They can find out about job opportunities, new techniques and tools used in their business, or problems they've run into that they think *surely* someone else has experienced. The mailing lists and discussion groups provide a fantastic way to meet other people in your business field.

Business Communications

As I write this book, every now and then I have a question for the editor. I simply write the message and click a button, and off it flies. Later, when I finish this chapter, I'll send the document file via email, too. Then later still, after the chapter's been edited, the editor can send it back via email. I'll change the edits back to what I originally wrote and then send it back yet again. (Editor's note: Yeah, that's what *he* thinks!)

Many businesses have discovered that the Internet provides a rapid communications tool. Why type a letter, memo, or report into a word processor, print it out, put it in an envelope, take it to a mailbox (or call FedEx), and wait a day or five for it to arrive when you can send the same word processing document and have it arrive a minute or two—even a few seconds—later?

Vacations and Flights

There are many places to help you with your travel plans, from picking a vacation spot to buying an airline ticket. Some services, such as Microsoft's Expedia (`http://www.expedia.com`) will even email you periodically to let you know about the lowest available rates to destinations you're particularly interested in. (Warning: "lowest available rate" is airline jargon that does not actually mean the "lowest available rate" in the airline industry. It means "the lowest rate from the list of rates we're looking at." Discount-ticket sites such as Cheap Tickets—`http://www.cheaptickets.com/`—will get you lower prices still.)

Product Information

We live in an instant gratification society, the entire purpose of which is to get toys into your hands faster and faster. Do you need information about that new car you want to buy, for instance? If so, go to `http://www.edmunds.com/` to check it out (you learned about Web addresses like this in Chapter 4, "The World of the World Wide Web"). As you can see in the following figure, the page contains the car's specifications as well as a picture of it. You can drool over it—and even find out just how much the dealer paid for it.

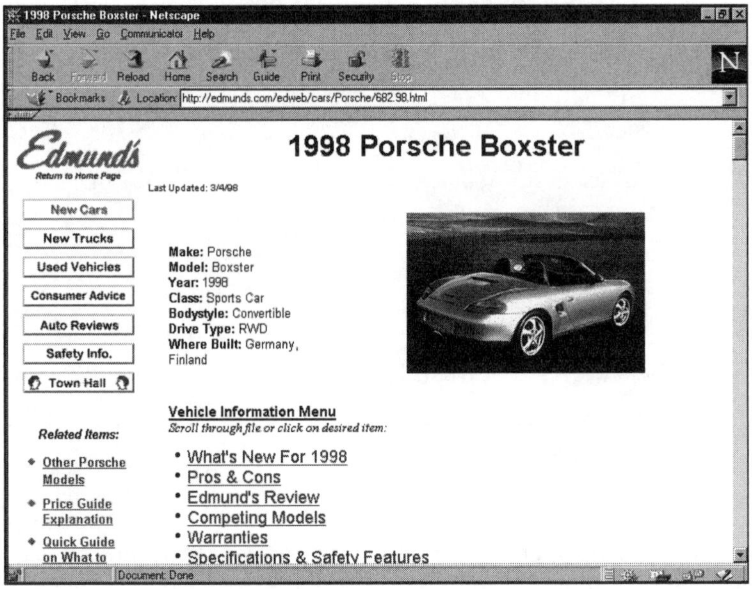

With what you'll save on this baby, you'll be able to buy Internet access for the rest of your life!

Product Support

There's a downside to the Internet, of course: It's run by computers, which, as we all know, are the work of Satan. Still, the next time your computer does something weird or you need a new print driver, go online and find the fix or software you need. Many computer and software companies, perhaps most, now have an online technical support site. Although it would be nice if all these sites were well-designed, some of them are as easy to use as running shoes on a frozen lake.

Getting Software

We're back to instant gratification. You know that program you just saw advertised in *Internet Windows Computing World* magazine? Want to try it out? Go online and download a demo right now! There's no more waiting. Pretty soon everybody will be buying software and transferring it straight to his computer.

You can use one of the Internet's great shareware libraries, too. (See Appendix C, "All the Software You'll Ever Need," for more information.) The following figure shows the TUCOWS site. TUCOWS, The Ultimate Collection of Winsock Software, is a library of shareware Internet programs for Microsoft Windows 3.x, 95, 98, and NT; they have Macintosh and OS/2 software, too. You can find it on the Web at `http://www.tucows.com/`.

TUCOWS: The Ultimate Collection of Winsock Software (they have Macintosh and OS2 stuff now, too).

Researching Stuff

If you are writing a school paper, researching a book, or planning a vacation, the Internet contains a cornucopia of illuminating tidbits. It's *not* a library (contrary to the nonsense of those in the Internet community who got a little carried away with their predictions), and it will be a long time before it can replace one. Still, it does give you access to huge amounts of useful information that's just waiting to be used.

Suppose you are planning to visit, oh, I don't know, how about Iceland? Get onto the World Wide Web and search for Iceland (you learned how to search for stuff in Chapter 17, "Finding Stuff"). What do you find? A hundred or more sites with information about Icelandic travel, sports, culture, media, real estate (there's no way *I'm* moving there), news, and more.

Visiting Museums

I suppose you can't afford to visit the Louvre *and* the Smithsonian this year. What a shame. Still, you can get online and see what you are missing (see the following figure). The potential here is greater than the reality. Maybe someday most of the masterpieces in the world's great museums will be online; but right now, many museums just provide one or two pictures and information about which subway to take to get there.

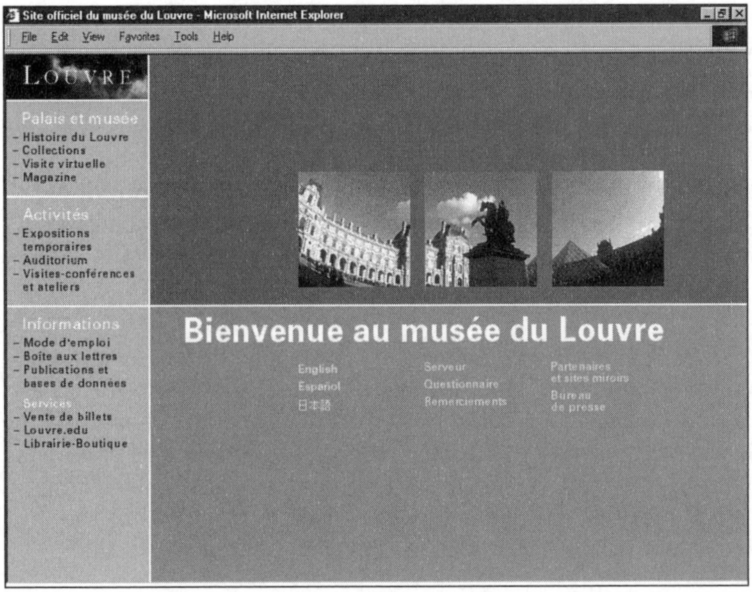

Visit the Louvre this summer from the comfort of your own home (`http://mistral.culture.fr/louvre/`).

Keeping Your Driver's License Up to Date

Moved recently? Need to update your driver's license's address information? If you're lucky, your state's Bureau of Motor Vehicles has a Web site from which you can download the necessary forms, along with forms to apply for special plates, order temporary tags, apply for a hearing-impaired ID card, or report a crash with an uninsured motorist. Start by searching for bureau of motor vehicles at a major search site.

Finding Financial Information

Want stock quotes? Want to invest online? Want to do your taxes online? How about information about competitors or about online banking services? You'll find it on the Internet. You can find links to great financial services at the search sites discussed in Chapter 17. Or try Yahoo! Finance (`http://quote.yahoo.com/`) or InvestorGuide (`http://www.investorguide.com/`). There are plenty of online investment services, too. All the major investment houses have online sites—Charles Schwab, Fidelity, Dreyfus, and so on. But there's also a new breed of brokerage house that grew up on the Internet, sites such as E*TRADE, which now has over a million accounts (`http://www.etrade.com/`).

Listening to Music

If music is your passion, you'll be happy to know that you can hear some of the latest from the music world when you find it on the Internet. Try IUMA, the Internet Underground Music Archive (`http://www.iuma.com/`). Would you prefer bagpipe music or film scores? Maybe you want to buy some CDs (see `http://cdnow.com/`). Whatever you're looking for, you can find it on the Internet.

The latest twist in the online-music scene is MP3, the sound format that has the music business terrified. It's used for pirating music—you can find just about anything in MP3 format online somewhere. But it's also used by thousands of small bands, singers, musicians, and even comedians to get their work out in front of people. To find out more about MP3, visit MusicMatch (`http://www.musicmatch.com/`), WinAmp (`http://www.winamp.com/`), and MP3.com (`http://www.mp3.com/`).

Reading Magazines and 'Zines

You'll find thousands of magazines and 'zines online. (For the not-quite-so-hip among you, a *'zine* is a small magazine, usually published on a shoestring by someone with three or more pierced body parts.) You'll find underground books and comics, as well as newsletters on almost anything you can imagine (and probably a few things you can't imagine). A good place to start is Liszt (`http://www.liszt.com/`) or the E-Zine List at `http://www.meer.net/~johnl/e-zine-list/`.

Hiding from the Real World

There's a wonderful cartoon that is legendary in the computer world. It shows a dog in front of a computer terminal, and it has the caption "Nobody knows you're a dog on the Internet." It's unfortunate that the need exists, but quite frankly, there are people who use the Internet to hide from the real world. For one reason or another, they have trouble with face-to-face relationships, yet on the Internet they can feel safe and part of a community.

If You *Can't* Get Out

Some people would love to have more face-to-face relationships but for some reason can't get out to meet people. Perhaps they are elderly or disabled or have been posted to the Antarctic. Or maybe they're not leaving their apartment for fear of being served a Kenneth Starr subpoena. Regardless of the reason, the Internet provides a link to the rest of the world for those times when you can't physically get somewhere.

Shakespeare on the Net

A little while ago I met a fellow computer book writer who stages Shakespeare plays in IRC (Internet Relay Chat). This chap (he's English) takes a play, modifies it slightly to his taste (he recently staged an updated version of *Macbeth*), and breaks it down into its individual character parts. He sends each "actor" his lines only, no more. Each line has a cue number, so the person playing the character will know when to type the lines. Then they start, each person typing his or her lines at the appropriate cue position. It's an act of discovery for all the "actors" because they don't know what the other characters will say until they say it. Strange, but strangely fascinating.

Remember Your Old Friend, Chat?

As you learned in Chapter 13, "Yak, Yak, Yak: Chatting in Cyberspace," IRC is a chat system. You type a message, and it's immediately transmitted to all the other people involved in the chat session. They respond, and you immediately see what they have typed.

Joining a Community of People with Common Interests

Suppose you have some, er, let's say unusual interests. You believe the U.S. government has been chopping up aliens for years—or maybe that it's in cahoots with aliens. Or suppose that, by chance, you are consumed with a hatred of purple dinosaurs (one in particular, anyway) or that you feel compelled to tell others of your latest, um, erotic experience in the air.

Now suppose that, in your neighborhood, there are few people who share your interests. Whom do you share your thoughts with? Where can you find a sense of community? On the Internet, of course, in the newsgroups and mailing lists (see Chapters 9-11). (And yes, the examples previously suggested are real examples.) You might be surprised at the sort of people you find online. It's not all techno-chat. I have a friend who's a member of a discussion group on the subject of renovating antique tractors, for instance!

You Don't Trust Your Doctor

I must admit I don't have a lot of faith in doctors. Grandma was right: Stay away from hospitals—they're dangerous! Many people go to the Internet in search of the answers their doctors can't provide. Whether you have a repetitive-stress injury, cancer, or AIDS, you'll find information about it on the Internet. Want to try homeopathy, acupuncture, or just figure out what leeches can do for you? Try the Internet. Be careful, though. Although you'll find a lot of useful information, you'll also run into some pretty strange ideas, many of which have as much relation to reality as Charles Manson does.

Shopping

Much of the press seems to think that the raison d'être for the Internet is for K-Mart and Sears to find another way to sell merchandise. Internet shopping has been grotesquely overrated for several years—but recently it's taken off. It's not living up to its potential yet, but nonetheless, millions of people are making purchases on the Internet. In particular, they're buying books, CDs, and software. But they're also buying telescope lenses, clothing, and even groceries.

Cybersex

The Internet provides a wonderful form of communication for those who seem to have trouble finding others with similar sexual proclivities. This is by no means a minor part of cyberspace; some commentators even claim that the sexual use of online services played a major part in their growth. (That's probably not so far-fetched an idea to anyone familiar with America Online's tremendously popular chat rooms.) You can get online and talk about things that your parents or spouse might consider *very* weird, with people who consider them quite normal.

Political Activism

As they say, political activism infects every form of human communication—or was that pornography? Anyway, the Internet is the latest frontier for political activities, providing militia groups a means of keeping in touch and providing Democrans and Republicats a place to seek votes.

Subversion

The Internet provides a great way to subvert the political system in which you live. That's right, you, too, can publish information that your government doesn't want published, whether it's information about how Nutrasweet was created as part of a plot to take over our minds or what was going on during the latest coup. Perhaps the most quoted such event was the last coup in Moscow, during which much information was exported through the Internet. Closer to home, the Internet has become a thorn in the side of the U.S. government as it makes the distribution of encryption software so easy.

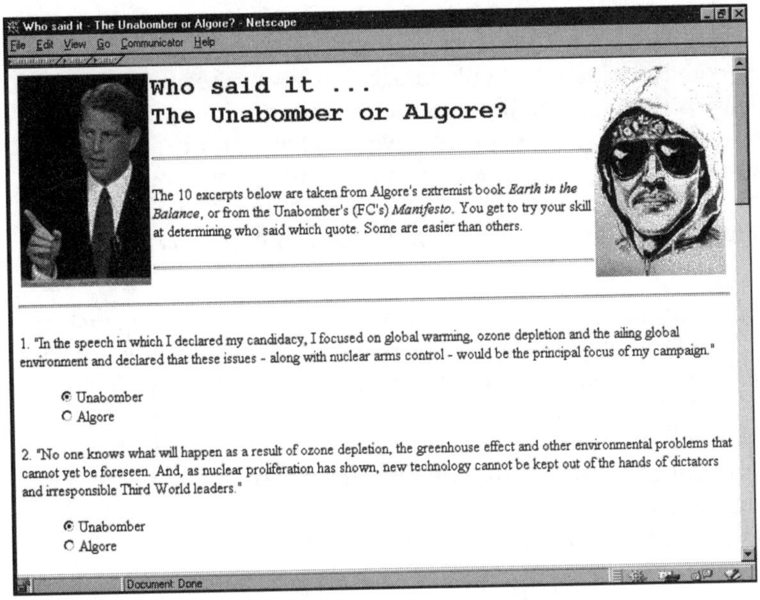

Here's a snap of the Political Activism section—or the Subversion section, perhaps.

Looking for Work (and Help)

Thousands of people are looking for work on the Internet, and thousands more are offering both full-time and contract positions. Many professional associations have special mailing lists used for transmitting job leads. Do a little research, and you could have dozens of leads arriving at your home every day. Check out this site for starters: `http://www.4work.com/`

Clubs and Professional-Association Information Sources

Are you running a large club or professional association? Why not set up a Web site? Your members can then check the Web site to find out when the next meeting is being held, search a database of fellow members, find out about the association's services, and more. Potential members can find out how to join, too.

Mating and Dating

Do people *really* meet online and get involved in romantic relationships of various kinds? Yes, they really do. I'd be inclined to make a joke about it, except that I have a friend who met a man online who eventually became her husband and the father of her child.

Long-Distance Computing

Being a computer geek comes with a real disadvantage: You always seem to be working. If you find yourself wishing you could get to the programs on your desktop computer while you are on vacation or are visiting relatives or clients, for example, you might have considered buying one of those remote control programs. You install the program on your laptop and then dial into your desktop machine. The program enables you to copy files between the computers and even run programs across the connection.

As you might guess, however, the long-distance phone calls can get very expensive, but now there's a new way to do it. Some of these programs let you make the connection across the Internet. So, if you use a national service provider that has phone numbers throughout the United States (or even an international provider or an online service that has numbers throughout the world), you can dial into a local number and connect to your computer across the Internet and pay only a fraction of the long-distance charge. Even if you don't want to go to quite these lengths, you can still log in and pick up your email wherever you happen to be.

Books

You can write books about the Internet. According to modern polls, there are now 5,357,131 people writing books about cyberspace, the Internet, and how we won't have to blow our noses ourselves 10 years from now because the Internet will do it for us. (Seriously, though, a survey not so long ago found that more money is spent on books and magazines about the Internet than is spent buying things on the Internet! So much for the computer revolution killing off paper publications!)

Keeping the Kids Busy

There's a lot of fuss about nasty stuff on the Internet that kids shouldn't see...but there's plenty of really good stuff out there, from sites that help them with science experiments, to sites that make history and geography fun. One of the best places to get started finding good kids' sites is Yahooligan! (`http://www.yahooligans.com/`).

What Did I Miss?

In addition to the ideas I've listed in this chapter, you could probably find a few thousand other uses or more. The Internet is huge, and it's diverse; it's whatever you make of it.

The beauty of the Internet is that although people begin as observers, they end up being participants. They become active in discussion groups and perhaps even start their own groups. They often create their own Web sites (it's surprisingly easy, as you saw in Chapter 20, "Setting Up Your Own Web Site").

Take a look at the Internet to see what's out there and how other people are using it. Who knows? You might soon find that it becomes part of your life. (Don't say I didn't warn you!)

The Least You Need to Know

- You can use the Internet for personal and business correspondence.
- Web sites provide product information, support, and purchasing options.
- You can access all kinds of online information, from research, to museums, to financial services, to medical information, to job searches.
- Listen to your favorite music group, or read your favorite author.

Chapter 23

WebTV and Other Unusual Internet Devices

In This Chapter

- Why other Internet-connection devices are needed
- The scoop on WebTV
- Receiving email on your pager
- Handheld computers
- Telephones, printers, and faxes
- Connecting elephants and other pets

The growth of the Internet is slowing because so many people who had computer hardware and computer *wetware* (a geek term for knowledge) are already on the Internet. For more people to get onto the Internet, two things must happen:

- More people need to begin using computers, so those computers can be connected to the Internet.
- Internet capabilities must be built into other devices, so people can connect to the Internet even if they don't have a computer.

Of course, the question is: Why would anyone want to connect to the Internet if he didn't have a computer? The answer is: He probably wouldn't. So don't expect a huge rush of non–computer-literate people trying to get onto the Internet. There are plenty of people who don't care about the Internet, so however easy it becomes to access the Internet, they won't.

Nonetheless, things will change. Email, for instance, will become pervasive, and eventually even people without Internet access will feel the pressure to use email. A number of Internet services will become so useful that nonusers will envy users. For instance, the Internet provides so many ways to get information when planning a trip, it's hard to beat. You can look up businesses in Internet Yellow Pages around the world and even print out maps and directions to those businesses (check to see that the hotel really is "just a short walk to the beach"). Need to meet someone at a local restaurant? Using the Web, you can get step-by-step directions from your hotel to the restaurant, along with a map. (For this type of information, by the way, visit `http://www.zip2.com/`.) You can see photographs of hotels, check airline schedules and prices, view information about the local climate and bar scene, and so much more.

Eventually, even non-computer-owning non-Internet users will want these services. Some will buy computers. Others will use some other kind of other Internet device. This chapter takes a quick look at alternatives to computers for accessing the Internet.

Before we start, Kent's First Law of Internet Connectivity:

> If it *can* be connected, it *will* be connected.

What sort of things can be connected to the Internet (and therefore *will* be connected to the Internet)? There are basically two types of devices: devices used to access information over the Internet and devices used to feed information to the Internet (some devices do both). Here are a few of the wonderful things that are already hooked up to the Internet or will be soon:

- Televisions
- Pagers
- Telephones
- Cars
- CD Players
- Printers and fax machines
- Pets
- Parking meters
- Police scanners
- Your house
- Hot tubs
- Elephants

If you want to see a sampling of the weird and wonderful things already connected, visit this Yahoo! page: `http://dir.yahoo.com/Computers_and_Internet/Internet/Interesting_Devices_Connected_to_the_Net/`. You'll find categories for Audio Equipment, Coffee Machines, Clocks, Calculators, Pagers, Robots, and Soda Machines.

We'll begin by looking at devices that can be used to get information from the Internet, replacements for your computer in effect. Then we'll take a quick look at the other side of the equation: things connected to the Internet to feed information into it.

WebTV

You've probably heard of WebTV. This is the first major noncomputer system to be widely available for retrieving information from the Internet (it's available in the U.S., Canada, and Japan). It now costs as little as $99 to buy WebTV Classic, $199 to buy WebTV Plus, and WebTV Plus service for Satellite, the latest and most advanced version, is about $499 for a 12-month subscription. You'll get what is basically a little box with a modem inside and a bunch of other circuitry. (The box is made by Sony, Philips Magnavox, or Mitsubishi; the service is owned by Microsoft.)

Why a modem? Many people seem to think WebTV uses the TV cable to access the Web, but it works with a phone line. A connection is made across the phone line to the WebTV Internet service, and the box uses the TV as a screen. You'll pay $19.95 a month for basic WebTV service, $24.95 a month for the WebTV Plus service or WebTV Plus Satellite service. If you choose to use your own service provider—perhaps you're in an area that doesn't have a WebTV phone number—you'll save $10 a month on your WebTV subscription.

WebTV also comes with a remote control—this is the Internet for couch potatoes—and, optionally, a wireless keyboard. The keyboard is $70, but it's almost an essential option, as "writing" using the remote control is like eating soup with chopsticks. On the other hand, you might find an ordinary computer keyboard more comfortable—you can connect any PS2-compatible keyboard. You can also connect a printer to the system, although there's a fairly limited range of printers that will work. (And the printer port is an optional add-on in the basic WebTV box.)

WebTV is a brand name, but it seems to me that it's turning into a generic term: WebTV meaning "a system that displays the Web on a television screen." WebTV is not the only player in the game; for instance, there's a French system called NetBox, a British system called SlipStream Internet Box, and a service called TVPC that incorporates a DVD (Digital Video Disk) player with an Internet-connected PC in a box (go to Yahoo! and search for set top box for more of these systems).

I think many WebTV owners are probably a little disappointed, though. Who would have bought one? People who want the Internet because they've heard all the hype, yet don't have a computer. The Internet has been hyped in many quarters, with images of exciting video rolling across Web pages for instance. But the reality is very different, and Web pages are not TV shows. Or perhaps there's another way to consider WebTV; it's whetted many people's appetites. Having used WebTV, they then move up to the "real thing" and get a PC.

What can WebTV do for you, then? Its basic feature is the ability to display Web pages. The WebTV box turns your TV into a Web browser. The more advanced systems, WebTV Plus and WebTV for Satellite, go much further, integrating TV and the Web in the following ways:

- It provides TV listings, showing what's on in your area.
- A feature named WebPIP (Web Picture in Picture) allows you to view a TV show and a Web page at the same time, even if your TV is not a Picture in Picture TV.
- TV Crossover Links provide access to Web pages designed in conjunction with TV shows. A small icon will appear at the bottom of the screen while the show is running; you can select the icon to open the related page.
- An IR Blaster feature allows the WebTV Plus box to control your cable box; selecting a channel on the WebTV Plus box would automatically change the cable box. Eventually, the system will allow you to program your VCR by clicking a show in the WebTV Plus listing.
- A 1.1GB hard drive is built into the system. It *won't* allow you to download programs in the same way you can with a computer. Rather, it's used for the Web browser's cache and will also be used for certain system enhancements. For instance, eventually you'll be able to read and write email even if you're not connected to the Internet—the email will be stored on the hard disk (right now the email is stored on the WebTV Internet server).
- Multimedia E-mail. You can grab still pictures from a TV show, from your video camera, or from your VCR, add 30 seconds of sound, and drop it into an email message.
- TV Pause. The satellite system comes with a feature that allows you to pause a program that you're watching, and come back and finish watching it later.

Visit `http://www.webtv.com/` to get all the details.

The Drawbacks

WebTV has a number of advantages, the main one being that it provides a cheap way to connect to the Internet. However, it's not the real thing, and even the WebTV people say that it's not intended to replace computers.

It can be awkward to use, particularly if you don't have a keyboard (as one reviewer put it, "it feels very much like using DOS or one of the old IBM 3270 terminals"). You can't download and run software, and you can't use many other non-Web Internet services—Telnet and FTP, for instance. The display is low-resolution, so you can't see much of a Web page without scrolling down; small text is often very difficult to read. You can't save documents you find on the Web (although you can print them if you add a printer to the system), and WebTV currently doesn't work with Java applets (see Chapter 6, "Forms, Applets, and Other Web Weirdness").

Still, WebTV has improved greatly over the past year or two. As long as you realize the limitations, it might be something that could be useful or perhaps just fun.

Intercast PC/TV

The next step joining TV and the Web is intercast PC/TV. That's the merging of Web pages into TV signals. There's a lot of empty space in a TV signal, and it's possible to transmit extra information, information that the TV doesn't need. For instance, closed captions for the deaf are transmitted in this way, as is the information used in teletext systems in Europe.

So a TV show can carry a Web page that is related to the show. A cooking show, for instance, could carry a Web page containing recipes. If you like what they're cooking, change to the Web page, read the recipe, and print it out on the printer connected to the TV. This is not the same as WebTV, by the way. WebTV grabs Web pages off the Web along the phone line the WebTV box is connected to. An intercast TV grabs the Web page from the TV signal, so it needs no Internet connection.

Of course, right now there are few intercast shows, and intercast TVs are not available, but they will be soon. On the other hand, Intercast PCs are available; Windows 98 comes with WebTV software built into it, so if you have the right sort of TV tuner card in your computer you can work with intercast broadcasts. Or you can install a program such as Intel's Intercast Viewer, which runs in Windows 95 or 98 (and is bundled with a number of PC tuner cards).

A number of broadcasters are now transmitting intercast data: CNN, CNBC, MTV, NBC, QVC, Lifetime, and so on. For example, while watching a CNN program, you can browse through story summaries in your Web browser, and use links to other resources on the CNN Web site. A good place to find more information is the Intel Intercast Web site at `http://www.intercast.com/`.

Handhelds

So-called *handheld* computers are gaining in popularity as businesspeople grow tired of lugging around laptops. If all you need while traveling is basic computing capabilities, then handhelds might be enough. Some of these machines even have modems, email programs, and, yes, Web browsers. (Just because a tiny little handheld has a Web browser doesn't mean you'll enjoy using it, though.)

A handheld with a modem begins at around $300, going up to around $1,000. Be very careful when buying one of these things, though. They're often difficult to use—after all, there's a limit to how far a computer can be shrunk. Compare the devices carefully, and find one that you can work with comfortably.

Pagers

Do you have an alphanumeric pager? Did you know you can receive email on it? A number of services will receive your email, and then forward it to your pager number. Some services even allow someone to enter a message into a Web page, and then click a button to send that message to a pager.

Some pager companies can set you up with an email address, so you can receive your messages. But even if your pager company doesn't do this, you can always get an account with a paging-service company, which might have better features than the pager company. For instance, you might be able to exceed the message limit. If your pager only accepts, say, 100 characters, you can use a service that will break your email messages into several pages, so you can exceed the limit. A service might also allow you to set filters to send some messages to the pager, but forward all others (for instance, pages from your spouse get sent to the pager and pages from your boss get forwarded to your email account, or vice versa depending on your relationships.)

Some services will also send news, weather, or stock reports at predetermined times and can retrieve email from your normal email account so you don't need a special email account just for your pager. If you'd like to track down these services, see `http://www.yahoo.com/Business_and_Economy/Companies/Telecommunications/Wireless/Personal_Communications/Pagers/Information_Delivery/Email/`.

Telephones

The idea of connecting telephones to the Internet is obvious. After all, the telephone is the world's most important electronic communication device. Chapter 14, "Internet Conferences: Voice on the Net, Whiteboards, and More," looked at speaking over the Internet, but that's not what I'm talking about now. I'm talking about an actual phone that can interface with the Internet to send and receive email (and perhaps more). There are around a dozen of these devices, maybe more. For instance, Nokia is selling what it calls "the world's first media phone" (although at the time of writing it's available only in Europe and Asia). It's a cell phone that lets you send and receive email—it even has a folder system to manage your messages. You can use the associated PC software to manage your address book (it comes with an interface cable). It even has access, with a built-in "microbrowser." If you want to find an Internet-capable phone, visit `http://www.allnetdevices.com/smart_phone/` for more information.

Refrigerators

Yep, that's right, you'll soon be able to buy a fridge that's Internet connectable. Why? The fridge should be able to keep an eye on food quantities, and order more from your grocer across the Internet. (The fridge is, apparently, to be released in Britain, where supermarkets are jumping into online commerce much more quickly than in North America.) It might also be able to connect to recipe databases and, er, online banking. Whether it can determine the age and digestibility of various things that have been sitting in the back of your fridge for a while before it reorders, I'm not sure. The Electrolux Screenfridge will, in theory, be on the market at the end of 1999.

Printers and Faxes

Need to send a fax to the corporate office in Kuala Lumpur? Why not send it over the Internet? If both offices had fax machines connected to the Internet, then the fax could go over the Net for free. If the office in Kuala Lumpur had a printer connected to the Internet, your computer could send a file directly to the printer; the printer would be, in effect, an Internet fax machine. Such devices will probably become commonplace not too long from now.

Cash Registers

Many fast-food store cash registers are already connected to the Internet. These "Point of Sale" (POS) terminals are mostly based on Windows PCs these days, so it's pretty easy to connect them. But why bother? Well, it allows a restaurant owner to sit at home and view the day's takings, across the Internet, in all his restaurants. It also, with an optional video camera, allows him to look in on the store and check up on the kids running it! Be sure they're wearing their hats the right way around, and so on.

It's a Wired, Wired, Wired World

Imagine a world in which everything that can be connected is connected. We're going to be seeing all sorts of things connected to the Internet over the next few years. For instance, you probably know that Bill Gates has wired his house—it's what's sometimes called an *intelligent* house. (Bill Gates might not be scared by the thought of Microsoft software controlling his living space, but it would scare the hell out of me.) I don't know whether his house is connected to the Internet, but there's no reason it couldn't be. And that's reason enough to think that eventually many houses *will* be connected to the Internet.

If you go on a vacation and forget to turn down the heat, don't worry; just connect to your house's heating interface on the Web, and set the heat to whatever you want. Want to check your phone messages? Get them over the Net. After houses are connected to the Internet, of course, new devices will be created—or old devices used in a new way—to provide reasons to connect over the Internet. For instance, you'll be able to view a snapshot of everyone who's rung your doorbell while you've been away, or view a picture of the front yard to see whether the kid next door kept his promise and mowed the lawn.

Some weird connections to the Internet are closer than you might think. Have you heard that parking meters will be networked soon? Networking meters provide all sorts of benefits (in general not to the parkers, of course, but to the cities that own the meters). For instance, meter monitors (or whatever they're called now; I understand the term *meter maid* is no longer politically correct) will be able to see exactly which meters are just about to run out of money and rush to get there before the person who parked the car. If you network something, you can connect that network to the Internet. So some people have been suggesting that cities might connect their parking-meter networks to the Internet, so parkers could feed the meters through a Web page. Of course, there are disadvantages to this, because it makes meter feeding way too easy and might cut down on meter availability, but I wouldn't be surprised if some cities try it.

How about elephants? Sound ridiculous? I've heard about a dairy research farm that considered networking its cows, and it's not so far from cows to elephants. Imagine a research project tracking the movement of Indian elephants. Many such projects already use radio trackers. It's not such a leap of imagination to consider connecting the radio signals to the Web, so people all over the world could watch the movement of the elephants. (It might not be a good idea in areas rife with ivory poachers, of course.) You heard it here first; elephants *will* be connected to the Internet.

Oops, I'm *almost* too late. I *swear* I didn't know about Elephant.net, the Malaysian Elephant Tracking Project, but after writing the previous paragraph, I thought I'd do a quick search. See for yourself: `http://www.asiaconnect.com.my/elephantnet/`. They use Java maps to show the movement of the elephants they're tracking. It's not real time—that is, you're not seeing the signal directly from the elephant—but I bet it will be one day.

Now we come to Kent's Second Law of Internet Connectivity:

> The degree of usefulness is no predictor of connectivity.

In other words, just because something is useful doesn't mean it will be connected before something that isn't useful. Remember this: Some of the first noncomputer devices connected to the Internet were drink machines. That's right, some bright computer-science undergraduates figured out that if they connected the department's drink machines to the Internet, they could view information about the machines over the Internet; no more arriving at the machine to discover that one's favorite drink was out of stock! Not too long after drink machines came hot tubs (as if anyone really cares about the temperature of a hot tub in someone's home on the other side of the world). So no matter how ridiculous or seemingly pointless the connection—it *will* be made! All sorts of useless stuff will be connected—and is connected—to the Internet. Luckily, plenty of useful stuff will be connected, too.

The Least You Need to Know

- Pretty much *everything* that's electronic can be connected to the Internet. If something's not electronic, an electronic device can be added. So elephants will soon be connected to the Net.
- WebTV provides a low-cost Internet connection, although it's nothing like using the Internet from a computer.
- Intercast PC/TV is the transmission of Web pages within TV signals. A number of broadcasters are already intercasting Web pages within their transmissions.
- It's very easy to send email and other information, such as news and weather, to a pager.
- Telephones, printers, and faxes will soon be connected to the Internet. Fridges, too.
- Handheld computers that can be connected to the Internet start at around $300; if you buy one, buy a pair of magnifying glasses, too.

Chapter 24

The Future of the Internet

In This Chapter

- Internet progress will slow down
- The future of high-speed connections
- Intercast PC/TV and $500 Internet boxes
- Multimedia
- The Internet backlash
- Open borders and free speech
- Software distribution

As physicist Niehls Bohr once said, "Making predictions is very difficult, especially about the future." Some things seem to be easy to predict, though. For instance, I predicted, in the last couple of editions of this book, that the Internet would get bigger, and that many more people would begin using the Internet. I'm happy to say that I was right on the money. On the other hand, so was just about every other Tom, Dick, and Harry making Internet predictions.

To get some predictions right, though, you have to step back and consider whether the crowd really knows what it's talking about. A prediction I've made on a number of occasions, for instance, was that if you held your breath until North America got the widely available high-speed Internet connections that the telephone and cable companies have been promising (along with Microsoft and various other people) for years, you could expect to turn blue several years before those high-speed connections actually appeared. These connections have been promised since 1994, and since 1994 I've been saying "wait until the next century." I'm glad to say I was right about that one, as I'll discuss a little later. So now I'm going to make a few more predictions, which, no doubt, will all come to pass.

Progress Will Slow Down

I'm happy with this prediction, because even though it seems fairly obvious to me that the rate of growth of Internet use had to slow down, many people disagreed with me. I made this prediction two or three years ago, and indeed it came to pass. I said that the rate of change on the Internet would slow down, and it did.

Although Internet changes between 1993 and 1996 were phenomenal, this level of progress couldn't be maintained for two reasons. First, most of the people who got on the Internet in the first few years of the boom were primed and ready to go. They were computer-literate, they had computers, and they had modems (or if they didn't, they could get them and install them). Few people went from being complete neophytes who had never used or owned a computer to being Internet junkies. Continuing this growth was difficult because newcomers to the Internet have to be new computer users as well as new Internet users, so they'll have bigger hurdles to jump. Getting the computerless and computer illiterate onto the Internet will be much more difficult than getting the already-computer-savvy up and running was. It might take the introduction of lots of new Internet devices, and introducing hardware takes time.

Second, the early years of the Internet boom (from 1993 to 1996) saw great technological changes on the Internet, but the changes were not quite as dramatic as they first seemed. Most of the changes came about as a result of companies taking existing technology and putting it together in a new way. For example, in 1994 most people used some form of terminal account to access the Internet. Now they are using TCP/IP access, which allows them to use graphical user interface software. However, TCP/IP had been around for years; what made it more popular was that a lot of companies wrote new TCP/IP software that would run on personal computers.

You can see this prediction in action. The rate of growth in Internet users has slowed down, and the technology isn't changing as fast as it did in the first few years of the boom. For instance, the major browsers used to release new versions every couple of months, but Netscape Navigator 4 has been around for a couple of years now, and Navigator 5 is nowhere in sight.

High-Speed Connections (Coming Soon)

An important cause of the Internet slowdown is the fact that connection speeds are still very slow. Since late in 1993 to now, we've gone from having "standard" modem speeds of 14.4Kbps to 56Kbps. But 56Kbps modems rarely reach full speed—they're more likely to be running around 33.6Kbps, which isn't much more than the 28.8Kbps modems that were already in development at the beginning of the Internet boom. In any case, it's just more of the same technology and not something radically different. And it appears that modems are very unlikely to get much faster. Modems are slow; the modem companies are just making them a little less slow.

Further improvements will be more difficult. The phone companies are promising to wire up the United States with fast connections soon, but it can't happen overnight. The phone companies have had enough trouble just providing everyone with enough phone lines, so where are they going to find all the people they need to install super-fast new lines such as ADSL? For two or three years, they've been telling me I'll be able to get an ADSL line to my house "soon," and it's still not available. Some of the predictions about high-speed lines were just plain ridiculous. Back in early 1998, Microsoft claimed that it and the telecommunications companies would bring fast connections to most people by the end of 1998. Whatever happened to that plan?

In 1994, the cable-TV companies promised that super-fast connections to the Internet were just around the corner, and most of us are still waiting. Cable connections are available to some of us, but the cable business expects that by the end of 1999 they'll have only two to three million users. That leaves the vast majority of users still working with those old telephone-line modems.

Wiring up the world with high-speed connections will still take a few more years. How many? I used to say, in 1994 and 1995, "early in the next century," but that doesn't mean a lot anymore. I'd bet we won't cross the 50% mark—50% of North American Internet home users working with ADSL or cable connections—until at least 2002, perhaps a little later.

Until these fast connections become available, the Internet can't live up to its hype and potential. Much of the hype about the Internet depends on high-speed connections to the Internet. For example, some pundits claim that Web sites need multimedia to make them more "compelling." (This claim seems to be rather insulting to the average Internet user, who supposedly values form over function; it indicates that he is so shallow that a bit of glitz keeps him happy.) Without high-speed connections, though, this multimedia stuff is more of a nuisance than a real benefit. Java, video, and animations are all very nice, but if you are getting the goodies over a phone line, even with a fast modem, the novelty soon wears off.

More Multimedia, but Much More Text

It's a foregone conclusion that the amount of multimedia (video, sound, animations, and such) on the Internet will increase. With new tools that make multimedia easier to create becoming available, it's inevitable. But the slow-connection problem will hold back multimedia for some time to come. Take a look at the online services—have they incorporated multimedia? Yes, a little, but not much; the connections most people have are too slow for multimedia to work well.

It's Not All That Common

I was once paid to put together a list of 50 Web sites that don't use sound (don't ask why, it's a long story!). It was laughably easy. Very few Web sites have sound or video, despite the fact that they are the most popular forms of multimedia and the easiest to work with.

Multimedia on the Internet gets much more attention right now than it deserves based on its level of use. Very few Web sites use multimedia (that is, sound and video). The vast majority of Web pages contain nothing more than text and pictures. For all the talk of multimedia and "cool" stuff, only a tiny fraction of Web sites—perhaps less than one percent—use sound, and that's probably the easiest multimedia format to work with. Very few Web sites have video or animation.

As people get past the hype, they're realizing that the Web is essentially text-based. Although multimedia use will grow, the amount of text on the Internet will grow much faster. In fact, according to an article in *Wired* magazine, one of the fastest growing areas on the Internet is email newsletter publishing.

Intercast PC/TV

Web browsers, computers, and TVs are merging, as detailed in Chapter 23, "WebTV and Other Unusual Internet Devices." Over the next few years, these components will be more tightly merged. More and more TV channels will *intercast* Web pages; more and more TVs will be built with Web browsers; and there'll be more interaction between TV and Web pages. For instance, although right now intercast allows a user to view a Web page associated with a TV show, you'll soon be able to respond through the Web page, perhaps voting in instant surveys or placing orders directly to infomercials.

How soon? Well, okay, not so soon. This whole TV/Internet integration thing hasn't grown anywhere near as fast as the pundits seemed to think it will. What's holding it back is the fact that most of the TVs in use today can't work with intercast pages, and are unlikely to be replaced anytime soon.

The Internet Backlash and the New Internet Business

In earlier editions of this book, I spoke of an Internet backlash that would occur. I said that companies would soon realize that making money on the Internet is not quite as simple as they had been told. The Internet is not paved in gold; conducting business on the Internet is not simply a matter of setting up a Web page and then raking in the cash. For example, Web publishing was in trouble—no large Web magazine had yet figured out how to make money (even today few companies make money publishing on the Internet). Some book publishers were even reducing their Internet presence after realizing that they couldn't sell enough books online to make it worthwhile.

I also said that I believed this backlash would be a good thing. There was too much Internet hysteria and too many inflated claims about what the Internet could do. I believe that the backlash has happened. Whereas a few years ago many people were rushing to the Internet for fear of missing out on an enormous business opportunity, they're now a bit more cynical. The most common question I hear when doing radio interviews is "Can you *really* make money on the Internet?"

My answer to that is, "You probably won't, but you most certainly can." Many businesses are now getting onto the Internet, but are approaching it with more rational expectations. Many businesses, even quite small businesses, *are* making money, not by posting a "billboard on the Information Superhighway" and then sitting back and taking orders, but by using sensible techniques for bringing people to the Web sites and incorporating other Internet systems, particularly email. (See Chapter 21, "Making Money on the Internet," for more information.)

The Internet Will Open Borders

The Internet opens borders. As more of the world runs on software, more of the software will become the focus of argument. Although it's rare these days for software to be banned, some software is now and again censored; violent games and encryption software are the targets of legislation in some countries.

Something to Think About

The idea of one country distributing software to a country in which it's banned brings up another issue that has to be dealt with by the courts: If you distribute something on the Internet, can you be held liable for the actions of people who download the software in countries in which your product is banned?

The problem is that software can slip across borders quickly and undetected when one's borders are punctured by the Internet. At one point, an organization of small telecommunications companies was trying to get the Federal Communications Commission to ban Voice on the Net programs (discussed in detail in Chapter 14, "Internet Conferences: Voice on the Net, Whiteboards, and More"). But how could such a ban work? One of the best programs comes from Israel, and that company can continue to distribute the software across the Internet, perhaps without breaking any U.S. laws. The U.S. government has tried to ban the export of encryption software and has totally failed. How can you stop the exportation of something that doesn't physically move, something that rides across the world on a wave of electrons? The encryption laws are falling apart as we speak, and there's a good chance that in 1999 or 2000 they'll finally go the way of Prohibition, another idea that seemed better than it actually turned out to be.

Another issue that's getting quite a bit of press right now is Internet gambling. There are hundreds of gambling Web sites. You can log on, give them your credit-card number, and start gambling right away. Although officials in the United States have claimed that these sites might be unsafe, there are few complaints from the gamblers, and most of these sites are probably quite reputable. But if gambling's illegal in your state, is it legal in your living room? If you can't gamble in your hometown, can you gamble in a Web site on a Caribbean island without leaving your hometown? U.S. lawmakers have been trying to figure this one out for several years now, but haven't quite worked out a plan that makes sense. They don't want you to gamble online, but you can still do it.

I think that many of these problems are insurmountable, that we might be entering an age in which the state will have to give up trying to control people and pay more than just lip service to the concept of personal choice and responsibility. But that doesn't mean there won't be many attempts to limit the power of the Internet. Governments around the world will set up programs to track transmissions of particular forms of data or might even employ people to sit at computers and watch what other people are doing. They might threaten other nations with economic penalties if those nations don't control some forms of Internet businesses. They will try to completely block portions of the Internet from their own countries. It's already happening today: China and Vietnam, for instance, are trying to let in the "good" bits of the Internet and block the "bad" bits. In the next few years, you'll hear of these and other actions being proposed in a variety of cases. The Internet crosses borders, and many people don't like that.

The Internet and the Fight for Free Speech

Another aspect of the borders issue is free speech. Some of the things you might say in the United States are unacceptable in, say, Indonesia. And some of the things a person might say in the Netherlands would be unacceptable in, say, the United States. Speech (and images) that is perfectly legal in some areas of the world is illegal in others.

Because the Internet is an international system, regulating it is very difficult. I think there are three possible paths:

- A few countries might cut their connections to the Internet (although in a world of satellite communications, they won't be able to do that completely).
- Others might declare the Internet to be a sort of no-man's land, where communications have to be unregulated (or at least, they might turn a blind eye).
- Others might try to regulate it the best that they can, if only to realize eventually that it can't be done without losing many of the benefits of the Internet.

It's not just "authoritarian" nations that will consider blocking and filtering the Internet, though, or at least try to find ways to control it a little better. The British Government recently tried to stop the distribution of a list of names of MI5 agents online. A renegade MI5 agent claimed harassment by his ex-employer, threatened to release this list on the Internet, and although he claims that he didn't actually do so, somehow the list did indeed wind up online. At the time of writing, it's not easy to find the list—but after something's posted online, it's very hard to remove it. You can intimidate Web-site owners to pull their sites down, but you can never be sure that somewhere someone else hasn't copied the information and is about to set up another site. And you can never be sure that "mirror sites" won't pop up around the world, in countries where you don't have much influence. It's happened before; as, for instance, when the Nottingham County Council in the United Kingdom tried to ban the distribution of a secret report about child abuse and satanism, only to find the report published at Web sites around the world (ultimately, the council's efforts to quash the report failed). It's happened when Canadian courts have stopped Canadian media from reporting facts about ongoing trials...yet Canadian citizens have been able to log onto the Internet and read the information on U.S. Web sites. And it'll happen many more times. "Information wants to be free" is a bit of a cliché, but certainly if someone wants the information to be free, he can make sure it takes on a life of its own by releasing it on the Web and seeing where it travels. (The more controversial the information, the farther it travels!)

France at one point banned the use of Netscape Navigator because its citizens are not allowed to use encryption software (Netscape rushed out a special French version of Navigator with the security features removed). Germany has tried to stop pornographic images coming into the country across the Internet (which anyone who's visited the Reeperbhan sex shop district in Hamburg will find amusing) and has prosecuted a man for merely creating a link to a foreign Web site (the site discussed how to sabotage trains). All over the world, the Internet will continue to be decried as a dangerous and evil place for the very reason that it can't be fully regulated. Remember, though, that the telephone was once cursed as a tool of vice because it allowed men to discreetly set up appointments with prostitutes.

Schools Use the Internet; Test Scores Continue to Plummet

Some people say that the Internet will save our schools. Some go so far as to say that schools will no longer be needed, that our kids will learn at home through the TV. To quote former Assistant Secretary of Education Dr. Diane Ravitch, "If little Eva cannot sleep, she can learn algebra instead...she'll tune in to a series of interesting problems that are presented...much like video games."

I don't know about your kids, but when mine can't sleep, the last thing on their minds is algebra. Lewis Perleman (author of *School's Out*) says that we don't need schools anymore because information is plentiful outside schools (as if all that education is about is piping information into kids). Anyway, who's going to be looking after these kids? Oh, I forgot, we'll all be telecommuting by then, won't we?

Information is everything, these people think. All problems are a result of a lack of information, so if the information flows freely, all our troubles will slip away. Put algebra on one channel and Power Rangers on another, and our children will make the right decision. If only life were so simple. Alan Kay, one of the founders of Apple Computer, says that problems schools cannot solve without computers won't be solved with them. He's dead right. Why would computers (and Internet connections) be a panacea? We've known how to educate kids well for centuries, so why would a sudden infusion of technology fix problems that have nothing to do with a lack of technology?

So my prediction is that computers with Internet connections will be found in greater numbers in schools. The price of education will increase correspondingly. Yet, overall, it will make very little difference to whether kids succeed in school. While schools across the country spend billions on computers, many poor schools still won't have enough books or enough money to keep the rain out.

Colleges Use the Internet; Enrollment Soars

Although schools might not become better educators of our children, distance learning across the Internet will become a major component of many people's education. Many colleges already use the Internet, and there are a number of Internet schools, training companies that set up business to teach people across the Internet. But we're nowhere near reaching the potential of this medium for college education.

Educating through the Internet is not merely a convenience (college courses have been taught through TV programs for many years, after all). It can also bring education to people who might not otherwise be able to take part, people living in remote regions, for instance, or even the Third World; major universities could set up offices in small towns, where local people could come in to use the computers. Even in large cities, the ability to study online might make it much easier for students to find time in a busy schedule or to study a course that's taught only one place in the country or even one place in the world. Online education will be an integral part of the knowledge explosion coming in the next century.

$500 Internet Boxes

Ha! I was right about this one! Early in 1996, there was a lot of talk about $500 Internet boxes. The theory is this: Produce a box that enables people to connect to the Internet at a low cost, and you'll sell millions of these boxes. The problem is this: You get what you pay for. The boxes were going to be so stripped down (no hard disk, lousy screens, useless for running games or software you buy at a store), that they'd be almost useless, and they never did appear.

On the other hand, computer prices have dropped so far that it won't be long until $500 buys a *real* Internet-capable computer. You can already get great little computers for around $700, so maybe the $500 Internet box isn't so far off. (In 1998, I said, "We won't have $500 Internet Boxes until computer prices have dropped so much that you can get a full computer for $500, anyway.")

Software over the Internet

Eventually, a lot of software will be purchased from the Internet. Why take software, package it in hardware (disk, cardboard, plastic wrapper, and so on), put it in a store, and have people buy it there, just so they can take it home and load it? Why not just sell it over the Internet as an electronic product delivered electronically? You can already buy some software across the Internet, but it's often "light" or demo software (see the following figure). Although millions of dollars' worth of software is already sold across the Internet, the primary sources remain the traditional retail channels: stores and mail order. One day, however, the Internet might become one of the primary channels for software distribution.

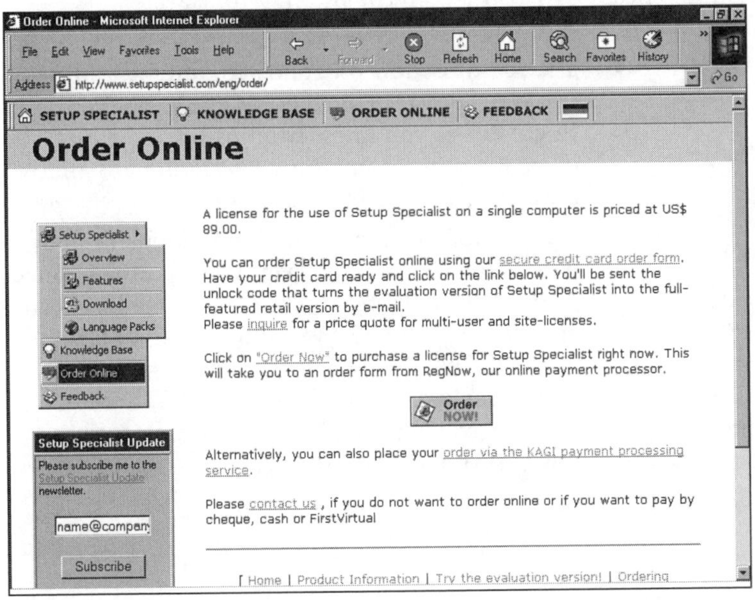

Fill out this form with your credit card information, and then you can download the software.

Geeks Versus Salespeople

Unfortunately, many geeks think that because something makes technological or financial sense, it will come to pass. They completely forget human nature, and consequently, their predictions are way off-target. Most software packaging is already unnecessary from a purely utilitarian point of view (big boxes with a small book and a smaller disk rattling around inside), but it makes perfect sense from a marketing point of view! That's why software will continue to be sold in stores for years to come.

I don't believe some people's claims that software will eventually be run across the Internet, though. Many people are saying that you won't own software—you'll rent it. When you need it, you'll log onto the Internet and run it from another site. Although some software might be successfully distributed like this, I doubt that most will, for a few reasons:

- Storing software on a hard disk is very cheap. With prices around 3 cents a megabyte—under 2 cents if you buy a big drive—and dropping, hard-disk storage is a negligible cost. You pay $100 for a program and 50 cents for the hard disk storage. If it's that cheap, why connect to the Internet to use it?
- "Why buy a program you can rent?" proponents ask. For those few programs you might want to use very occasionally, renting might be the way to go. But as you know from real-world experience, if you use something frequently, it's almost always cheaper to buy than to rent.
- Connections to the Internet are unreliable and will be for a long time. Even voice phone connections are unreliable, and the telephone has been around for about 120 years. It's going to be a long time before we have very high speed and very reliable data connections to the Internet that are available at a cost that competes with the low cost of hard disk storage.

The LAN Example

Do you have a network at work? How often is it down? How often is it sluggish because everyone's doing something at once? That's what the Internet will turn into if this idea ever becomes reality.

- The more the Internet grows, the more traffic it will have to bear. A lot of traffic is unavoidable; the whole purpose of the Internet is communication, after all. But if everyone were logging onto the Internet just to run programs that could run on their hard disks instead, the data that would have to be transferred would be immense. It's not necessary, so why do it? We won't.

I've praised cable connections, but I must admit I had a *9-day* period when my connection stopped working. If I'd been renting software, I'd have been out of business for 9 days! There are a lot of drawbacks and few benefits to running software across the Internet. The next time you hear someone claiming this is what we are headed for, ask the question "Why?" I haven't heard a convincing answer yet.

On Predictions...

"The more things change, the more they stay the same" might be a cliché, but the more I look at failed predictions, the more it seems to make sense. The car, for instance, is 110 years old. Has it changed? A little. Cars are more comfortable, faster, and more fuel-efficient, but it's more of the same. Do they hover or fly? No. Can they navigate themselves? No. We were promised these things decades ago. Do they have four wheels and a steering wheel? Why, yes. They had those things 110 years ago, and they still do.

The Internet has seen phenomenal change in the past few years, but remember one thing: Most of the technology in use today was just sitting there waiting to be used. Some of the wild predictions depend on technology that doesn't yet exist, and new technologies take a very long time to develop and become widely used. The Automated Teller Machine was introduced in 1965 in the United Kingdom, but it wasn't widely used in the United States until the mid-'80s. Twenty years for a relatively simple technology. The Internet is supposed to have far more dramatic effects—it's supposed to turn the world upside down. It might, but not anytime soon.

Here's my final prediction then: Most of the predictions you hear about the Internet won't come to pass. (Not my predictions, of course; everything you read here is absolutely correct and most certainly *will* come to pass!) All the wild predictions about how the Internet will create a new world, how "nothing will ever be the same," how it will bring about world peace (seriously, some people are predicting this) and a new form of electronic democracy, and so on—all this is nonsense.

How do I know that? Because all-encompassing, far-reaching predictions are always wrong. The Green Revolution was supposed to end world hunger, antibiotics were supposed to eradicate infectious diseases, and the PC was supposed to lead to fantastic increases in productivity. True, the Green Revolution did raise crop yields, we did eradicate smallpox, and the PC allows ordinary people to do things they wouldn't have been able to afford before (such as create professional-looking business documents). But we still have world hunger, infectious diseases seem to be making a comeback, and economists have been unable to find more than negligible gains in productivity that are attributable to the PC.

Me, a cynic? Why, yes!

The Least You Need to Know

- Progress on the Internet will continue to slow. Whereas most of the initial development was just waiting to happen, future gains will be more difficult.
- We're still at least five years away from widespread, low-cost fast Internet connections in North America.
- Intercast PC/TV is one way that the Internet (specifically the Web) can be merged with TV; but we're still waiting for high-speed connections to make it all work well.
- The Internet backlash is perhaps ending; businesses are more cynical about the hype, but many businesses are finding the Internet to be essential.
- As the Internet opens borders, it will lead to fights over what might be distributed—and what might be said—across the Internet.
- Software will be more widely distributed across the Internet. However, we won't get rid of our hard disks and run programs over the Internet.

Part 4

Resources

You'll find reference information in this part of the book. There's a glossary of Internet terms and a quick look at the new Internet tools built into Windows 98. I'll tell you where to find the software you need: programs to help you on your travels around the Internet, games, print drivers, and unlimited other things. I'll also give you some background information about picking a service provider, in case you don't have Internet access yet or you want to find a new provider.

You'll also find out how to use the email responder, a system some readers might want to use to retrieve chapters that explain how the Internet used to work (and still does for the unfortunate users stuck with old technology).

Appendix A

Speak Like a Geek: The Complete Archive

ActiveX A multimedia-authoring system for the World Wide Web from Microsoft.

ADSL Asynchronous Data Subscriber Line, a very fast digital line provided by the phone company if you're very lucky. It's available here and there, but there's a good chance it won't be available in your area for some time.

alias A name that is substituted for a more complicated name, usually in an email program. For example, you can use a simple alias (pkent) instead of a more complicated mailing address (`pkent@topfloor.com`) for a mailing list.

America Online (AOL) A popular online information service and generous donator of floppy disks to just about every North American household.

anchor A techie word for an *HTML* tag used as a link from one document to another.

anonymous FTP A system by which members of the Internet "public" can access files at certain *FTP* sites without needing a login name; they simply log in as anonymous.

Archie An index system that helps you find files in more than 1,000 *FTP* sites.

archive file A file that contains other files (usually compressed files). It is used to store files that are not used often or files that might be downloaded from a file library by Internet users.

ARPANET The Advanced Research Projects Agency (of the U.S. Department of Defense) computer network, which was the forerunner of the Internet.

article A message in an Internet newsgroup.

ASCII American Standard Code for Information Interchange, a standard system used by computers to recognize text. An ASCII text file can contain the letters of the alphabet, the punctuation characters, and a few special characters. The nice thing about ASCII is that it's recognized by thousands of programs and many different types of computers.

backbone A network through which other networks connect.

bandwidth Widely used to mean the amount of information that can be sent through a particular communications channel.

baud rate A measurement of how quickly a modem transfers data. Although, strictly speaking, this is not the same as bps (*bits per second*), the two terms are often used interchangeably.

BBS See *bulletin board system.*

beta test A program test based on the premise, "This program is virtually finished, but because we need a little help smoothing out the rough edges, we'll give it to a few more people."

BITNET The "Because It's Time" network (really!). A large network connected to the Internet. Before the Internet became affordable to learning institutions, BITNET was the network of choice for communicating.

bits per second (bps) A measure of the speed of data transmission; the number of bits of data that can be transmitted each second.

bookmark A URL that has been saved in some way so that you can quickly and easily return to a particular Web document.

bounce The action of an email message being returned because of some kind of error.

bps See *bits per second.*

browser, Web A program that lets you read *HTML* documents and navigate the Web.

BTW An abbreviation for "by the way;" it's commonly used in email and newsgroup messages.

bug A malfunction in a computer program. Internet software seems to have led the software business to new levels of bug inclusion.

buglike feature When a programmer or technical support person, talking about the stupid way in which a program handles a particular procedure, says, "That's not a bug, that's the way we designed it"—that's a buglike feature. This term might have been coined by the *Mosaic* programmers at *NCSA*, who understood that just because you designed something one way, it doesn't mean you *should have* designed it that way.

bulletin board system (BBS) A computer system to which other computers can connect so their users can read and leave messages or retrieve and leave files.

cable modem A device that connects a network card in your computer to a cable-TV line, to provide Internet access. Some of these systems are very fast, at a very good price—probably the best value in Internet connectivity that you can find. If you can get one of these (it might not be available in your area yet), you should do it!

cache A place where a browser stores Web documents that have been retrieved. The cache might be on the hard disk, in memory, or a combination of the two. Documents you "return to" are retrieved from the cache, which saves transmission time.

CDF Channel Data Format, a system used to prepare information for *Webcasting*.

CERN The European Particle Physics Laboratory in Switzerland, the original home of the World Wide Web.

chat A system in which people can communicate by typing messages. Unlike email messages, chat messages are sent and received as you type (like a real chat—only without the voice). The most popular Internet chat system is Internet Relay Chat. There are a number of Web-site based chat systems, too. The best and most popular of all the chat systems, however, are on the online services. See also *talk*.

CIX The Commercial Internet Exchange, an organization of commercial Internet service providers.

client A program or computer that is "serviced" by another program or computer (the *server*). For instance, a Web client—that is, a Web *browser*—requests Web pages from a Web server.

compressed files Computer files that have been reduced in size by a compression program. Such programs are available for all computer systems (for example, PKZIP in DOS and Windows, tar and compress in UNIX, and StuffIt and PackIt for the Macintosh). Sometimes known as *archive* files, although the terms are not really synonymous; an archive file is not necessarily compressed (although many are).

CompuServe A large online information service, recently bought by AOL.

cracker Someone who tries to enter a computer system without permission. This is the correct term, although the term *hacker* is often mistakenly used in its place.

CSLIP (Compressed SLIP) See *Serial Line Internet Protocol (SLIP).*

cyberspace The area in which computer users travel when navigating a network or the Internet.

DARPANET The Defense Advanced Research Projects Agency network, which was created by combining *ARPANET* and *MILNET*. The forerunner of the Internet.

DDN The Defense Data Network is a U.S. military network that is part of the Internet. *MILNET* is part of the DDN.

dedicated line A telephone line that is leased from the telephone company and is used for one purpose only. On the Internet, dedicated lines connect organizations to service providers' computers, providing dedicated service.

dedicated service See *permanent connection.*

dial-in direct connection An Internet connection that you access by dialing into a computer through a telephone line. Once connected, your computer acts as if it were an Internet host. You can run *client* software (such as Web *browsers* and *FTP* programs). This type of service is often called *SLIP, CSLIP,* or *PPP.* Compare to *dial-in terminal connection.*

dial-in service A networking service that you can use by dialing into a computer through a telephone line.

dial-in terminal connection An Internet connection that you can access by dialing into a computer through a telephone line. Once connected, your computer acts as if it were a terminal connected to the service provider's computer. This type of service is often called *interactive* or *dial-up.* Compare to *dial-in direct connection.*

dial-up service A common Internet term for a *dial-in terminal connection.*

direct connection See *permanent connection.*

DNS See *Domain Name System.*

domain name A name given to a host computer on the Internet.

Domain Name System (DNS) A system by which one Internet host can find another so it can send email, connect *FTP* sessions, and so on. The hierarchical system of Internet host domain names (`domainname.domainname.domainname`) uses the Domain Name System. The DNS, in effect, translates words into numbers that the Internet's computers can understand. For instance, if you use the domain name `poorrichard.com`, DNS translates it into 207.33.11.236.

dot address An informal term used for an *IP address,* which is in the form *n.n.n.n,* where each *n* is a number. For instance, 192.17.3.3.

download The process of transferring information from one computer to another. You download a file from another computer to yours. See also *upload.*

EARN The European network associated with BITNET.

EFF See *Electronic Frontier Foundation.*

EFLA Extended Four-Letter Acronym. Acronyms are essential to the well-being of the Internet. See *TLA.*

Electronic Frontier Foundation (EFF) An organization interested in social, legal, and political issues related to the use of computers. The EFF is particularly interested in fighting government restrictions on the use of computer technology.

email Short for electronic mail, the system that lets people send and receive messages with their computers. The system might be on a large network (such as the Internet), on a bulletin board or online service (such as CompuServe), or over a company's own office network.

emoticon The techie name for small symbols created using typed characters, such as *smileys* :)

encryption The modification of data so that unauthorized recipients cannot use or understand it. See also *public-key encryption.*

etext Electronic text, a book or other document in electronic form, often simple ASCII text.

Ethernet A protocol, or standard, by which computers might be connected to one another to exchange information and messages.

FAQ (Frequently Asked Questions) A document containing a list of common questions and corresponding answers. You'll often find FAQs at *Web sites*, in *newsgroups*, and at *FTP* and *Gopher* sites.

Favorites The term used by Internet Explorer for its *bookmark* list.

Fidonet An important network that is also connected to the Internet. Well known in geek circles.

file transfer The copying of files from one computer to another over a network or telephone line. See *File Transfer Protocol.*

File Transfer Protocol A *protocol* defining how files transfer from one computer to another; generally abbreviated as *FTP*. FTP programs transfer files across the Internet. You can also use FTP as a verb to describe the procedure of using FTP, as in, "FTP to `ftp.demon.co.uk`," or "I FTPed to their system and grabbed the file."

Finger A program used to find information about a user on a host computer. Often used in the early days of the Internet boom, this system has now been largely forgotten.

flame An abusive newsgroup or mailing list message. Things you can do to earn a flame are to ask dumb questions, offend people, not read the FAQ, or simply get on the wrong side of someone with an attitude. When these things get out of control, a flame war erupts. Sometimes also used to refer to an abusive email message.

flamer Someone who wrote a flame.

form A *Web* form is a sort of interactive document. The document can contain fields into which readers can type information. This information might be used as part of a survey, to purchase an item, to search a database, and so on.

forms support A Web *browser* that has forms support can work with a Web *form.* Not all browsers can use forms (more recent ones can, though).

forum The term used by CompuServe for its individual bulletin boards or discussion groups (similar to Internet *newsgroups*).

frames Some Web pages are split into different frames (or panes); in effect, these frames create two or more independent subwindows within the main browser window.

Free-Net A community computer network, often based at a local library or college, which provides Internet access to citizens from the library or college or (sometimes) from their home computers. Free-Nets also have many local services, such as information about local events, local message areas, connections to local government departments, and so on.

freeware Software provided free by its creator. (It's not the same as *public domain software*, for which the author retains copyright.) See also *shareware*.

FTP See *File Transfer Protocol*.

gateway A system by which two incompatible networks or applications can communicate with each other.

geek Someone who knows a lot about computers, but very little about communicating with his fellow man—and, perhaps more importantly, with his fellow woman. (Vice versa if the geek happens to be a woman, although the majority of geeks are men.) Geeks spend more time in front of their computers than talking with real people. The term "geek" might have started as a derogatory term, but many geeks are proud of their geekness—and many have become very rich because of it. As Dave Barry (who got rich before becoming a computer geek) once said, "I'm a happy geek in cyberspace, where nobody can see my haircut."

GEnie An online service owned by General Electric.

Gopher A system using Gopher *clients* and *servers* to provide a menu system for navigating the Internet. Most Web browsers can act as Gopher clients. Gopher was started at the University of Minnesota, which has a gopher as its mascot.

Gopherspace Anywhere and everywhere you can get to using *Gopher* is known as Gopherspace.

GUI (Graphical User Interface) Pronounced *goo-ey*, this is a program that provides a user with onscreen tools such as menus, buttons, dialog boxes, a mouse pointer, and so on.

hacker Someone who enjoys spending most of his life with his head stuck inside a computer, either literally or metaphorically. See also *geek* and *cracker*.

helper See *viewer*.

history list A list of Web documents that you've seen in the current session (some browsers' history lists also show documents from previous sessions). You can return to a document by selecting it in the history list.

home page 1. The Web document your browser displays when you start the program or when you use the browser's Home command. 2. A sort of main page at a Web site. (Personally, I don't like this second definition, but there's not much I can do about it.)

host A computer connected directly to the Internet. A service provider's computer is a host, as are computers with permanent connections. Computers with *dial-in terminal connections* are not; they are terminals connected to the service provider's host. Computers with *dial-in direct connections* can be thought of as "sort of" hosts: They act like hosts while connected.

host address See *IP address*.

host number See *IP address*.

hostname The name given to a *host*. Computers connected to the Internet really have *host numbers*, but hostnames are easier to remember and work with. A hostname provides a simpler way to address a host than using a number.

hotlist A list of URLs of Web documents you want to save for future use. You can return to a particular document by selecting its *bookmark* from the hotlist.

HTML (Hypertext Markup Language) The basic coding system used to create Web documents.

HTTP (Hypertext Transfer Protocol) The data-transmission *protocol* used to transfer Web documents across the Internet.

hyperlink See *link*.

hypermedia Loosely used to mean a *hypertext* document that contains, or has links to, other types of media such as pictures, sound, video, and so on.

hypertext A system in which documents contain links that allow readers to move between areas of the document, following subjects of interest in a variety of different paths. With most browsers, you use the mouse to click a link to follow the link. The *World Wide Web* is a hypertext system.

HYTELNET A directory of *Telnet* sites. A great way to find out what you can do on hundreds of computers around the world.

IAB See *Internet Architecture Board*.

IAP Internet Access Provider, another term for *service provider*.

IE A common abbreviation for *Internet Explorer*.

IETF See *Internet Engineering Task Force*.

IMAP Internet Message Access Protocol, a system used to provide access to Internet email. Although this system is often used by corporations that link their networks to the Internet, most Internet service providers use a system called *POP*.

IMHO An abbreviation for In My Humble Opinion, which is often used in email and newsgroup messages.

index document A *Web* document that lets you search some kind of database. This term and *index server* are not used much these days; you'll hear the simple term "search page" instead.

index server A special program, accessed through an *index document*, that lets you search some kind of database.

inline images A picture inside a Web document. These graphics must be GIF, JPG, or XBM format files because those are the formats browsers can display.

Integrated Services Digital Network (ISDN) A digital telecommunications system that everyone's been waiting for but that the telephone companies seem unable to get installed in a decent time. ISDN allows voice and data to be transmitted on the same line in a digital format—instead of the normal analog format—and at a relatively high speed. ISDN is an Albanian acronym for "Yesterday's Technology Tomorrow." Despite the fact that ISDN was invented around the time of the Spanish-American War, the telephone companies just can't seem to figure out how to install this technology—and now ISDN's days are numbered because it's rapidly being superceded by *ADSL*.

interactive service See *dial-in terminal connection*.

internet Spelled with a small i, this term refers to networks connected to one another. "The Internet" is not the only internet.

Internet II The Internet used to be a nice little secret, a special toy for members of academia and the military-industrial complex. But since all you plebs got onto the Internet, it's been pretty crowded and slow. So a new network, called Internet II, is being created just for academia and military research. Don't expect them to make the same mistake twice and invite you to join!

Internet address See *IP address*.

Internet Architecture Board (IAB) The council of elders elected by *ISOC*; they get and figure out how the different components of the Internet will all connect.

Internet Engineering Task Force (IETF) A group of engineers that makes technical recommendations concerning the Internet to the IAB.

Internet Explorer A Web browser from Microsoft. It's one of the two best browsers, giving Netscape Navigator a run for its money.

Internet Protocol (IP) The standard protocol used by systems communicating across the Internet. Other protocols are used, but the Internet Protocol is the most important one.

Internet Relay Chat (IRC) A popular *chat* program. Internet users around the world can chat with other users in their choice of IRC channels.

Internet Society (ISOC) The society that, to some degree, governs the Internet; it elects the Internet Architecture Board, which decides on technical issues related to how the Internet works.

InterNIC The Internet *Network Information Center*. Run by the National Science Foundation, this center provides various administrative services for the Internet.

IP See *Internet Protocol.*

IP address A 32-bit address that defines the location of a host on the Internet. Such addresses are normally shown as four bytes, each one separated by a period (for example, 192.156.196.1). See *dot address* and *hostname.*

IRC See *Internet Relay Chat.*

ISDN See *Integrated Services Digital Network.*

ISOC See *Internet Society.*

ISP An abbreviation for Internet Service Provider that's much loved in geekdom. See also *service provider.*

Java A programming language from Sun Microsystems. Programmers can create programs that will run in any Java "interpreter," so a single program can run in multiple operating systems. (That's the theory at least; in practice, the programs often malfunction.) Netscape Navigator and Internet Explorer both have built-in Java interpreters.

JavaScript A sort of subset of Java, JavaScript is a scripting language that's simpler to use than Java. Both Netscape Navigator and Internet Explorer can run JavaScripts at least some of the time.

JPEG A compressed graphic format often found on the World Wide Web. These files use the .jpg or .jpeg extension.

JScript Microsoft's version of *JavaScript*; it contains as much of JavaScript as Microsoft can manage to add (Netscape develops JavaScript, so they're always ahead of Microsoft), plus some JScript-specific commands.

Jughead Jonzy's Universal Gopher Hierarchy Excavation And Display tool. A *Gopher* search tool that's similar to *Veronica*. The main difference between Veronica and Jughead is that Jughead searches a specific Gopher server whereas Veronica searches all of Gopherspace.

KIS See *Knowbot Information Service.*

Knowbot A program that can search the Internet for requested information. Knowbots are in an experimental stage.

Knowbot Information Service (KIS) An experimental system that helps you search various directories for a person's information (such as an email address).

LAN See *local area network.*

leased line See *dedicated line.*

link A connection between two *Web* documents. Links are generally pieces of text or pictures that, when clicked, make the browser request and display another Web document.

linked image An image that is not in a *Web* document (that's an *inline image*), but is connected to a document by a *link*. Clicking the link displays the image. Often known as an external image.

LISTSERV list A *mailing list* that is handled by the popular LISTSERV mailing list program.

local area network (LAN) A computer network that covers only a small area (often a single office or building).

log in The procedure of *logging on* or logging in. Also sometimes used as a noun to mean the ID and password you use to log on.

logging off The opposite of *logging on* or logging in; telling the computer that you've finished work and no longer need to use its services. The procedure usually involves typing a simple command, such as **exit** or **bye**, or, in more recent days, clicking a **Disconnect** button.

logging on Computer jargon for getting permission from a computer to use its services. A logon procedure usually involves typing a username (also known as an account name or user ID) and a password. This procedure makes sure that only authorized people can use the computer. Also known as logging in.

lurker Someone involved in *lurking.*

lurking Reading newsgroup or mailing list messages without responding to them. Nobody knows you are there.

mail reflector A mail program that accepts email messages and then sends them on to a predefined list of other email addresses. Such systems provide a convenient way to distribute information to people.

mail responder A system that automatically responds to a received email message. For instance, many companies use `info@hostname` addresses to automatically send back an email message containing product and company information.

mail robot An email system that automatically carries out some sort of email-related procedure for you.

mail server 1. A program that distributes computer files or information in response to email requests. 2. A program that handles incoming email for a host.

mailing list 1. A list of email addresses to which a single message can be sent by entering just one name as the To address. 2. Discussion groups based on a mailing list. Each message sent to the group is sent out to everyone on the list. (*LISTSERV lists* are mailing-list groups.)

MB Abbreviation for *megabyte*.

MCImail An email system owned by MCI.

megabyte A measure of the quantity of data. A megabyte is a lot when you are talking about files containing simple text messages, but not much when you are talking about files containing color photographs.

meta-search site A search site that allows you to search many other search sites. For instance, enter a question into Ask Jeeves (`http://www.askjeeves.com/`), and the system will search WebCrawler, Yahoo!, Infoseek, Excite, and AltaVista all at once.

MILNET A U.S. Department of Defense network connected to the Internet.

MIME (Multipurpose Internet Mail Extensions) A system that lets you send computer files "attached" to email. Also used to identify file types on the Web.

mirror site A copy of another site. (There are *FTP* mirror sites and *Web* mirror sites.) Every so often the contents of the other site are copied to the mirror site. The mirror site provides an alternative location so that if you can't get into the original site, you can go to one of the mirror sites.

modem A device that converts digital signals from your computer into analog signals for transmission through a phone line (modulation) and converts the phone line's analog signals into digital signals your computer can use (demodulation). (So-called ISDN modems are not true modems; they don't modulate and demodulate.)

Mosaic The first popular *GUI Web browser*, created by *NCSA*. This was the first graphical browser; some of the original Mosaic programmers helped to found Netscape Communications, the publisher of *Netscape Navigator*.

MPEG A computer video format. With the right software and, in some cases, hardware, you can play MPEG video files on your computer.

MUD A type of game popular on the Internet. MUD means Multiple User Dimensions, Multiple User Dungeons, or Multiple User Dialogue. MUDs are text games. Each player has a character; characters communicate with one another by the users typing messages.

navigate Refers to moving around on the Web using a *browser*. When you jump to a Web document, you are navigating.

navigator A program that helps you find your way around a complicated online service. Several navigator programs are available for CompuServe, for instance. Navigators can save you money by letting you prepare for many operations (such as writing mail) offline and then go online quickly to perform the operations automatically.

NCSA National Center for Supercomputing Applications, the people who make the *Mosaic* Web *browser*.

netiquette Internet etiquette, the correct form of behavior to use while working on the Internet and in *Usenet* newsgroups. These guidelines can be summarized as "Don't waste computer resources, and don't be rude." Apparently neither dictum is widely observed.

Netnews See *Usenet*.

Netscape Communicator A suite of programs based on *Netscape Navigator*; it contains Navigator (a *Web browser*), Messenger (*email* and newsgroups—the newsgroups portion is called *Collabra* in some versions), AOL Instant Messenger (*talk*), and Composer (a *Web*-page editing program). Some versions also include Netcaster (a *push* program), Conference (a *chat* and *VON* program), IBM-Host-on-Demand (*tn3270*), and Calendar (a scheduling program), although Netscape seems to have lost interest in these programs.

Netscape Navigator At one time the Web's most popular browser, created by some old *NCSA* programmers who started a company called Netscape Communications. Recently dropped down to second position, after *Internet Explorer*.

Network Information Center (NIC) A system providing support and information for a network. See also *InterNIC*.

Network News Transfer Protocol (NNTP) A system used for the distribution of *Usenet newsgroup* messages.

newbie A new user. The term might be used to refer to a new Internet user or a user who is new to a particular area of the Internet. Because everyone and his dog is getting onto the Internet, these loathsome creatures have brought the general tone of the Internet down a notch or two, upsetting long-term Internet users who thought the Internet was their own personal secret.

news server A computer that collects newsgroup data and makes it available to *newsreaders*.

newsgroup The Internet equivalent of a *BBS* or discussion group (or *forum* in CompuServe-speak) in which people leave messages for others to read. See also *LISTSERV list*.

newsreader A program that helps you find your way through a *newsgroup*'s messages.

NIC See *Network Information Center.*

NNTP See *Network News Transfer Protocol.*

NOC Network Operations Center, a group that administers a network.

node A computer device connected to a computer network. That device might be a computer, a printer, a router, or something else.

NREN The National Research and Education Network.

NSF National Science Foundation; the U.S. government agency that runs the *NSFnet.*

NSFnet The National Science Foundation network, a large network connected to the Internet.

offline The opposite of *online*; not connected.

offline browser A program that automatically collects pages from Web sites and then makes them available for viewing *offline.*

online Connected. You are online if you are working on your computer while it is connected to another computer. Your printer is online if it is connected to your computer and ready to accept data. (Online is often written "on-line," although the non-hyphenated version seems to be gaining acceptance these days.)

online service A commercial service (such as *CompuServe*, *The Microsoft Network*, and *America Online*) that provides electronic communication services. Users can join discussion groups, exchange email, download files, and so on. These services now have Internet access, too, so they might also be considered as *Internet service providers (ISPs).*

packet A collection of data. See *packet switching.*

Packet InterNet Groper (PING) A program that tests whether a particular host computer is accessible.

packet switching A system that breaks transmitted data into small *packets* and transmits each packet (or package) independently. Each packet is individually addressed and might even travel over a route different from that of other packets. The packets are combined by the receiving computer.

permanent connection A connection to the Internet using a *leased line.* The computer with a permanent connection acts as a host on the Internet. This type of service is often called *direct*, *permanent direct*, or *dedicated service* and is very expensive to set up and run. However, it provides a very fast, high *bandwidth* connection. A company or organization can lease a single line and then allow multiple employees or members to use it to access the Internet at the same time.

permanent direct See *permanent connection.*

personal certificate An electronic certificate containing *encryption* data used to encrypt and sign email or computer files or to identify the owner to a *Web site.* See also *public-key encryption.*

PING See *Packet InterNet Groper.*

plug-in A special type of *viewer* for a *Web browser.* A plug-in plays or displays a particular file type within the browser's window. (A viewer is a completely separate program.)

point of presence Jargon meaning a method of connecting to a service locally (without dialing long distance), often abbreviated *POP.* If a service provider has a *POP* in, say, Podunk, Ohio, people in that city can connect to the service provider by making a local call.

Point-to-Point Protocol (PPP) A method for connecting computers to the Internet via telephone lines; similar to *SLIP,* although a preferred, and these days more common, method.

POP See *point of presence* and *Post Office Protocol.*

port Generally, port refers to the hardware through which computer data is transmitted; the plugs on the back of your computer are ports. On the Internet, port often refers to a particular application. For instance, you might *Telnet* to a particular port on a particular host.

Post Office Protocol (POP) A system for letting hosts get email from a server. This system is typically used when a dial-in direct host (which might have only one user and might be connected to the Internet only periodically) gets its email from a service provider. The latest version of POP is POP3. Do not confuse this with another type of POP, *point of presence.*

posting A message (article) sent to a newsgroup or the act of sending such a message.

postmaster The person at a host who is responsible for managing the mail system. If you need information about a user at a particular host, you can send email to `postmaster@hostname`.

PPP See *Point-to-Point Protocol.*

private key The code used in a *public-key encryption* system that must be kept secure (unlike the *public key,* which might be freely distributed).

Prodigy An online service founded by Sears.

protocol A set of rules that defines how computers transmit information to one another, allowing different types of computers and software to communicate with one another.

public domain software Software that does not belong to anyone. You can use it without payment and even modify it if the source code is available. See also *shareware* and *freeware*.

public key The code used in a *public-key encryption* system that might be freely distributed (unlike the *private key*, which must be kept secure).

public-key encryption A system that uses two mathematically related keys: a *private key* and a *public key*. Information that has been encrypted using one key can be decrypted only by using the associated key. The private key is used to digitally sign an electronic document or decrypt files that were encrypted using the public key.

push A push program periodically retrieves data from the Internet and displays it on the user's computer screen. A push program is a sort of automated *Web browser*. See also *Webcasting*.

RealAudio A well-known streaming audio format.

reflector, mail Messages sent to a mail reflector's address are sent automatically to a list of other addresses.

reload (or **refresh**) A command that tells your browser to retrieve a Web document even though you have it in the cache. Microsoft uses the term refresh for this command in its Internet Explorer browser. (In Netscape Navigator, the Refresh command simply redisplays the Web page to clear up any display problems).

remote login A BSD (Berkeley) UNIX command (rlogin) that is similar to *Telnet*.

rendered An *HTML* document has been rendered when it is displayed in a Web browser. The browser renders it into a normal text document by removing all the HTML codes, so you see just the text that the author wants you to see. An unrendered document is the *source HTML* document (with codes and all).

rlogin See *remote login*.

rot13 Rotation 13, a method used to scramble messages in *newsgroups* so that you can't stumble across an offensive message. If you want to read an offensive message, you'll have to decide to do so and go out of your way to decode it.

router A system used to transmit data between two computer systems or networks using the same *protocol*. For instance, a company that has a permanent connection to the Internet will use a router to connect its computer to a leased line. At the other end of the leased line, a router is used to connect it to the service provider's network.

RTFM Abbreviation for (Read the F***ing Manual), which is often used in reaction to a stupid question (or in response to a question which, in the hierarchy of *newbies* and long-term Internet users, is determined to be a stupid question).

Serial Line Internet Protocol (SLIP) A method for connecting a computer to the Internet using a telephone line and modem. (See *dial-in direct connection*.) Once connected, the user has the same services provided to the user of a permanent connection. See also *Point-to-Point Protocol*.

server A program or computer that services another program or computer (the *client*). For instance, a *Gopher* server program sends information from its indexes to a Gopher client program, and *Web servers* send Web pages to Web browsers (which are Web clients).

service provider A company that provides a connection to the Internet. *Online services*, although generally regarded as different from service providers, are in fact also service providers because in addition to having their own services, they provide access to the Internet.

SGML Standard Generalized Markup Language. *HTML* grew out of SGML.

shareware Software that is freely distributed, but for which the author expects payment from people who decide to keep and use it. See also *freeware* and *public domain software*.

shell account Another name for a simple *dial-in terminal* account.

Shockwave A popular multimedia *plug-in*.

shopping cart A program that enables visitors to a Web site to place orders and purchase products.

signature A short piece of text transmitted with an email or newsgroup message. Some systems can attach text from a file to the end of a message automatically. Signature files typically contain detailed information on how to contact someone: name and address, telephone numbers, Internet address, CompuServe ID, and so on—or some strange little quote or poem.

Simple Mail Transfer Protocol (SMTP) A *protocol* used to transfer email between computers on a network.

SLIP See *Serial Line Internet Protocol*.

smiley A symbol in email and newsgroup messages used to convey emotion or provide amusement. Originally, the term referred to a symbol that seems to smile, but the term now seems to refer to just about any small symbol created with text characters. You create smileys by typing various keyboard characters. For example, :-(means sadness. Smileys are usually sideways: Turn your head to view the smiley. The more technical term for a smiley is *emoticon*.

SMTP See *Simple Mail Transfer Protocol*.

snarf To grab something off the Web and copy it to your computer's hard disk for future use. Snarfing is often illegal if done without permission (a copyright contravention).

source document An *HTML* document, the basic ASCII file that is *rendered* by a browser.

spam The term given to unsolicited email sent to large numbers of people without any regard to whether those people want to receive the mail. Originally, the term referred specifically to a single message sent to large numbers of newsgroups. The term comes from the Monty Python Spam song, which contains the refrain, "Spam, Spam, Spam, Spam, Spam, Spam, Spam, Spam."

stack See *TCP/IP stack*.

start page A term used by Microsoft in some versions of its Internet Explorer browser to refer to the *home page*. Just to confuse users, some versions of Internet Explorer refer to the home page as Home Page.

streaming In the old days, if you transferred an audio or video file, you had to wait for it to be transferred to your computer completely before you could play it. Streaming audio and video formats allow the file to play while it's being transferred.

tags The codes inside an *HTML* file. Web *browsers* read the tags to find out how they should *render* the document.

talk A program that lets two or more Internet users type messages to each other. As a user types a character or paragraph, that text is immediately transmitted to the other user. There are several common talk programs: talk, ntalk, and Ytalk are old UNIX systems, but these days AOL Instant Messenger and ICQ are becoming very popular. Talk is similar to *chat*, although chat systems are intended as meeting places, whereas talk programs are private. See also *chat*.

tar files Files *compressed* using the UNIX tape archive program. Such files usually have filenames ending in .tar.

TCP/IP (Transmission Control Protocol/Internet Protocol) A set of *protocols* (communications rules) that control how data transfers between computers on the Internet.

TCP/IP stack The software you must install before you can run TCP/IP programs across a dial-in direct connection. You might think of the TCP/IP stack as an Internet driver. In the same way you need a printer driver to send something from your word processor to your printer, you need the TCP/IP stack to send information to (and receive information from) your dial-in direct programs.

Telnet A program that lets Internet users log in to computers other than their own host computers, often on the other side of the world. Telnet is also used as a verb, as in "Telnet to debra.doc.ca."

Telneting Internet-speak for using Telnet to access a computer on the network.

The Microsoft Network A major online service (at one point the fastest growing service in history) that was launched in 1995 when Windows 95 was released. Also known as MSN.

TLA Three-Letter Acronym. An acronym for an acronym. What would we do without them? See also *EFLA*.

tn3270 A *Telnet*-like program used for *remote logins* to IBM mainframes.

trojan horse A computer program that appears to carry out a useful function but which is actually designed to do harm to the system on which it runs. See also *virus*.

UNIX A computer operating system. Many—probably most—host computers connected to the Internet run UNIX.

upload The process of transferring information from one computer to another. You upload a file from your computer to another. See also *download*.

URL (Uniform Resource Locator) A Web address.

Usenet The "User's Network," a large network connected to the Internet. The term also refers to the *newsgroups* distributed by this network.

UUCP UNIX-to-UNIX copy program, a system by which files can be transferred between UNIX computers. The Internet uses UUCP to provide a form of email, in which the mail is placed in files and transferred to other computers.

UUCP network A network of UNIX computers connected to the Internet.

uudecode If you use *uuencode* to convert a file to ASCII and transmit it, you'll use uudecode to convert the ASCII file back to its original format.

uuencode The name given a program used to convert a computer file of any kind (sound, spreadsheet, word processing, or whatever) into an ASCII file so that it can be transmitted as a text message. The term is also used as a verb, as in "uuencode this file." There are DOS, Windows, UNIX, and Macintosh uuencode programs. In Windows, a program called Wincode can uuencode and *uudecode* files. Most email programs handle *MIME* transmissions properly these days, so uuencode is falling out of use.

VBScript A scripting language from Microsoft, which is similar in concept to *JavaScript*.

Veronica The Very Easy Rodent-Oriented Netwide Index to Computerized Archives, a very useful program for finding things in *Gopherspace*.

viewer A program that displays or plays computer files that you find on the Web. For instance, you need a viewer to play video files you find. These programs are sometimes known as *helpers*.

virus A program that uses various techniques for duplicating itself and traveling between computers. Viruses vary from simple nuisances (they might display an unexpected message on your screen) to serious problems that can cause millions of dollars' worth of damage (such as crashing a computer system and erasing important data).

Voice on the Net (VON) A service through which you can talk to other Internet users. You need a sound card, microphone, speakers, and the right software; then you can make Internet phone calls. They're warbly, but very cheap.

VON See *Voice on the Net*.

VRML Virtual Reality Modeling Language, a system used to create three-dimensional images. Internet pundits claimed, in 1995, that most Web sites would be using VRML by now and lots of it, but the pundits forgot that VRML doesn't run well on most people's computers. Since then, people have lost interest in VRML, despite the fact that now many people's computers do run VRML well. VRML's time has not yet arrived.

VT100 The product name of a Digital Equipment Corporation computer terminal (DEC). This terminal is a standard that is emulated (simulated) by many other manufacturers' terminals.

W3 See *World Wide Web.*

WAIS See *Wide area information server.*

Web Pertaining to the *World Wide Web.*

Web forum A discussion group running on a Web site.

Web server A computer system—a computer running special server software—that makes *Web* documents available to Web browsers. The browser asks the server for the document, and the server transmits it to the browser.

Web site A collection of *Web* documents about a particular subject on a *host.*

Webcasting Distributing information via *push* programs.

Webspace The area of cyberspace in which you are traveling when working on the *Web.*

WebTV A system used to display Web sites on a television. A box containing a *modem* is connected to a TV; the signals from the Internet are transmitted on the phone lines (not along the TV *cable* line) and displayed on the TV screen. WebTV is manufactured by Sony and Philips/Magnavox (and recently bought by Microsoft), although the term is also widely used to describe the technology in generic terms. If you're excited about getting onto the Internet, a good way to dissipate some of that excitement is to buy WebTV. On the other hand, some people love it. Takes all kinds.

Web-hosting company A company that sells space on a Web server to people who want to set up Web sites.

White Pages Lists of Internet users.

Whois A UNIX program used for searching for information about Internet users.

Wide area information server (WAIS) A system that can search particular databases on the Internet.

Winsock A *TCP/IP stack* for Microsoft Windows.

World Wide Web A *hypertext* system that allows users to travel through linked documents, following any chosen route. World Wide Web documents contain topics that, when selected, lead to other documents.

WWW See *World Wide Web.*

X.500 A standard for electronic directory services.

XBM X Bitmap graphics format, a bitmap from the UNIX X Window system. These simple images are one of only three types that can be used as inline graphics; the others are GIF and JPG. They're rarely seen on the Web these days, though.

XML Extensible Markup Language, a subset of SGML. *HTML*-like tags that extend HTML by allowing designers to create their own tags. Particular industry groups could then create programs that would recognize those tags. For instance, the medical industry could create special programs that recognize tags such as <MD>, <RX>, and <VERYSICK>.

Appendix B

Windows 98's Internet Features

Microsoft has integrated the Windows operating system more closely with the Internet, and the latest version of its operating system, Windows 98, has a plethora of Internet-related tools. Tight integration of the operating system and the Internet enables Microsoft to update the operating system frequently. This is a real boon for all Windows users, ensuring that we can all work with the very latest bugs available.

The U.S. Justice Department claimed that Microsoft uses unfair practices to destroy competition, and that one of those practices is adding features to the operating system—in other words, by adding various utilities to the operating system, Microsoft is harming the companies that would otherwise be creating and selling similar software. That might be so, but do we need a government department overseeing the development of Microsoft Windows? The operating system presents enough problems as it is without lawyers and bureaucrats helping design it! (This strikes me as akin to letting lawyers design a kids' playground—"You can have any structure you want, as long as it's not more than six inches off the ground.") At the time of writing, this problem has not really been resolved—Microsoft and the Justice Department are still battling. However, Microsoft was allowed to release Windows 98 with all the Internet-related tools it originally intended.

Justice Department Versus Microsoft

I'm no cheerleader for Microsoft. But on the other hand, I'm not sure I want the Justice Department designing software, either. Consider, in relation to the fuss about Microsoft adding its browser to the operating system, the following:

- Microsoft is not the only operating-system publisher to believe that people buying an operating system should get a free browser; IBM provides one with OS2, and the current version of the Apple operating system includes two browsers!
- Microsoft was not the first company to bundle a Web browser with an operating system; IBM included a browser in OS2 in mid to late 1994, long before Microsoft had even released the beta of Internet Explorer.
- Web browsers were "traditionally" free; in 1994, there were dozens of Web browsers available, and most were available at no cost.
- Netscape claims that Microsoft hurt it by giving away a browser in the operating system, but if Netscape's executives really believed they could build a multibillion dollar business based on a simple utility such as a Web browser, a utility that had a history of being free, they must have been smoking something pretty strong.

Anyway, this appendix is a quick summary of the features included in Windows 98 at the time of writing, with information on how to find each program. Note that some of the Internet features might not be installed on your computer yet—it all depends on the choices made by the person who installed Windows 98 onto your computer. You can add any missing programs by running Windows Setup (assuming you have the installation disk, that is). If the item you want has not been installed, select **Start**, **Settings**, **Control Panel**, and then open the **Add/Remove Programs** icon, and click the **Windows Setup** tab. In the list box that you'll see, click the category, then the **Details** button, and then select the item you want to install.

These are the optional programs, sorted by category (the category you'll see in the Add/Remove Programs dialog box).

Table B.1 The Optional Internet Features in Windows 98

Category	Feature
Communications	Dial-Up Networking
	Microsoft Chat
	Virtual Private Networking
Internet Tools	MS FrontPage Express
	Microsoft VRML Viewer
	Microsoft Wallet
	Personal Web Server
	RealAudio Player
	Web Publishing Wizard
	Web-Based Enterprise Management
Microsoft Outlook Express	(Email, newsreader, and address book; this is a category by itself)
Multimedia	Macromedia Shockwave Director
	Macromedia Shockwave Flash
	Microsoft Media Player
	Online Services America Online
	AT&T WorldNet Service
	CompuServe
	Prodigy Internet
	The Microsoft Network
WebTV for Windows	(Category by itself)

To further complicate the issue, Microsoft has online upgrades (**Start**, **Windows Update**). If you upgrade your system, it might not match exactly what's shown here. You should be able to find the latest programs in this Windows Update area, though.

Online Services

Thanks to Bill Gates's battle with the U.S. Justice Department, America Online, and Netscape, Windows 98 includes software for several online services. In other words, America Online will be able to save millions of dollars by not including a free disk in all its junk mail to American homes. Instead, Windows 98 users can simply select AOL or one of several other online services and log right in. To find these online service programs, select **Start**, **Program Files**, **Online Services** (see the following figure). Windows 98 currently includes software for America Online, CompuServe, AT&T WorldNet, Prodigy Internet, and, of course, The Microsoft Network.

Thanks to the Justice Department, choosing an online service is easier than ever (which is bad news for thousands of small Internet service providers, of course).

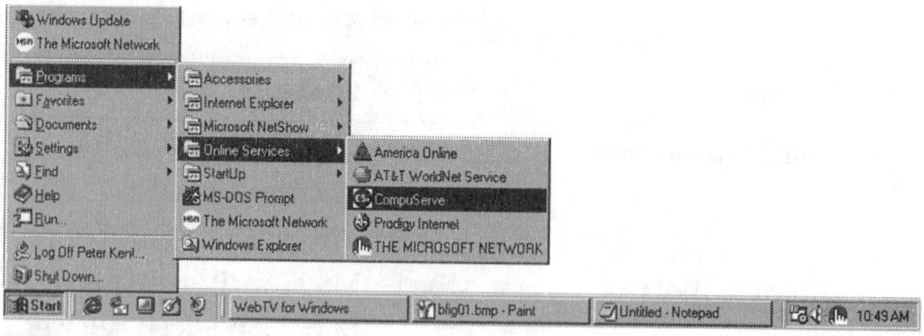

System Setup Tools

Windows 98 has several tools to help you set up your Internet connection:

- **Dial-Up Networking** This utility creates connections to Internet service providers, so you can get onto the Internet. In theory, it provides a simple point-and-click configuration system. In practice, it doesn't. Note, however, that in many cases you don't need to use this utility at all. For instance, if you use one of the online services already built into Windows 98; the connection will be configured for you automatically. You can use the Connection Wizard to help you set up Dial-Up Networking. You can open Dial-Up Networking by selecting **Start**, **Programs**, **Accessories**, **Communications**, **Dial-Up Networking**, but you'll probably want to use the Connection Wizard instead.
- **Connection Wizard** This program leads you through the process of setting up Dial-Up Networking. In theory, it "automatically handles the software configuration steps necessary for gaining access to the Internet." Although I almost let my cynicism get away with me (having seen, in Windows 95, what phrases such as "automatically handles" really mean), I must say that the Connection Wizard is quite good, a great improvement (why wasn't this in Windows 95?). It even has a referral service that helps you find a service provider in your area. Select **Start**, **Programs**, **Internet Explorer**, **Connection Wizard**.
- **ISDN Configuration Wizard** Dial-Up Networking is designed to work with ordinary phone lines, but this program helps you set up a connection to an ISDN line (see Appendix D, "Finding Internet Access and the Right Equipment"). To open this program, select **Start**, **Programs**, **Accessories**, **Communications**, **ISDN Configuration Wizard** (if you haven't installed an ISDN device, this option won't appear).

Email and Newsgroups

Microsoft Outlook Express combines an email program (see Chapter 2, "The Premier Internet Tool: Email," and Chapter 3, "Advanced Email: HTML and Encryption,"), a newsreader (see Chapter 9, "Newsgroups: The Source of All Wisdom," and Chapter 10, "Your Daily News Delivery,"), and an address book. If you're working on a computer set up by your corporate employer and are connected to the corporate network, there's a good chance you'll be using Outlook Express. If you get to pick your own software, you might want to find something else.

Microsoft often creates software based on the principle "It might not be the best, but at least it's the biggest." I've used Microsoft Exchange, the clunky forerunner to Outlook Express, so I just can't bring myself to use this new incarnation (although admittedly it looks, at first glance, like a bit of an improvement). Much better programs are available. (I like Gravity for newsgroups and AKMail for email, but you might find something that suits you better.)

To start Outlook Express, use the **Outlook Express** icon on the desktop or on the taskbar, or select **Start**, **Programs**, **Internet Explorer**, **Outlook Express**. You can get to the Address book directly using **Start**, **Programs**, **Internet Explorer**, **Address Book**.

Internet Explorer Web Browser

Internet Explorer is the Web browser that the Justice Department (and Netscape) is so upset about. Explorer is a very good browser, although I'm not convinced it's a great one; I currently prefer Netscape Navigator, although there have been times when I thought Explorer was better; these programs seem to leapfrog each other. To start Internet Explorer, click the Explorer icon in the taskbar, or select **Start**, **Programs**, **Internet Explorer**, **Internet Explorer**.

Browser Plug-Ins

You learned about browser plug-ins and viewers in Chapter 7, "Web Multimedia," and Windows 98 provides several. Do you really need all these? Being a Web-multimedia cynic, I'd say no (the Web could really do with a little less multimedia, and a little more good writing), but who knows, perhaps you feel you have to experience the "best" that the Web has to offer. Now and again even I, the Internet Curmudgeon, feel that I just *have* to see *why* a Web author feels that I just *must* view his site using the Shockwave plug-in (when it's all over I rarely find myself in agreement with him). Perhaps the most useful plug-in is the RealAudio plug-in; RealAudio is used a fair bit on the Internet.

These are the Windows 98 plug-ins:

- **Microsoft VRML Viewer** This program is a Virtual Reality viewer. If you find any 3D images on the Web, this plug-in can probably handle them. You won't find many, though.
- **Microsoft Wallet** You can use this special commerce plug-in to pay for purchases at Web sites. It provides a convenient way to store and transfer your credit card information. (You can protect the credit card numbers by providing a password.) It will also store your address and other contact information. The

only problem is that few Web sites are set up to work with the Wallet. It still keeps useful information close at hand, though (no more running off to find your credit cards before buying something). To add your information, open the Internet Properties dialog box by using the **Internet** icon in the Control Panel or by selecting **View**, **Internet Options** inside Internet Explorer. Then click the **Content** tab to find the Wallet settings.

- **NetShow Player** This program plays streaming video and audio. (*Streaming*, you'll remember from Chapter 7, means that the information plays at the same time it's being transferred across the Internet; a nonstreaming data file has to transfer completely before it can begin playing.) For instance, the MSNBC news Web site (`http://www.msnbc.com/`) uses data that plays through NetShow Player.
- **RealAudio Player** This program plays sounds; it's often used at music and news Web sites.
- **Shockwave Director** This program plays Macromedia Director files, which are animation files that you'll sometimes run across.
- **Shockwave Flash** This program plays another form of smaller and "lighter" animation file.

When Internet Explorer needs to run one of these plug-ins, it will automatically open the right one.

Microsoft Chat

Microsoft Chat, which you saw in Chapter 13, "Yak, Yak, Yak: Chatting in Cyberspace," is built into Windows 98. To open the program, select **Start**, **Programs**, **Internet Explorer**, **Microsoft Chat**.

Web Publishing Tools

Windows 98 provides several Web publishing tools. You can find all these items in the Internet Explorer folder; select **Start**, **Programs**, **Internet Explorer**.

- **MS FrontPage Express** This editor from Microsoft FrontPage creates Web pages for you, as you can see in the following figure). It's a sort of Web-page word processor; you type the text and select formats, font types, colors, and so on, and FrontPage Express adds all the HTML codes for you (see Chapter 20, "Setting Up Your Own Web Site").
- **Web Publishing Wizard** This program simplifies the process of transferring pages from your computer to the computer that will host your Web pages.

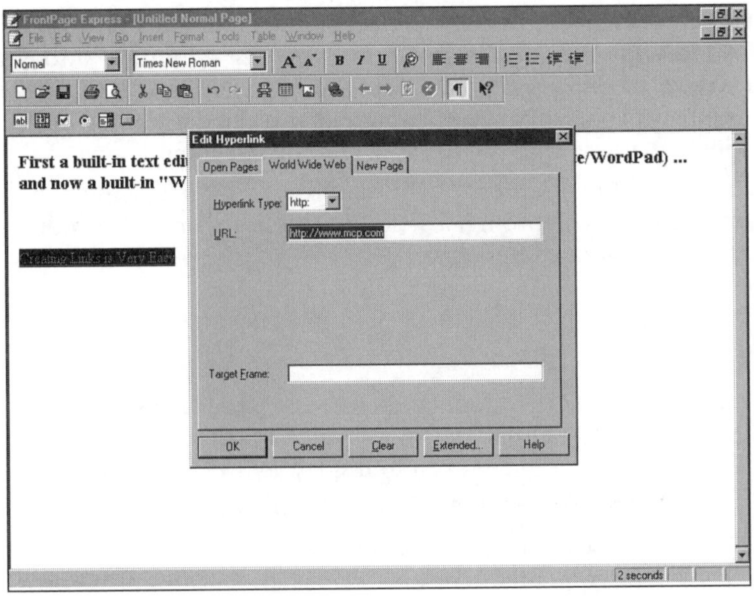

Windows has a text editor, a simple word processor, and now it has an HTML editor, too.

- **Personal Web Server** You can set up a Web site on your own computer and make it available to other people on your corporate network (if the network is running the TCP/IP protocol, ask your system administrator) or even on the Internet (if people on the Internet have access to your computer). You can also use it to test a Web site on your own computer before publishing it on the Internet. The Personal Web Server is a very simple Web server that you configure by filling in forms in your Web browser. (Remember, the server is the program that receives browsers' requests for Web pages and transmits those pages to them.)

"Corporate" Tools

Windows 98 has several tools that I think of as "corporate" tools, that is, programs that you're unlikely to use at home, but might work with if you are employed by a medium to large corporation.

- **Microsoft NetMeeting** This "conference" program enables you to communicate with people across the Internet instantly by typing messages, drawing on a whiteboard, or transferring files (see Chapter 14, "Internet Conferences: Voice on the Net, Whiteboards, and More"). You might even be able to include voice and video. Open this program by using **Start**, **Programs**, **Internet Explorer**, **Microsoft Netmeeting**.

- **Virtual Private Networking** This system can be used to build a private network on the World Wide Web. Authorized people can use a "tunnel" through the World Wide Web to access the corporate network. So wherever you happen to be traveling, as long as you can access the Internet you can get to the network. This system is something that the network administrator must set up.
- **Web-Based Enterprise Management** This tool is used for managing various corporate and network tasks through a series of Web pages on the network. It's another toy for the network administrator.

WebTV for Windows

This system is *not* the same as the WebTV product discussed in Chapter 23, "WebTV and Other Unusual Internet Devices," although it was created in conjunction with that product. Rather, it's a system that enables you to display TV information and Web pages carried by TV signals on your computer.

WebTV for Windows likes to have a TV tuner card available, which is a card installed in your computer that allows the computer to display TV signals, but it can still do a few things even if your computer can't display TV. Without a TV tuner, it can display television schedules, downloaded from the Web, for you. If you have a TV tuner installed in your computer, you can quickly select a program in the schedule and watch the program on your computer (see the following figure). If that program is carrying Web pages embedded in the signal, those pages can be displayed.

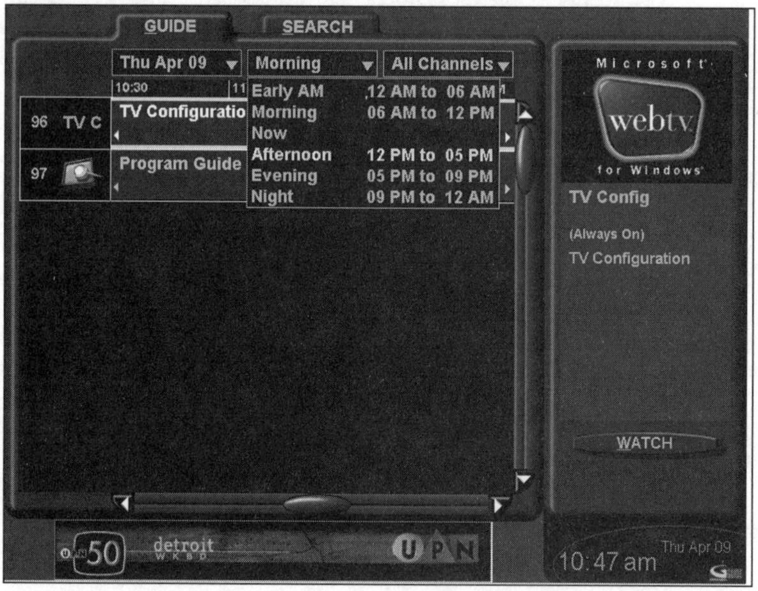

If you don't get enough TV already, now you can watch it when you should be working or at least figure out what you'll watch when you escape from your cubicle this evening.

How can a TV signal carry a Web page? There's a lot of empty space in a TV signal, and because a Web page doesn't take up much room, relatively speaking, it's possible to cram the page into the dead space in the TV signal (into the vertical blanking interval). A TV with some kind of processor in it can then pull the Web page out and display it separately. This technology is nothing particularly new; such systems have been used for years in Europe to transmit data on television screens. In Great Britain, for instance, TV viewers can switch from the normal TV broadcasts to a special TeleText menu, from which they can select news articles, weather reports, and so on.

The main problem with using WebTV to view Web pages carried by TV signals is that very few TV signals carry Web pages, although that will probably change over the next year or so. You can start WebTV by clicking the **WebTV** taskbar icon or by selecting **Start**, **Programs**, **Accessories**, **Entertainment**, **WebTV for Windows**.

Web Integration

Windows 98 attempts to integrate the computer desktop with the Web and even provides Web-like features on the desktop. (Of course, it would work a little better if we all had fast, permanent connections to the Internet, which is what Bill Gates and various telecommunications companies promised we'd all have by Christmas of 1998. By the time you read this, it'll be close to Christmas of 1999, perhaps much later...and the nation still won't have widely available, fast, permanent connections to the Internet.)

- **Active Desktop** This feature makes your Windows desktop work like a Web page. Instead of double-clicking an icon, you can just single click (and the icon labels look like Web links). Windows Explorer looks like a browser and works like a browser to some degree; click a file, and Explorer displays the file, for instance. To set up Active Desktop, select **Start**, **Settings**, **Active Desktop**.
- **Push** Windows 98 has a built-in "push" system (see Chapter 8, "Push Information to Your Desktop"). You can embed Web pages into the desktop. Want the latest sports news every morning? Find a good sports Web site, and then embed the page into your desktop so it's always there. Windows 98 also provides a variety of preconfigured push *channels*, which are essentially Web pages specially configured to work with the push system. Eventually, you'll be able to receive push channels via satellite transmissions. (Don't you love the word "eventually"? Writers use it to mean "I've no idea when.") There's a View Channels icon on the taskbar, and when you first start Windows, you'll see a special Channel box on the right side of the window.

Maintenance and Configuration

Look in the Control Panel (**Start**, **Settings**, **Control Panel**), and you'll find an Internet Properties icon. The Internet Properties dialog box provides all sorts of Internet-related settings, from how to automatically dial the Internet to how to keep your kids away from "bad" Web sites. You can also open this dialog box from inside Internet Explorer; select **View**, **Internet Options** inside Internet Explorer.

You'll also find a number of Help Troubleshooters for Internet-related subjects: The Modem, Microsoft Network, and Dial-Up Networking. These little interactive programs try to help you figure out why something isn't working (if you're lucky, they might even succeed). Choose **Start**, **Help**. On the **Contents** tab, click **Troubleshooting** and then **Windows 98 Troubleshooters**.

Finally, you can update Windows 98 across the Internet. Open the **Start** menu, and you'll see a **Windows Update** option. This option opens your browser, connects to a Microsoft upgrade Web site, and runs the Windows Upgrade Wizard. If there are any bug fixes waiting for you—ahem, I mean "system enhancements"—the Wizard will automatically transfer and install them.

Windows Update

The Windows Update area of the Microsoft Web site has lots of goodies you can download for free. Microsoft knows its Web site is as easy to navigate as the London docks during a heavy fog, so they've kindly added a menu option to your Start menu. Simply select **Start**, **Windows Update**, and Internet Explorer will open and connect to the appropriate page. Perhaps. Sometimes it doesn't work too well. Still, if you *do* get through, you'll find toys such as these:

- The latest and greatest updates to all your favorite Windows 98 utilities.
- **Agent 2.0** Used to display "characters used in interactive guides and entertainment features on some Web sites," an invaluable business tool. If you hate those little characters who tell you how to use Word or Excel, you won't want this.
- **AOL ART Image Format Support** Download America Online art now…so you don't have to later.
- **DirectAnimation** Speed up animations.
- **Web Folders Internet Publishing Utility** Work with files on your Web server in the same way you work with files on your computer.
- **Web Publishing Wizard** A tool for posting Web pages to a Web server.
- **Language Support** View Web pages in languages such as Arabic, Japanese, Hebrew, Korean, and many others.

Techno Talk

Bug-Fix Watch!

It can be fun to visit the Windows Update area. See whether you can spot the bug fixes cleverly disguised as product improvements! Here's a tip. If you can't understand exactly what the file is supposed to do, yet Microsoft says it's a critical or recommended update, it's probably a bug fix. Or if you download it and find the new features are so minimal as to be almost worthless, it's probably a bug fix.

Appendix C

All the Software You'll Ever Need

You've read about a lot of software in this book, and there's much more that hasn't been mentioned. Thousands of shareware, freeware, and demoware programs for the Macintosh, Windows 3.1, Windows 95, Windows 98, Windows NT, and all flavors of UNIX are available for you to download and use. "How do I find all these programs?" you ask. It's easy to find software once you know where to look.

Different Types of Software

Shareware is software that is given away free, but which you are supposed to register (for a fee) if you decide to continue using it. *Freeware* is software that is given away with no fee required. *Demoware* is software that is generally free, but is intended to get you interested in buying the "full" program. There are many other related terms, such as *crippleware* (shareware that will stop working in some way—perhaps the entire program stops working, or maybe just one or two features—after the trial period is over).

The Search Starts at Home

You can always begin looking at home. If you use one of the online services, you'll find stacks of software within the service—no need to go out onto the Internet. All the online services have Internet-related forums (or BBSs, or areas, or whatever they call them). These are good places to begin, and you can usually download the software more quickly from there than from the Internet. In addition, many online services have forums set up by software vendors and shareware publishers. These are good places to get to know, too.

If you are with a true Internet service provider, you'll often find that your service has a file library somewhere. The library will have a smaller selection than the online services do, but it might be a good place to start nonetheless. On the other hand, you might want to go straight to the major Internet software sites, which will have a much greater range of programs.

Finding a Browser

In this book, I've mentioned two programs in particular— Netscape Navigator and Internet Explorer—that you need to know how to find. You might already have one or the other of these. Many online services and service providers already provide one of them in the software package you get when you sign up. If you want to get the latest version or try the competing program, go to one of these sites:

Netscape Navigator: `http://www.netscape.com/`

Internet Explorer: `http://www.microsoft.com/ie/`

I've mentioned dozens of other programs throughout this book. You can find most of those programs at the sites I discuss next.

The Internet's Software Libraries

The Internet is full of wonderful software libraries. Check out some of the following sites, but remember that there are more, which you can find using the links mentioned in the section "Finding More," later in this appendix.

- **TUCOWS (Windows)** (`http://www.tucows.com/`) TUCOWS (shown in the following figure) originally stood for "The Ultimate Collection of Winsock Software," but these days it has software for the Macintosh and OS2, as well as Windows 3.1, 95, 98, and NT.
- **Stroud's Consummate Winsock Applications Page (Windows)** (`http://cws.internet.com/`) Another excellent Windows software archive.

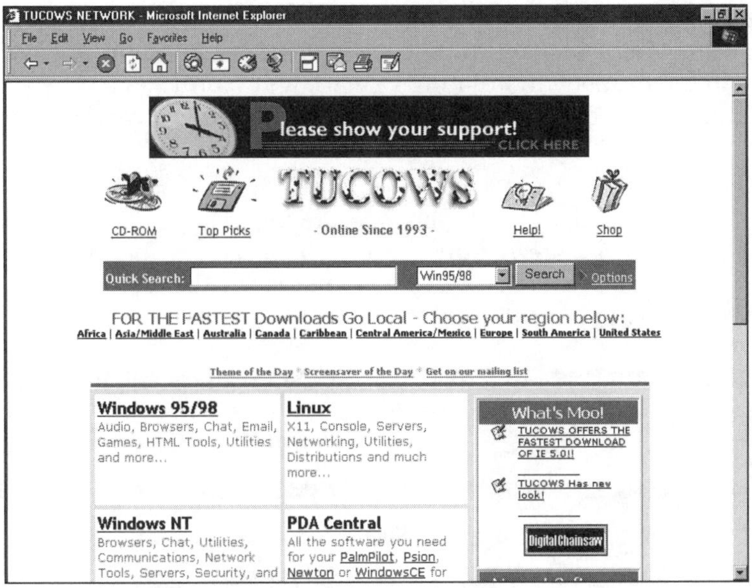

The TUCOWS site is an excellent place to find all sorts of useful Windows software. (The more cows a program's been awarded, the better it is.)

- **Winsite (Windows)** (`http://www.winsite.com/` or `ftp.winsite.com`) Another good Windows archive. Winsite claims to be the "Planet's Largest Software Archive for Windows." It now has a special section, Casino Winsite, containing gambling software. Note that it's often difficult to get to the FTP site.
- **TopSoft (Windows, Macintosh, UNIX)** (`http://www.topsoft.com/`) This relatively small site has a nice selection of useful programs, and you'll find a detailed description for each one (many other sites have very simple descriptions, or none at all, for the programs they store).
- **ZDNet Software Library** (`http://www.hotfiles.com/`) This site contains many Windows programs (over 10,000 files). It's well-organized, with detailed descriptions of the files.
- **ZDNet Mac (Macintosh)** (`http://www.zdnet.com/mac/download.html`) Go to this site to find a large Macintosh software archive.
- **Nonags (Windows 95, Windows 98, and Windows NT)** (`http://www.nonags.com/`) This site is dedicated to software that has "no nags, no time limits, no disabled features, or any other tricks. Most are really free, a few are shareware..."
- **Shareware.com (Windows, Macintosh, UNIX, OS2, Atari, Amiga, DOS)** (`http://www.shareware.com/`) This site contains a huge collection of software for all major operating systems. You can search for a keyword and come up with all sorts of interesting things here. Shareware.com claims to have more than 250,000 files.

- **Jumbo (Windows, DOS, Macintosh, UNIX)** (`http://www.jumbo.com/`) Another excellent site, Jumbo contains thousands of programs (it claims to have more than 300,000) for a variety of operating systems. It also provides a variety of "starter kits," collections of programs for decompressing files and checking them for viruses.
- **Keyscreen (Windows)** (`http://www.keyscreen.com/` or `http://www.screenshot.com/`) This unusual site (see the following figure) doesn't have many programs—around 425 shareware and freeware applications—but it provides pictures of programs (over 2,100), so you can see whether you might like them before bothering to download them.

Keyscreen lets you see what you're downloading before you do so.

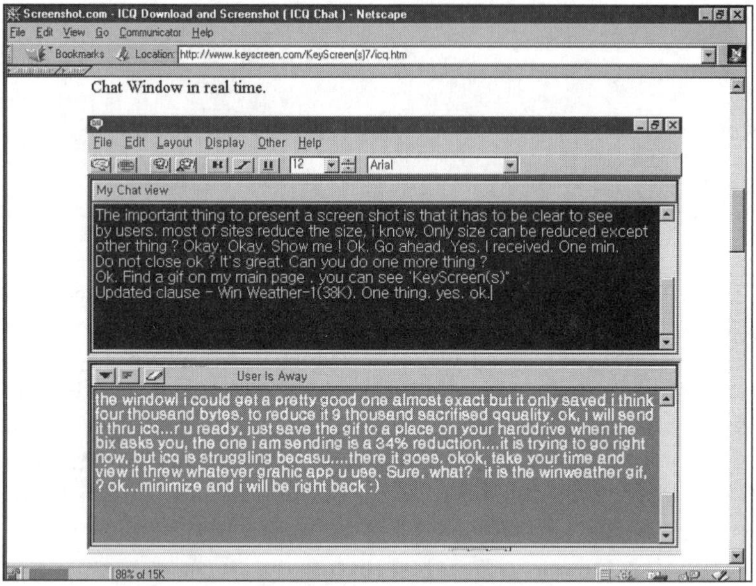

- **Info-Mac HyperArchive (Macintosh)** (`http://hyperarchive.lcs.mit.edu/HyperArchive.html`) This large collection of Macintosh software contains lots of files, but it's not very easy to work with.
- **The Ultimate Macintosh Site (Macintosh and Apple)** (`http://www.ultimatemac.com/` or `http://www.flashpaper.com/umac/`). You'll find lots of information about the Macintosh, along with software, at this Web site. You'll find links to Apple shareware sites, too.
- **WUGNET (Windows User's Group Network)** (`http://www.wugnet.com/shareware/`) You'll find hundreds of handpicked Windows shareware programs at this site (many of them Internet-related applications). WUGNET picks a great program each week, and the archives store previous weeks' choices going back a couple of years.

Plug-Ins and Viewers

You can find many viewers at the software sites already mentioned, but you can also find them at a few sites specifically created for viewers and plug-ins. You can find links to viewers and plug-ins that will work in Internet Explorer at `http://www.microsoft.com/ie/download`. A good place to find plug-ins for Netscape is at `http://home.netscape.com/plugins/`. For viewers, you can try `http://home.netscape.com/assist/helper_apps/` or one of the following sites:

- **The NCSA Mosaic Home Page** (`http://www.ncsa.uiuc.edu/SDG/Software/Mosaic`) Select the appropriate operating system—Windows, Macintosh, or UNIX—and you'll find a link to viewers that can be used with any browser, not just Mosaic.
- **The WWW Browser Test Page** (`http://www-dsed.llnl.gov/documents/WWWtest.html`) This page provides test files, so you can see whether your plug-ins and viewers are working—and find others if they're not.
- **The IUMA Utilities Pages** (`http://www.iuma.com/IUMA-2.0/help/`) This site is a good place to go for audio and video utilities.
- **Browsers.com** (`http://www.browsers.com/`) This site has links to all sorts of browser-related software and information.

Finding More

New software archives appear online all the time, and many are specialized sites, providing software for particular purposes. You can search for more at the search sites discussed in Chapter 17, "Finding Stuff." For example, you can go to Yahoo!'s `http://www.yahoo.com/Computers_and_Internet/ Software/` page and find links to all sorts of software sites—software for amateur radio, CAD (Computer Aided Design), astronomy, and just about everything else. Also try Pass The Shareware (`http://www.passtheshareware.com/`), a site with loads of links to shareware sites.

Don't Forget Demos and Drivers

Thanks to the Internet, the distribution of demo software has increased greatly. Commercial software publishers often create versions of their software that they give away. Some of these programs are full working versions that just stop working after a while; others are "crippled" in some way from the very

Looks Can Be Deceiving

Many demos are created by companies that think the way to make sales is to create a totally worthless demo that doesn't even show what the full product could do. Sometimes you're better off working with shareware or freeware than a demo.

beginning (perhaps a few important features don't work). These demos offer a good way to find out whether the company's product is worth buying, and in some cases they even have enough features to make the demo worth keeping. You'll often see these demos advertised in the computer magazines with the URL of the company's Web page.

Many companies also give away software such as drivers, a fact that came in handy for me when I wanted to print something on a color printer at a local copy store. The store had an Apple printer, so I went to the Apple Web site, dug around a little, and found the Windows driver for that printer. I was then able to print the page to a file using that print driver and take it to the copy shop.

Looking for Something Strange?

If you're looking for a program that you can't find at the popular software libraries, remember that you can always search for it using the techniques discussed in Chapter 17. It's amazing what those search sites can turn up sometimes! So if you're looking for something really obscure that the average library doesn't hold, don't give up too soon. You can even try Archie (see Chapter 16, "Gopher and Telnet—Still Alive, but Barely") to search for a file at an FTP site if you have a good idea of the filename.

Appendix D

Finding Internet Access and the Right Equipment

If you are reading this, either you don't have an Internet service provider (ISP) or you are considering changing the one you have. Let's deal with the first major question: Which is the best Internet service provider?

I Want the Best! Where Do I Get It?

Where do you find the best deal in Internet access? The cable-TV company. The best value in Internet access in North America is a bidirectional connection from a cable company. Note that there are two types of connection being sold. The best is a system in which a network card in your computer is connected to a cable modem, which is then connected to the TV cable—all data, both uploads and downloads, travels along the cable. Some companies have been installing a system that requires your computer to have a modem connection at the same time. Data from your computer to the Internet passes along the phone line, whereas data from the Internet to your computer passes along the cable.

If you can get one of the bidirectional systems, go for it. It's cheap, around $80 to install and $40 a month. You'll transfer more data per dollar on a cable system than any other Internet connection you can find. You'll get super fast connections, and it's always on—no need to log onto the Internet when you start your computer, because as soon as your computer boots up and starts its network software, it's automatically connected.

One caveat—beware of the security problems inherent with these systems. You're connected to the same network as your neighbors—it's like being on a corporate network. So if you turn on network file sharing, and don't password protect your directories, your neighbors can get onto your hard disk and dig around! Be sure you ask the installer how to avoid this problem.

Of course, there's another problem with cable connections—most people in North America don't live in an area in which they are being installed. (And even if you do, you might have to wait on the phone for an hour or two to get through to someone who can set up an appointment for an installation.)

If you can't get a cable modem, you might try an ADSL connection from your phone company. But these connections are slower than cable, and more expensive. They're also not widely available yet. And they come from the phone company, the same people who spent several decades trying to figure out how to install ISDN connections (and not quite getting it right).

What, then, are the options for the rest of you (hey, I'm okay, I've got my cable modem!). There's no easy answer to that, unfortunately. It's rather like asking, "What makes the best spouse?" Everyone has a different answer. A service that you think is good might prove to be a lousy choice for someone else.

Basically, what you need to do is pick a service provider that is cheap, helpful, and has a reliable and fast connection to the Internet and easy-to-install software. Of course, that's very difficult to find. I've had Internet accounts with a couple of dozen providers, and I haven't found one yet that I would rave about. They've ranged from pretty good to absolutely awful.

What's a Reasonable Cost?

Over the past few years, Internet-account charges have gradually moved away from a per-hour basis and toward a flat fee. You pay for unlimited access, so whether you use the service for one hour a month or a hundred, you pay the same price. For instance, you can get a CompuServe account that allows you to log on for as long as you want for $24.95 a month (or just $19.95 if you use the CompuServe 2000 software); America Online (AOL) will charge you $21.95. Special offers can sweeten the deal; both CompuServe and AOL, for instance, will give you a free month's access (up to 100 hours during that month). For a while, $19.95 seemed to be the normal flat fee charged, but the rates seem to have crept up a little—and then down a little. But it's still possible to find much cheaper rates. MCI WorldCom is $16.95 a month for the first three months, for instance (and that rate is permanent if you're an MCI telephone customer), and many small ISPs charge even less—I've seen rates as low as $12.00 a month. If you rarely use the Internet, you can probably find a company that will charge by the hour; CompuServe charges $9.95 for five hours (20 hours if you use their new CompuServe 2000 software) and $2.95 for additional hours, for instance.

Unlimited Access

What does unlimited access *really* mean? It means that you can use the service for as many hours as you can connect and remain connected. Which might be many hours less than the number of hours in a month! Busy signals might often thwart your attempts, and even if you can connect, you might find that your connection is dropped frequently.

Note, however, that some Internet service providers—as opposed to online services such as CompuServe and AOL—might charge a sign-up fee, perhaps as much as $25 to $50. And they generally don't offer a free trial period (although some of the larger companies do give the first month free).

Free Internet access might be on the way. Industry analysts say that a number of large companies are planning to provide their customers with free Internet account—open a bank account, get a free Internet account—as a way of creating customer loyalty. So the pressure on access rates seems to be downward, perhaps all the way down to zero.

Tips for Picking a Provider

Consider the following guidelines when you're trying to find an Internet service provider:

- The major online services often make it very easy to connect to the Internet: You just run the setup program and away you go.
- On the other hand, the major online services tend to be a bit more expensive (although their prices have dropped greatly, and the difference is no longer so significant). Some of them also have a reputation for having very slow and unreliable connections to the Internet. But then, so do many Internet service providers!
- There are a lot of low-priced Internet service providers (in Colorado, for example, there are about 70), and the competition is stiff!
- Unfortunately, many low-priced services have customer service that matches their prices—they are often not very helpful. To work on those services, you need more than a little of the geek gene inside you.
- On the other hand, some of these services *are* very good and will help you hook up to the Internet at a very good price.

- Be sure the service has a toll-free or local support telephone number—you'll almost certainly need it!
- A number of large national Internet service providers, such as WorldNet (owned by AT&T), EarthLink, and PSINet, often have very good prices ($20-$25 a month for unlimited usage, for instance). In addition, in some areas, they might even have good service.
- There are no hard and fast rules! A service that is very good in one area might be lousy in another. And a service that your friend says is really good might be very good right now and absolutely awful next month.

Finding a Service Provider

If you don't have an Internet account yet, but you want to find one, I can help. Here are a few ideas for tracking down service providers:

- If you're using Windows 98, try the Internet Connection Wizard (see Appendix B, "Windows 98's Internet Features"). This program has a referral service that might help you find a service provider in your area.
- Look in your local paper's computer section; local service providers often advertise there.
- Look in your city's local computer publication for ads.
- Check the Yellow Pages' "Internet" category.
- Ask at your local computer store.
- Check for ads in one of the many new Internet-related magazines.
- Look in a general computer magazine (many of which *seem* to have turned into Internet magazines).
- Ask your friends and colleagues which local service providers are good (and which to avoid).
- If you know someone who has access to the World Wide Web, ask him to go to `http://dir.yahoo.com/Business_and_Economy/Companies/Internet_Services/Access_Providers/`. Or, better still, say, "Go to Yahoo! and search for *service provider*." You might not know what that means, but your friend probably will (check out Chapter 17, "Finding Stuff," for more information). You'll find information about many service providers and even some price comparisons. (You might also try using the Web at your local library; most libraries have Internet access these days.)
- Another good Web site to try is The List (`http://thelist.internet.com/`), a directory of more than 4,000 service providers. Also, you can try ISP Finder (3,031 service providers and climbing) at `http://ispfinder.com/`.

Find a Free-Net

You might also want to look for a *Free-Net*. Free-Nets are community computing systems. They might be based at a local library or college, and you can dial into the system from your home computer. As the name implies, they don't cost anything. (Well, some might have a small registration fee of around $10, but if it's not actually free, it's pretty close to it.)

Free-Nets offer a variety of local services, as well as access to the Internet. You might be able to find information about jobs in the area or about local events and recreation. You might be able to search the local library's database, find course schedules for local colleges, or ask someone questions about Social Security and Medicare.

Free-Nets usually have a menu of options based on a simulated town. There might be a Community Center, Teen Center, and Senior Center, for example. In addition, there might be an Administration Building (where you can go to register your account on the Free-Net), a Social Services and Organizations Center (where you can find support groups and local chapters of national organizations such as the Red Cross), and a Home and Garden Center (where you can find out about pest control). There might even be a Special Interests Center, where you can chat about UFOs, movies, religion, travel, or anything else. Free-Nets also have a system that lets you send messages to other users.

Free-Net or Freenet?

You'll see the terms Free-Net, freenet, and FreeNet, and maybe even some other variations. All of these terms were service marks of NPTN (National Public Telecommuting Network), which preferred to use the term Free-Net. Note, however, that NPTN is bankrupt and out of business, so feel free to use whatever spelling you want.

Even without Internet access, Free-Nets are a great community resource, especially for homebound people such as the elderly and handicapped. However, they have serious limitations. Not all Free-Nets will provide full access to the Internet. For security reasons, some might limit certain services. For instance, they might not want you to use FTP to bring possibly virus-laden files into their systems. Free-Nets are often very busy and difficult to connect to. Most importantly, they are generally dial-in terminal connections or shell accounts. You probably won't be able to use the fancy graphical software that makes the Internet so easy to use.

If you still want to find a Free-Net or other form of free access in your area, contact the Organization for Community Networks. It has a Web site (`http://ofcn.org/`), where you can find a listing of Free-Nets and other community networks. (Again, take a trip to your library to use its Internet access, or find a friend with access.) You can also contact this organization at the following address:

Organization for Community Networks
P.O. Box 32175
Euclid, Ohio 44132
Phone: 216-731-9801

This organization does not have a full list of all the free Internet access systems available, though. Check your local computer paper, and ask at local computer stores (not the big chains, but the mom-and-pop type computer stores staffed by people who actually know what they are selling).

Equipment You Will Need

You're going to need the following items to connect to the Internet:

- A computer
- A modem
- A phone line
- Software

Which computer? You know the story, the faster the better; the more RAM (Random Access Memory), the better. Ideally, you need a computer that will run the nice graphical software that's available for Windows and the Macintosh. If you don't have a computer that will run this sort of software, you can still access the Internet, but you'll have to use a dial-in terminal (shell) account.

For instance, you'll probably want at least a 486, or better, if working in the PC world. You might be able to scrape by with a 386. But most software won't run well on a 286, if at all. (For a shell account, just about any machine is okay.)

A modem takes the digital signals from your computer and converts them to the analog signals that your phone line uses. You plug the phone line into the modem, and, if it's an external modem, you plug the computer into the modem, too. (If it's an internal modem, you install it in a slot inside your computer, and the phone line connects to a socket on the edge of the card.)

When buying a modem, remember the rule of "the faster, the better." Service providers generally have connection speeds of at least 33,600bps connections these days, and many have added 56Kbps connections recently. You can buy a good 33,600bps modem for $50 to $60 (you'll have trouble buying a slower modem than this these days). The 56Kbps modems are more expensive, but see the following discussion of these modems.

By the way, don't buy a modem from the *Acme Modem and Hiking Shoe Company* (or from any of the other hundreds of budget modem makers). Anyone can build and sell a modem; however, building a *good* modem is difficult. Modems are complicated things, and the cheap generic modems often do not connect reliably. Buy a modem from one of the well-known modem companies, such as US Robotics, Hayes, Practical Peripherals, or MegaHertz. (Look in a computer magazine, and you'll soon see which modems are being sold by most of the mail-order companies.) It will cost you a few bucks more, but it might save you hours of hassle. You might also ask your service provider for a recommendation on the kind of modem to buy; they should be able to tell you about the ones that work well, and those that don't.

The 56K Problem

Before you buy a 56K modem, you need to understand a few things. First, there were two rival techniques used for making modems transmit at this speed. It took a little while to agree upon a standard for these modems, but now all modem manufacturers are selling what are known as V.90 modems—be sure you get one of these and not an older 56K modem. Also, before getting a modem, be sure that the service provider you want to work with can provide 56K connections (many can't, or perhaps don't yet have 56K numbers in your area) and that the modem you want to buy will work okay with that service.

Note also that although a modem might be rated at 56K, it can transfer data at high speed only one way. Transfers *from* the Internet will occur at the highest connection speed, but transfers *to* the Internet will go at the slower 33,600bps rate. That's okay for most users, who are viewing information on the Web or downloading files.

Finally, even if you do get a 56K modem, it might not transfer at that speed across some phone lines (if it can't reach top speed, it'll still be able to transmit at a lower speed). No phone lines can handle full 56K transmissions, and some lines are completely incompatible with 56K transmissions.

56K modem prices range from around $90 to $149 for a name brand. If you've already got a 33,600bps modem, it might not be worth upgrading. If you're buying your first modem, or if you have a 28,800bps modem or slower, you should seriously consider getting a 56K modem.

If you'd like more information about 56K modems, including lists of service providers who work with them, ways to test your local phone lines to see whether they'll handle 56K modems, and lots more, check out these sites:

- 3Com, the manufacturer of the US Robotics modems: `http://www.3com.com/56k/`
- The 56K Modem Info Center: `http://www.sirius.com/~rmoss/`
- 56K.com: `http://www.56k.com/`

You Want Something Faster

Yes, there are faster connections—for some of us. The following sections give a quick rundown of other possible types of connection that might be available in your area.

Cable

You already know what I think about cable connections—if they're available in your area, get one. They're fast, very fast. In the time that it takes to transfer half a page across a 56K connection, a TCI @Home cable connection can transfer 26 pages. (That doesn't mean it's always 52 times as fast—although the cable connection's fast, the Web server from which you're pulling pages might be slow, or the lines across the Internet might be busy.)

ADSL

This is a new telephone technology that the phone company said would be introduced in late 1996. Even in 1998, when it was supposed to be available in most of North America...it wasn't. And although now, in 1999, I'm running into people who do have ADSL connections (and are very happy with them), it's still not available in most areas. Hey, maybe in the next millennium. I tried to get an ADSL connection. I was told June of 1998. And indeed it was "available" in my area at that time...just not for my home, apparently. ("Available" in telephone-company speak means "we've installed some of these systems somewhere near you, but that doesn't mean you'll get one.") Then I was told "the second half of 1998." We're almost into the second half of 1999, and it's still not available.

Even if you can get an ADSL line, what will you connect to? You might have to sign up for Internet service with your local phone company, and the local phone companies have proven themselves completely incompetent at providing Internet access. (Here's an example: My phone company once changed their login script without telling their subscribers, so people could no longer connect. I guess they were looking for a way to cut back on system congestion.)

ADSL provides fast connections, but generally not as fast as cable (unless you want to spend a lot of money). There are various choices, beginning at around 256Kbps (about five or six times the speed of a fast modem) and going up to 7Mbps (about 125 times faster!). Prices begin at around $60 a month (including Internet access). There's also a setup charge, and you'll have to buy a card to go into your computer.

ISDN

ISDN is an old Albanian acronym for "Yesterday's Technology Tomorrow—Perhaps." ISDN phone lines are fast digital phone lines. This technology has been around for years, but the U.S. phone companies, in their infinite wisdom, figured that we really didn't need it. For a while they were scrambling to provide it, spurred on by the increasing number of people who use the Internet. Then they figured out they should be installing ADSL. If ADSL isn't available in your area, you might be able to install ISDN. But the rather modest speed gains over a fast modem—perhaps two to three times the speed—might not be worth the hassle.

ISDN Modem

An ISDN modem is not really a modem. The word *modem* is a contraction of two words: modulate and demodulate, which are the terms for the processes of converting digital signals to and from analog phone signals. Although the ISDN adapters are called ISDN modems, the signals are digital all the way: There's no modulating and demodulating being done.

Don't bother to get an ISDN line until you find a service provider who also has an ISDN connection; currently most don't. You'll be charged at both ends, by the phone company (who will charge to install and maintain the line) and the service provider (who will charge extra for the privilege of connecting to the Internet with it).

Not surprisingly, prices are all over the place. To use ISDN, you'll need a special *ISDN modem*, as it's known (more correctly, an ISDN *adapter*). That'll cost around $350 to $450, but prices are falling. Then you pay the phone company to install the line (between $0 and $600—don't ask me how they figure out these prices), and you'll pay a monthly fee of $25 to $130. You'll have to pay both the phone company *and* the service provider an extra fee for this special service. I had ISDN installed in 1997 and discovered a few oddities about this technology. It requires that large holes be dug in your yard, generally by a small group of rotund men who stand around in front of your house staring at the hole. It might take a dozen visits from the phone company—they might even try to install it a couple of times after they've already installed it once. It might also require the destruction of the neighbor's shrubbery. Even then, it might not work well; I eventually gave up and went back to using a normal modem, and prayed every night for a cable modem.

Satellite

For the next few years, only one satellite service will be available in North America, the DirecPC from Hughes Network Systems (`http://www.direcpc.com/` or call 800-347-3272). Other companies plan to introduce satellite service, but the earliest such service can begin is around 2002.

It costs about $250–$300 to buy the equipment, and $180 to pay someone to install it. (There's also a product called DirecDuo, which combines Internet and TV service, for around $100 more.)

DirecPC connections are at 400Kpbs, seven times faster than fast modems. Note, however, that DirecPC transmits data only *to* your computer. You still need a phone line and an Internet service provider to transmit data out (you can use Hughes's Internet access service, or use a service provider of your choice). When you connect to a Web site, for instance, the instructions to the Web server go along your phone line to the service provider; then the data from the Web site goes up to the satellite and down to you.

The lowest rates are around $30 a month, including Internet access; that rate provides only 25 hours a month, though, with extra hours costing $1.99. To get 100 hours a month you'll pay $50. Rates for businesses are higher. I've heard complaints about satellite access being unreliable. Indeed Hughes has this disclaimer on their Web site: "To ensure equal Internet access for all DirecPC subscribers, Hughes Network Systems maintains a running average fair access policy. ...To ensure this equity, customers might experience some temporary throughput limitations. DirecPC Turbo Internet access is not guaranteed."

T1 Line

This special type of digital phone line is about 10 times faster than ISDN, but it costs a couple of thousand dollars or more for the equipment and then somewhere from a few hundred to a couple of thousand dollars a month to run. Although this solution is okay for small businesses who really need fast access to the Internet (very few really do), it's out of the price range of most individuals.

For now, most of you are stuck with modems. With luck, they're 56Kbps modems, which are relatively slow but affordable. But don't get too jealous of people using faster connections. The Internet can be very slow at times, and even if you have a very fast connection from your service provider to your computer, you might still find yourself twiddling your fingers. For instance, when you're using the Web or an FTP site, the server you've connected to might be slow. Or the lines from that server across the world to your service provider might be slow. Or your service provider's system might be clogged up with more users than it was designed to handle. So just because you have all the equipment you need for a fast connection doesn't mean you'll get a fast connection.

Oh, all right, I'll tell you the truth. A fast connection is fantastic—the Internet is a completely different experience. Sure, you'll run across slow servers now and then, but there seem to be fewer and fewer of them. But all of a sudden you'll find that things that make absolutely no sense over a slow modem—in particular video—really can work well. News sites' news clips, for instance, can be more trouble than they're worth if you're working on a phone-line modem, but over a cable connection they really do work well. Before I had a cable modem, I rarely used the RealPlayer video player. These days, I routinely click on videos at new sites. Jealous? Never mind; those fast connections will be in your area soon. Well, maybe not soon, but eventually.

Appendix E

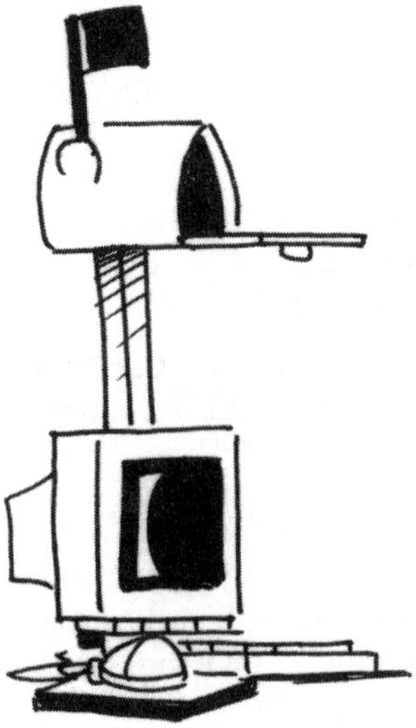

The Email Responder

You can find additional information related to this book using a mail responder. The mail responder will automatically send you chapters from the first edition of *The Complete Idiot's Guide to the Internet* or a chapter from *The Complete Idiot's Next Step with the Internet* in response to a special message from you.

About the First Edition

Why might you want to see the first edition of this book? The book you are reading is completely different from the first edition. Back in 1993, when the first edition was written, most people were using the command-line interface to work with the Internet. Now most are using some kind of graphical user interface. But because some people are still stuck at the command line, I've provided information from the first edition so that these people can get to all the funky little UNIX commands they're going to need.

Using the Email Responder

Here's how to use the email responder:

1. Send an email message to `ciginternet@mcp.com`.
2. In the Subject line of the message, enter the appropriate command from the following list. When the email responder receives your message, it automatically sends a message back to you containing the requested chapter.
3. When you receive the message, save it to your hard disk, and then open the chapter in a word processor or text editor. (Or simply read the chapter in your mail program if you want.)

Don't bother to include text in the message. Your message will be received by a computer (not an actual person) and whatever you write in the body of the message won't be read anyway. (If you want to contact Que, see the contact information at the front of this book. If you'd like to contact the author, email `cig6@topfloor.com`.)

With the email responder, you can receive any of the following chapters from the first edition of *The Complete Idiot's Guide to the Internet* by typing the appropriate command.

Chapter	Command
5 Let's Get Physical: What You Need to Get Started	physical
7 Your First Trip to the Internet	first
8 Menus and Shells, Oh My!	shells
9 A UNIX Survival Guide	unix
10 Please Mr. Postman: An Intro to E-mail	email
11 UNIX Mail: Down to the Nitty Gritty	unixmail
12 Still More on Mail	moremail
Chapters 10, 11, and 12	allmail
13 Return to Sender, Address Unknown	sender
14 Finding Folks with Fred and Whois	fred
Chapters 13 and 14	who
15 Newsgroups: The Source of All Wisdom	wisdom
16 More on Newsgroups and Mailing Lists	maillist
Chapters 15 and 16	news
17 Telnet: Inviting Yourself onto Other Systems	telnet
18 Grabbing the Goodies: Downloading Files with FTP	ftp
19 More Neato FTP Stuff	moreftp
Chapters 18 and 19	allftp
20 Archie the File Searcher	archie
21 Digging Through the Internet with Gopher	gopher

Chapter	Command
22 Finding Your WAIS Around	wais
23 Think Global: World Wide Web	web

The autoresponder also has Chapter 1, "Yak, Yak, Yak, Talking on the Net," from *The Complete Idiot's Next Step with the Internet*, which contains detailed information about Internet Relay Chat. To get this chapter, enter **irc** in the Subject line.

Finally, you can retrieve the OWNWEB.HTM file, mentioned in this book's Chapter 20, "Setting Up Your Own Web Site," by typing **ownweb** in the Subject line.

Index

Symbols

A

B

D

F

G

H

I

J

K

L

M

N

O

Q

R

S

T

U

V

W

X-Y

Z